THE ROMAN TRIUMPH

THE ROMAN TRIUMPH

MARY BEARD

THE BELKNAP PRESS OF HARVARD UNIVERSITY PRESS

CAMBRIDGE, MASSACHUSETTS

LONDON, ENGLAND

Copyright © 2007 by the President and Fellows
of Harvard College
All rights reserved
Printed in the United States of America
First Harvard University Press paperback edition, 2009.
Set in Adobe Garamond
Designed by Gwen Nefsky Frankfeldt

Frontispiece: Giovanni Battista Tiepolo,
The Triumph of Marius, 1729.
A re-creation of the triumphal procession of January 1, 104 BCE.
Jugurtha, the defeated king of Numidia, stands a proud prisoner in
front of the chariot—threatening to upstage the victorious general
Marius in the background. To left and right are the spoils of victory—
precious vessels and sculpture, including a bust of the goddess
Cybele with distinctive turreted headdress, just as Mantegna
had envisaged in his *Triumphs of Caesar* (Fig. 28).

Library of Congress Cataloging-in-Publication Data
Beard, Mary, 1955–
The Roman triumph / Mary Beard.
p.   cm.
Includes bibliographical references and index.
ISBN 978-0-674-02613-1 (cloth : alk. paper)
ISBN 978-0-674-03218-7 (pbk.)
1. Triumph.   2. Rites and ceremonies—Rome.
3. Processions—Rome.   4. Rome—Military antiquities.
5. Triumph in art.   6. Triumph in literature.
7. Rites and ceremonies—Rome—Historiography.   I. Title.
DG89.B43 2007
394'.50937—dc22   2007002575

Contents

THE ROMAN TRIUMPH

The Question of Triumph

"Petty sacrilege is punished; sacrilege on a grand scale is the stuff of triumphs." Those are the words of Lucius Annaeus Seneca, first-century CE philosopher and tutor of the emperor Nero. He was reflecting in one of his philosophical letters on the unfair disparity in the meting out of punishment and reward, and on the apparent profit that might come from wrong-doing.[1] As we might gloss it, following the wry popular wisdom of our own day, "Petty criminals end up in jail; big ones end up rich."

In referring to the "stuff of triumphs," Seneca meant those famous parades through the city of Rome that celebrated Rome's greatest victories against its enemies (or its biggest massacres, depending on whose side you were on). To be awarded a triumph was the most outstanding honor a Roman general could hope for. He would be drawn in a chariot—accompanied by the booty he had won, the prisoners he had taken captive, and his no doubt rowdy and raucous troops in their battle gear—through the streets of the city to the Temple of Jupiter on the Capitoline hill, where he would offer a sacrifice to the god. The ceremony became a by-word for extravagant display.

Seneca's quip is uncomfortably subversive. For, by implication, it questions the morality of some of those glorious victories that were celebrated in this most lavish of all Roman rituals; and it hints that the spoils on show might sometimes have been the fruits of sacrilege rather than the just rewards of imperial conquest. It puts a question mark over the triumph and triumphal values.

Roman triumphs have provided a model for the celebration of military success for centuries. Through the last two millennia, there has been hardly a monarch, dynast, or autocrat in the West who has not looked back to Rome for a lesson in how to mark victory in war and to assert his own personal power. Renaissance princelings launched hundreds of triumphal celebrations. Napoleon carted through the streets of Paris the sculpture and painting he had seized in Italy, in a pointed imitation of a Roman triumph. It is a kind of ironic justice that the Romans' own masterpieces should find themselves put on parade in a foreign city—just as the masterpieces looted from the Greek world had been paraded through Rome two thousand years earlier. As late as 1899 the victories of Admiral George Dewey in the Spanish-American War were celebrated with a triumphal parade in New York. True, no live captive or spoils were on show; but a special triumphal arch was built, in plaster and wood, at Madison Square.[2]

Scratch the surface of these apparently self-confident ceremonies and time and again "Senecan" doubts begin to emerge—in sometimes surprising places. Donatello's wonderfully sensuous bronze statue of David (now in the Bargello in Florence) was probably commissioned by Cosimo de' Medici in 1428 after victory over some rival Italian potentates.[3] David is shown with his foot on the head of Goliath; on the giant's helmet is a scene of triumph, and in the triumphal chariot—in an imaginative variant we shall meet again—stands not a human general but a victorious Cupid, the god of love. Donatello is directing us to the erotic charge of his young David. But he is also pointing to the transitory nature of triumphal glory: Goliath who blazoned the emblem of the triumph on his armor is now himself the victim of his triumphant successor.[4]

In a completely different medium, a *New Yorker* cartoon gives similar anxieties a humorous touch (Fig. 1). We shall shortly see that in ancient Rome itself "triumphal arches" were not quite so closely linked to trium-

"So far so good. Let's hope we win."

FIGURE 1: Boris Drucker, *New Yorker* cartoon, 1988. The anxious Romans are putting the finishing touches on an imaginary arch—a composite loosely based on the Arch of Constantine in Rome and the Arch of Trajan at Beneventum (Fig. 10).

phal processions as they have been in the modern world, and in the modern imagination. But, anyway, here the cartoonist pictures a group of Roman workmen finishing off just such a structure—when the dark thought strikes them that Rome might not actually be victorious in whatever war this arch is intended to celebrate. The joke is partly on the dangers of anticipation, on "counting your chickens before they are hatched." But it is also on the fact that a triumph involves both winners and losers—that those who triumph today may one day be *triumphed over.*

This book will write those doubts and quizzical reflections back into the history of the Roman triumph. Most modern accounts of the ceremony stress the militaristic jingoism of the occasion, its sometimes brutish celebration of conquest and imperialism. It is cast as a ritual which, throughout the history of Rome, asserted and reasserted the power of the Roman war machine and the humiliation of the conquered. Cleopatra of Egypt is famously supposed to have killed herself rather than be triumphed over. That is certainly one side of it. But I shall argue that the very ceremony which glorified military victory and the values underpinning that victory also provided a context within which those values could be discussed and challenged. It has too often been convenient to dismiss Roman culture as unreflectively committed to warfare and imperial domination, and to regard members of the Roman political elite individually as obsessed with achieving military glory. Of course, Rome was "a warrior state."[5] The Romans were not a crowd of proto-pacifists. But, as a general rule, it is warrior states that produce the most sophisticated critique of the militaristic values they uphold. I hope to show that this was the case with Rome; and that within Roman culture the triumph was the context and the prompt for some of the most critical thinking on the dangerous ambivalence of success and military glory.

On the usual calculation, the triumph was celebrated more than three hundred times in the thousand-or-so-year history of the ancient city of Rome. It made an impact far beyond the commemoration of victory, and on aspects of Roman life as diverse as the apotheosis of emperors and the passion of erotic pursuit ("conquest," that is, in the bedroom, not on the battlefield). It has been the subject of study and hot debate by scholars and cultural commentators from antiquity until the present day.

This book is driven in part by curiosity—about the ritual itself and its insistent presence in Roman literature, scholarship, and art, and about the controversies and debates, ancient and modern, that it has raised. Through an exploration of the triumph, I aim at the same time to communicate something of my own enthusiasm for the sophistication, nuance, and complexity of Roman culture (notwithstanding my distaste for much of what those sophisticated men—and I mean *men*—got up to). I also try to grapple with some of the biggest questions in the understanding of ancient ritual in general and of the triumph in particular that, despite centuries of inspiring work, still get fudged or passed by. In fact, the approach that I follow in the rest of the book is intended to challenge many of the ways Roman ritual culture is studied, and the spurious certainties and prejudices that dog it. This is a manifesto of sorts.

Also at the heart of what I have written is a conviction that, at its best, the study of ancient history is as much about *how* we know as *what* we know. It involves an engagement with all the processes of selection, constructive blindness, revolutionary reinterpretation, and willful misinterpretation that together produce the "facts" about the triumph out of the messy, confusing, and contradictory evidence that survives. With this in mind, I have taken care, where it is most relevant, to indicate if, say, a key piece of evidence actually derives from a possibly tendentious medieval summary of an ancient text or if it depends on accepting some nineteenth-century "emendation" (put simply, clever "alteration") of the words transmitted to us in the manuscripts. Factors like this are usually side-stepped, except in the most scholarly and technical academic articles—and sometimes even there. This book is intended not only for those who are already expert in ancient Roman culture but also for those who wish to discover it. I shall be making clear why some of the best-loved "facts" about the triumph are nothing of the sort. But more important, I hope to convey to nonspecialists the intellectual pleasure—and the sheer fun—of making sense of the ancient world from the complex layers of different kinds of evidence that we have. This is a book which, as mathematicians would say, shows its working.

The first chapter plunges into the middle of things. It takes a single triumphal ceremony—the triumph of Pompey the Great in 61 BCE—and explores its celebration and commemoration in depth. It offers a glimpse of the intriguing richness of the evidence for this ritual, from the miniature images on Roman coins to the disapproving accounts of austere Roman moralists; and it shows how far the impact of a single triumphal ceremony can extend. Chapters 2 and 3 stand back to reflect on the general role of the triumph in Roman culture and to wonder just how reliable (or reliable *in what sense*) is the evidence that remains. They show that we know both more and less about the triumph than we might suppose. At the heart of the book, Chapters 4 through 8 home in on particularly revealing aspects of triumphal culture—the victims, the spoils, the successful general, the rules and regulations that determined who was allowed to triumph, and the variety of triumphlike celebrations that emerged in Rome and elsewhere.

The final chapter reflects on the history of the triumph. It goes without saying that over a thousand years the character of the ceremony must have changed drastically, as well as reactions to it. We should not imagine that anything like Seneca's clever quip could plausibly have fallen from the lips of the men and women who observed any such ritual in the fifth or fourth centuries BCE. How those early Romans would have responded and how their ceremony itself was conducted is now practically irrecoverable. As I shall argue, most later Roman accounts of primitive triumphal history—from clever reconstruction to elaborate fantasies—tell us more about the period in which they were written than the one they purport to describe. It fits appropriately with the approach of the book as a whole that the "origins" of the ceremony are, intentionally, left till last. Please do not start there.

CHAPTER

I

Pompey's Finest Hour?

BIRTHDAY PARADE

September 29, 61 BCE, was the forty-fifth birthday of Pompey the Great. It was also—and this can hardly have been mere coincidence—the second and final day of his mammoth triumphal procession through the streets of Rome. It was a ceremony that put on show at the heart of the metropolis the wonders of the East and the profits of empire: from cartloads of bullion and colossal golden statues to precious specimens of exotic plants and other curious bric-à-brac of conquest. Not to mention the eye-catching captives dressed up in their national costumes, the placards proclaiming the conqueror's achievements (ships captured, cities founded, kings defeated . . .), paintings recreating crucial moments of the campaigns, and a bizarre portrait head of Pompey himself, made (so it was said) entirely of pearls.[1]

Over the previous six years, Pompey had dealt decisively with two of the greatest dangers to Rome's security, and boasted a range of conquests that justified comparison with King Alexander himself (hence the title "the Great"). First, in 67, he had dispatched the pirates who had been terrorizing the whole Mediterranean, with the support of "rogue states" in the East. Their activities had threatened to starve Rome of its seaborne grain supply and had produced some high-profile victims, including the young Julius Caesar—who, so the story went, managed to raise his own ransom and then proceeded to crucify his captors. Pompey is reputed to have cleared the sea in an impressively (and perhaps implausibly) short three months, before resettling many of the old buccaneers in towns at a safe distance from the coast.

His next target was a more formidable opponent, and another imitator of Alexander, King Mithradates Eupator of Pontus. Some twenty years earlier, in 88 BCE, Mithradates had committed an atrocity that was outrageous even by ancient standards, when he invaded the Roman province of Asia and ordered the massacre of every Italian man, woman, or child that could be found; unreliable estimates by Greek and Roman writers suggest that between 80,000 and 150,000 people were killed. Although rapidly beaten back on that occasion, he had continued to expand his sphere of influence in what is now Turkey (and beyond) and to threaten Roman interests in the East. The Romans had scored a few notable victories in battle; but the war had not been won. Between 66 and 62 Pompey finished the job, while restoring or imposing Roman order from the Black Sea to Judaea. It was a hugely lucrative campaign. One account claims that Mithradates' furniture stores ("two thousand drinking-cups made of onyx inlaid with gold and a host of bowls and wine-coolers, plus drinking-horns and couches and chairs, richly adorned") took thirty days to transfer to Roman hands.[2]

Triumphal processions had celebrated Roman victories from the very earliest days of the city. Or so the Romans themselves believed, tracing the origins of the ceremony back to their mythical founder, Romulus, and the other (more or less mythical) early kings. As well as the booty, enemy captives, and other trophies of victory, there was more light-hearted display. Behind the triumphal chariot, the troops sang ribald songs ostensibly at their general's expense. "Romans, watch your wives, see the bald adulterer's back home" was said to have been chanted at Julius Caesar's triumph in 46 BCE (as much to Caesar's delight, no doubt, as to his chagrin).[3] Conspicuous consumption played a part, too. After the ceremonies at the Temple of Jupiter, there was banqueting, occasionally on a legendary scale; Lucullus, for example, who had been awarded a triumph for some earlier victories scored against Mithradates, is reputed to have feasted the whole city plus the surrounding villages.[4]

At Pompey's triumph in 61 the booty had flowed in so lavishly that two days, instead of the usual one, were assigned to the parade, and (superfluity always being a mark of success) still more was left over: "Quite enough," according to Plutarch, in his biography of Pompey, "to deck out another triumphal procession." The extravagant wealth on display certainly prompted murmurings of disapproval as well as envious admiration. In a characteristic piece of curmudgeon, the elder Pliny, looking back on the occasion after more than a hundred years, wondered exactly whose triumph it had been: not so much Pompey's over the pirates and Mithradates as "the defeat of austerity and the triumph, let's face it, of luxury." Curmudgeon apart, though, it must count as one of the most extraordinary birthday celebrations in the history of the world.[5]

GETTING THE SHOW ON THE ROAD

Ancient writers found plenty to say about Pompey's triumph, lingering on the details of its display. The vast quantity of cash trundled through the streets was part of the appeal: "75,100,000 drachmae of silver coin," according to the historian Appian, which was considerably more than the annual tax revenue of the whole Roman world at the time—or, to put it another way, enough money to keep two million people alive for a year.[6] But the range of precious artifacts that Pompey had brought back from the royal court of Mithradates also captured the imagination. Appian again notes "the throne of Mithradates himself, along with his scepter, and his statue eight cubits tall, made of solid gold."[7] Pliny, always with a keen eye for luxury and innovation, harps on "the vessels of gold and gems, enough to fill nine display cabinets, three gold statues of Minerva, Mars and Apollo, thirty three crowns of pearl" and "the first vessels of agate ever brought to Rome." He seems particularly intrigued by an out-sized gaming board, "three feet broad by four feet long," made out of two different types of precious stone—and on the board a golden moon weighing thirty pounds. But here he has a moral for his own age and a critical reflection on the consequences of luxury: "The fact that no gems even approaching that size exist today is as clear a proof as anyone could want that the world's resources have been depleted."[8]

In some cases the sheer mimetic extravagance of the treasures on display makes—and no doubt *made*—their interpretation tricky. One of the most puzzling objects in the roster of the procession was, in Pliny's words, "a mountain like a pyramid and made of gold, with deers and lions and fruit of all kinds, and a golden vine entwined all around"; followed by a "musaeum" (a "shrine of the Muses" or perhaps a "grotto") "made of pearls and topped by a sun-dial." Hard as it is to picture these creations, we might guess that they evoked the exotic landscape of the East, while at the same time instantiating the excesses of oriental luxury.[9] Other notable spectacles came complete with interpretative labels. The historian Dio refers to one "trophy" carried in the triumph as "huge and expensively decorated, with an inscription attached to say 'this is a trophy of the whole world.'"[10] This was a celebration, in other words, of Pompey the Great as world conqueror, and of Roman power as world empire.

Almost all of these treasures have long since been lost or destroyed: the agate broken, gems recycled into new works of art (or monstrosities, depending on your taste), precious metals melted down and refashioned. But a single large bronze vessel (a *krater*) displayed in the Capitoline Museum at Rome might possibly have been one of the many on view in the procession of 61 BCE—or if not, then a close look-alike (Fig. 2). This particular specimen is some 70 centimeters tall, in plain bronze, except for a pattern of lotus leaves chased around its neck and inlaid with silver; the slightly rococo handles and foot are modern restorations. It was found in the mid-eighteenth century in the Italian town of Anzio, ancient Antium, and given to the Capitoline Museum—where it currently holds pride of place as the center of the "Hall of Hannibal" (so-called after its sixteenth-century frescoes depicting a magnificently foreign Hannibal perched on an elephant but showing also, appropriately enough, a triumphal procession of an allegorical figure of "Roma" over a captive "Sicilia").[11]

FIGURE 2: Bronze vessel, late second–early first century BCE. Originally a gift from King Mithradates to a group of his own subjects (as an inscription around the neck records), it may have reached Italy as part of the spoils of Pompey—a solitary survivor of the treasures on display in his triumphal procession in 61?

The connection with Mithradates is proclaimed by an inscription pricked out in Greek around the rim: "King Mithradates Eupator [gave this] to the Eupatoristae of the gymnasium." In other words, this was a present from Mithradates to an association named after him "Eupatoristae" (which could be anything from a drinking club to a group involved in the religious cult of the king). It must originally have come from some part of the Eastern Mediterranean where Mithradates had power and influence, and it could have found its way to Antium by any number of routes; but there is certainly a chance that it was one tiny part of Pompey's collection of booty. It offers a glimpse of what might have been paraded before the gawping spectators in September 61.[12]

A triumph, however, was about more than costly treasure. Pliny, for example, stresses the natural curiosities of the East on display. "Ever since the time of Pompey the Great," he writes, "we have paraded even trees in triumphal processions." And he notes elsewhere that ebony—by which he may well mean the tree, rather than just the wood—was one of the exhibits in the Mithradatic triumph. Perhaps on display too was the royal library, with its specialist collection of medical treatises; Pompey was said to have been so impressed with this part of his booty that he had one of his ex-slaves take on the task of translating it all into Latin.[13] Many other items had symbolic rather than monetary value. Appian writes of "countless wagonloads of weapons, and beaks of ships"; these were the spoils taken directly from the field of conflict, all that now remained of the pirate terror and Mithradates' arsenal.[14]

Further proof of Pompey's success was there for all to contemplate on the placards carried in the procession (see Figs. 9 and 28). According to Plutarch, they blazoned the names of all the nations over which he triumphed (fourteen in all, plus the pirates), the number of fortresses, cities, and ships he had captured, the new cities he had founded, and the amount of money his conquests had brought to Rome. Appian claims to quote the text of one of these boasts; it ran, "Ships with bronze beaks captured: 800. Cities founded: in Cappadocia 8; in Cilicia and Coele-Syria 20; in Palestine, the city which is now Seleucis. Kings conquered: Tigranes of Armenia, Artoces of Iberia, Oroezes of Albania, Darius of Media, Aretas of Nabatea, Antiochus of Commagene."[15]

No less an impact can have been made by the human participants in the show: a "host of captives and pirates, not in chains but dressed up in their native costume" and "the officers, children, and generals of the kings he had fought." Appian numbers these highest ranking prisoners at 324 and lists some of the more famous and evocative names: "Tigranes the son of Tigranes, the five sons of Mithradates, that is, Artaphernes, Cyrus, Oxathres, Darius, and Xerxes, and his daughters, Orsabaris and Eupatra." For an ancient audience, this roll-call must have brought to mind their yet more famous namesakes and any number of earlier conflicts with Persia and the East: the name of young Xerxes must have evoked the fifth-century Persian king, best known for his (unsuccessful) invasion of Greece; Artaphernes, a commander of the Persian forces at the battle of Marathon. The names alone serve to insert Pompey into the whole history of Western victory over Oriental "barbarity."[16]

An impressive array of captives made for a splendid triumph. By some clever talking, Pompey is said to have managed to get his hands on a couple of notorious pirate chiefs who had actually been captured by one of his Roman rivals, Quintus Caecilius Metellus Creticus, who had been hoping to show them off in his own triumphal parade. At a stroke, Pompey had robbed Metellus' triumph of two of its stars, while enhancing the line-up in his own.[17] Even so, some of the defeated were unavoidably absent. Tigranes *père* of Armenia, Mithradates' partner in crime, had had a lucky escape. Thanks to a well-timed surrender, he was restored by Pompey as a puppet ruler on his old throne and did not accompany his son to the triumph. (In the treacherous world of Armenian politics, young Tigranes had actually sided with the Romans, before disastrously quarreling with Pompey and ending up a prisoner.) Mithradates himself was already dead. He was said to have forestalled the humiliation of display in the triumph by his timely suicide; or rather he had a soldier kill him, his long-term precautionary consumption of antidotes having rendered poison useless.[18]

In place of Tigranes and Mithradates themselves, "images"—*eikones* in Appian's Greek—were put on display. Almost certainly paintings (though three-dimensional models are known in other triumphs), these were said to capture the crucial moments in the conflict between Romans and their absent victims: the kings were shown "fighting, beaten and running away . . . and finally there was a picture of how Mithradates died and of the daughters who chose to die with him." For Appian, these images reached the very limits of realistic representation, depicting not only the cut and thrust of battle and scenes of suicide but even, as he notes at one point, "the silence" itself of the night on which Mithradates fled. Thanks to triumphal painting of this type, art historians have often imagined the triumph as one of the driving forces behind the "realism" that is characteristic of many aspects of Roman art.[19]

Pompey himself loomed above the scene, riding high in a chariot "studded with gems." Parading his identification with Alexander the

Great, he was said to have been wearing a cloak that had once belonged to Alexander himself. We are not told how he combined this with the traditional costume of the triumphing general, which included an ornate purple toga and tunic that modern studies have traced back variously to the costume of the early kings of Rome or to the cult image of the god Jupiter himself. In any case, Appian on this occasion chooses to be skeptical ("if anyone can believe that," he writes), although he does go on to offer an implausibly plausible account of just how Pompey might have got his hands on this heirloom of a king who had died some 250 years earlier: "He apparently found it among the possessions of Mithradates—the people of Cos having got it from Cleopatra." This Cleopatra, like her more famous later name-sake, was a queen of the Ptolemaic royal house of Egypt and a direct descendant of Alexander's general Ptolemy. The treasure she had left on the Greek island of Cos had come into Mithradates' possession in 88 BCE; it is just possible (though not very likely) that this included some genuine memorabilia of Alexander, for Ptolemy was not only a close associate of the king but had also taken charge of his corpse and burial.[20]

Dressed as Alexander or not, Pompey chose to display his power by a show of clemency rather than cruelty. "He put none of the prisoners to death as he arrived at the Capitol . . . instead he sent them back home at public expense—except those of royal blood. Of these, only Aristoboulus [of Judaea] was put to death at once, and Tigranes [junior] later." Pompey's blaze of restraint served, of course, to hint just how deathly a ceremony a triumph might be. Other victorious generals were reputed to have taken the crueler course. The idea was that for the most powerful, news-worthy, or dangerous of the captives the procession might culminate in execution, rather than in feasting.[21]

TRIPLE TRIUMPH

The ceremony of 61 BCE was not Pompey's first triumph. After a triumphal celebration for victories in North Africa in probably 81 or 80, and another for victories in Spain in 71, he now belonged to that select group of Roman generals—including Romulus himself and a clutch of less mythical republican heroes—who had triumphed three times. It was an achievement that quickly became his crowning glory, his identifying device, almost his nickname: he was the man who, in the words of the poet Lucan, "thrice had mounted the Capitol in his chariot"—"three-triumph-Pompey," as we might put it.[22] In fact, his own signet ring made exactly that point: according to Dio, Pompey sealed his letters with a design that blazoned three trophies of victory, presumably in the traditional form of a suit of enemy armor pinned to a tree trunk or stake (see Fig. 4).[23]

True, other Romans celebrated even more triumphs than Pompey: Julius Caesar, for example, was to notch up five; and Camillus, who saved Rome from the Gauls, is supposed to have had no fewer than four in the early fourth century BCE. But Pompey, in a sense, could outbid even these. As Plutarch put it, "The greatest factor in his glory, and something that had never happened to any Roman before, was that he celebrated his third triumph over the third continent. For others before him had triumphed three times. But he held his first triumph over Africa, his second over Europe, and this final one over Asia, and so in a way he seemed to have brought the whole world under his power in his three triumphs." Pompey's three triumphs marked out the planet as his, and as Rome's, domain.[24]

Glory, however, courts controversy; the proudest and richest of ceremonies are also those most liable to backfire. Pompey's first triumph, in particular, became renowned as much for its own-goals as for its glorious celebration of victory. Pompey was at that time still in his twenties, his career launched and accelerated in the blood-thirsty campaigns of Roman civil war between the rival factions of Marius and Sulla. Too young ever to have held an elected office, he was already a terrifyingly successful and ruthless general in Sulla's camp and was instrumental in Sulla's rise to "dictatorship" in the city. "Murderous teenager" was the famous taunt thrown at him in a courtroom altercation by an elderly adversary. (This ageist banter had, in fact, been started by Pompey, who asked his opponent whether he had been sent back from the underworld to make his charge.)[25] In North Africa, he managed to destroy the remaining Marian forces who did not immediately desert to his side, and to oust their African ally, King Iarbas of Numidia, from his throne—before, according to Plutarch, going on a hunting expedition to round up some exotic African animals, against whom, as much as against the human inhabitants, he apparently wanted to display the overwhelming strength of Rome.[26]

Returning home, he was greeted warmly by Sulla who, according to one version, hailed him for the first time as "Magnus," "the Great." Pompey also asked to celebrate a triumph. It would have been unprecedented, in Roman memory at least, for a man so young who had as yet held no magistracy to be granted such an honor, and, whether for this or other reasons, the dictator at first refused. The story goes that his change of heart was brought about by a bold and prescient quip of Pompey. "You should bear in mind," he is reported to have said, "that more people worship the rising than the setting sun." As Plutarch explains, the implication that Pompey's power was on the rise, while his own was on the wane, was not lost on Sulla: "Let him triumph," he finally conceded.[27]

The exact date of the celebration is not known. Pompey's age on the occasion is given variously as "in his twenty-fourth year," twenty-four, twenty-five, and twenty-six. But if they differ on the precise chronology, ancient writers agree in identifying Pompey's extreme youth and lack of formal status—he was not yet a member of the senate—as the triumph's most memorable feature. As Plutarch put it, vividly if inaccurately, "He got a triumph before he grew a beard." To some, this seemed a dazzling honor, proof of Pompey's precocious military genius, and a blow for youth and talent against the conservative closed-shop of senatorial tradition; and it is said to have increased his popularity among the common people. To others, such flouting of precedent and traditional hierarchy represented another step in the dissolution of republican politics. "It goes absolutely against our custom that a mere youth, far too young for senatorial rank, should be given a military command . . . It is quite unheard of that a Roman equestrian should hold a triumph," as Cicero had caricatured the huffing and puffing of Pompey's opponents.[28]

The controversies of this triumph did not stop there. One picturesque detail concerns a team of African elephants. Pompey had brought these back to Rome, caught perhaps on his own hunting expedition. His plan was to hitch his triumphal chariot not to the customary horses but to four of these lumbering beasts. It was a dramatic gesture which would serve to emphasize Pompey's far-flung conquests of exotic foreign territory, and at the same time cast a divine light over the conqueror himself. For, in Greco-Roman myth, the victorious return of the god Bacchus from his conquest of India was often staged in a wagon drawn by elephants.[29]

How Pompey's aides succeeded in training these animals and yoking them to the chariot is a matter of guesswork. But the project came to a premature end at one of the gates through which he was to pass on his way up to the Capitol. The elephants were too big to go through. Pompey apparently tried a second time, again unsuccessfully, and then replaced them with horses. This too-tight squeeze may possibly have been stage-managed to emphasize the idea that Pompey had literally grown too big for the constraints of the city. More likely, it was an embarrassing *impasse,* followed by an awkward hiatus while the outsized animals were removed and the replacements yoked in their place, to the horror (and glee) of the more conservative senators. As the story was later told, at any rate, the moral was not far below the surface: even the most successful of triumphing generals should take care not to get above themselves.[30]

Some of Pompey's own troops might also have taken pleasure in his discomfiture. For in the run-up to the celebration, relations between the soldiers and their general had become, at the very least, strained. The enthusiastic participation of the troops in a triumph could usually be guaranteed by a generous hand-out from the spoils. On this occasion, Pompey's golden touch failed him, and the men complained about the meanness of what they received: the story was that they not only threatened to mutiny but to give in to the obvious temptation and loot the cash on display in the procession itself. Pompey's reaction was to stand firm and—in what was to become another famous slogan—to say that he would rather have no triumph at all, indeed he would rather die, than give in to his soldiers' insubordination. This went down predictably well in some quarters. According to Plutarch, one of the leading opponents of his triumph changed his mind after this display of old-fashioned discipline; and the anecdote is recounted elsewhere as an example of proper determination on the part of a general.[31] It can hardly, however, have endeared him to the rank and file.

He did not make the same mistake after the Mithradatic war, when the size of the donative distributed before the triumph (in fact, while the troops were still out in the East) reached legendary proportions. One hundred million sesterces are said to have been shared out between his "legates and quaestors," Pompey's immediate subordinates, probably about twenty in all. These men must have been wealthy already, but an extra 5 million sesterces each would have been the equivalent of a substantial inheritance, and on its own a sizeable aristocratic fortune. For Pompey, it was a good investment in political loyalty.

The lowest ranking soldiers received 6,000 sesterces each—a tiny proportion of what was given to the commanders, but at roughly six times a soldier's annual pay it must, even so, have seemed a major windfall.[32] Certainly this triumph was remembered centuries later, long after the end of antiquity, for its lavish generosity—as an early sixteenth-century document from the archives of Florence vividly brings home. This was written by an adviser to the Medici, suggesting a detailed programme for celebrating the feast of John the Baptist. To fill one afternoon, this anonymous apparatchik proposed the recreation of four particular ancient triumphs, giving in each case the reasons for his choice. One of them is the (third) triumph of Pompey; the reason is Pompey's liberality and his generosity to friends and enemies alike. A good model for the Medici.[33]

THE ART OF MEMORY

Public spectacles are usually ephemeral events. At the end of the day, when the participants have gone home, when the props, the rubbish, the barricades, and the extra seating have all been cleared away, the show lives on only in memory. It is, of course, in the interests of the sponsors to ensure that the memory lasts, to give the fleeting spectacle a more permanent form, to spread the experience beyond the lucky few who were present on the day itself. That is one function, in modern ceremonial, of souvenir programmes, commemorative mugs, postage stamps, and tea towels. In the case of Pompey's triumphs, the written accounts of the events offered by ancient historians, antiquarians, and poets are crucial in the whole process of its memorialization; and we shall return to these later in this chapter. But art and architecture also played an important part in fixing the occasions in public consciousness and memory.[34]

Coins, for example, replicated Pompey's great day in miniature and distributed it into the pockets of those who could never have witnessed the ceremony. A striking gold coin or *aureus* (Fig. 3) depicts the head of Africa (wearing a tell-tale elephant's skin) with a border in the form of a laurel wreath, one of the distinctive accessories of the general and his soldiers at a triumph; the clear link with Pompey is made by the title MAGNUS running behind Africa's head, and more allusively by the jug and *lituus* (a curved staff) which were the symbols of the augurate, the priesthood he held. It can only be Pompey then in the triumphal chariot

FIGURE 3: Gold coin (*aureus*) minted to celebrate one of Pompey's triumphs, c. 80, 71, or 61 BCE. On the reverse (right), a miniature scene of triumph. On the obverse (left), a laurel wreath encircles the name "Magnus," a head of Africa, and the symbols of Pompey's priesthood.

FIGURE 4: Reverse designs of two silver *denarii* commemorating Pompey's victories, minted 56 BCE. The three trophies (left) call to mind Pompey's three triumphs. The globe surrounded by wreaths (right) hints at worldwide conquest—and at the globe carried in the triumphal procession of 61.

on the reverse of the coin, being crowned by a flying figure of Victory. The rider of the nearest horse in the team is presumably Pompey's son, for the children of the triumphant general regularly seem to have shared his chariot or to have ridden next to him on trace-horses. PRO·COS, for *pro consule,* written beneath, is the formal title of Pompey's military command. Whether it is linked to his first, second, or third triumphs (it has been variously dated to c. 80, 71, and 61 BCE) or even seen as a later issue celebrating all three, the image acted as a visual reminder of Pompey's triumphal career.[35] Alongside their obvious economic functions, these coins would have been a prompt to reimagining the spectacle maybe years after, or miles distant from, its original performance.

Another set of coins, silver *denarii* issued in 56 BCE by Pompey's son-in-law, Faustus Sulla (the dictator's son), recall Pompey's triumphs using different visual clues.[36] These fall into two main types (Fig. 4). The first depicts on its reverse three trophies of victory, plus the symbols of Pompey's priesthood. The other features a globe surrounded by three small wreaths, with a larger wreath above; below are an ear of corn and what is usually—and over-confidently, I suspect—identified as the stern-post of a ship (together perhaps a reference to Pompey's naval command against the pirates and his control of Rome's corn supply in 57). The three trophies must call to mind Dio's description of Pompey's signet ring. The globe evokes not only his world-wide conquests but also, more specifically, that "huge and expensively decorated . . . trophy of the whole world" carried in the procession of 61, while the laurel wreaths signal the triumphal context.[37]

The appeal of these designs lies partly in their sheer bravura in reducing the vastness of the ceremony and the victories lying behind it to a space no larger than a postage stamp. But, predictably enough, triumphs had their colossal memorials too. Part of the profits of Roman warfare in the Republic regularly went into the construction of public buildings, for the most part temples. (The tradition of "triumphal arches," as we call them, became fully established only later, and even then were not exclusively connected with triumphs.) These temples simultaneously commemorated the power of Rome, the prowess of the general, and the support of the gods for Roman victory, as well as acting as memorials of the triumphal celebrations themselves. For they were not only funded out of the very riches that were paraded in procession through the streets, but they also provided permanent showcases for some of the prize spoils that would have been merely glimpsed on the day of the triumphal spectacle.[38]

Pompey's name is associated with a Temple of Minerva, which—as Pliny's quotation of its dedicatory inscription makes clear—he founded out of the spoils of his eastern campaigns: "Dedicated to Minerva, in proper fulfillment of his vow, by Cnaeus Pompeius Magnus, *imperator,* at the completion of the thirty years' war, following the rout, ruin, slaughter, or surrender of 12,183,000 men, the sinking or capture of 846 vessels, the submission of 1538 towns and fortresses, and the subjection of lands from the Sea of Azov to the Red Sea."[39] He was also linked with a Temple of Hercules, which Vitruvius in his manual of architecture refers to as "Hercules Pompeianus." To judge from Vitruvius' description of its decidedly old-fashioned architectural style, Pompey probably financed a restoration rather than the original foundation, but a sufficiently lavish restoration for his name to become attached to the building. There is a fair chance that its statue of Hercules—by Myron, so Pliny has it, the famous fifth-century BCE Greek sculptor (best known now for his *Discus Thrower* but in antiquity more renowned for his extremely life-like *Cow*)—was part of the spoils of victory of one of Pompey's campaigns. Certainly, such a connection is implied by another of the triumphal coins of Faustus Sulla, which features a head of Hercules, in characteristic lion's skin.[40]

It is, however, another design in the same series of coins—Venus crowned with a laurel wreath—that signals Pompey's most extravagant attempt to set his triumph in stone.[41] For they were minted the year before the spectacular inauguration of the theater and porticoes that were built out of the profits of Pompey's eastern campaigns and destined to display many of his triumph's choicest spoils. The term "theater and porticoes" hardly does justice to this vast building complex, which stretched from the present day Piazza Campo dei Fiori to the Largo Argentina, covering an area of some 45,000 square meters (Fig. 5). A daring—and, for Rome, unprecedented—combination of temple, pleasure park, theater, and museum, it wrote Pompey's name permanently into the Roman cityscape. Even now, though no trace remains visible on the ground, its buried foundations (and particularly the distinctive curve of the theater) determine the street plan and housing patterns of the city above; it remains a ghostly template which accounts for the surprising twists and turns of today's back-streets, alleyways, and mansions.[42]

Add to this the lucky survival of exactly the right part of the third-century CE inscribed plan of the city of Rome (the so-called "Marble Plan" or "Forma Urbis"), combined with a series of references in ancient authors and some modern excavation, and we are able to reconstruct the main lines of its design and use—even if intense controversy surrounds the details.[43] At one end of the multi-storey complex perched a Temple of Venus "Victrix." This was the goddess who as "giver of victory" could be seen as the divine guide of Pompey's military success; one ancient writer made the understandable mistake of calling it simply a Temple of Victoria.[44] But Venus "victorious" (both translations are correct) must also have evoked the success of the goddess herself in the mythical con-

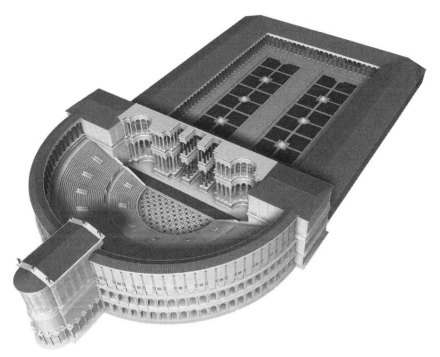

FIGURE 5: Pompey's theater and porticoes. There have been many attempts to recapture the daring design and lavish scale of the whole complex. This three-dimensional reconstruction, based on nineteenth-century drawings, shows the Temple of Venus Victrix (bottom left) overlooking the auditorium; beyond the porticoes, gardens and a sculpture gallery.

test with Juno and Diana for the apple of Paris, and so too the whole history of the Trojan War—and Rome's descent from Venus' son, the Trojan Aeneas—which that contest sparked.

On this upper level stood other smaller shrines to a clutch of notably military virtues (including Virtus itself, the personification of manly courage, and Felicitas, the kind of divinely inspired good fortune that was essential to successful generalship). More eye-catching, though, was the dramatic feat of engineering that adapted and expanded the steps of the Temple of Venus into the seating of a vast theater, cascading down to a performance area and extensive gardens beyond. According to Pliny's no doubt exaggerated figures, it could hold 40,000 spectators.[45]

Whether this scheme was inspired by the so-called "theater-temples" of Italy (where temple steps doubled with theater seating) or was a piece of new-fangled Hellenism copied, as Plutarch claimed, from the architecture of the Greek city of Mytilene is hard to say. What is certain is that this was the first permanent stone theater built in the city of Rome, and as such it caused some muttering about luxury and immorality among the old guard.[46] No less of an innovation were the gardens, walkways, and porticoes that stretched for almost two hundred meters (this was effectively Rome's first public park) toward a new senate house that stood at the far end of the complex. This was the spot "even at the base of Pompey's statue" where Julius Caesar was murdered in 44 BCE.[47]

The whole development was littered with sculpture and painting, in part the booty from the east, in part (as Pliny remarks about statues of a pair of heroines, one of whom was famous for giving birth to an elephant) specially commissioned. There are a number of references to prize items from this gallery in surviving ancient literature. Pliny notes, for example, in addition to Alcippe the elephant's mother, a painting of Cadmus and Europa by the fourth-century artist Antiphilos and another by the fifth-century painter Polygnotos, originally hanging in Pompey's senate house and showing "a shield bearer" (a talking point, it seems: was he shown mounting or dismounting from his horse?).[48] Traces of this gallery in surviving marble or bronze, still less in paint, have been much harder to pin down. The survivals include a group of five outsized Muses, plus a matching Apollo (now split between galleries in Rome, Naples, and Paris), a similarly colossal seated female figure, and a number of inscribed statue bases, all discovered in this area of Rome.[49]

Beyond this general outline, our detailed understanding of the decorative programme of the building is much more limited than most of the reconstructive fantasies of modern archaeologists would suggest. These have often rested on the ingenious but doubtful speculation that a list of risqué pagan statues denounced for their immorality by Tatian, a second-century Christian polemicist, in fact represents (though Tatian himself does not say so) a partial roster of the statues from Pompey's temple, theater, and porticoes.[50] This has launched a variety of theories: that the sculptural decoration was themed around Greek poetesses, courtesans *(hetairai)*, and extraordinary mothers (fitting neatly with Pliny's Alcippe, of course); that it offered a "quintessentially Roman formulation" of the equation of "libido with tyranny," within an artistic programme that put on show a particularly loaded version of the union of Greek and Roman culture; or, taking a more cerebral turn, that it recreated in stone the theological theories of that most influential first-century polymath Varro, under perhaps the directly guiding hand of Varro himself.[51] Whether these scholarly fantasies are just that or whether they reflect in part the fertile imagination of the Romans themselves is a moot point. But, either way, it should not cloud the fact that this was, or was also, a monument of Pompey's triumph.

With its array of treasures from the conquests, any walk through Pompey's porticoes must also have entailed a re-viewing of the spoils first seen on September 28 and 29, 61—the procession being re-enacted in the movement of each and every visitor, as they passed the objects on display.[52] But more than that, some individual works of art explicitly evoked Pompey's triumphal moment. Pliny refers to a portrait of Alexander the Great by the painter Nikias (prompting recollections of the cloak said to have been worn by Pompey in the procession), as well as to a group of statues of "fourteen *nationes*" or "peoples" that stood "around Pompey" or (depending on the exact reading of a possibly corrupt text) "around the porticoes/theater of Pompey."[53] These were presumably new commissions, personifications of the peoples conquered in his campaigns; significantly or not, the number fourteen coincides with the total number of nations whose names, according to Plutarch, were carried at the front of the triumphal parade itself (or, alternatively, with the list of conquests that Pliny quotes from the "announcement" of the triumph). The statues certainly continued to make an impression well into the Empire: Suetonius claims that, after he had murdered his mother, the emperor Nero dreamed that was he was being menaced by them; it was a nightmare that foreboded provincial uprising from the peoples whom Pompey had once conquered.[54]

One surviving statue may even represent Pompey in his role as triumphant conqueror: a colossal statue of a nude male, some three meters tall, which since soon after its discovery in the sixteenth century has stood in the Roman mansion now known as the Palazzo Spada (Fig. 6). In the mid-seventeenth century it was identified as the very statue beneath which Caesar was assassinated. The arguments were based on its findspot in the right area of the city, the presumed likeness of its head to other portraits, and (for those with vivid imaginations) the red stains in the marble of his left leg—traces of Caesar's blood. This identification appeared to crumble when the head was shown to be entirely modern, a sixteenth-century restoration.

Nonetheless, leaving the blood aside, the findspot does make some connection with Pompey's theater complex plausible, as does the scale of the piece and some of its attributes: the figure is supported by a palm trunk (a plant strongly connected with victory and triumph), while in his hand he holds a globe, the symbol of world conquest. True, these are also well-known attributes of Roman emperors, and a detailed case has been made for seeing here a figure of the emperor Domitian. But it is no less likely that the seventeenth-century scholars had it right (albeit for the wrong reasons): that this is what is left of the triumphant Pompey from his senate house.[55]

The triumphal aspects of this whole building complex were emphasized even more starkly in the celebrations that marked its inauguration in 55 BCE—a characteristic Roman combination of tragic theater, music, and athletics, horse racing and wild beast hunts (the hunts alone lasted for five days). The date chosen for the festivities is itself significant. Although not explicitly recorded in any surviving ancient evidence, it was almost certainly the closing days of September (shortly after Cicero delivered his speech *In Pisonem [Against Piso]*, as that speech makes clear).[56] In other words, the inauguration of the buildings took place over the anniversary of the third triumph—making in the process another stupendous birthday celebration for Pompey.

The plays chosen for the occasion, too, could be seen as an imaginative re-performance of the triumph. According to Cicero, two re-

FIGURE 6: Colossal statue of Pompey, now in the Palazzo Spada, Rome. The head was shown to be modern, when the statue was moved in 1798 to provide a backdrop in a performance of Voltaire's *Death of Caesar*; but the rest may be what is left of the general that once stood in the senate house that was part of his theater-and-portico complex.

vivals featured prominently in the theatrical programme: Accius'
Clytemnestra and the *Equus Troianus (Trojan Horse)* of either Naevius or
Livius Andronicus. We can do no more than guess at the details of their
plots, but *Clytemnestra* certainly focused on the return of Agamemnon
to Greece after his victory at Troy, the *Equus Troianus* on the devious
Greek scheme to bring that victory about. Cicero, in a letter written
shortly after the event, strongly suggests that the spoils of war played a
starring role in both productions: he writes of the "six-hundred mules"
that tramped across the stage in the *Clytemnestra* (no doubt carrying Agamemnon's returning army, its baggage, and its treasure) and the "three-
thousand kraters" in the *Equus Troianus* (presumably a parade of booty
the Greeks stripped from the Trojans). It may be fanciful to imagine
that Pompey's Mithradatic booty came back on stage to act the part of
Agamemnon's spoils. But where else did those "three-thousand kraters"
come from?[57]

As with the triumph itself, however, despite its lavishness (or perhaps,
rather, because of it), Pompey's inaugural celebration prompted cyni-
cism and disapproval as well as admiration. This was, no doubt, partly
because Pompey's political pre-eminence had been eroded in the six
years since his third triumph. The kind of razzmatazz that accompanied
the triumphal procession of the Roman Alexander risked appearing
faintly ridiculous when it was revived to celebrate the triumphal monument of a man who had been forced to protect his own position through
an uneasy alliance with Julius Caesar, who had been the butt of abuse—
and worse—from all sides, and whose third consulship in the very year
of 55 BCE had only been achieved by even more obvious corruption and
violence than usual.[58]

Cicero's "memorably dyspeptic letter" describing the events threw
some predictable cold water on quite how successful the spectacles had
been. An elderly star actor brought out of retirement specially for the occasion had apparently dried up at a key moment, the general extravagance of the proceedings had been more off-putting than admirable,
and the wild beast hunts gave "no pleasure at all" to gentlemen of taste.
"What pleasure can there be for a man of refinement when some feeble

human being is being torn to pieces by a mighty beast, or a noble beast run through with a hunting spear?" he asked, in that tone of carefully contrived superiority sometimes adopted by the Roman elite in discussing the bloodier aspects of the games. But in fact, the elite were not alone in feeling some disquiet at the fate of the animals. Pompey's bad luck with elephants came back to haunt him: a group of twenty that had been assembled for the show attempted a mass break out from the arena, causing (as Pliny rather calmly puts it) "trouble in the crowd," and finally—thwarted in the escape attempt—trumpeted pitifully to the spectators as if making a plea for release. Just as the noble prisoners in the triumphal procession itself were (as we shall see) always liable to upstage the victorious general himself in the play for the audience's attention, so here it was animal victims who stole the show.[59]

But more than that, some of the chosen spectacles raised particularly uncomfortable questions. It was one thing for the theatrical programme to showcase the return of Agamemnon and so inevitably to cast Pompey's eastern victories in the light of the mythical Greek victory over Troy. But how could the rest of Agamemnon's story be kept out of the frame, notably his murder immediately after that triumphant arrival home at the hands of his wife, Clytemnestra, and her lover, Aegisthus? It may be that the image of Agamemnon as the great western conqueror of the East was powerful enough, for most of the people, most of the time, to keep the other associations at bay. But Suetonius, in his biography of Caesar, reports the story that Pompey divorced his wife on his return from the East "because of Caesar" and that he used to call Caesar "Aegisthus." This is as clear a hint as you could wish that the subversive potential of the mythical stories on display was not lost on all Romans.[60]

Other attempts to memorialize the triumph, or to extend its display beyond the day of the procession itself, had a more personal focus—and, in some cases, were no less double-edged. Triumphal spoils were not only displayed in major building projects; they also adorned the private houses of victorious generals. Pliny stressed the permanence of the triumphal message entailed by such displays. He explained that, as the spoils were not removed with a change of owner, the "houses themselves went on triumphing for ever, even when they changed hands" and that for new owners the spoils acted as an incentive to glory ("Every day the walls of the house reproach an owner who has no taste for war for intruding on someone else's triumph").[61]

Pliny may have had in mind here a famous passage in one of Cicero's attacks on Mark Antony, who occupied Pompey's house after his death (having bought it for, no doubt, a knock-down price during the civil wars). The rams of ships captured by Pompey, probably in his campaign against the pirates, still stood in its entranceway; and these spoils could hardly believe, as Cicero imagines it, that the drunken and dissolute Antony was really their new owner. In this case the captured weapons remained—maybe for centuries—as the carriers (and protectors) of the glory of the triumphing general, and as an incentive to follow his example. Even in late antiquity, Pompey's house (or a house that was believed to be Pompey's) went under the name of the "House of the Rams" *(domus rostrata).*[62]

The special costume worn by the triumphing general offered the possibility of a different type of permanent honor. Traditionally this had been worn on the day of the triumph alone. But Pompey in 63 BCE, between his second and third triumphs, was granted the almost unprecedented right to wear various elements of the dress on particular public occasions—including, according to the historian Velleius Paterculus, the right to "the golden crown and full triumphal costume at all circus games." This grant probably accounts for the presence of the mysterious fourth wreath, or crown, on the coin of Faustus Sulla, and its implications are clear to us: the temporary glory of the triumphal procession was being turned into a permanent mark of status and prestige. The implications were also clear to (and resisted by) some Romans, including, if we are to believe Velleius, Pompey himself: "He did not have the nerve to use this honor more than once; and that was once too often."[63]

Even so, in January 60 BCE, in a letter to his friend Atticus, Cicero could pillory Pompey's obsession with the baubles of triumphal glory. While the senatorial heavyweights were preparing to gang up to defeat a bill that would have distributed land to his veteran soldiers, Pompey himself was keeping his head down; or, as Cicero put it, "He's safeguarding that dinky little triumphal toga of his by keeping quiet."[64] What does this exactly mean? That Pompey was unwilling to do anything to jeopardize his rights to triumphal dress, voted in 63 BCE? Or, more loosely, that he wanted above all to hang on to the fleeting renown of his third triumph, celebrated only a few months earlier? Either way, the attributes of triumphal glory are here cast as an unworthy obsession, the trinkets of honor rather than the real thing.

THE HEART OF THE TRIUMPH

This story of Pompey exposes many of the issues that lie at the heart of Roman triumphal culture. Some of these need very little exposing. It would be hard to overlook the role of the ceremony, and its memorials, in the celebration of Roman military prowess and imperial expansion, and in the glorification of the victorious general himself; this is why, after all, kings, dynasts, and autocrats have chosen to imitate it ever since, parading their power and their conquests in recognizably Roman style. In fact, the triumphal entry of the French king, Henri II, into the city of Rouen in 1550 was explicitly likened in contemporary records to Pompey's ceremony: "No less pleasing and delectable than the third triumph of Pompey . . . seen by the Romans as magnificent in riches and abounding in the spoils of foreign nations" (Fig. 7).[65]

The triumph was about display and success—the success of display no less than the display of success. As the Greek historian Polybius put it in his analysis of Roman institutions in the second century BCE, it was "a spectacle in which generals bring right before the eyes of the Roman people a vivid impression of their achievements." The general was, in other words, the impresario of the show and almost (as Polybius' language strongly hints) a consummate artist, restaging his own achievements in front of the home crowd.[66] So it certainly must have seemed in 61. Some of Pompey's conquests were, quite literally, brought to Rome (the booty and treasure, the beaks of wrecked pirate ships, the exotic trees, the captives all paraded through the streets). But also on show was

FIGURE 7: Soldiers in the triumphal entry of Henri II into Rouen in 1550. As in some Roman triumphs, they carry models of forts captured by the victorious army. Enthusiastic accounts of the procession held these models to be so accurate that the places were "easily recognizable" to the participants in the various battles.

a notable range of different representations of both the processes and the profits of victory (the placards detailing the money gained and the peoples conquered, the paintings capturing details of Mithradates' defeat, the trophy of the whole world). The triumph, in other words, re-presented and re-enacted the victory. It brought the margins of the Empire to its center, and in so doing celebrated the new geopolitics that victory had brought about.

This is what Pompey himself suggested in a famous quip he is supposed to have uttered before his triumph, at an assembly at which he detailed his successes to the Roman people: "The very pinnacle of his glory, as he himself said, was to have found Asia a frontier province and to have left it at the very center of the state *(mediam patriae)*." This was more than showy rhetorical exaggeration. It was a clever play on words; for as a proper noun, *Media* means the "country of the Medes," and so a part of Asia ("he turned Asia into Media . . . "). It was also, surely, a knowing allusion to the nature of Roman victory itself and to its representation in the triumph; for Asia did indeed come to the very heart of Rome.[67]

Almost equally clear is the fact that the glory of the triumph was bound up in the rivalry and competition of Roman republican politics. Each individual ceremony was a celebration in its own right, of course; it reflected the particularities of an individual campaign and an individual moment of politics. But, long before the first century BCE, it was also part of the history of the triumph, to be judged against, to upstage or be upstaged by, the triumphs of predecessors and rivals. True, the hothouse competitiveness of Roman political life may have been over-emphasized by modern scholars; among the hundreds of triumphs celebrated through the Republic, many must have been modest occasions where the victorious general was entirely content with a few cart-loads of spoils and the regulation plaudits. All the same, this ceremony—as almost every other Roman institution—could hardly have escaped being implicated in the struggles for supremacy between the great dynasts of the first century. It was certainly written up in these terms by ancient commentators. Hence the repeated rhetoric of innovation and inflation, the stress on triumphs which were bigger and better than those that had gone before or which launched new forms of display. In Pompey's case we have already noted the emphasis on the unprecedented size of the profits and the vast quantity of booty, as well as on the elephants (who for the first time, albeit unsuccessfully, pulled the triumphal chariot) and on the novelty of treating exotic trees as spoils of war.

The sense of direct triumphal rivalry is most vividly captured by the story of his relations with Metellus Creticus, who was also scoring victories over the pirates that threatened to upstage Pompey's own. In telling how Pompey stole two of Metellus' prize captives to adorn his own triumph, Dio prompts us to reflect on how triumphal glory is achieved and calibrated, and on the fact that in the celebration of victory even the successful general can be a loser as well as a winner. Plutarch goes further, claiming that Pompey sent his own men to fight on the pirates' side against Metellus. Resorting to an extravagant comparison with the traditional stories of Greek myth, Plutarch suggested that this was an even more flagrant piece of glory-hunting than that of Achilles in Homer's *Iliad*, who prevented his comrades from attacking his enemy, Hector, so that no one else should have the honor of the first blow. Pompey "actually fought on behalf of enemies of the state and saved their lives, in order to rob of a triumph a general who had worked hard to achieve it."[68]

Losers in the race for triumphal glory, however, were not only those who were upstaged by their rivals in the lavishness of the spectacle they could provide. One of the most important lessons of Pompey's triumphs (and one to which I shall return several times) is the risk and the danger attached even—or especially—to the most spectacular of celebrations. Not far under the surface of that image of self-confident success usually associated with the triumphing general in most modern writing ("his greatest moment of glory ever") is the specter of failure and humiliation.[69]

It was not just a question of things going wrong, although that must have been a frequent enough event in even the best-planned ceremonial. Pompey's discomfiture with the elephants was more than matched by Caesar's, when the axle of his chariot broke during the first of his series of triumphs in 46 BCE, ironically enough in front of a Temple of Felicitas (Good Fortune). Caesar was almost toppled out and had to wait for a replacement.[70] Nor was it primarily a matter of the predictable sneers of rivals and friends. Sneers and strident satire have always been an occupational hazard of the successful, and are a fairly reliable marker of celebrity renown. A much more significant concern in ancient writing on the triumph is the underlying problem of glory and its representations. Did the panoply of triumphal display on the scale launched by Pompey necessarily risk overplaying its hand? Was true glory to be measured in terms of luxury or of restraint? Did the pomp and circumstance invite retribution as well as admiration? In the fullness of time, would the triumph be remembered as the general's finest hour or the presage of his fall?

For Pliny, one notorious object carried in the procession of 61 provoked reflections of this type: the portrait head of Pompey himself made out of pearls. "That portrait, that portrait was, I repeat, made out of pearls," he carped, in full tirade. "This was the defeat of austerity and the triumph, let's face it, of luxury. Never, believe me, would he have been able to keep his title 'Magnus' ('The Great') among the heroes of that earlier generation if he had celebrated a triumph like this after his first victory. To think, Magnus, that it was out of pearls that your features were fashioned—things you would never have been allowed to wear, such an extravagant material, and meant for women. Was that how you made yourself seem valuable?"

But this portrait was not for Pliny simply a symbol of Pompey's extravagant effeminization. There was a yet nastier implication, which he goes on (gleefully, one feels) to insinuate. "It was, believe me, a gross and offensive disgrace, except that the head on display without the rest of his body, in all its eastern splendor, ought really to have been taken as a cruel omen of divine anger; its meaning could easily have been worked out." Or, at least, it could have been with hindsight. For Pliny is referring to Pompey's murder on the shores of Egypt, where he had fled after his defeat by Caesar's forces at the battle of Pharsalus in 48 BCE. Decapitated by a treacherous welcoming party, his head "without the rest of his body" was eventually presented to Caesar, who reputedly wept (crocodile tears?) at the sight. The head of pearls in his greatest triumphal procession already presaged Pompey's humiliating end.[71]

Other ancient writers also drew an unsettling connection between Pompey's death and his moments of triumphal glory. Lucan's magnificently subversive epic on the civil war between Pompey and Caesar, the *Pharsalia,* written a hundred years later during the reign of Nero (and with a cynical eye on the imperial autocracy that stemmed from Pompey's defeat), repeatedly plays on ideas of triumph. Its opening verses herald the subject of the poem as "wars that will win no triumphs," an oxymoron pointing to the illegitimacy of the civil conflict that is Lucan's theme.[72] Throughout, Pompey himself is both defined and dogged by his triumphal career. The "Fortune" who brought him victory over the pirates has abandoned him, because she is "exhausted by his triumphs."[73] And after his humiliating death, what is burnt on the funeral pyre by his widow is not his body at all but his weapons and clothes, in particular his "triumphal togas" and "the robes thrice seen by Jupiter supreme."

Lucan seems to be hinting not only at the close identification of Pompey with his triumphs (to cremate Pompey is also to cremate his triumphs), but also—as Cicero once saw it—at his solipsistic obsession with the superficial trappings of triumphal glory (to cremate Pompey is *only* to cremate this fancy dress).[74] The most pointed scene, however, occurs in his camp on the night before the disastrous battle of Pharsalus itself, when Pompey dreams that he has returned to Rome: he is sitting in his own theater—his triumphal monument—and is being applauded to the skies by the Roman people; this, in turn, takes him back to the celebration of his first triumph and to the applause of the senate and people on that occasion. Once again the triumph (or its memory) accompanies and directly presages defeat.[75]

There is a final uncanny twist. As Dio emphasizes, Pompey was murdered "on the very same day as he had once celebrated his triumph over Mithradates and the pirates"; or, in Velleius' formulation, "in his fifty-eighth year, on the eve of his birthday." In Roman cultural memory Pompey's whole life—his death no less than his birth—was tied to his moment of triumph.[76]

THE TRIUMPH OF WRITING

Pompey's triumph of 61 was one of the most memorable—or, at least, the most remembered and, for us, the best documented—in the whole history of Rome. For all the undoubted importance of the memorials in marble, bronze, and gold, it was *writing*, more than anything else, that inscribed the occasion in Roman memory; it was recalled, rethought, and resignified through the tales in Pompey's biographers, the poetic imagination of Lucan, the sometimes grinding narratives of ancient historians, the encyclopedic curiosity (and moralizing fervor) of the elder Pliny, and more.[77] These are the accounts that underlie the story of Pompey's triumph told in this chapter. Yet even the least suspicious of readers must by now have felt a few reservations about just how plausible some of the descriptions are. Did the procession really feature such extravagant quantities of precious metals as we read? A statue of Mithradates eight cubits high (that is some three and a half meters) in solid gold? Do the figures for cash acquired, captives on parade, or enemy defeated (more than 12 million, according to the dedication to Minerva that Pliny quotes) make any sense? Has not a good deal of exaggeration, or wishful thinking, crept into these ancient accounts, and so too into our own story of the triumph? After all, Appian himself was skeptical enough to sound a warning note about that unlikely story of Alexander's cloak.

There are obvious reasons for being suspicious. For a start—with the exception of Cicero's sarcasm on the inauguration of Pompey's theater—not one of the surviving ancient accounts is from the pen of an eyewitness to the ceremonies; and the fullest descriptions of the triumph itself were written at least a century (and in Dio's case almost three centuries) later. They are almost bound to be, in part at least, the product of years of anecdote, hyperbole, and popular myth-making, of later reformulations of Pompey's image and importance, and of their authors' experience of triumphal ceremonies in their own day, projected back—even if indirectly—onto the parade of 61 BCE. Of course, some good "primary" evidence, even archival records, may lie behind some of these accounts, but that is harder to pin down than we might imagine.

We can be fairly certain that Plutarch's bibliography included the (now lost) account of the Mithradatic wars by Pompey's own tame historian, Theophanes of Mytilene, and that Appian made use of the histories of Pompey's contemporary Asinius Pollio. But we do not know whether either of these men were present at the triumph of 61 or whether they included a description of it in their books; and even if they did, we could not be sure that the triumphal details in Plutarch and Appian were drawn directly from them.[78] Besides, there is also the question of the intellectual and ideological agenda of the ancient writers. Pliny, for example, was not setting out to offer a historical description of Pompey's triumph. His various references to the ceremony all serve quite different aims, whether to exemplify the consequences of excess, the characteristics of extraordinary human beings, or the history and use of ebony. This will inevitably have affected the selection and adaptation of the material at his disposal.

Scratch the surface of the surviving ancient accounts and all kinds of particular difficulties emerge. Sometimes we find awkward inconsistencies between writers. It was reassuring to note that Pliny and Plutarch both offer a list of fourteen peoples conquered by Pompey. It was reassuring, too, to be able to match this figure to the number of statues of the *nationes* who formed that notable group of sculpture in Pompey's theater. Far less reassuring is the fact that the names of the countries cited are significantly different in each case, that they do not exactly match any other list we have of Pompey's conquests, fourteen or not, and that we have no reliable way now of establishing which peoples were officially the object of Pompey's triumph.[79]

Sometimes it is a matter of detecting clear hints of literary embellishment and invention. So, for example, when Appian reports that Mithradates' reason for suicide was his desire not to appear in Pompey's triumphal procession, we can be almost certain that he is not relying on any evidence for the king's motives but exploiting what was by then a well-known cliché of the triumph (seen most famously in the story of the suicide of Cleopatra) that foreign rulers would do anything rather than suffer the humiliation of a Roman triumph. Even the quotations of, or from, various official documents are not necessarily quite what they seem. We do not know whether the ancient writers saw and transcribed the documents themselves, or took them from earlier literary accounts, reliable or not. And we cannot always work out what the original document was.

For example, a copy of one inscription, listing Pompey's conquests in detail and noting his generous offering to "the goddess," was included in a (now lost) book of the *Bibliotheca Historia (Library of History)* by the Greek historian Diodorus—and is known to us only because of its curious preservation in a tenth-century Byzantine anthology. Some scholars take it to be a Greek translation of the original dedicatory inscription of Pompey's Temple of Venus Victrix (or of Minerva). Others argue that it is not from Rome at all but the original Greek record of some dedication by Pompey in the East, perhaps at the famous Temple of Artemis at Ephesus. Others imagine that it is not a single text, but a composite of a number of documents translated by Diodorus then sewn together probably by his Byzantine anthologizer. Which of these solutions is correct is an entirely open question.[80]

The numbers given for cash or captives, for spoils or ships taken, remain the most tendentious area of all. Ancient records of figures such as these are almost always controversial: not only were they easily susceptible to exaggeration (more euphemistically, "rounding up") in antiquity itself, but in the process of transmission by later scribes, who most likely had very little idea of the significance or plausibility of these numbers, they were very easily corrupted. The question is which ones have been corrupted, by how much, and on what principle they can be corrected.[81] Various suggestions have been made for regularizing some of the figures cited for Pompey's triumphs. For example, Pliny's impossible 12,183,000 for the number of enemy prisoners and casualties has been ingeniously reduced to 121,083 and in the process brought into line with the sum total of enemy troops said to have been killed, imprisoned, or put to flight at different stages of the campaign in Plutarch's account: an aggregate (though Plutarch does not do the calculation himself) of 121,000.[82]

In general, however, modern historians have been more inclined than we might expect to give some credence to the raw numbers cited for the profits of the campaigns and the cash distributed to the soldiers. This is partly because, for all their problems, these figures have proved too tempting a historical source to discard: it is only from the total amount said to be distributed to the soldiers, combined with the level of individual donatives, that any estimate has been possible of the number of troops under Pompey's command; and it is from Plutarch's claims about the annual tax revenue of the Roman Empire and Pompey's additions to it that many an ambitious theory on Roman economic history has been launched.[83] This has meant turning a relatively blind eye to inconvenient contradictions between different figures in different ancient writers. Pliny, for example, claims that from his booty Pompey paid 50 million denarii into the treasury, while Plutarch gives a figure more than twice as much: 120 million denarii.[84] It has also meant not giving weight to other, conflicting indications. It seems implausible—even if not impossible—that Pompey should have made distributions to his troops on the scale reported without some noticeable impact on the quantity of Roman coins minted. But in so far as we can reconstruct the pattern of Roman minting and coin circulation through this period, Pompey's donatives and the influx of booty into Rome and subsequent public expenditure seem to have made (suspiciously) no impact at all.[85]

So where does this leave our understanding of Pompey's triumph? We are confronted with what is a common dilemma in studying the ancient world. Some of the information transmitted to us must be inaccurate, even flagrantly so; some of it may well be broadly reliable. But we have few clear criteria (beyond hunch and frankly *a priori* notions of plausibility, compatibility, and coherence) that enable us to distinguish what is "accurate" from what is not. How, for example, do we evaluate the objects said to have been displayed in the procession? Reject the eight-cubit solid gold statue because it is simply too big to be true? Accept the wagonloads of precious vessels because we have a specimen that seems to match up, and the pearl head because Pliny is so insistent about it? Suspect some exaggeration (but not perhaps outright invention) when it comes to the golden mountain with the vine or that extraordinary sundial?

Yet to think about this triumph principally in terms of the "accuracy" of our sources—and so how best we might reconstruct the events as they happened on the day—is in many important ways to miss the point. It is, of course, right and proper to recognize that the surviving written accounts do not offer a direct window onto the ceremonies; not even eyewitness narratives do that (as we know from our own experience, as well as from the study of numerous Renaissance and early modern rituals, where an abundance of primary documentation in fact proliferates the problems of reading and reconstructing).[86] But the point is that "the events as they happened on the day" are only one part of the story of this, or any, triumph.

The triumph of Pompey is not simply, or even primarily, about what happened on September 28 and 29, 61 BCE. It is also about the ways in which it was subsequently remembered, embellished, argued over, decried, and incorporated into the wider mythology of the Roman triumph as a historical institution and cultural category. Like all ceremonies—from coronations to funerals, graduation to mardi gras—its meaning must lie as much in the recollection and re-presentation of the proceedings as in the transient proceedings themselves. Its story is always in the telling. The exaggerations, the distortions, the selective amnesia are all part of the plot—as this book will show.

II

The Impact of the Triumph

ROMAN TRIUMPHAL CULTURE

The triumph left a vivid mark on Roman life, history, and culture. At some periods the ceremony was more or less an annual event in the city. In the ten years between 260 and 251 BCE, for example, twelve triumphs are recorded, thanks to successful Roman campaigns against the Carthaginians. Pompey's triumph in 71 was the last in a bumper year that had already seen three triumphal processions. Many of these occasions were memorialized by Roman writers who recounted—and, no doubt, embroidered—the controversies and disputes that sometimes preceded them, as well as the character of the processions themselves, with their placards and paintings, captives, precious booty, and occasionally unexpected stunts. Some were more unexpected than others. In 117–118 CE a triumph celebrated the emperor Trajan's victory over the Parthians. But Trajan himself was, in fact, already dead; his place in the triumphal chariot was taken by a dummy.[1]

Triumphs offered a suitable climax to poems celebrating Roman achievement. Silius Italicus, writing in the first century CE, made the triumph of Scipio Africanus the culmination of his verse account of the war against Hannibal. He probably had in mind the precedent of Ennius, the "Father of Roman Poetry." Although only a few hundred lines survive of Ennius' great epic on Roman history, the *Annales,* its final book very likely featured the triumph of his patron, Marcus Fulvius Nobilior, in 187 BCE.[2] Completely imaginary celebrations added to the picture, as writers retrojected the triumph back into the world of Greek history and myth, to honor the likes of Alexander the Great and the god Bacchus. In a particularly striking piece of Romanization, at the end of his epic on the legends of the Greek city of Thebes (the *Thebaid*), Statius invents a Roman-style triumph for the Athenian king Theseus after his victory over that classic symbol of female barbarity, the Amazons. The king rides through the streets, to the cheers of the crowd, in a chariot decked with laurel and pulled by four white horses; in front stream the captives, the spoils, and the weapons taken from enemy, carried shoulder-high. But there is a twist. In this story, the enemy leader is under no threat of execution as the procession reaches its end; Hippolyte, the Amazon queen, is Theseus', her conqueror's, bride.[3]

Monuments depicting or commemorating triumphs came to dominate the cityscape of Rome; some of them still do. The Arch of Titus, erected in the early 80s CE, is a highlight of the modern tourist trail, being one of the few monuments in the Roman Forum to remain standing to its full height (albeit with the help of a radical rebuild in the early nineteenth century). In its passageway are two sculptured panels with the most evocative images of the triumph to have survived from antiquity. On one side, Titus in his chariot celebrates his triumph over the Jews, held jointly with his father Vespasian, after the sack of Jerusalem in 70 (Fig. 8). On the other side, the booty from the Temple, including the distinctive menorah, is carried shoulder-high in procession through Rome (Fig. 9).[4] The triumphal imagery of other buildings we may reconstruct from fainter traces, combined with ancient descriptions.

The Forum of Augustus, for example—the showpiece monument of Rome's first emperor and a match for Pompey's theater-complex in grandeur, if not in size—seems to have been packed with allusions to triumph. It too was built from the profits of successful campaigns *(ex manubiis).* In the center of its great piazza stood a four-horse triumphal chariot or *quadriga,* possibly carrying a statue of Augustus himself along

FIGURE 8: The triumphal procession in 71 CE of the future emperor Titus, from the passageway of the Arch of Titus in the Roman Forum. A typically Roman combination of documentary realism and idealizing fantasy: Titus stands in his chariot, crowned by a winged Victory; in front, another female figure (perhaps the goddess Roma, or "Virtue") leads the horses. The *fasces*, Roman rods of office, fill the background.

with a figure of Victoria, the personification of victory (or so an elegant bronze female foot found on the site has been taken to suggest). Statues of heroes of the Republic lined the colonnades, each one (according to Suetonius) "in triumphal guise." And, in a classic instance of a Greek subject being reinterpreted in Roman triumphal terms, two famous old masters by the fourth-century BCE painter Apelles showing "War as a captive"—or, according to another writer, "Madness"—"hands bound behind his back, and Alexander triumphing on a chariot." As if to drive the point home, the emperor Claudius later had the face of Alexander cut out and Augustus' substituted.[5]

Outside Rome too there were plenty of visual reminders of triumphs. One of the most spectacular must have been the vast monument over-

FIGURE 9: The procession of triumphal spoils from the passageway of the Arch of Titus (facing Fig. 8). The sacred treasures of the Jews, taken by the Romans at the destruction of the Temple in Jerusalem, are paraded through the streets: in the center the menorah, to the right the Table of Shewbread. The placards identify the objects or record the details of the victory.

looking the site of the battle of Actium, on the northwest coast of Greece, which commemorated the defeat there in 31 BCE of Antony and Cleopatra and the founding moment of Augustus' domination of the Roman world. Here, recent excavations have brought to light thousands of fragments of marble sculpture, which make up an elaborately detailed sculptural narrative of the triumph that followed in 29. If one of the functions of the triumphal procession was, as Polybius had it, to bring the successes of battle before the eyes of the people in Rome, at Actium that process was reversed: the triumph was replayed in marble on the site of the battle.[6]

A more familiar sight on the Roman landscape were the so-called "triumphal arches" which by the first century CE had become a characteristic marker of Roman presence and power across the Empire, from Britain to Syria. Most of these had a less direct connection with triumphal celebrations than their modern title implies (the term *arcus triumphalis* is not known in Latin until the third century CE). They were built to commemorate particular events, to honor individual members of the imperial family, or, earlier, to vaunt the prestige of republican aristocrats. We know, for example, of a series of three arches decreed in honor of the imperial prince Germanicus after his death in 19 CE. The important fact is not that such arches regularly commemorated triumphs (though some did), but—in a sense, the other way round—that they used the imagery of triumphal celebrations as part of their own rhetoric of power.

Triumphal chariots once perched on the tops of many arches, while the Arch of Trajan at Beneventum (modern Benevento) in south Italy, built in 114 CE to mark the construction of the road between Brindisi and Rome, incorporates a miniature frieze showing a triumphal procession that winds its way around all four sides of the monument (Fig. 10).[7] But the triumph was commemorated not only in these great piles of masonry; the ceremony invaded domestic space too. We know of one anonymous grandee, the proprietor of a villa outside Pompeii that was destroyed in the eruption of 79 CE, who must regularly have faced up to the triumph at his dinner table. For the design of one of the exquisite silver cups from the famous dinner service discovered at Boscoreale features a triumphing general—almost certainly the future emperor Tiberius—with his retinue, standing proud in his triumphal chariot (Fig. 11).[8]

The impact of the triumph was not confined to the realm of imperialist geopolitics or military history; it extended far beyond the general, his friends and rivals among the Roman elite, the victorious soldiers and the noble, or pathetic, captives dragged along in the procession. To be sure, these figures enjoy the spotlight in most ancient accounts of the ceremony. But, as with all such public ceremonials at any period of history, there must have been a wide range of different experiences of the triumph and all kinds of different personal narratives prompted by it. What, for example, of those who flogged refreshments to the crowds, who put up the seating or cleared up the mess at the end of the day? What of the spectators who found the sun too hot or the rain too wet, who could hardly see the wonderful extravaganza that others applauded,

FIGURE 10: The Arch of Trajan at Beneventum, 114–118 CE. Its sculpture commemorates the achievements of the emperor in both peace and war; the small triumphal procession (Fig. 21) runs around the whole monument, just below the attic storey. Further sculpture would originally have stood on top, above the attic.

FIGURE 11: Triumph of Tiberius, on a silver cup from Boscoreale. The future emperor stands in the chariot, holding a scepter and laurel branch; behind, a slave holds a wreath or crown over his head. The exact date of the piece depends on which of Tiberius' two triumphs is depicted: 7 BCE or 12 CE.

or who found themselves mixed up in the outbreaks of violence that could be prompted by the spectacle? The historian Dio reports "bloodshed" at a controversial triumph in 54 BCE.[9] What kind of experience was *that* for the by-standers?

These experiences are not entirely lost to us, even if we know much less about them than most historians would now wish. Ovid, for example, in his *Ars Amatoria (Art of Love),* turns his, and our, attention to the fun and games in the audience and to "conquests" of a different sort. He presents the triumphal procession as a good place for a pick-up and explains to his learner-lover how to impress the girl in his sights with pseudo-erudition:

. . . Cheering youths will look on, and girls beside them,
    A day to make every heart run wild for joy;
And when some girl inquires the names of the monarchs,
    Or the towns, rivers, hills portrayed
On the floats, answer all her questions (and don't draw the line at
    Questions only): pretend
You know even when you don't.[10]

We even catch an occasional glimpse of the infra-structure beneath the lavish ceremonial, a glimpse of the workers and suppliers who made the whole show possible. A tombstone in Rome, for example, commemorates a gladiator from Alexandria who came to the capital specially "for the triumph of Trajan" in 117–118 and lists his bouts in the games that followed the triumph: a draw on the second day, a victory on the ninth against a man who had already fought nine fights—and then the text breaks off.[11] From a different angle, Varro in his treatise on agriculture could see the triumph, and particularly the banquets that regularly came after the procession itself, as a money-spinner for farmers. The aviary on his aunt's farm, he insists, had provided 5,000 thrushes for the triumph of Caecilius Metellus in 71 BCE. At twelve sesterces a piece, auntie had raked in a grand total of 60,000 sesterces. All pomp and glory aside, she and her fellow farmers had their own good reasons for welcoming the announcement of a triumph.[12]

Yet the grip of the triumph on Roman culture is evident not only in the details of performance and preparation, or in the memory or anticipation of the great day itself. The triumph was embedded in the ways that Romans wrote, talked, and thought about their world; it was, as the old cliché aptly puts it, "good to think with." Sometimes the association with victory, in a literal sense, remained strong. Seneca, for example, refers to a gladiator optimistically called "Triumphus." A town in the province of Spain went under the name "Triumphale." Vegetius, in his military handbook, cites the phrase "emperor's triumph" as a typical army security password. And, appropriately enough, during Rome's war against Hannibal, two prodigious infants were supposed to have uttered the words traditionally chanted in the triumphal procession: "io triumpe." The first infant was aged just six months; the second, even more incredibly, made his voice heard from the womb. These did not turn out to be good omens; the dreadful Roman defeat at Lake Trasimene in 217 BCE shortly followed the first utterance, and more than a decade would pass after the second before Hannibal was finally defeated.[13]

Often, however, the forms, conventions, and hierarchies of the triumph provided a vocabulary for discussing quite different aspects of Roman life. Modern English too, of course, uses the word "triumph" and its derivatives in a wide range of contexts, to mark out "triumphant" theatrical performances or to brand motor cars and female underwear. ("Triumph has a bra for the way you are," as the advertising slogan ran.) But our words evoke little more than a general sense of resounding success. In ancient Rome, the ceremony itself remained a live presence in almost every usage. Slaves in Roman comedy represented their clever victories over their masters in parodies of technical triumphal vocabulary. Seneca neatly encapsulated the virtue of clemency as a "triumph over victory," using exactly the same Latin formulation ("*ex victoria sua*") as for a triumph "over Spain" or wherever; and the triumph was repeatedly turned to in Roman philosophical debates on glory, morality, and ethics. Early Christians reworked its conventions to express the "triumph" of Jesus.[14]

Poets did more than celebrate triumphs of their patrons; they found in the ceremony a model for activities as diverse as the pursuit of love and the production of poetry itself. In a famous poem celebrating the immortality of writing ("I have completed a monument more lasting than bronze") Horace deploys the technical vocabulary of the triumph to vaunt his own achievements in bringing the traditions of Greek verse into Latin. In appealing to the Muse to crown him with "Delphic laurel," he further blurs the boundary between poetry and triumph—laurel being an emblem of both.[15] Propertius exploits a similar theme, beginning his third book of poems with a flamboyant image of himself and his Muse in a triumph. On board his chariot (just like the young children of a triumphant general) are his "little Loves" *(parvi Amores)*—Cu-

FIGURE 12: "The Triumph of Love." Maarten van Heemskerck (1498–1574) captures the theme of Petrarch's *Trionfi*, with a victorious Cupid riding on a triumphal chariot. Around him are his prisoners—famous victims of Love, including the Latin poets Ovid and Tibullus, Hercules, King Solomon, and the tragic lovers Pyramus and Thisbe. As the Latin verse beneath explains, they are making their way not to the Temple of Jupiter (who, philanderer that he is, shares the chariot with Cupid) but to the Temple of Venus on the hill.

pids, or perhaps his "love poems" themselves; and, behind, like the general's soldiers, a "crowd of other writers," his poetic imitators who share in his victory.[16] Even more subversively, in his series of *Amores (Love Poems),* Ovid exploits the conventions of the triumph to explore the predicament, or success, of the lover. This way of rethinking the ceremony was to have an enormously successful afterlife in Renaissance allegories of the triumph, notably in Petrarch's series of six moralizing poetic *Trionfi (Triumphs),* the Triumph of Love, Chastity, Death, Fame, Time, and Eternity (Fig. 12).[17] But Petrarch looked back directly to Ovid, and to one poem in particular where the love-sick poet pictures himself as a wounded captive in the triumphal procession of a victorious Cupid:

With your train of prisoners behind you, besotted youths
   and maidens,
      Such pomp, such magnificence, your very own
Triumph: and I'll be there too, fresh-wounded, your latest
      Prisoner . . .[18]

It is a joke that simultaneously pokes fun at the militaristic ethos of
the ceremony and re-appropriates its conventions to reflect on erotic
conflict.

Ovid's clever playfulness hints at yet another role for the triumph in
Roman intellectual culture. It was not only "good to think *with*"; it was
also good to think *about.* Roman academics and antiquarians regularly
directed their energies to wrestling with the history and meaning of the
ceremony, and to explaining its (even to them) peculiar customs and
symbols. They puzzled, and disagreed, over its origins and the etymology of the word *triumphus* itself. It was not merely the imagination of
poets and story-mongers that gave the triumph an Eastern pedigree. If
some scholars held the ceremony to be the invention of Rome's founder
Romulus, for others it was the brainchild of the god Bacchus. In fact,
the Bacchic origin meshed conveniently with the derivation of the word
triumphus itself from one of Bacchus' Greek epithets *(thriambos).* But
that did not convince those who preferred to see it as a perfectly Roman
term. Suetonius apparently explained it as *bona fide* Latin: *tri-umphus* reflecting the *three* sections of Roman society—army, senate, and people—involved in granting the honor.[19]

The significance of the triumphal laurel was also a particularly hot
topic of debate. Masurius Sabinus, a first-century CE antiquarian, saw it
as a fumigator or purifier (and so saw the origin of the triumph itself as a
ritual of purification after the bloodstains of war). Pliny preferred to
stress its links with the god Apollo and its symbolic connections with
peace (while also noting that it was a plant that was never struck by
lightning).[20]

Where they could not explain, they could at least try to bring sense
and order. Repeated attempts were made to reconstruct or establish the

rules of the triumph. Who was allowed to celebrate one, after what kind of victory, and against what kind of enemy? Was a triumph allowable, for example, after the defeat of such "inferior" enemies as pirates or slaves?[21] Even the victims in the triumph became the targets of an academic obsession with classification. In one particularly far-fetched (or fine-tuned) attempt at systematization, Porphyrio, an ancient commentator on the poetry of Horace, claimed to be able to distinguish the different types of wagon assigned to transport different ranks of royal captives in the procession: *esseda* for "conquered kings"; *pilenta* for the "conquered queens"; *petorrita* for the "king's relations."[22] The triumph brought out the best and the worst in Roman scholarship.

THE MODERN TRIUMPH

These Roman writers would, no doubt, be gratified to learn of the impact of the triumph on later historians. From the scholarly world of Byzantium, through the rediscovery of classical antiquity in the Renaissance and its reassessment in the Enlightenment, right up to the present day, this distinctive piece of Roman ceremonial has stirred historical and antiquarian curiosity, prompting a huge variety of reconstructions, analysis, and explanation. What Andrea Mantegna recaptured in his cycle of paintings of the *Triumphs of Caesar*—originally for the Gonzaga family of Mantua, now in Hampton Court Palace, London (see Figs. 27, 28, and 29)—others discussed in essays, treatises, and poetry. Petrarch again, for example, headlined the triumph in the ninth book of his Latin epic *Africa,* linking the triumphal procession of Scipio Africanus to the poetic triumph of Ennius.[23]

Some early historical work is particularly notable, and still useful. Italian humanists eagerly gathered together the widely scattered references to the triumph in ancient writers. So efficient and accurate were they that Onofrio Panvinio's study of the triumph in his *Fastorum Libri V* first published in the 1550s—an analytical list of Roman office holders from Romulus to Charles V in the sixteenth century—remains even today one of the most comprehensive collections of evidence for the cere-

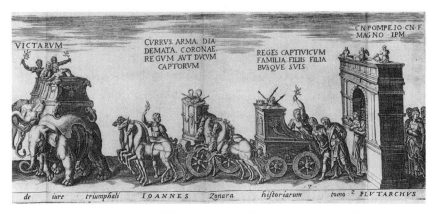

FIGURE 13: A Renaissance view of the Roman triumph. Panvinio's version of the ceremony is here brought to life in a series of contemporary engravings, which pick out highlights of famous processions as he—following the main ancient accounts—described them. In this section: elephants, the chariots and regalia of the defeated kings, and the royal captives themselves.

mony (Fig. 13).[24] Just over two hundred years later, Edward Gibbon's essay "Sur les triomphes des Romains," written in 1764 as a prelude to his classic *History of the Decline and Fall of the Roman Empire,* is a strikingly intelligent account of the triumph, its few pages still one of the best introductions of all to the significance of the ceremony. In an unnervingly modern vein, Gibbon reflects on—among other things—Roman constructions of glory and military virtue, and the relationship between the audience and the spectacular display.[25]

Inevitably, very different interests have attracted scholars to the triumph over the centuries. In the Renaissance, triumphal ceremonies that claimed links with ancient Rome lay at the heart of politics and civic spectacle. "Invented tradition" or not, this gave a particular edge and urgency to the humanists' studies of the triumph. Flavio Biondo, for example, in his *Roma Triumphans* of 1459, saw the Christian church as the direct inheritor of the Roman triumphal tradition, albeit with the explicitly pagan elements redefined. Just as the city of Rome had hosted the long series of ancient triumphs, now it was the center of the triumphant Church, with all its Christian ceremonial and its military conquests over the religious enemy in the shape of the Turks. For Biondo, it was almost too good to be true (and, in fact, we now know it was *not* true) that the site of St. Peter's could be identified with that very tract of land where the ancient Romans had assembled to start their triumphal processions.

Panvinio, by contrast, traced the line of succession from ancient Roman traditions through to the Holy Roman Empire, its rulers and its rituals—as the paraded continuity in office-holding from Romulus to Emperor Charles V in his *Fastorum Libri V* underlines. It was a continuity acted out in the streets of Rome during Panvinio's lifetime, notably in 1536 when Charles V made a triumphal entrance into the city after his African victories, in a spectacle choreographed by Pope Paul III. For this event, Paul attempted to reconstruct the exact route of the ancient triumph, demolishing so much of the city in the process that it had Rabelais, famously, leaving town in disgust. Charles himself appeared as a Christian triumphant over the infidel and as a second Scipio Africanus—a Romulus and St. Peter combined.[26]

Humanists turned also to investigate many of the questions put on the agenda by their ancient counterparts: the rules governing the ceremony, its origins, etymologies, and so on. Recent work has focused on these issues, too, though driven by different scholarly priorities. The legal basis of the triumph and the constitutional position of the general himself proved a particular fascination for historians in the nineteenth century and beyond, whose aim was to reconstruct (or, as skeptics might now see it, *devise*) the "constitution" of ancient Rome. A lawyer's version of the triumph was inevitably the result, as they attempted to see through the mass of often conflicting evidence to the fundamental legal principles and sources of authority that underpinned the ceremony.[27]

The preoccupations of the twentieth century with the operation of politics in the Roman Republic shifted the focus slightly, but still tended to keep the spotlight on the rules and regulations of triumphal celebrations. On what grounds were some successful generals refused a celebration? Whose right was it to grant or refuse a triumph anyway? How did the rules change over time, particularly as the expansion of Roman overseas territory changed the nature of military engagement and the structure of military command?[28]

The origins and early history of the ceremony have also remained firmly on the agenda of modern scholarship on the triumph. The crucial questions here have been concerned not only with where exactly the ceremony originated (though many recent analysts, as we shall see in Chapter 9, have advocated a foreign, or at least Etruscan, origin with even more enthusiasm than ancient writers). No less central has been the idea that the details of the ceremony as they have come down to us offer a rare window onto the religion and culture of the earliest phases of Rome's history. The triumph was, after all, an institution stretching back into the remote past, and Roman ritual practice was notoriously conservative. The chances are that many triumphal conventions, customs, and characteristic symbols—some of which puzzled later Roman writers—preserve their archaic form, and that they are explained by (and also help to explain) the shape and meaning of the triumph in distant prehistory.

This series of inferences is, in fact, a shaky one. In particular, the unchanging conservatism of Roman ritual is at best a half-truth that has increasingly been challenged, and will be further challenged in the course of this book.[29] Nonetheless, these notions underlie some of the most powerful modern readings of the triumph. J. G. Frazer, for example, in his founding text of comparative anthropology, *The Golden Bough,* saw in the general—whose costume he believed combined distinctively regal aspects with features drawn from the god Jupiter himself—a direct descendant of the original "divine kings" of Rome (and so a marvelous confirmation of his whole theory of primitive divine kingship). H. S. Versnel, in *Triumphus,* a book that has become the standard modern reference point on the ceremony, thinks in terms of a primitive New Year festival, harking back ultimately to the ancient Near East via Etruria. It is indicative of the general direction of modern interests that *Triumphus,* though subtitled "an inquiry into the origin, *development* and meaning of the Roman triumph," shows little concern with the ceremony as it was practiced after the fourth century BCE.[30]

In the increasingly wide range of classical scholarship over the last fifty years or so, very few triumphal stones have been left entirely unturned. Studies have appeared on the role of women at the triumph, on the development of triumphal ceremonial into Christian antiquity, on the similarities (and differences) between triumphal processions and funeral processions, on the iconography of triumphal monuments, on triumphal themes in Roman poetry, on the social semiotics of the procession, on the triumph as a means of controlling Roman elite rivalry or of "conflict resolution," as well as on a number of individual ceremonies— real or imagined.[31] And that is to cite only a few.

All the same, given the richness of triumphal culture at Rome and in surviving Roman literature, it is surprising that so much attention overall has been devoted to the origins and earliest phases of the ceremony in that misty period of Roman prehistory before we have any contemporary literary evidence at all, and only the most controversial of archaeological traces; and that so little attention, by comparison, has been devoted to the triumph in periods of which we know much more and where we can hope to see, if not "how it actually happened," then at least how it was recorded, remembered, imagined, debated, and discussed. As others have pointed out, there is no reliable modern guide to the triumph during the Roman Principate, over the three centuries between the reign of Augustus and the beginning of the Christian empire—and one should probably include the last three centuries BCE as well.[32]

This book aims to fill some of that enormous gap, opening up and exploring the triumphal culture of Rome in the late Republic and Principate. It will bring together material—visual and archaeological as well as literary—from that period and will bring back to center-stage texts that have often been marginalized because they do not play to dominant modern interests: poetic evocations of entirely imaginary triumphs, for example, or unbelievably extravagant and inevitably inaccurate accounts of processions such as Pompey's. At the same time, it will take a fresh look at texts that have often been interrogated, narrowly, for the information they might provide on the prehistory of the ceremony.

I shall suggest, for example, that the ingenious speculations of Plutarch or Aulus Gellius may tell us less about the proto-triumphs of the eighth century BCE than about the triumphal scholarship and culture of the second century CE, a millennium later; that even Livy's detailed accounts of the triumphal controversies of the middle Republic are as much about the configurations of the triumph in the late first century BCE as they are about the rules, regulations, and contests of the late third. In short, I shall be looking carefully *at* the surviving ancient writing on the triumph, rather than merely *through* it to some more distant world (or lost system or even lost reality) beyond.

The book is also prompted by a series of reflections—my own puzzlement, if you like—about Roman ritual and public spectacle. I am not so much concerned with definitions of ritual as a symbolic, social, semiotic, or religious activity. Nor am I concerned with the tricky boundary disputes that can still provoke intense academic debate. Is there a difference (and, if so, what) between "ritual" and "ceremonial"? Is ritual always focused on the sacred? Is there such a thing as "secular" ritual? In fact, one singular advantage of some of the most recent theoretical studies of ritual in a cross-cultural perspective is that they transcend such narrow definitional problems. I am thinking particularly of work by Catherine Bell and by Caroline Humphrey and James Laidlaw. All of these stress the idea of "ritualization" rather than "ritual." On this model, ritual actions are not seen as intrinsically different from nonritual actions. What is crucial in distinguishing ritual from nonritual behavior is the fact that participants themselves think of what they are doing in ritual terms and mark it out as separate from their everyday, nonritual practice.[33]

But if an approach of this kind makes it easier to take the triumph as "ritualized activity" without becoming embroiled in the dead-end arguments that have sometimes dogged its study (Is it a "religious" ceremony? If not, can it count as "ritual"?), all sorts of other questions still remain. How can the history of an ancient ceremony best be studied? How should we understand the relationship between written ritual ("rituals in ink," as they have been termed) and ritual practice?[34] What were large-scale public ceremonies and processions *for?* Can we get beyond the easy, even if sometimes correct, conclusion that such rituals, in classical antiquity no less than in any other historical period, acted to reaffirm society's core values? Or beyond the more subtle variant that sees them rather as the focus of reflection and debate on those values, and as such always liable to disruption, subversion, and attack no less than to enthusiastic participation, patronage, and support?[35] In pondering these questions, and in setting up an interplay between such theoretical reflections and the rich texture of the primary evidence (rather than attempting to reach for neat solutions and definitions), I have found the Roman triumph a uniquely telling object lesson. This is for a combination of reasons.

First, the triumph is the only public ceremony at Rome—with the exception of the infrequent Secular Games, the semi-private festival of Dea Dia recorded by the priesthood of the Arval Brethren, and some elements of the funerary tradition—for which we can reconstruct a historical series of individual, identifiable performances. True, the Roman calendar included a whole variety of annual festivals whose celebration likewise was supposed to extend back into the earliest periods of Rome's history and lasted as long as the pagan city itself, or longer: the Parilia, the Vinalia, the Consualia, and so on. But each of these is usually represented to us as an undifferentiated cycle of more or less identical traditional ceremonies. Although ancient writers may dwell on the colorful myths of these festivals' origins, only rarely are later innovations or changes in the ritual explicitly recorded.[36]

Even more rarely do we catch a glimpse of any individual occasion, and then usually for reasons of political controversy: the memorable celebration of the Lupercalia on February 15, 44 BCE, for example, when Mark Antony took advantage of his lead role in the proceedings to offer a royal crown to Julius Caesar; or the procession of the Hilaria (in honor of the goddess Cybele, the "Great Mother") on March 25, 187 CE, which, with its elaborate fancy dress, provided the cover for an (unsuccessful) assassination attempt on the emperor Commodus.[37] Because the triumph, though frequent, was not regular in this sense, because a fresh decision to celebrate a triumph was required on each occasion, and because it was by definition tied to outside events, the circumstances and honorand different each time, it has a *history* unlike any other ritual at Rome.

Second, ancient writers offer a wealth of detail on the performance and spectacle of the triumph, and of individual triumphs, as for no other Roman ceremony. Pompey's triumph in 61 BCE is one of the most richly, if not the most richly, documented. But the lavish accounts, fanciful or not, of many other triumphs also go far beyond descriptions of anything else in the repertoire of ritual at Rome. This is due in large part to the triumph's centrality in Roman political and cultural life and to the undoubted impact of its celebration. Writers lingered on their triumphal descriptions because the ceremony seemed important to them.

But more strictly literary factors are also relevant. It would be wrong to imagine that the details of the triumph were necessarily more compelling than those of other rituals, certainly not for everyone all the time. It would have been possible to write up ceremonies such as the Lupercalia or Hilaria in a way that focused on the individual performance, the variations in their picturesque procedures, and the tensions and conflicts that lay behind the yearly celebrations. Conversely, there were, as we know, numerous triumphs in the course of Roman history—the pinnacle of glory for the general concerned, maybe—which figure in surviving literature as briefly and routinely as any minor annual festival: "Marcius returned to the city, celebrating a triumph over the Hernici," "a triumph was held over the Privernates."[38] Yet the competitive individualism of the triumph, its association with many of the most prominent names in Roman public life, as well as its links to the powerful narrative of imperialism and Roman military success gave it a rhetorical charge which those other ceremonies could not often match.

Third, the triumph attracted the interest and energies of Roman scholars themselves more than any other ritual or festival. The combination of, on the one hand, the researches of ancient anthropologists and antiquarians in their interrogation of the various features of the ceremony and its organization and, on the other, the work of literary commentators, puzzling over the more obscure vocabulary and difficult passages in the written versions of the triumph, offers us an unusually nuanced view of ancient attempts to explain and make sense of a ritual. It presents Roman intellectuals in action, themselves trying to understand the traditions of their own culture; and it gives us a memorable opportunity to work with them. In this respect, again, no ritual can touch it.

"FASTI TRIUMPHALES"

The single most impressive monument—in both the literal and metaphoric sense—of this ancient scholarly interest in the triumph is the register of triumphant generals, that once stood inscribed on marble, in the Roman Forum. Part of an ensemble erected during the reign of Augustus, the names of the generals were listed, side by side with those of the consuls and other chief magistrates of the city, stretching right back to the beginning of Rome's history. Though the monument does not survive intact, a large cache of fragments was excavated near the Temple of Antoninus and Faustina (see Plan) in the mid-sixteenth century—a discovery that partly inspired the researches of Panvinio and his contemporaries, who saw in them the chronological key to Roman history. The fragments were reconstructed, reputedly by Michelangelo (such was their importance), in the Palazzo dei Conservatori on the Capitoline, first in its courtyard, then moved to an upstairs room shared with the famous Roman bronze wolf, where they still remain; hence their modern title *Fasti Capitolini*, "The Capitoline Chronology" or "Calendar." Pieces unearthed since the Renaissance have been incorporated in the reconstruction, or are displayed alongside (Fig. 14).[39]

Despite numerous gaps in the surviving text, it is absolutely clear that the register of generals (*Fasti Triumphales*, as it is sometimes now known) originally offered a complete tally—or so it was presented—of those who had celebrated triumphs, from Romulus in the year of the city's founding (traditionally 753 BCE) to Lucius Cornelius Balbus in 19 BCE (see Fig. 36). The *Fasti* still preserves the full or partial record of

FIGURE 14: The modern display of the *Fasti Capitolini* in the Capitoline Museums, Rome. The combination of the iconic wolf with the list of magistrates and generals makes a particularly powerful symbol of ancient Roman culture—as those who devised this layout no doubt intended.

more than two hundred triumphs, making it the most extensive ancient chronology of the ceremony that we have. Each entry is given in a standard format, with the full name of the general, the formal title of the office he held, the name of the peoples or places over which he triumphed, and the date of the ceremony—the day, month, and year from the founding of Rome: "Quintus Lutatius Cerco, son of Gaius, grandson of Gaius, consul, over the Falisci, first of March, year 512."[40]

The list adopts a generous definition of the "triumph" and notably includes the record of two forms of celebration that ancient writers often took care to distinguish from the triumph "proper": the ovation *(ovatio)* and the triumph on the Alban Mount *(triumphus in Monte Albano)*.[41] The ovation differed from the triumph mainly in that the general processed to the Capitoline either on foot or horseback, not in the triumphal chariot, and he was crowned with myrtle, not laurel. Ancient scholars dreamed up a variety of unconvincing theories to explain this ceremony: Aulus Gellius, for example, claimed it was used when the war had not been properly declared, or when it had been against "unsuitable" enemies, such as slaves and pirates—though these conditions match very few of the thirty *ovationes* known to us. In practice it seems to have been often seen, and used, as a consolation prize for generals who, for whatever reason, were refused a full ceremony; and it was sometimes known as the "lesser triumph."[42]

The triumph on the Alban Mount was a more drastic response to refusal. A few generals between the late third century and the early second, who had been turned down for a triumph in Rome, chose instead to celebrate one on the hill, now known as Monte Cavo, about 27 kilometers outside the city—presumably, though we have no details of the ritual, processing up to the shrine on the summit by the ruggedly paved road that still survives.[43] Both these ceremonies are given their place in the inscribed list (distinguished only by the addition of *"ovans"* in one case, and *"in Monte Albano"* in the other), suggesting that for some purposes they too could count as *bona fide* triumphs. Also noted are other variants to the triumphal ceremony and occasionally special honors. "Naval triumphs"—that is, those for naval victories—are consistently indicated (the first being for Caius Duilius in 260 BCE), even though we know of no specific difference in their procedures. And the dedication in 222 of the so-called *spolia opima* appears on the list too, a ceremony supposed to have taken place only when the general himself killed the enemy commander in single combat and then dedicated the captured armor to the god Jupiter Feretrius.

Although the content and overall layout of the text is clear enough, the *Fasti Capitolini* are puzzling in several ways. The question of where exactly in the Forum they were originally displayed has been an issue of intense dispute for centuries. Panvinio himself imagined that they originally stood near the Temple of Vesta. But this idea was based on an emendation of a passage in Suetonius' treatise *De Grammaticis (On*

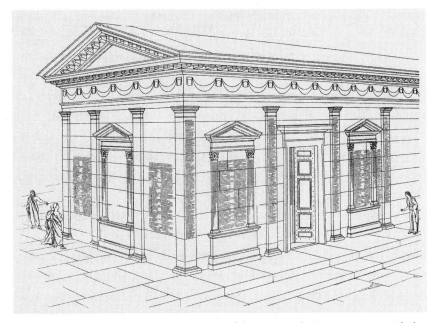

FIGURE 15: Nineteenth-century reconstruction of the Regia in the Roman Forum, with the inscribed lists of generals and consuls. The triumphs fill the tall pilasters, the magistracies the broader panels—and both are eagerly scanned by Roman passers-by. A nice idea, but we now think that the Regia was the wrong shape and too small for any such arrangement.

Grammarians) referring to *fasti* at "Praenestae," which he erroneously read as *pro aede Vestae* ("in front of the Temple of Vesta").[44] By the nineteenth century, the location favored by most archaeologists was the Regia (see Plan and Fig. 15), which served as the headquarters of the priestly college of *pontifices,* who were themselves traditionally associated with the calendar and historical record-keeping. But excavations of this building have suggested that it was hardly large enough to accommodate the whole of the text, encouraging most recent studies to opt instead for one of the commemorative arches erected in the Forum by Augustus; though, frankly, which arch is anyone's guess (Fig. 16).[45] Nor is it certain at what precise date the texts were inscribed, whether the consular and triumphal lists were planned together, or what process of decision-making lay behind the later emendations and additions (the consuls were continued down to the end of Augustus' reign and

FIGURE 16: Reconstruction of an arch erected in the Roman Forum to commemorate Octavian's victory at the battle of Actium in 31 BCE. This is one of many attempts to pin the inscribed list of generals and consuls to one of the Augustan arches in the Forum—though the history of these, their date, location, and appearance, remain controversial.

a note of the performance of the Secular Games was added as late as 88 CE).[46]

Even more crucially, we do not know who compiled the lists, by what methods, or drawing on what sources of information. Texts inscribed on stone rarely blazon their authors, and we can easily fall into the trap of assuming them to be neutral documentary records, free from the interests, prejudice, or priorities of any particular writer. In fact, some individual or group must have been responsible for the choice of words carved into the marble—whether that responsibility entailed merely selecting an existing document to copy or adapt, or a much more active process of research and composition, delving into archives, family records, and earlier historical accounts to reconstruct a complete chronology of the ceremony. There have been some imaginative theories. Panvinio, following his misreading of Suetonius, deduced that the main hand behind the compilation was the Augustan antiquarian Verrius Flaccus (in fact, Flaccus had been responsible for the calendar, or *fasti,* at Praenestae). Others have detected the influence of Cicero's friend Atticus, who is known to have compiled a chronology of Rome and its magistrates. But this is little more than a guess, for there is no firm evidence on the processes of composition.[47]

We shall return to some of the problems of the *Fasti Capitolini* in the next chapter—not only how they were compiled but also the nagging question of how accurate they are. For the moment the most important point to stress is that the Romans themselves saw—and were confident that they could reconstruct—a historical sequence of triumphal ceremonies stretching back into the earliest phases of their city. This point is confirmed by some, admittedly scanty, surviving fragments of two other inscribed lists of triumphs.

First are a couple of scraps listing some late second-century BCE triumphs, rather grandly known as the *Fasti Urbisalvienses,* after the town (modern Urbisaglia in north Italy) where the larger piece turned up; these are so close to the *Fasti Capitolini* as to make it almost certain that they were a direct copy, intended to replicate the metropolitan text in an Italian municipality. The second group is made up of five more substantial fragments found somewhere in Rome during the Renaissance, listing triumphs between 43 and 21 BCE and known as the *Fasti Barberiniani* after the family who once owned them (see Fig. 37). These not only fill in some of the gaps of the *Fasti Capitolini,* but their use of a distinctively different formula ("Appius Claudius Pulcher over Spain, first of January, *triumphed [and] dedicated his palm*") suggests an independent tradition.[48]

Nonetheless, the clear impression given by these documents is that, by the end of the first century BCE, a broad orthodoxy had become established on the overall shape of triumphal history, even if, as we shall see, particular details and individual triumphs could be matters of dispute and disagreement.

THE LESSONS OF HISTORY

That historical sequence of individual celebrations was more than a matter of simple chronology. For it provided the basis on which Roman writers theorized and sometimes puzzled over the development of the triumph in a more general sense. In many ways the triumph came to be seen as a marker of wider developments in Roman politics and society. So, for example, the increasingly far-flung peoples and places over which triumphs were celebrated represented a map of Roman imperial expansion and of the changing geopolitical shape of the Roman world. This aspect certainly struck Florus, when he reflected on Rome's victory in wars of the fifth century BCE over two settlements that by his day had long been as Roman as Rome itself (one not much more than a suburb of the city): "Over Verulae and Bovillae, I am ashamed to say it—but we triumphed." It made the point, even if at the cost of some creative invention; there is no other reference to a triumph over either of these towns.[49]

Even more powerfully, though, triumphal history was conscripted into moralizing accounts of the pernicious growth of luxury and corruption. The decline of the sturdy peasant virtues of early Rome could be traced in the increased ostentation of the triumph. If Caius Atilius Regulus (who triumphed in 257 BCE) was supposed to have held the reins of his triumphal chariot in calloused hands that only recently "guided a pair of plough oxen" or if the Manius Curius could be said (in Apuleius' memorable phrase) to have "had more triumphs than slaves," the same was not true later.[50] Dionysius of Halicarnassus concluded his account of Romulus' founding triumph in 753 BCE with some uncomfortable thoughts on the changed character of the ceremony in his own day: "In our life-time it has become extravagant and pretentious, making a histrionic show more for the display of wealth than for the reputation of virtue; it has departed in every respect from the ancient tradition of frugality."[51] Dio too seems to have echoed these sentiments, though (so far as we can gauge from the Byzantine historian who is our main access to the lost sections of his early books) he pinpointed the cause of decline in the influence of "cliques and political factions" in the city.[52]

This moralizing was given a particular edge by the fact that triumphal processions themselves were one of the main conduits through which wealth and luxury were introduced to Rome. Triumphs did not simply reflect the rise of extravagance. As they celebrated richer and richer conquests and displayed the costly booty through the streets, they were partly responsible for it. So Livy emphasizes in his discussion of the victory of Cnaeus Manlius Vulso against the Galatians (in modern Turkey), and of the subsequent triumph in 187. It was then, he writes, that Roman banquets began to feature "lute-girls and harpists, and other seductive dinner-party amusements"; "it was then that the cook began to be a valuable commodity, though for men of old he had been the most insignificant of slaves, both in cash-value and the work he did, and then that what had been servile labor began to be considered an art." With no less disapproval, both Livy and Pliny (who quotes a writer of late second century BCE as his authority) add "sideboards and one legged tables" to the roster of deleterious novelties introduced by this triumph.[53]

The chronology of the triumph was, in other words, more than a scholarly game for Roman antiquarians. The sequence of triumphal celebrations from Romulus onward provided a framework onto which other developments in Roman politics and society could be mapped.

THE AUGUSTAN NEW DEAL

The *Fasti Capitolini* themselves signal one of the most striking links between triumphal chronology and Roman history more generally. For their layout of the complete sequence of triumphs on four pilasters, starting with the victory celebration of Romulus, comes to an end with that of Lucius Cornelius Balbus in 19 BCE. Balbus' triumph for victories in Africa (over a perhaps misleadingly impressive roster of towns and tribes listed by Pliny) occupies the final centimeters at the bottom of the fourth pilaster, leaving no space for any further celebrations to be recorded.[54] This was not a matter of chance. It must have taken careful calculation on the part of the designers and carvers to ensure this perfect fit. Nor was Balbus' merely the most recent celebration to have taken place when the decision was made to inscribe the whole triumphal chronology. As the design shows, this triumph was intended to represent the end of the series, or at least a rupture in the pattern of celebrations that had held good for centuries.

So far I have referred to the sequence of triumphs as an unbroken series, from the mythical foundation under Romulus to whatever celebration is deemed to count as the last (the triumph of Diocletian and Maximian in 303 CE is one favorite modern candidate, but there are plenty of rivals stretching into Byzantium—as we will see in Chapter 9). And so, in a sense, it is. At the same time, a notable change occurred under the emperor Augustus, both in the generals to whom the honor was awarded and in the frequency at which it was celebrated. After Balbus in 19 BCE, no one triumphed in ancient Rome apart from the emperor himself or, occasionally, members of his closest family. The only partial exception is the ovation, or "lesser triumph," awarded in 47 CE to Aulus Plautius, the general responsible for the initial conquest of Britain—as much a parade, no doubt, of the traditionalism of the ruling emperor Claudius as of Plautius' success.[55]

This restriction partly explains why the number of triumphs decreases dramatically at this point. In the course of his gloating over the triumph of the emperor Vespasian and his son Titus over the Jews in 71 CE ("a most glorious victory over those who had offended God the Father and Christ the Son"), the Christian historian Orosius, writing in the fifth century CE, calculated that it was the three hundred and twentieth triumphal celebration in eight centuries of Roman history. Of those 320, only 13 took place in the hundred years after 29 BCE; and of those, only 5 were staged in the ninety years following Balbus' triumph. And during some periods of the Empire no triumph is known for decades: in the twenty-six years between the triumph of Claudius over Britain in 44 and the Jewish triumph, for example, or in the more than forty years that separated the posthumous triumph of Trajan in 117–118 from that of Marcus Aurelius over the Parthians in 166. It is not, however, quite so rare as some modern miscalculations claim: only thirteen between 31 BCE and 235 CE, as one particularly glaring piece of faulty arithmetic has it.[56]

For successful generals outside and sometimes inside the imperial family, triumphal *ornamenta* or *insignia* replaced the celebration of a triumph proper and were awarded until the second century CE. It is clear enough what these "ornaments" did *not* include: namely, the traditional public procession to the Capitol, accompanied by the spoils, captives, and victorious troops. Much less clear is what exactly they *did* include. We assume, rather vaguely, that they amounted to the "paraphernalia of a triumph," in the sense of the distinctive triumphal toga and tunic, plus the crown or wreath and scepter. But in fact the only direct piece of evidence (a confusing description of Claudius' triumph over Britain) may well indicate that men granted this honor wore only the usual *toga praetexta* of a magistrate.[57] It is also a matter of guesswork how, and with what ceremony, they were bestowed—though they seem to have been accompanied by the grant of a statue of the honorand in that most triumphal of monuments, the Forum of Augustus.[58] Second best or not, this series of honors must have served to keep the triumph on the political and cultural agenda, while at the same time perhaps investing the full ceremony itself with rarity value and yet more celebrity status.

The reasons for the restriction of the triumph to the innermost imperial circle are, in broad terms, obvious enough: it was not in the interests of the new autocracy to share with the rest of the elite the fame and prominence that a full triumphal ceremony might bring, particularly military prominence. Modern historians have laid great emphasis on this, writing of the "elimination" of "a major element in senatorial public display" and of the projection of the emperor "as the sole source of Roman military success," while building up the triumph of Cornelius Balbus as the swansong of the traditional ceremony.[59]

In fact, the picture is more complicated. To be sure, the *Fasti Capitolini* chime in with this modern orthodoxy, by ending so decisively with the triumph of Balbus at the bottom of the final pilaster. As we shall see in Chapter 9, ancient observers are far less emphatic or univocal than their modern counterparts. Suetonius, for example, offers a dramatically divergent view, painting the reign of Augustus as a bumper period for the triumph.[60] Several other writers do point to a change in triumphal practice around this date, but they focus on different pivotal moments and theorize the change in a variety of different ways.[61]

However we resolve these details, the change in triumphal practice has significant implications for how we read ancient descriptions of the ceremony and ancient investigations of the rules, origins, and meaning of the ritual. For the majority of these—including such rich accounts as Plutarch's description of Pompey's triumph or Valerius Maximus' discussion of various aspects of "triumphal law"—were written not only much later than the events which are their subject but in a period when the full triumph in the traditional republican sense was no longer a regular sight in the Roman streets but an element in the ceremonial of imperial monarchy. Some of the authors who wrote in such detail about triumphs may never have witnessed one; almost none could have participated in the kind of controversies that surrounded some triumphal celebrations in the Republic.[62]

This disjunction between the flourishing of the "culture of the triumph" (the ritual in ink) and the relative rarity of the ceremony in practice is one of the creative paradoxes that drives this book.

CHAPTER

III

Constructions and Reconstructions

AN ACCURATE RECORD

The study of ancient history is necessarily stereoscopic. We have one eye on how the ancients themselves understood their own culture and their past. But at the same time, with the other eye, we are constructing our own story; we are subjecting theirs to critical scrutiny and enjoying the privilege of those who come later to "know better" about the past than our predecessors. In Chapter 2 I stressed the importance of taking seriously Romans' own accounts of triumphs and their own attempts to make sense of the history and meaning of the institution. Yet taking the Roman view seriously is not the same as suspending all critical judgment; it is not the same as imagining it to be "correct."

The way that the ceremony was described, debated, and theorized by the ancients themselves is an important subject of study in its own right. But that approach must always be in dialogue with shrewd historical skepticism and a cool suspicion about just how much the Roman writers themselves knew about the ceremony and its history. The inscribed *Fasti Triumphales* were an extraordinary achievement of Roman historical reconstruction and the backbone of many modern studies of the ceremony's history, to be sure. But how accurate a document is it? To what extent is a (more than symbolic) chronology of Roman triumphal celebrations within our grasp—whether we rely on this inscribed text or on the records transmitted by historians such as Livy?

Suppose we were faced with an inscribed list—from Westminster Abbey, maybe—of English monarchs from King Arthur to Elizabeth II, each reign precisely dated and its major achievements summarized. At either end of such a roster we would have little difficulty in assessing the historicity of the kings and queens concerned. The status of Queen Victoria (1837–1901) or even Edward VIII (whose brief "reign" in 1936 would have posed its own problems to the compilers of the list) is of an entirely different order from that of King Arthur. Whatever shadowy historical character or characters may, or may not, lie behind the story of the Lord of the Round Table, there is no doubt that he is exactly that—a story, an ideological fiction, a mythical ancestor of English kings and kingship.

So too with the roster of triumphing generals inscribed in the Roman Forum. It would be perverse to be too skeptical about the general accuracy of the triumphal record of the last two centuries BCE, which amounts to well over a hundred ceremonies in all. Even if the details of these occasions were embellished, invented, or disputed by historians in antiquity, we usually have no good cause to doubt the occurrence of the recorded triumphs, some of which—such as Pompey's in 61—are documented in a wide variety of different sources and media. Nor is it likely in this period that any celebration has fallen out of the record (though later, after 19 BCE, where we rely almost entirely on now-patchy literary accounts, some ceremonies have almost certainly been lost to us, even if for a time they retained a place in Roman memory).

Conversely, it would be just as perverse *not* to be skeptical about the historicity of the earliest triumphs recorded, in the mythical period of the foundation of the city and its more or less legendary early kings. The triumph of Romulus that opens the *Fasti Triumphales* certainly played an important role in the symbolic history of the ceremony, much as the reign of King Arthur does in the symbolic history of British kingship. But no one would now imagine that it could be pinned down to a particular historical occasion or real-life honorand. Besides, the differences between ancient writers in their reconstructions of the early history of the triumph reinforce the sense of a fluidity in the tradition. Livy's Romulus does not triumph, for example (though he does dedicate the *spolia opima* after killing the enemy commander, Acro); Dionysius of Halicarnassus' Romulus does—not just once but, as in the inscribed *Fasti,* three times.[1] Indeed, by and large Dionysius' chronology in his *Antiquitates Romanae (Roman Antiquities)* is much closer to the *Fasti* than Livy, but even he, significantly or not, omits any mention of the two triumphs of the last king, Tarquin the Proud, that have a place on the inscription.[2]

The more difficult problem lies not in identifying the clearly mythical, and the equally obviously historical, examples but in how to draw a line between them. In the English case, this would be the "King Alfred dilemma," a monarch caught in that difficult territory between "myth" and "history" (a *bona fide* ruler of the late ninth century, maybe, but hardly the founder of the British navy or absent-minded dreamer who burnt the peasant's cakes in anything but legend). So where in the list of triumphs does myth stop and history start? How far back in time can we imagine that the compilers of the inscribed *Fasti,* or other historians working in the late Republic and early Empire, had access to accurate information on exactly who triumphed, when and over whom? And if they had access to it, did they use it? To what extent were they engaged in fictionalizing reconstruction, if not outright invention? This is the kind of dilemma that hovers over most of our attempts to write about early (and not so early) Rome. Why believe what writers of the first century BCE or later tell us? Or, to push the argument back a step, how trustworthy were the historical accounts composed in the third or second centuries BCE, now largely lost to us, on which the later writers relied?

Modern critics have generally divided into two opposing camps on these questions, or hesitated awkwardly between them. On the one hand stand the optimists, who argue that the traditions of archival and other forms of record-keeping were well enough, and early enough, established at Rome for reasonably reliable data to be available for even a period as remote as the last phases of the monarchy in the sixth century

BCE; and that some of this information, whether transmitted through priestly records (the notorious *Annales Maximi,* for example), family histories, or traditional ballads, was incorporated into the historical narrative that survives.

On the other hand are the skeptics who not only doubt the existence, or (if it existed) the usefulness, of the supposed archival tradition but also question the process by which any early "information" was transmitted to the later historical narrative. It was not a matter of wholesale one-off invention. But over time, so this argument runs, the repeated attempts of Roman historians to systematize such fragmentary evidence as they had and to massage it into a well-ordered series of events and magistracies, combined with the powerful incentive to elevate the achievements of the ancestors of families prominent in later periods, drastically compromised the accuracy of the Romans' view of their early history.[3] As Cicero summed it up, the "invented triumphs and too many consulships" with which leading families glamorized their own past distorted the Roman historical tradition.[4]

INVENTED TRIUMPHS?

It is no easier to resolve this historiographical dilemma in the case of the triumph than in the case of any Roman institution. Leaving aside whatever information may have been recorded in Roman archives, we certainly have evidence of a range of public documents specifically associated with triumphal celebrations. On an optimistic reading, these might underpin the accuracy of the triumphal chronology. A scholar of the first century CE, for example, discussing a particular form of archaic Latin verse, refers to "the ancient tablets which generals who were going to celebrate a triumph used to put up on the Capitoline"; and he quotes lines (in the so-called "Saturnian" meter which is his subject) from two of them, vaunting the military success of generals who triumphed in 190 and 189 BCE.[5] Likewise, Cicero implies that scrupulous generals submitted accounts that were filed away in the state treasury (and, in principle at least, retrievable from it)—accounts that noted not only the quantity of triumphal booty but also systematically inventoried the size, shape, and attitude of each sculpture.[6]

Pompey's triumphs were, as we have seen, trumpeted on inscriptions in the temples that his victories funded, and Livy quotes the text attached to a dedication to Jupiter in the Temple of Mater Matuta, which details the achievements of Tiberius Sempronius Gracchus in Sardinia and his subsequent triumph in 175. (The dedication was a tablet or painting in the shape of the island, decorated with representations of the battles concerned.)[7] In fact, some aspects of triumphal chronology seem to have been so well established in the Roman world that Varro could treat a notable triumph in 150 BCE as a fixed date against which to calibrate prices of wheat and other staples.[8]

Yet how far back in Roman history such documentation goes remains quite unclear. None of the examples just quoted is earlier than the second century BCE, nor do we have any indication that material of this kind was regularly used by historians and scholars in antiquity in determining or checking the history of the triumph. Moreover, the details of triumphal history as it has been transmitted to us present all kinds of difficulties and discrepancies. Livy, in fact, echoes Cicero when he complains of the conflicting evidence for the campaigns, victories, and commanders of the year 322 BCE and laments the lack of any contemporary history of that period, the misleading influence of family histories, and the outright "falsehoods" found in the eulogistic inscriptions attached to the portrait statues of the republican elite.[9] The compilers of the *Fasti Capitolini* must have got their data from somewhere, but for us to imagine hard-nosed archival research on their part, still less an accurate source, would be an act of faith.

In fact, to follow the skeptics, there can be no doubt whatsoever that some of the information on republican triumphs recorded in the inscribed *Fasti* as well as in literary accounts has been, at the very least, "touched up" at some stage. Even supposing that we were prepared to suspend disbelief and accept that the exact date of all triumphs, as well as the full name of the general (including father's and grandfather's name), could have been transmitted accurately from the fifth century BCE, a number of specific cases must arouse suspicion.

The very first triumph of the newly founded Republic in 509 BCE, supposedly celebrated by Publius Valerius Publicola, offers a usefully glaring example. Dated to the first of March (the opening, appropriately enough, of the month of Mars, the god of war), it falls on the anniversary of that first triumph of Romulus which launched the whole series. It is, in theory, possible that we are dealing here with a lucky coincidence, or with some canny politicians in the late sixth century who already "knew" the date of the (mythical) first triumph and chose to replicate it. Much more likely is that, in the retrospective construction of republican triumphal history, the first triumph of the Republic (mythical or not) was mapped onto the very first triumph of all, as a second founding moment of the city and of its most distinctive ritual.[10]

Similar issues arise with the six other celebrations assigned to the first of March, making it, to judge from the *Fasti,* the single most popular date for the ceremony through the Republic.[11] Generals may well have found this an attractive and symbolically resonant date to choose for their own big day. But no less likely is it that, in the course of the long scholarly process of fine-tuning and filling the gaps in the triumphal record, the first of March would have seemed a particularly appropriate date to assign to dateless triumphs.

Besides, despite the generally consistent overall picture of triumphal history given by the inscribed documents and different ancient writers, there are very many individual discrepancies long after the obviously mythical period of the early kings. We are not dealing, in other words, with a single orthodox triumphal chronology publicly memorialized in the *Fasti Capitolini,* but a number of chronologies, similar in outline, while divergent—even conflicting—in detail. Several triumphs, for example, are recorded in the *Fasti* but nowhere else, even at periods when Livy's detailed year-by-year historical narrative survives. We know nothing at all, apart from what is inscribed on the stone, of the triumph of Publius Sulpicius Saverrius over the Samnites on October 29, 304 BCE. Likewise, no mention is made in any surviving literary account of the triumphs of Gaius Plautius Proculus in 358, Gaius Sulpicius Longus in 314, or Marcus Fulvius Paetinus in 299, though in each case Livy does refer to an appropriate victory or campaign (one is tempted to ask whether a triumph has been extrapolated from a victory, or even vice versa).[12]

It is not simply, however, that the *Fasti* are fuller, more gullible, or more systematic in their records. For in other instances, even bearing in mind the fragmentary nature of the surviving text, the inscription omits triumphs that are claimed in some literary accounts: a group at the start of the Republic (in 504, 502, and 495), but a couple later too—including a celebration in 264 for the victory of Appius Claudius Caudex in Africa, which is featured in Silius Italicus' *Punica,* his epic on the Punic Wars, as the subject of a painting that roused Hannibal's indignation.[13]

What accounts for these discrepancies? Sometimes presumably the partisan or self-serving inventions that Cicero and Livy imply. But—although one modern critic has not unreasonably concluded that "triumphs are more likely to be invented than ignored"—a variety of factors, not the least of which was sheer carelessness, could lead to the exclusion of a ceremony from a particular record. So, for example, the omission of Octavian's triumph for his victory at Actium in 29 BCE from the *Fasti Barberiniani* may be the fault of an inattentive stone carver (even though other more sinister explanations are possible, as we shall see).[14] In other cases it seems clear enough that, in constructing their historical narratives, Roman writers failed to mention individual triumphs because they had other historical priorities in mind. This may explain the fact that two celebrations which took place during the Civil Wars of the 30s BCE (the triumph of Lucius Marcius Censorinus in 39 and Gaius Norbanus Flaccus in 34) are recorded only in the inscribed *Fasti.*[15]

Yet on other occasions a deeper level of uncertainty or more radically different versions of the details of triumphal history were at stake. Polybius, for example, writes of the "very splendid" triumph of Scipio for victories in Spain in 206 BCE; Livy, by contrast, claims not only that Scipio did not celebrate a triumph, but that he requested one only half-heartedly, as it would have breached precedent. For up to that point, no one who, like Scipio, had held command without being at the same time a magistrate had triumphed.[16] On the other hand, Livy makes much of the triumph of Cnaeus Manlius Vulso in 187, as we have already seen, noting the fifty-two enemy leaders led before the general's chariot, the wagonloads of coin, weapons, and precious metals, and the songs chanted by the victorious troops, as well as lingering on its moral consequences; yet the historian Florus explicitly states this triumph was requested by Vulso but refused.[17]

An instructive case is the disputed triumphal career of Lucius Aemilius Paullus, whose three-day triumph in 167 over King Perseus of Macedonia was later written up almost as extravagantly as Pompey's of 61. But how many triumphs did Paullus celebrate? We can identify this one and an earlier celebration in 181 BCE, for victory over the Ligurians of north Italy. Both of these, and these only, were recorded on the inscription beneath the statue of Paullus that stood among the republican worthies in the Forum of Augustus.[18]

Yet we find a different story in the inscription accompanying another statue of Paullus put up by one of his descendants in the mid-50s BCE to embellish the so-called *Fornix Fabianus* in the Forum—an arch originally erected in 121 BCE to commemorate the victories of Paullus' grandson, Quintus Fabius Maximus Allobrogicus. Here, Paullus is clearly stated to have "triumphed three times."[19] This second tradition is followed by Velleius Paterculus, in his history of Rome written during the reign of the emperor Tiberius. Before his great triumph over Perseus, Paullus had, Velleius states, "triumphed both as praetor and as consul."[20] Paullus was praetor in 191, when he campaigned in Spain; but there is certainly no space for such a triumph in the *Fasti,* which indeed explicitly marks the triumph of 167 as his *second.*

This is very likely an example of an "invented triumph." We cannot be absolutely certain that a triumphal celebration in 191 has not fallen out of the mainstream of the historical record. But more likely, within the traditions of family loyalty, exaggeration, and hype (as represented on what is effectively a dynastic monument of Paullus' family), two triumphs were massaged into three; at some point, too, an appropriate campaign, in Spain, was found to fit the fictive triumph. And as Cicero and Livy feared, the invention got a foothold, even if a precarious one, in the historical narrative of Paullus' career. If so, this is a rare instance where we not only suspect invention but can see its process in action, largely because of its relatively late date; earlier inventions presumably became so established in the triumphal record that they are no longer easily identifiable as such.[21]

That late date is in itself striking, for the second century BCE is well within the period when the historicity of recorded triumphs in general seems hardly to be in doubt. It serves as a powerful reminder that the incentives to embellish triumphal careers did not stop even at a time when the historical narrative was more carefully policed. It is also a warning that no firm chronological line can be drawn between a period of "mythical" and one of "historical" triumphs. Although the record of the late Republic reflects the historical sequence of triumphs celebrated much more closely than that of the early Republic, there was never a period when distortion of all kinds—from wishful thinking to subtle readjustments—was entirely off the agenda.

We cannot now reconstruct the processes of compilation, reading, or research that lay behind the finished inscribed text of the *Fasti Capitolini.* We can only guess at its relationship with the literary records of triumphal history embedded in the writing of Livy, Dionysius, and their lost predecessors. We can often do little to explain or resolve the discrepancies between the various sources of evidence. It is clear nevertheless that underneath the self-confident parade of triumphs from Romulus to Balbus lurked more controversy, dispute, and uncertainty than immediately meets the eye. Of course, part of the point of the inscription was precisely to create such a public orthodoxy, to mask the conflicts and to exclude the variants. In that sense it tried to monopolize the history of the triumph and is about the most spectacular example of triumphal ideology to survive. One of the tasks of a modern historian must be to question the version of history offered by the *Fasti,* and expose the self-serving myths, the uncertainties, and half-truths within.

RECONSTRUCTING A RITUAL

Nostalgia, anachronism, exaggeration, creative invention, scrupulous accuracy—all these, in different combinations, determined how individual triumphs were written up by ancient authors. Yet the particular appeal of this ceremony for scholars since the Renaissance has, nevertheless, been the sense that the richness of the ancient evidence does allow us for once to reconstruct the programme of a major Roman ritual in its entirety. Ask the question: "What happened at the Lupercalia, or the Parilia?" and the answer will come down to the one or two picturesque details: the dash round the city at the Lupercalia; the bonfire-leaping at the Parilia. We could not hope to give any kind of coherent narrative of the festivals. Even the inscribed records of the Arval Brethren mostly give a relatively spare account of the annual ritual of Dea Dia.[22]

In the case of the triumph, by contrast, thanks to a host of ancient references to location and context, participants and procedures, it has been possible to sketch out a richly detailed "order of ceremonies," from beginning to end. In fact, at the center of most modern discussions of the triumph, for all their differences in interpretation and their different theories on triumphal origins and meaning, lies a generally agreed picture of "what happened" in the ceremony, at least in its developed form. It looks something like this:[23]

> The triumphal party assembled early in the morning on the Campus Martius (outside the sacred boundary of the city, the *pomerium*), from where the procession set off on a prescribed route that was to lead through the so-called "Triumphal Gate", on past the cheering crowds in the Circus Maximus, through the Forum to culminate on the Capitoline hill.
>
> The procession was divided into three parts. The first included the spoils carried on wagons or shoulder-high on portable stretchers *(fercula)*; the paintings and models of conquered territory and battles fought; the golden crowns sent by allies or conquered peoples to the victorious general; the animals that were to be sacrificed, trumpeters and dancers; plus the captives in chains, the most important of them directly in front of the general's chariot.
>
> The second part was the group around the general himself. He stood in a special horse-drawn chariot, sometimes expensively decorated with gold and ivory, with a phallos hanging beneath it (to avert the evil eye); his face painted red, he was dressed in an elaborate costume, a laurel crown, an embroidered tunic *(tunica palmata)* and a luxurious toga (originally of purple, *toga purpurea,* later decorated with golden stars, *toga picta*); and in one hand he held an ivory scepter, in the other a branch of laurel. Behind

him in the chariot stood a slave, holding a golden crown over his head, and whispering to him throughout the procession, "Look behind you. Remember you are a man". His children went with him, either in the chariot itself if they were small, or on horseback alongside. Behind the chariot came his leading officers and Roman citizens he had freed from slavery, wearing "caps of liberty".

The final part was made up of the victorious soldiers, wearing laurel wreaths and chanting the ritual triumphal cry of "io triumpe", interspersed with those ribald songs about the general himself.

When they reached the foot of the Capitoline, some of the leading captives might have been taken off for execution; the rest of the procession made its way up to the Temple of Jupiter. There the animals were sacrificed to the god and other offerings were made by the general, before feasts were laid on for the senate on the Capitol, and elsewhere in the city for soldiers and people. At the end of the day, the (presumably exhausted) general was given a musical escort back home.

Many of the elements of this reconstruction will already be recognizable from the ancient discussions of Pompey's triumph. Indeed, every single part of it is attested in Roman literature or the visual arts—in some cases many times over. It captures an image of the triumph that is embedded in all modern literature on the subject, this book no less than others. And it is an image that would no doubt strike a chord with Romans themselves (unsurprisingly perhaps, as it is directly drawn from ancient material). In comparison with the usual games of hypothesis, guesswork, hunch, and "filling the gaps" that lie behind most ancient historical reconstruction, this must count as uniquely well documented.

At the same time, it is grossly misleading. In a sense, all such generalizations always are. Any attempt to sum up a thousand years of ritual practice must involve drastic processes of selection, and the smoothing out of inconsistencies; it must consistently ungarble the garbled evidence and systematize the messy improvisations and the day-to-day changes that inevitably characterize ritual as practiced, even in the most conservative and tightly regulated society.[24] It takes only a few moments' reflection to realize that dozens and dozens of triumphal ceremonies must have matched up to this standard template in only some respects. The lavish displays of booty, for example, can only have become an op-

tion at a relatively late stage, when Rome was involved in lucrative foreign wars. And however much the literary tradition may have magnified
even modest ceremonies, small-scale triumphs with little on show, only
a few accompanying soldiers hardly raising a ribald song, and an unimpressive handful of captives no doubt easily outnumbered the blockbuster occasions celebrating the conquests of Pompey, Aemilius Paullus,
or Titus and Vespasian. Lucius Postumius Megellus, for example, who
celebrated a triumph in 294 BCE, the very next day after he had put his
case to the senate, would hardly have had time to get a lavish show on
the road (unless it had all been prepared in advance).[25]

But simplification is precisely what generalizations are *for.* The price
we pay for highlighting the structure is the loss of difference and the rich
particularity of each occasion. This is no better or worse than modern
generalizations about the procedures at, for example, funerals or church
weddings. The claim that "the bride wears white" remains true at a certain level, no matter how many women choose to take themselves down
the aisle in pastel peach or flaming red.

The problems, however, run deeper than that. The very familiarity of
this reconstruction of the Roman triumph (from Mantegna's *Triumphs
of Caesar* to the film *Quo Vadis*) and its confident repetition by historians over the last half millennium have tended to disguise the fragility, or occasionally the implausibility, of some of its most distinctive elements. What kind of balancing act, for example, would be required of a
general simply to stay upright in a horse-drawn chariot traveling over
the bumpy Roman streets, both hands full with a scepter and laurel
branch, sharing the ride with a couple of children and the obligatory
slave? Scratch the surface of some of the most central "facts" about the
triumph and an uncomfortable surprise may be in store.

The notorious phallos, for example, hanging under the triumphal
chariot (or "*slung* beneath" it, as more than one distinguished historian
has recently put it, obviously envisaging a sizeable object) turns out to
be much harder to track down than is usually implied. It is not a major
element in any of the ancient discussions of the triumph, and it is never
depicted in any of the numerous visual representations of the triumphal
chariot we have. In fact, in the whole of surviving ancient literature it

is mentioned precisely once: in Pliny's encyclopedic *Naturalis Historia* *(Natural History)*.[26] It could be, of course, that Pliny has done us the greatest good turn in preserving this crucial piece of evidence, over which our other sources of information have drawn a polite veil. Plenty of respectable theories about Roman culture are based on a single passing reference in Pliny, after all; and many modern historians would take pride in their ability to rescue and deploy such apparently curious pieces of information. Nevertheless, Pliny's isolated remark remains a long way from the confident assertion that "a phallos hung beneath the triumphal chariot." You would need a very strong commitment to the idea that Roman ritual never changed and that a single instance was by definition typical (once a phallos, always a phallos) to bridge that gap.

The same is true for several other elements in the reconstruction: the golden stars on the triumphal toga (known only from Appian's description of the triumph of Scipio); the historical development from *toga purpurea* to *toga picta* (no more than a learned deduction noted by Festus in the second century CE); the red-painted face (more widely attested; but Pliny, who is again our main source of evidence, actually refers to something more disturbingly exotic—a red painted *body*).[27]

Conversely, a blind eye is consistently turned to some of the less convenient records of triumphal custom. Although we are happy to rely, when it suits our purposes, on the Byzantine historians who preserved the gist of the lost sections of Dio, we steer very clear when it does not. John Tzetzes' claim, for example, that the triumphing general ran around the "place" (presumably the Capitoline temple) three times before dedicating his garland has not entered our tradition of the triumph.[28] The "bell and whip" which—according to several Byzantine historians, almost certainly drawing on Dio—hung on the triumphal chariot usually lose out to the much more intriguing and satisfyingly primitive, even if no better attested, phallos, though one modern commentator has dreamed up the economical solution of using "bells and whips" to decorate the phallos.[29]

In the final section of this chapter, I shall look in finer detail at just two features of our standard image of the triumphal procession: the slave who stood in the chariot behind the general, and the prescribed route taken by the procession through the city to the Temple of Jupiter. My questions are simple. How are these elements of the triumph reassembled by modern historians? What gets lost in the process? What assumptions underlie it? The fact is that the same wealth of ancient evidence which has encouraged the detailed reconstruction of the procession also provides the material with which that standard reconstruction can be challenged.

REMEMBER YOU ARE A MAN

The slave standing in the triumphal chariot behind the general, holding a golden crown over his head and whispering "Look behind you. Remember you are a man" has become one of the emblematic trademarks of the triumph. So emblematic a figure has he become, in fact, that his role featured in the voice-over of the closing sequence of the 1970 movie *Patton*—where his words, summing up the story's moral lesson, were more simply rendered as "All glory is fleeting." But he has also been integral to one of the most influential modern theories of the ceremony: that the triumphing general himself was seen as, in some way, divine (or, more precisely, that he represented the god Jupiter). For what was the point of warning someone that he was (only) a man, unless he was on the verge at least of thinking of himself, or being seen, as a god?

The words of warning that I have quoted are drawn from the late-second-century CE Christian writer Tertullian, whose reflections on the custom are reassuringly compatible with modern explanations: "He is reminded that he is a man even when he is triumphing, in that most exalted chariot. For at his back he is given the warning: 'Look behind you. Remember you are a man.' And so he rejoices all the more that he is in such a blaze of glory that a reminder of his mortality is necessary." Tertullian, however, makes no mention of a slave. Nor does Jerome, writing at the end of the fourth century CE: he repeats the phrase "Remember you are a man" (almost certainly borrowing it directly from this passage of Tertullian), but he does at least refer to a "companion" of the general, who traveled behind him in the chariot and muttered the key words each time the crowds roared their acclamation.[30]

A handful of other ancient writers offer a similar, but not identical, account; some of them offer very different explanations of the words spoken; and a few hint more allusively at the slave's role. According to Arrian, the hard-line philosopher Epictetus saw in the reminder of mortality (delivered by whom he does not say) a lesson in the transience of human possessions and affections. And this pointedly philosophical angle is possibly shared by Philostratus, who writes of the emperor Trajan parading his pet philosopher before the city of Rome in his triumphal chariot. In what could be a parody of the practice of the triumph and a humorous reversal of the warning, the emperor "turns round to him and says 'I do not know what you are saying but I love you as I love myself.'"[31]

Dio seems to have referred explicitly to the "public slave" in the chariot and to his repeated "Look behind you." No mention here, though, of "Remember you are a man," and Dio's interpretation of the warning strikes a rather different note. For him, if his later excerptors and summarizers have transmitted his sense correctly, it means "Look at what comes next in your life and do not be carried away with your present good fortune and puffed up with pride." Juvenal, by contrast, exploited the scene for a satiric sideswipe at the Roman elite. In describing the procession that opened the circus games (which overlapped closely with the triumphal procession), he hints that the mere presence of the sweaty slave in the same chariot was enough to take the bigwig down a peg or two.

Pliny, meanwhile, in discussing the iron ring traditionally worn by the triumphing general, alluded to the presence of a slave but assigned him the job of holding "the golden Tuscan crown" over the general's head. Elsewhere, without reference to the exact words or to who might have spoken them, he refers to the phrase, like the phallos, as a "defense against envy"—or, in the primitive gloss that some modern translators choose to put on it, "protection against the evil-eye." His sense here is hard to fathom, partly because the text itself is now corrupt and exactly what Pliny originally wrote is difficult to reconstruct. But he seems to have suggested, in extravagant terms, that the words were intended to "win over Fortune, the executioner of glory" *(Fortuna gloriae carnifex)*. Confusing enough for us—and it certainly confused Isidore, Bishop of Seville, who drew heavily on Pliny in the compilation of his own multi-volume encyclopedia in the seventh century CE. In a memorable piece of creative misunderstanding, Isidore has "an executioner" *(carnifex)* instead of the slave in the chariot—a particularly gruesome warning of the "humble mortal status" of the general.[32]

The implications of all this are clear enough. First, the standard claim that "a slave stood behind the general in his chariot and repeated the words 'Look behind you. Remember you are a man'" is the result of stitching together different strands of evidence. No ancient writer presents that whole picture. Jerome is perhaps the closest, with half the full phrase and a "companion" in the chariot. Otherwise, Tertullian's quotation, broadly confirmed by Epictetus and, on a generous reading, Philostratus and Pliny, must be combined with the testimony of Dio, Juvenal, and Pliny again on the presence of the slave (even though Dio offers a rather different form of the words spoken, and Juvenal says nothing about them at all—and is, in any case, describing the circus procession, not the triumph!).

Second, each of these different strands of evidence comes from a different date and context. None is earlier than the middle of the first century CE. Only Dio (albeit writing in the third century CE and filtered through much later Byzantine paraphrases) is offering a description of triumphal practice. The rest are conscripting the symbols of triumph into second-order theorizing or moralizing; even Pliny's reference to the use of an iron ring in the triumph is prompted by his lamentations over the decadence and corruption of gold ("A terrible crime against humanity was committed by the man who first put gold on his fingers"). Several are driven by a distinctive ideological agenda. For Juvenal, the slave is invoked as a weapon against aristocratic pride; for Jerome, the general's "companion" provides an analogy for Christian reminders of human frailty. But Tertullian provides the most glaringly partisan example. For he quotes the words in the context of a Christian attack on the idea that the Roman emperor was a god. The triumphing general he has in mind is the emperor; and, using that standard Christian tactic of twisting pagan practice to convict itself, he trumpets the words "Remember you are a man" as a clinching argument for the emperor's mortality. Where Tertullian picked up this piece of triumphal custom we do not know. There is no clear evidence that he ever went to Rome, still less that he witnessed a triumph.[33] But he would certainly have been horrified to think that his comments were used to support any argument that the general represented the pagan Jupiter.

The picture becomes even more puzzling if we include the visual evidence for the triumphal procession. On the diminutive triumph that decorates the silver cup from Boscoreale, we see a plausible figure of a slave standing behind Tiberius in his chariot, holding a crown or wreath over his head (see Fig. 11). He appears again on a fragment of a substantial relief sculpture from Praeneste (Palestrina), apparently showing a triumph of the emperor Trajan (Fig. 17).[34] But with the exception of a solitary clay plaque and possibly a lost sarcophagus of the late Empire (known from Renaissance drawings) that depicted the "triumphal" opening of the circus games (see Fig. 35), there is no trace of the slave on any other visual representation of the ceremony.[35]

It is not that he is simply omitted (though that is sometimes the case). More often his place is taken by the entirely imaginary figure of a winged Victory.[36] It is she, for example, who stands in the chariot and crowns Titus on his Arch (see Fig. 8), Trajan on the Beneventum frieze (see Fig. 10), and Marcus Aurelius on the triumphal panel now in the Capitoline Museum (see Fig. 31). Augustus had this treatment too, more than once, to judge from that solitary female foot found in the Forum of Augustus and a coin that depicts an arch topped by a triumphal chariot, and Victory on board with (presumably) the emperor (Fig. 18).[37] On other coins she is shown swooping in from the skies to crown the general (or zooming off again).[38] But again there is no sign of the slave, nor does he appear on what is often taken to be the very earliest coin repre-

FIGURE 17: Part of a relief panel from Praeneste (Palestrina) showing the emperor Trajan (98–117 CE) in triumph; the right-hand section is lost. The emperor—recognizable by his distinctive features and hairstyle—is accompanied in the chariot by a slave who holds a large, jeweled crown over his head.

FIGURE 18: Gold coin (*aureus*) minted 17–16 BCE to celebrate Augustus' road repairs—commemorating, in particular, the arches erected in honor of his restoration of the Via Flaminia. On top of the arch is a statue of Augustus, riding in a chariot pulled by a pair of elephants and crowned by a winged figure of Victory.

sentation of a historical triumph, commemorating Marius' triumph in 101 BCE (Fig. 19).[39]

This is an extraordinary discrepancy between the texts and (most) images. We are not simply dealing with different conventions of representation in different media, textual and visual. That is no doubt part of it. But the problem is that the "message" of the different representations of the triumphal scene is so entirely contradictory. If the figure of the slave and his words of warning acted in some sense to humble the general at his triumph or to draw the sting of what might be seen as his excessive glory, putting the figure of Victory in his place signaled precisely the reverse: it showed the crowning of the general by the divine agent of the gods, a shameless display of power, honor, and prestige.

This contradiction has proved impossible to solve. The few modern attempts to make sense of it are frankly unconvincing. The idea, for example, that the replacement of the slave by a Victory reflects a historical development of the ceremony, from a primitive religious ritual (where such ideas as the "evil eye" were taken seriously) to a naked display of power and success, flies directly in the face of the pattern of the evidence. In strictly chronological terms, Victory is attested long before the

FIGURE 19: Reverse design of a silver *denarius* minted in 101 BCE, commemorating Marius' triumph of that year. The general in his chariot is accompanied by a horse and rider, probably Marius' son.

slave; but, in any case, the contrast is much more one of medium and context than of date.[40]

Nor is it clear what lies behind those rare occasions when the slave *is* depicted in visual images.[41] In fact, a closer look at the relief from Praeneste uncovers some absurd paradoxes. If, as has been argued, the triumph in question on that sculpture is Trajan's posthumous celebration of 117–118 CE, then (on a literal reading) we are being asked to imagine the slave uttering his warnings of mortality to the dummy of an emperor who is already dead—and about to become, *pace* Tertullian, a god.[42] We do better, I suspect, to celebrate rather than explain (away) the contradictions, and to see them rather as a reflection of different ancient "ways of seeing" the triumph and different conceptions of the position of the general and the nature of military glory.

These issues bring us face to face with the fragility of the "facts of the triumph." The slave, with his warning for the general, certainly has some part in the history of the ritual. But there is nothing to prove that he was the original, permanent, and unchanging fixture in the ceremony as performed that he is often assumed to be. Besides, different versions of his words were clearly current, and they were interpreted in different ways. Even supposing he were a constant presence in the procession, his role could be emphasized, effaced, or substituted according to different priorities of representation and interpretation. If the slave holds a warning for *us,* it is of the risks we run in attempting to turn all these various versions of the triumph in art and literature—the moralizing turns, the Christian polemic, the glorifying images, the anthropological speculation—back into ritual practice.

PLOTTING THE ROUTE

The triumphal route, from its starting point somewhere outside the sacred boundary *(pomerium)* of the city to its culmination on the Capitoline hill, offers a different but no less revealing angle on the processes of historical reconstruction that underlie most modern accounts of the ceremony. Over the centuries of triumphal scholarship this aspect has generated considerably more controversy than the figure of the slave. Admittedly, only a few historians have ever contested the basic principle that there *was* a prescribed route for the procession. There is a broad consensus too that a better understanding of the path it took might well lead to a better understanding of the triumph as a whole. The meaning of a procession, as several studies in the Greek world have shown, regularly "feeds off" the buildings and landscapes by which it passes. The overall shape of the route too might offer an indication of the procession's original function. For example, a circular course right around the city, reminiscent of various purificatory ceremonies of lustration, might suggest a similar purificatory purpose for the early triumph (and fit nicely with one strand of ancient scholarship, which sees the prominence of laurel in the ceremony as connected with its role in purification).[43]

But matching up the various passing allusions to the route in ancient literature to the topography of the city on the ground has proved extremely difficult. Mapping the triumph is a much more tendentious process than any of the more self-confident scholarly reconstructions care to hint. I shall not summarize here all the twists and turns of the arguments for and against different routes, as they have been played, replayed, and sometimes literally re-enacted over the last five hundred years. I want instead, by looking closely at one or two controversial details, to reflect on why the apparently simple question "Where did the triumph go?" has proved so difficult to answer.

This is, once again, a fascinating case study in historical method. It also raises important issues of conservatism and innovation in the ritual practice of the triumph, which have implications for Roman ritual culture more generally. How conservative a ritual was the triumph? How rigid were the rules or conventions governing its performance? What does "conservatism" mean in the case of a ceremony carried out over more than a thousand years, through the streets of a city that was itself transformed over that period from a rural village of wattle and daub to a cosmopolitan capital—with all the display architecture, extravagant urban planning, and squalid slums that go with it?

Every attempt to reconstruct the triumphal route must start from the account by the Jewish historian Josephus of the triumph of the emperor Vespasian and Titus in 71 CE. Josephus himself had been a participant in the Jewish war, had defected to the Roman side, and, if not an eyewitness to the triumph, then was at least drawing on contemporary accounts. His is the only description of a triumphal procession to provide more than a series of snapshots of the performance and to offer a connected narrative and something approaching a route map for at least the start of the occasion.

> All the soldiery marched out, while it was still night, in proper order and rank under their commanders, and they were stationed on guard not at the upper palace but near the Temple of Isis. For it was there that the emperor and prince were resting that night. At break of day Vespasian and Titus emerged, garlanded with laurel and dressed in the traditional purple costume, and went over to the Portico of Octavia. For it was here that the senate, the leading magistrates and those of equestrian rank were awaiting their arrival. A platform had been erected in front of

the colonnade, with thrones of ivory set on it. They went up to these and took their seats. Straightaway the troops broke into applause, bearing ample testimony one and all to their leaders' valor. They were unarmed, in silken costume, garlanded with laurels. Acknowledging their applause, although the men wanted to continue, Vespasian gave the signal for silence.

When it was completely quiet everywhere, he rose, covered most of his head with his robe, and uttered the customary prayers. Titus prayed likewise. After the prayers, Vespasian briefly addressed the assembled company all together and then sent the soldiers off to the traditional breakfast provided by the emperors. He himself meanwhile went back to the gate which took its name from the fact that triumphs always pass through it. Here he and Titus first had a bite to eat and then, putting on their triumphal dress and sacrificing to the gods whose statues are set up by the gate, they sent off the triumphal procession, riding out through the theaters so that the crowds had a better view.

At this point Josephus changes focus to enthuse about the displays of spoils and special stunts in the procession. He does not pick up the route again until Vespasian and Titus are on the Capitoline, waiting for the shout that would indicate their celebrity prisoner had been put to death in the prison *(carcer)* in the Forum, at the foot of the hill.[44]

The general area of the start of this procession is clear enough from Josephus' description. The Portico of Octavia is firmly located in the south of the Campus Martius, between the surviving theater of Marcellus and the theater and porticoes of Pompey; the Temple of the Egyptian goddess Isis, from which a considerable quantity of Egyptian and Egyptianizing statuary and bric-à-brac has been unearthed, was some five hundred meters to the north, just east of the Pantheon. Vespasian and Titus, in other words, were conducting the preliminaries in the Campus Martius, outside the *pomerium,* while the procession proper presumably moved on its way southward, past the western slopes of the Capitoline and into the Forum Boarium (the so-called "Cattle Market"; see Plan). Beyond that, despite all the apparently precise details of Josephus' narrative, the locations or movements of the procession are very hard to pin down. It is to fill that gap, between text and map, that some of the most seductive but unreliable scholarly certainties have been generated.[45]

Where, for example, did Vespasian and Titus spend the night, guarded by the serried ranks of their troops? Josephus' Greek (just like my translation) could mean that they lodged in the Temple of Isis. If so, it would seem a significant choice: a careful allusion to the fact that in the civil wars of just two years earlier, Titus' younger brother Domitian was said to have escaped his opponents thanks to an ingenious disguise as an attendant of the Egyptian goddess.[46] What better place for this new imperial team to sleep over than the temple of the goddess whose protection had saved the young hope of the dynasty?[47] Yet the Greek can equally well mean that Vespasian and Titus spent the night "*near* the Temple of Isis." At this point practical modern logic has often come into play. The pair of generals, plus their army, would need a good deal of space, more than the Temple of Isis could possibly provide. Somewhere close by (the exact location is not absolutely certain) was the so-called *villa publica:* a building originally connected with the Roman census, used occasionally to house ambassadors and with surrounding parkland large enough to hold an army levy.

Neither Josephus nor any other ancient writer mentions the *villa publica* in connection with the triumph. But this has not stopped modern scholars from confidently identifying the *villa publica* as the place where the Flavian pair lodged on this occasion. More than that, it has not stopped them from identifying it as the *traditional* place where triumphing generals stayed on the eve of their celebration: the building "whose function it was," as one recent authority has it, "to accommodate the generals and victorious armies before the triumph." Another even imagines the returning general plus army "wait[ing] in the Villa Publica," where he "would apply to the senate for the right to hold a triumph."[48] If so, even with the capacious parkland, it must have been impossibly (and implausibly) overcrowded at some periods in the late Republic, when more than one general was simultaneously waiting for his triumph, sometimes over a period of years. This process of conjecture, wild extrapolation, and over-confidence is how many of the "facts" of the triumph are made. To repeat: no ancient evidence whatsoever links the *villa publica* with the ritual, beyond the ambivalent and uncertain implications of Josephus' description.

RECONSTRUCTING THE "TRIUMPHAL GATE"

Even more confusion surrounds the "gate" where Vespasian and Titus went after addressing the senate and others in the Portico of Octavia—a monument that has been the subject of more pages of learned dispute than any other part of the triumphal route. Josephus' rather awkward periphrasis ("the gate which took its name from the fact that triumphs always pass through it") has always been taken to be a gloss on the monument known in Latin as the *porta triumphalis* ("the triumphal gate"). This is mentioned for certain on only four other occasions in ancient literature. It is referred to once by Cicero, in his attack on the ignominious return to Rome in 55 BCE of his adversary Cnaeus Calpurnius Piso: "It doesn't matter what gate you entered the city by," he sneers at one point in the proceedings, "so long as it wasn't the triumphal one." And it appears three times in connection with the funeral of the emperor Augustus: Tacitus and Suetonius both record a proposal that Augustus' body should be carried to its pyre "through the triumphal gate." Dio goes further and states that this was exactly what did happen "by decree of the senate" (all implying that the gate was not usually open or a free thoroughfare).[49]

None of these writers give any hint of its form; the term "porta" (in Greek *pulē*) rather than "arcus" or "fornix" more easily suggests a gate in a city wall than a free-standing arch (as is also implied by Cicero's description of Piso "entering" the city), though many recent theories have opted for a free-standing structure. None refer to its function in the triumph. None, apart from Josephus, give any clue to where it stood; though, if Augustus' body was to be carried through it in his funeral cortège without a vast detour, we should probably have in mind some place between the Forum (where the eulogies were delivered) and the northern Campus Martius (where the pyre and his mausoleum stood).

Despite this vagueness, most modern scholars have been convinced that this structure represented a significant point at the start of the procession. The idea of the ceremonial passage through an arch or gate (whether as *rite de passage,* a purificatory ritual, or an entry ritual) has proved predictably seductive.[50] And most scholars have also been convinced that, with the help of a variety of other evidence, the location of the gate might be pinpointed. Only one independent mind of the early twentieth century ventured to suggest that the *porta triumphalis* may not have been a fixed structure at all but the name applied to whatever gate or even temporary arch the general passed through as he began his procession. And she has been much ridiculed for it (rightly maybe; for the idea certainly seems to conflict with Josephus' account).[51]

Leaving to one side the various hypotheses of Renaissance scholars (who regularly, and quite wrongly, conscripted the Vatican into the itinerary), enthusiastic arguments have been advanced over the last two hundred years for placing the gate in the Circus Maximus, the Circus Flaminius, the Campus Martius near the *villa publica,* as well as on the road that led from the Forum to the Campus Martius around the east side of the Capitoline hill.[52] The most recently fashionable theory, though floated as long ago as the 1820s, is that the triumphal gate was identical with, or at least closely linked to, the Porta Carmentalis, a gate in the old city wall at the foot of the Capitoline hill to the west, not far from where the Theater of Marcellus still stands. Originally (part of) the city gate itself, the triumphal gate was later replaced—so the most influential version of the argument goes—by a free-standing arch. This is so much the modern orthodoxy that it can now be treated as "fact."[53]

It is, of course, not "fact" at all; and no ancient author states directly or indirectly that the *porta triumphalis* was identical, or nearly identical, with the Porta Carmentalis. Yet a careful look at the arguments used to support this case offers a marvelous object lesson in the methods of modern historians of the triumph. We can trace the decidedly flimsy series of inferences and sleights of hand that claim to transform the mysterious and frankly opaque references in a few ancient texts into a physical structure whose form we can reconstruct—and whose image survives.

The idea takes off from what is almost certainly a Renaissance commentary on Suetonius, explaining that "the *porta triumphalis* seems to have been between the Porta Flumentana and the Porta Catularia." We do not know whether or not the Renaissance scholar was here drawing on reliable ancient evidence. Nor do we know where in the old city wall the Porta Catularia was situated (it is itself referred to in only one surviving passage of ancient literature, without any precise location). But assuming that our Renaissance informant is correct and assuming that we can conveniently pinpoint the Catularia between the Capitoline and the Campus Martius, then the implication would be that the *porta triumphalis* belonged just where we believe the Porta Carmentalis to have stood (though no agreed traces have been discovered).[54]

At this point, a story in Livy and Ovid helps out. When in 479 BCE the ill-fated posse of the Fabian clan marched out of Rome, to be defeated in their battle against the Veientines, Livy explains (according to the usual translation) that they left by the *wrong side* of the Porta Carmentalis, under the right-hand arch. Ovid chimes in with a reference to the curse of the right-hand arch ("Don't go through it anyone, there's a curse on it"). This story is, of course, much later elaboration; and even as told by Livy and Ovid, the exact significance of the "wrong" arch is far from clear. Was there one side for entrances and the other for exits, which the Fabii got wrong? Or was the right-hand side not in regular use at all? It does seem to show, however, that the Porta Carmentalis was a double gate, one side of which, or maybe both, was governed by special customs or regulations. Notwithstanding all the difficulties (and, frankly, none of the proposed solutions make sense of all the evidence), one of the arches of the Porta Carmentalis has become the prime candidate for being the *porta triumphalis,* which was, the theory goes, ritually opened on special occasions, such as triumphs.[55]

The rabbit out of the hat is a short poem by Martial celebrating a new Temple of Fortuna Redux ("Fortune the Home-Bringer") erected by his patron the emperor Domitian after his return (hence "Home-Bringer") from wars in Germany, and a new arch to go with it nearby. The poem opens with the temple built on what was "till now an open space"; and

then Martial turns to the arch "standing exultant over subjugated nations . . . with twin chariots numbering many an elephant"; it is, as the
poet insists, "a gate *(porta)* worthy of the emperor's triumphs" and a
fitting "entrance way to the city of Mars." Where exactly was this temple? The temptation to see it as a reconstruction of an old Temple of
Fortuna that stood near the Porta Carmentalis has proved almost irre-
sistible (despite the fact that Martial strongly suggests that his temple
was entirely new and built on open ground, not a reconstruction). Because if that were the case, the adjacent arch could be seen as a rebuild of
the *porta triumphalis,* this time as a free-standing structure.[56]

Why stretch the argument to such tenuous lengths? Because if the
theory is correct, the pay-off is rich. For the poem describes this arch in
some detail, as topped by a pair of chariots pulled by elephants, plus a
golden figure of the emperor. This can be matched up not only to an
image on a Domitianic coin but also to an elephant-topped arch in various scenes in later Roman commemorative sculpture. In other words,
the *porta triumphalis* which risked being a hazy phenomenon, documented allusively by a couple of ancient writers and of entirely uncertain form, has not merely been located but been given concrete form before our very eyes.[57]

We may judge these arguments and identifications a brilliant series of
deductions, a perilous house of cards, or a tissue of (at best) half truths
and (at worst) outright misrepresentations and misreadings. But impressed or not, we will find it hard to reconcile this reconstruction of the
triumphal gate and its location with the single surviving piece of ancient
literary evidence that provides an explicit context for the gate in the topography of the city. For, if we return to Josephus, we find that he gives
clear directions to it in the itinerary taken by Vespasian and Titus at the
start of their procession. After addressing the assembled company in
the Porticus of Octavia, Vespasian *"went back to* the gate which took
its name from the fact that triumphs always pass through it." It is difficult to see how anyone could describe movement from the Porticus to
the Porta Carmentalis as "going back," when the start of the journey had
been further north near the Temple of Isis.[58] The text would seem to in-

dicate that the gate was, as several earlier scholars suggested, "back" toward the beginning of the route that Vespasian and Titus had taken from the Isiac temple. Turning the Porta Carmentalis into the *porta triumphalis* demands sidelining this particular detail of Josephus' account.[59]

Whatever we decide about the gate, we must still face the question of just how accurate a template in general the road map provided by Josephus is. In particular, how correct is the common assumption that Josephus' route reflects the traditional pattern of behavior if not of all triumphing generals (what happened before the definition of the early city wall and its gates must be anyone's guess) then at least of those from the mid-Republic on? Filippo Coarelli takes a strong line in his own influential attempt to plot the route, claiming that Vespasian and Titus were "preoccupied with following exactly the forms of the most ancient ritual."[60] Josephus certainly, as Coarelli points out, glosses the *porta triumphalis* as the gate through which triumphal processions "always" pass; and he writes of Vespasian uttering the "customary" prayers. Leaving aside the question of how on earth Josephus knew what was customary (so far as we know the last triumph had been some twenty-five years earlier and Josephus had been in Judaea anyway), it takes only a moment's reflection to see that this was not a traditional triumph, following the most ancient rules, at all.

Not only was the culminating location of the ceremony, the Temple of Jupiter Optimus Maximus, still a pile of rubble after its complete destruction during the recent civil war (the final sacrifices must have been carried out amidst the devastation).[61] But also, unless we are to imagine that both Vespasian and Titus had carefully avoided the center of the city—the Palatine and Forum—since their arrival back in Rome from the East (and all the evidence, Josephus included, is that they had not), then, like other triumphing emperors, they had certainly flouted the republican tradition that the general should remain outside the *pomerium* until the ceremony.[62] As anthropologists have long since shown, performing a ritual "just as our ancestors have always done" is never exactly that. It is always a mixture of scrupulous attention to precedent, convenient amnesia, and the "invention of tradition." The triumph of 71 can have been no different; though it is now impossible for us, given the evidence we have (and it may well have been just as tricky for Josephus), to disentangle the various constituent strands of innovation and conservatism.

SIGNIFICANT DEVIATIONS

Similar issues undermine most attempts to map the rest of the triumphal route (and indeed to reconstruct the ceremony as a whole). From the point the procession goes through the triumphal gate and on through "the theaters" (and which theaters, of course, depends on where you put the gate), there is no narrative such as Josephus provides, and no clear markers on the ground. Some commemorative arches were probably planned with proximity to the procession in mind, some equally certainly were not (and it is not always easy to decide which falls into which category). The title *via triumphalis,* which used to be attributed to the modern Via S. Gregorio, running between the Colosseum and the great fountain known as the Septizodium (see Plan), is an entirely modern coinage. In antiquity itself *via triumphalis* was actually the name given to a road outside the city, on the right bank of the Tiber, leading to south Etruria (and its connection with the ceremony of triumph, if any, is a matter of guesswork).[63] Essentially, the method that has been adopted in tracing the route is one of connecting the dots, that is, plotting all the scattered topographical references to points on any triumphal procession, at any period and in any author, and then drawing a line between them, on the assumption that the triumph took a single orthodox route throughout Roman history, notwithstanding the changing face of the city's monuments and other new buildings.

One dot goes in the Forum Boarium, where the statue of Hercules stood; according to Pliny, it was dressed up in triumphal costume on the days of the procession. Another dot pinpoints the Circus Maximus, for Plutarch writes of the people watching the triumph of Aemilius Paullus "in the horse-racing stadia, which Romans call 'circuses.'" These are usually taken to be the Circus Flaminius at the start of the procession, though it is not mentioned by Josephus, and the Circus Maximus, which is what Josephus *may* have meant by the "theaters" that gave the crowds "a better view."[64] Add to these locations the references to triumphal processions on the Sacra Via (or "sacred way"), which led somehow—its exact path and extent is disputed—between the lower slopes of the Palatine into and perhaps through the Forum; the story of Julius Caesar's anger when one of the tribunes did not rise to his feet when his procession passed the "tribunes'" benches (near the senate house); and the need sometimes to drop off prisoners for execution at the *carcer* at the foot of the Capitoline.[65] Join all these points together and it is easy enough to trace a route round the city and up to the Temple of Jupiter on the Capitol, such as the one marked out on our Plan (see p. 335).

The result is by no means implausible as a ceremonial route, though several scholars have felt that at something less than 4 kilometers it would have been hardly long enough for the number of participants and the quantity of booty that is sometimes reported. Ernst Künzl, for example, compares it with the Rose-Monday procession in Mainz—where, in the year in which he observed it, some six thousand participants, one hundred tractors and other motor vehicles, and almost four hundred horses occupied a good 7 kilometers. By contrast, just one day of Aemilius Paullus' extravaganza in 167 BCE is said in one report to have included 2,700 wagonloads of captured weapons alone, never mind the soldiers and captives and booty on display.[66] But beyond such practical difficulties (which might always be taken as a further hint that the figures reported are wildly exaggerated), one final puzzling reference to the triumphal route shines a terrifyingly clear light onto modern assumptions, and modern disputes, about the ceremony as a whole.

According to Suetonius, "As Caesar rode through the Velabrum on the day of his Gallic triumph [46 BCE], the axle of his chariot broke and he was all but thrown out." This story appears to be matched in the account of Dio, who refers to the incident taking place "in front of the Temple of Fortune [or Felicitas] built by Lucullus."[67] The location of that temple is not otherwise known, and no archaeological traces have been identified; but the combination of these references appears to locate it in "the Velabrum," the valley between the Capitoline and the Palatine that joins the Forum to the Forum Boarium. So far, so good. But what was Caesar doing riding through the Velabrum? It is at first sight a puzzling detour from the generally accepted route I have sketched out. Two main solutions have been proposed. The first is that Caesar's triumph was taking a shorter route into the Forum. This involves imagining that there were at least two possible triumphal itineraries: a long version that went through the Circus Maximus then circled the Palatine and made its way back to the Forum by the Sacra Via; and a much shorter version that went directly down through the Velabrum into the Forum. On this occasion, with a show of uncharacteristic modesty and restraint, Caesar was taking the abbreviated path.[68]

The other argues precisely the reverse: namely, that all triumphs must have gone this way. The standard route, instead of making its way directly from the Porta Carmentalis to the Circus Maximus through the Forum Boarium, must have turned left down the street known as the Vicus Iugarius as far as the Forum, then retraced its steps back up the street on the other side of the Velabrum (the Vicus Tuscus) and then on to the Circus Maximus. The presence of an Arch of Tiberius at the point (probably) where the Vicus Iugarius meets the Forum is taken to support this version of the route.[69]

This second solution invests heavily in the idea of the conservatism of Roman ritual. According to this line, it is inconceivable that any processional route in a religious system "as rigid and conservative as the Roman state religion" could ever have varied: if Caesar took this path, then so must have all triumphing generals from time immemorial.[70] But more than that, the very peculiarity of this detour down the Velabrum is itself taken as proof of just how fossilized Roman ritual was. By the late Republic the Velabrum was a bustling commercial and residential zone, but in the days of the early city it was believed to have been an undrained marsh. Any triumphing general wanting to complete a circuit of the city before the sixth century BCE (when the area was supposed to have been drained) would have been prevented from proceeding straight across the marsh in this part of the city and would have been forced to take a detour that clung to the sides of the valley. Caesar's route then, so the argument goes, shows us just how obsessively the topography of early Rome was preserved in the ritual practice of later periods.[71]

The paradox of this apparently precious piece of evidence about Caesar's accident as he was riding through the Velabrum is that it is used to justify two completely contradictory claims about "the triumphal route"—first, that the route could vary, with more than one possible itinerary through the city, and second, that it was rigidly fixed, reflecting even in the historical period the topographical constraints of the archaic city. But this story has an even more surprising sting in the tail than that. Never mind the problem that recent geological analysis suggests that the Velabrum had not actually been a permanent bog since the neolithic period.[72] In our scholarly eagerness to follow Caesar down the Velabrum, we have generally failed to ask if that is exactly where Suetonius claims that he went. In fact, Suetonius' Latin almost certainly means nothing of the sort.

The phrase in question, *Velabrum praetervehens,* is usually translated as "riding through" the Velabrum. This is not an impossible translation, but all the same the verb *praetervehor* would be an odd choice to indicate a route down *through* the Velabrum. The word is commonly used for riding or sailing *past* something, even skirting or avoiding it.[73] In this case, a glance at the map would suggest that Caesar was not going *through* or *down* the Velabrum at all but *skirting* or going *past* it—keeping it on his left, in other words—as he made straight (let's suppose) from the Campus Martius across the Forum Boarium to the Circus Maximus. In which case, we are dealing neither with an alternative triumphal route here nor with a curious detour fossilized in the itinerary from the remote Roman past. Much more plausibly, the "Velabrum loop" is the product of some loose reading of the Latin, over-enthusiastically interpreted.[74]

The fact is that we cannot map with certainty the route of any individual triumphal procession; still less can we reconstruct "the" triumphal route or even be certain that such a thing existed. No ancient author refers to any such fixed itinerary; the closest we come to that is Josephus' remark about triumphs "always" passing through the (triumphal) gate. That said, few students of Roman ritual would imagine that the triumphal itinerary was invented completely new each time. After all, what "ritualizes" ritual is the prescribed nature of its actions; and the constraints of the topography of the city itself, combined with the fixed endpoint on the Capitoline, the casual literary references, even the murky tradition on the *porta triumphalis,* are enough to give us some idea of a likely framework within which to plot the triumph's layout.

The route sketched out on our map may not be too far from that taken by some—maybe many—triumphs. But any more detailed reconstruction than this must rest on all kinds of different imponderables, and on different preconceptions. What degree of improvisation flourished under the convenient alibi of ritual conservatism? How far did the monumentalization of the city center shift (or, alternatively, fossilize) the ritual route? What other factors prompted change or adaptation in the itinerary? What role, for example, did the choices of individual generals play? Or the sheer amount of booty that had to be dragged through the streets? For none of these crucial questions can we now do much more than guess the answer or adduce more or less plausible parallels in other cultures. Overall, as I have already noted, the main message from the comparative evidence of more recent ritual traditions is that there is likely to be much more innovation in the ceremony than any claims of rigid ritual conservatism (whether vaunted by the Romans or their modern observers) would appear to allow. The triumph is likely to have been much more conservative in theory than it was in practice.

ASKING THE RIGHT QUESTION

This close look at just two aspects of the procession has been intended to show just how perilous is the process of reconstruction that lies behind what we think we know about the triumph. It has been a lesson in the limitations of our knowledge of the ceremony as it was actually performed. But the issue is not simply one of the inadequacy of our historical "sources," as we like to term them (and in so doing, painting ancient texts as the passive object of modern historical inquiry, rather than one voluble and loaded side of a difficult dialogue). As I have repeatedly stressed, the triumph is the most lavishly documented Roman ritual there is. If this lavish documentation fails to answer convincingly the questions we are setting before it, then the chances are that we are asking the wrong questions. However seductive the question of "what happened on the day," this is not necessarily the question that produces the most telling answers from the range of texts and images that we now have: texts, in particular, that are recreating triumphs of centuries earlier, fantasizing about imaginary ceremonies, or deploying the ritual (as we saw in the case of Tertullian and the slave) as a way of thinking about other aspects of Roman culture and ideology.

In the next four chapters, I shall therefore change my focus back to the triumph and its conventions as a major part of the Roman cultural economy, the Roman imaginary. Looking first at the victims and spoils, then at the triumphing general himself, I shall not be turning my back entirely on the practice of the ceremony and the hard material evidence; wherever possible, I shall attempt to throw light on "what happened." But for the most part I shall be dealing with a richer subject. What did the triumph and its participant signify in Roman culture? What did "Romans"—and inevitably that shorthand often comes down to "elite Romans of the first century BCE through the second century CE," think when they thought "triumph"?

Captives on Parade

THUSNELDA STEALS THE SHOW

One of the highlights of the Vienna World Exhibition in 1873 was a vast new canvas by the German painter Karl von Piloty entitled *Thusnelda in the Triumphal Procession of Germanicus* (Fig. 20). Though this is to many modern eyes an uncomfortably overblown nineteenth-century extravaganza, measuring some five by seven meters, it was chosen as the work of art to represent Germany by the international jury then in charge of selecting "the outstanding creations of all nations" to adorn the show. Plaudits soon followed. It was a masterpiece, as one critic enthused, which showed the capacity of modern art "to work on our deepest feelings"—outclassing, as a history painting, even Rubens and Veronese.[1]

The painting takes as its subject the triumph of the Julio-Claudian prince Germanicus celebrated on May 26, 17 CE, after his military successes against various German tribes. His campaigns had been launched in retaliation for one of the most resounding "barbarian" victories over the occupying power: the "Varian disaster" of 9 CE (as it is usually called, from a Roman perspective), when three legions under Publius Quinctilius Varus were more or less annihilated in the Teutoburg Forest. Germanicus had certainly done something to restore Roman fortunes, notching up a few victories against the insurgents, taking a handful of

FIGURE 20: K. T. von Piloty, *Thusnelda in the Triumphal Procession of Germanicus*, 1873.
Spotlit in the center of the painting is the German heroine Thusnelda, wife of the rebel
leader Arminius, under the disgruntled eye of the emperor Tiberius watching from his dais.
The triumphing general himself is only just coming into view in the background.

prominent captives (including Thusnelda, the wife of Arminius, the
German hero of the "Varian disaster"), and recovering two of the legionary standards lost with Varus. Yet Arminius himself was still at large
and inflicting serious damage on the Roman forces. The triumph was
a potentially awkward celebration, since it was far from clear that
Germanicus had definitively won the war.[2]

Not that any such awkwardness necessarily impinged on the splendor of the occasion or of its celebration in history. Velleius Paterculus,
always as eager to support the imperial dynasty as some other writers
were to undermine it, praised Tiberius for laying on a triumphal spectacle "which matched the importance of Germanicus' achievements." At
least one roughly contemporary calendar of festivals, inscribed on stone,

appears to have memorialized May 26 as the day on which "Germanicus Caesar was borne into the city in triumph," while coins issued under the emperor Gaius (Germanicus' son) depicted the young prince on his triumphal chariot, and on the reverse blazoned the slogan "Standards Recovered. Germans Defeated."[3]

The most detailed surviving eulogy of the ceremony is given by the geographer Strabo, who refers to Germanicus' "most brilliant triumph" and then proceeds to list the famous captives on parade in the procession, including: Thusnelda and her three-year-old son, Thumelicus; her brother Segimuntus, the chief of the Cherusci tribe; Libes, a notable priest of another tribe, the Chatti; and an impressive roster of other German leaders, their wives, and children. Only one German, Strabo explains, found a different place: Segestes, Thusnelda's father and a Roman collaborator, "was present at the triumph over his nearest and dearest, as guest of honor."[4]

Tacitus, however, strikes a discordant note, with a characteristically cynical narrative of the triumph. It is a nice reminder that the very same ceremony can for some observers be a glorious celebration, for others a hypocritical sham. Tacitus opens his account of the year 15 with implications, already, of impropriety: "A triumph was decreed to Germanicus, *while the war was still going on.*"[5] Precedents can be found for such a premature anticipation of victory.[6] And, in any case, exactly what counted as the definitive end of a war must often have been harder to determine at the time than it appears with the benefit of hindsight. In fact, the declaration of a triumph might more than once have been a useful device for drawing a final line under an uncertainly completed campaign, asserting—rather than merely recognizing—its end. But Tacitus presents the train of events and the culminating procession as yet another example of the corruption of imperial rule, and in particular of Tiberius' jealousy of the dashing young prince and of his attempts to rein in Germanicus' success under the veil of empty honor.

"The procession," he writes, "displayed spoils and captives, replicas *(simulacra)* of mountains, of rivers and of battles." But it was not only the geographical features on show that were a pretense (*simulcra* in the pejorative sense). So too the whole victory being celebrated: "Seeing that he had been forbidden to finish off *(conficere)* the war, it was taken as finished *(pro confecto)*." The very success of the sham spelled danger. "The impressive sight of the general, and his five children who shared his chariot, riveted the attention of the spectators. But this concealed an underlying anxiety, as they reflected that popularity had not turned out well for his father, Drusus, that his uncle Marcellus had died at an early age despite the passionate support of the plebs, and that the enthusiasms of the Roman people were short-lived and ill-omened."[7]

Piloty's painting combines the accounts of Tacitus and Strabo. The scene on the imperial dais echoes all the Tacitean misgivings. A distinctively clad German, who must be Segestes, can hardly bear to watch as his family members walk by as captives. Tiberius himself, flanked by his sinister right-hand man Sejanus, looks decidedly grumpy—if not half asleep—at having to sit through the lavish celebration, sham or not. (It is, of course, in the very nature of successful shams that they merge into what they are pretending—but, at the same time, trying not—to be.) Only the imperial ladies seem to be having a good time, gawping at the exotic display.

But, unlike the image conjured by Tacitus, all eyes are *not* on the triumphing prince. He is only just entering the scene, a small figure in the background, half in shadow, crammed into the chariot with his five youngsters. The foreground is dominated instead by the captives listed by Strabo. The priest Libes is dragged along by a leering Roman soldier who tugs at the old man's beard. An assortment of German women look alternately fearsomely wild or resigned to their fate. But unquestionably the star of the show is the central, spotlit figure of Thusnelda, captive wife of the rebel Arminius, with little Thumelicus at her side. She is passing directly in front of the emperor and cuts a fine contrast with Tiberius: for it is she who behaves as a proud monarch, tall and unbowed; the ruler of the Roman world is hunched up on his dais, with his minders, merely a bit-part in the grand display. Here the triumphal victim has become the victor; all eyes are on her.

Piloty is playing with one of the commonest tropes of nineteenth-century nationalism, taking the most prominent victims of Roman conquest and transforming them into heroes of the nation-states of Europe. Boudicca, Vercingetorix, Thusnelda, and Arminius ("Herman the German") were all conscripted into the patriotic pantheon of their home countries in northern Europe. But, knowingly or not, Piloty is also picking up key themes in Roman commentaries on the celebrations of triumph: that the gaze of the audience was perilously hard to control; that the general risked being up-staged by his exotic victims; that the noble (or pitiful) captives might always steal the show. At the center of the parade lay a dynamic tension—a competition for the eyes of the spectator—between victor and victim (see Frontispiece).

Most modern studies of the triumph have focused on the successful general. This chapter offers a new perspective by concentrating on the defeated. It aims to explore the victims' role in the culture of the triumph: from the (not so) simple facts of their number, identity, and ultimate fate to the moral lessons they had to teach and their potential rivalry in the economy of the spectacle with the general himself.

THE VICTIM'S POINT OF VIEW?

The second poem in Ovid's collection of *Amores (Love Poems)* written in the late 20s BCE opens with the poet complaining of a sleepless night, tossing and turning. The diagnosis is soon clear: our poet has become a victim of the fire-power of Love ("Yes, Cupid's slender arrows have lodged in my heart"). Resistance is futile, and indeed will only make matters worse. So he opts for unconditional surrender and (as we have already glimpsed in Chapter 2) takes his due place as a captive in Cupid's triumphal procession.

> So I'm coming clean, Cupid: here I am, your latest victim,
>   Hands raised in surrender. Do what you like with me.
> No need for military action. I want terms, an armistice—
>   You wouldn't look good defeating an unarmed foe.

Put on a wreath of myrtle, yoke up your mother's pigeons—
  Your stepfather himself will lend you a fine
Chariot: mount it, drive in triumph through the cheering
  Rabble, skillfully whipping your birds ahead,
With your train of prisoners behind you, besotted youths and
  maidens,
    Such pomp, such magnificence, your very own,
Triumph: and I'll be there too, fresh-wounded, your latest
  Prisoner—displaying my captive mind—
With Conscience, hands bound behind her, and Modesty, and all
  Love's
    Other enemies, whipped into line.
You'll have them all scared cold, while the populace goes crazy,
  Waves to its conquering hero, splits its lungs.
And what an escort—the Blandishment Corps, the Illusion
  And Passion Brigade, your regular bodyguard:
These are the troops you employ to conquer men and immortals—
  Without them, why, you're nothing, a snail unshelled.
How proudly your mother will applaud your triumphal progress
  From high Olympus, shower roses on your head;
Wings bright-bejewelled, jewels starring your hair, you'll
  Ride in a car of gold, all gold yourself.
What's more, if I know you, even on this occasion
  You'll burn the crowd up, break hearts galore all round:
With the best will in the world, dear, you can't keep your arrows
  idle—
    They're so hot, they scorch the crowd as you go by.
Your procession will match that of Bacchus, after he'd won the
  Ganges
    Basin (though *he* was drawn by tigers, not birds).
So then, since I am doomed to be part of your—*sacré* triumph,
  Why waste victorious troops on me now?
Take a hint from the campaign record of your cousin, Augustus
  Caesar—*his* conquests became protectorates.[8]

This is a wonderfully evocative image of a triumph: the roaring crowds; the victims chained and bound; the general's mother looking on, proudly applauding as she scatters rose petals over his head; the soldiers and comrades on whom the success depended; and of course the victor himself in his splendid chariot and rich ceremonial dress. (Cupid here sports not triumphal laurel but a wreath of myrtle, as worn in the "lesser" ceremony of *ovatio*—appropriately enough, as myrtle was the sacred plant of Venus, and perhaps a hint that the erotic victory over Ovid had anyway been too easy to deserve a full triumph.)

At the same time, the poem is, as many critics have pointed out, dazzlingly subversive in a variety of ways. The most public celebration of Roman military prowess is playfully (and pointedly) conscripted into the celebration of private passion. The role of the lover, often presented in Latin poetry as a *soldier* in Love's army (*militat omnis amans,* "every lover is a soldier," as Ovid's own slogan from later in this book has it) is overturned, to make the lover the defeated *victim,* not the comrade, of Cupid.[9] And as the final couplet must prompt us to reflect, the relationship of this imaginary triumph to the military celebrations of the emperor himself raises awkward questions: how far are we to see the figure of the triumphant Augustus ("Caesar") in this Cupid? Augustus and Cupid were, after all, as Ovid insists, following the logic of the emperor's claimed descent from Venus herself—*cognati,* "cousins."[10]

But the poem offers something rather more unexpected. Frustrating as it is to admit it, this clever allegorizing, this manipulation of the conventions of the ceremony to explore the idea of erotic capture, must count as the closest we get to a surviving first-person account from a triumphal victim. Of course, that is not very close at all. Ovid's attempt here to rethink the predicament of the poet-lover by imagining what it might have felt like on the wrong side of the triumph was a quintessentially Roman fantasy; it was one of the games only victors could play. The same goes, and even more so, for the motivations and reactions ascribed to *bona fide* historical captives by various Roman writers. However tempting it might be to read these as if they gave us the victim's own perspective on the triumph, they are inevitably Roman projections of those motivations and reactions onto the mute victim. They are more an exercise in ventriloquism than reportage—a different angle on the ceremony, maybe, but still the victor's story. Characters such as Thusnelda and the rest did not find their own triumphal voice, in surviving literature at least, until centuries after the Roman Empire had collapsed.

THE CLEOPATRAN SOLUTION

The classic case of this ventriloquism is the reported reaction of that most famous of all triumphal *refuseniks,* Cleopatra. Her suicide, after the death of Mark Antony, was the stuff of ancient, no less than modern, legend. Plutarch's account of the deadly asp(s) hidden in the basket of figs has—despite Plutarch's own doubts about the story and thanks, in large part, to Shakespeare's reworking of it in *Antony and Cleopatra*—become canonical. And the motive for the suicide has become equally enshrined in ancient and modern literary tradition. As Horace insisted in his "Cleopatra Ode," written soon after the event, the Egyptian queen killed herself because she was not prepared to face the humiliation of appearing in a Roman triumph; she preferred to cheat her enemy Octavian (later Augustus) of the pleasure of parading her through the streets of Rome.

> Fiercer she was in the death she chose, as though
> she did not wish to cease to be a queen, taken to Rome
>   on the galleys of savage Liburnians
>   to be a humble woman in a proud triumph.[11]

We read the same explanation in Plutarch, Florus, and Dio, and it provided Shakespeare with Cleopatra's memorable line to the dying Antony: "Not th'imperious show / Of the full-fortuned Caesar ever shall / Be brooch'd with me." Livy too put similar defiant words in her mouth. Though this portion of his history of Rome no longer survives in full, an ancient commentator on Horace quotes from its account of the queen's final days: "She used to repeat, again and again, 'I shall not be led in triumph.'"[12] These are vivid vignettes and memorable slogans. And it is tempting indeed to imagine, as many modern critics have, that they offer us some direct insight into the psychopathology of a notable captive and her reactions to the victory and its parade.

But it is not so simple as that. Partly, the bizarre details of the suicide account are decidedly unlikely: Plutarch and Dio were not the only writers to have had their doubts about the asp—or the "Egyptian cobra," in modern zoological terminology—and to suggest alternative versions; modern scholars too have queried the plausibility of many aspects of the tale. "The Egyptian cobra is about two metres long and hard to conceal in a basket (especially if there were two of them)," as one recent commentator on Plutarch puzzles.[13] Cleopatra may not, in any case, have been as eager to take her own life as the standard story suggests. As many military victors at all periods have found, some of the most prominent captives are much more trouble than they are worth to keep alive, too "hot," glamorous, or disruptive to risk bringing back home. Octavian may have publicly regretted the absence of the queen from his triumphal parade; but many modern historians have suspected that, at the very least, he gave her every opportunity to take her own life, even if he did not actually arrange her murder.[14]

Even more to the point, however, is the fact that the tale of suicide preempting the appearance in the triumphal procession is not restricted to this one famous incident. It is one of the commonest tropes of Roman triumphal narratives. When Mithradates decided to die rather than face Pompey's Roman triumph, he said to the officer chosen for the task, so Appian reports: "Your strong arm has done me great service in struggles against my enemies. It will do me the greatest service if you would now make an end of me, in danger as I am of being led off to a triumphal procession after being for so many years the absolute monarch of so great a realm."[15]

Likewise runs the story of Vibius Virrius, rebel leader in the city of Capua, which had rashly sided with Hannibal during Rome's war against Carthage. When defeat appeared inevitable, Virrius persuaded some twenty-seven of the Capuan senate to join him in drinking poison. "I shall not be bound and dragged through the city of Rome as a spectacle in a triumph" are the words that Livy put in his mouth.[16] There are hints too that similar sentiments were sometimes ascribed to Zenobia, the queen of Palmyra, whose territorial expansion in the East (at Rome's expense) was quashed by the emperor Aurelian in 272 CE. Various stories were told of what happened to Zenobia after her defeat. According to some writers she was paraded in Aurelian's triumph; but the historian Zosimus records the tradition that she died on the way back to Rome, either from illness or self-imposed starvation. Again, we are meant to infer, this might have been suicide to preempt the humiliation of the triumphal procession.[17]

An obvious explanation for this series of look-alike incidents is that they are all reappropriations of the original story of Cleopatra. Zenobia, in the literary tradition at least, was often seen as a warrior queen closely on the model of Cleopatra. One ancient biography alleges that she claimed descent from the Egyptian queen herself, even using some of the banqueting vessels that had once belonged to Cleopatra, while dressed—as if to add another anti-Roman queen to her repertoire— in the cloak of Dido.[18] It is hardly surprising that some versions of the story cast her death too in Cleopatran colors. Appian and Livy were also writing after Cleopatra's defeat, even if their subjects, Mithradates and Virrius, predated her by decades or centuries. It would be a nice example of the complexity of triumphal chronology, of the mismatch between the chronology of the celebrations themselves and that of their literary representations, to imagine the ancient writers retrojecting a (true) Cleopatran story back onto earlier captives facing the prospect of a triumphal parade.

In fact, however, the story of Cleopatra is not the first to suggest death as an option preferable to a parade through the streets of Rome. We can trace the idea of defiant suicide back to the late Republic in an anecdote about Aemilius Paullus and his triumph over the Macedonian King Perseus in 167 BCE. The king is said to have begged not to be paraded in the triumphal procession; Paullus to have taunted him in reply with the "Cleopatran solution." The matter had been, the victor observed, in Perseus' power; if he had wished to avoid that disgrace, he could always have killed himself. We have no reason to suppose that this is a more genuine exchange than any of the words ascribed to triumphal victims. But that is not the point. For while this particular anecdote is recounted twice by Plutarch in the early second century CE, it also used by Cicero in his *Tusculanae Disputationes (Tusculan Disputations)* as an example of how one might escape from suffering—almost fifteen years before the defeat of Antony and Cleopatra at the battle of Actium.[19]

We are dealing then with something more significant in the long history of Roman triumphal culture than an elusive glimpse of a genuine captive's perspective on his or her own predicament. Whatever those feelings were, the repeated stress on the suicide of the noble prisoner is part of that ambivalent power struggle between victor and victim that lies embedded at the center of the triumph and its representations. On the one hand, so the narrative logic runs, Cleopatra—or Mithradates, or whoever—*did* snatch victory from the jaws of defeat by the (reported) act of suicide. Their death deprived their conqueror of the clearest proof of his victory. As one recent account has it, "Cleopatra's suicide . . . denied to the triumph of 29 BC her physical presence as an assured token of . . . submission"; the female prisoner thwarted the ambitions of the general, trumped his military might, by removing her body from his control.[20]

On the other hand, these stories also celebrated the inexorable power of Roman conquest and triumph. As Paullus pointedly reminded Perseus, there was no escape but death; this was a zero-sum game in which for the victim the price of reclaiming victory was self-annihilation. This was a logic that lurked also behind those triumphal processions in which the living prisoners were on show. They offered not only proof of their own submission; in the high stakes of triumphal competition they also demonstrated the capacity of Roman power to serve up its victims to the public gaze. The bottom line of the "Cleopatran solution" is that Roman power correlated with its ability to parade those proudly defeated monarchs in the center of Rome itself; their only escape, death.

FACTS AND FIGURES

As the complexities of these apparently simple stories must hint, many of the basic "facts" and practical details about triumphal prisoners are hard, if not impossible, to pin down. Even for triumphs in relatively well-documented periods, the question of how many captives were on display on any occasion is difficult to answer with any confidence. Ancient figures—especially, but not only, when they concern battle casualties or other tokens of Roman military success—are notoriously unreliable.[21] But very few of the ancient literary accounts hazard a number at all, except (suspiciously) for a handful of early triumphs, where we read of round numbers in the thousands.

The maximum is the 8,000 claimed by Eutropius (writing more than half a millennium after the event) for the prisoners paraded in 356 BCE in a triumph over the Etruscans. This is followed by Dionysius' total of 5,500 for a procession at the start of the fifth century BCE and Livy's record of 4,000 captives at the triumph of Marcus Valerius Corvus over the town of Satricum in 346 BCE, who were subsequently sold.[22] Accounts of later triumphs, if they quantify the prisoners at all, tend to refer only to "lots of them" (as in Appian's account of a "host" of captives and pirates in Pompey's parade in 61). Occasionally they note the complete absence of captives on display. So it was in 167 BCE, for example, at the triumph of Cnaeus Octavius, who had scored a naval victory in the war against King Perseus. "Minus captives, minus spoils," as Livy remarks: Octavius had been upstaged by the triumph of Aemilius Paullus which took place the day before, with its impressive complement of booty and prisoners.[23]

The usual assumption—based, as so often, on common sense, backed up by passing references in ancient authors where they happen to fit—is that, by the time the Romans were fighting at any distance from home, only a selection of those captured in war were normally brought back to decorate a triumph. The majority would have been disposed of, most commonly sold off as slaves, near the war zone and would have figured in the triumph only in the form of the cash their sale raised.[24] The general would have had to strike a balance between creating a powerful impression on the day and the expense, inconvenience, and practical difficulties of transporting, feeding, guarding, and managing a large number of unwilling captives. In fact, we have no idea how any of those arrangements were handled. Where, for example, were the mass of prisoners kept before the triumph? This must have been an especially pressing question when, as often in the late Republic, a period of months or even years elapsed between the victory and the parade itself.

A strategic selection of some of the most impressive captives is certainly the model suggested by Josephus, writing of the aftermath of Titus' suppression of the Jewish revolt. He refers to "the tallest and most beautiful" of the young prisoners being reserved for the triumph, while the others (after the hard core or the particularly villainous had been put to death) were sent to the mines and amphitheaters or sold into slavery. Scipio Aemilianus, too, according to Appian, picked out fifty of the survivors of the siege of Numantia for his triumph of 132 BCE (though these could hardly have been fine specimens, given the terrible conditions of the siege); the rest were sold.[25]

Other ancient writers, however, refer to the large-scale transport of prisoners to Rome: Tiberius Sempronius Gracchus' captive Sardinians in 175 BCE, who were so numerous (and therefore cheap) that, according to one ancient theory, they gave rise to the puzzling Roman catchphrase "Sardi venales!" "Sardinians for sale!" Or the full complement of prisoners who, Polybius implies, were sent to Rome in 225 BCE for Lucius Aemilius Papus' triumph over the Gauls.[26] All kinds of circumstances might have encouraged a mass display of prisoners; Gracchus, for example, may have used the human profits, in the shape of slave captives, to make up for the absence of rich booty from Sardinia.[27]

KINGS AND FOREIGNERS

This vagueness over the number of captives put on show—however frustrating for us—is not a mere lapse on the part of the ancient writers on whom we depend for our information. They were concerned with significantly different issues, in particular with the rank, status, and exotic character of the headline captives. On these topics they offer detailed and specific accounts, even if not always consistent and compatible. Livy, for example, underlined his disagreement with Polybius on the parade of the Numidian prince Syphax in Scipio Africanus' triumph of 201 BCE. Polybius had claimed that he *was* exhibited in the procession, Livy at one point claimed to know better—that Syphax had actually died at Tibur before the triumph took place.[28] Likewise, as we have already seen, different traditions were handed down of Zenobia's role in Aurelian's triumph: did she die en route to Rome or was she the chief captive on parade?

What seems to have counted for most, in the written versions of the Roman triumph at least, was the display of defeated monarchs and their royal families. Augustus pares this down to its essentials, boasting in his own account of his *Res Gestae (Achievements):* "In my triumphs nine monarchs or children of monarchs were led before my chariot."[29] But this emphasis on celebrity captives has a long history throughout triumphal narratives. In contrast to the austere anonymity of Augustus' description (perhaps he was well advised to disguise the fact that two of the "children of monarchs," Alexander and Cleopatra [junior], were also children of a leading Roman senator, Mark Antony), writers often lovingly recorded the resonant names of these high-status prisoners. We have already seen that the triumph of Pompey in 61 BCE was adorned with a royal family whose names prompted memories of famous past conflicts between West and East. Livy makes just this point about the family of King Perseus on display in Aemilius Paullus' parade in 167 BCE. The two young princes were called, with an eye on the glorious Macedonian past, Philip and Alexander, "tanta nomina" ("such great names").[30]

The roll call of these monarchs, princes, princesses, and "chieftains" (the belittling title we like to give to the proud kings of "barbarian tribes") is an evocative one; it includes Gentius, king of Illyricum, plus his wife, children, and brother, in the triumph of Lucius Anicius Gallus in 167 BCE (only a few months after Aemilius Paullus' extravaganza with King Perseus); Bituitus, king of the Gallic Arverni, in the triumph of

Fabius Maximus in 120; Jugurtha, king of Numidia, and his two sons in Marius' triumph in 104; Arsinoe, Cleopatra's elder sister, young prince Juba of Mauretania, and the Gallic chieftain Vercingetorix in Caesar's triumphs in 46.[31] And this is not to mention all the vaguer references, projected as far back as the early Republic, to "the noble captives" in the procession, "the enemy generals" or "the purple-clad" walking before the triumphal chariot. "The royal generals, prefects, and nobles, thirty-two of them, were paraded before the victor's chariot," as Livy typically notes of the celebration of Scipio Asiaticus' defeat of King Antiochus in 189 BCE. It was even something of a cliché of Roman word play that triumphs involved the enemy *duces* ("leaders") themselves being *ducti* ("led" as prisoners) in the victory parade.[32]

The triumph, as it came to be written up at least, was a key context in which Rome dramatized the conflict between its own political system— whether the Republic or the autocratic Principate that officially disavowed the name "monarchy"—and the kings and kingship which characterized so much of the outside world. Of course, many Roman triumphs did not actually celebrate victories over kings; still less did they have a king on display in the parade. Nevertheless, kings were seen as the ideal adversaries of Roman military might. They dominated the imaginative reconstructions of historical triumphs; and the inscribed triumphal *Fasti* in the Forum specified carefully when the celebration had boasted a royal victim, by adding the king's name to the usual formula of defeat—"de Aetolis et rege Antiocho," "over the Aetolians *and King Antiochus*."[33] No other category of enemy was picked out in the inscription in this way.

Kings also provided an image of triumphal victims that was repeatedly reworked in Roman fantasy, humor, and satire. When the younger Pliny, in the published (and no doubt much embellished) version of the speech he delivered on taking up his consulship in 100 CE, projects an image of the emperor Trajan's future triumph, it is a triumph over Dacian kings that he calls to mind, with a stress once more on the royal *names*. "I can almost see the magnificent names of the enemy leaders— and the physique which is a match for those names." He goes on to imagine single combat between Trajan and the enemy king, "if any of those kings would dare to engage with you hand to hand." (Not so honorable, the behavior of the later emperor Lucius Verus, who is said to have "brought actors from Syria as if he were bringing a group of kings to his triumph.")[34] This same focus on triumphal royalty underlies the quip of Florus about the celebration in 146 BCE which followed Metellus Macedonicus' victory over Andriscus, an implausible adventurer who had claimed to be the son and heir of King Perseus of Macedon. The joke was that he did achieve royal status in the end, for in his defeat "the Roman people triumphed over him as if over a real king."[35] Unsurprisingly, this stereotype makes its mark on entirely mythic celebrations too. The Christian writer Lactantius refers to some poem (now lost) on the triumph of Cupid, on the model perhaps of Ovid's treatment of that theme—except that here it is Jupiter, the king of the gods, who is the chief victim, led in chains in front of the triumphal chariot.[36]

If not royal, then the best triumphal prisoners were at least exotic and recognizably foreign. Pompey's captives in his procession of 61 BCE—pirates as well as the Eastern princes and generals—were said to be kitted out in their native costume. Even better still, literary invention or not, was the parade of the conquered in the triumph over Zenobia in 274 CE. As often, the semi-fictional excesses of late Roman biography expose some important truths at the heart of Roman culture. Here, in the biographer's account of Aurelian's procession, we read first of a marvelous roster of foreign prisoners: "Blemmyes, Axiomitae, Arabs from Arabia Felix, Indians, Bactrians, Hiberians, Saracens, Persians, all bearing gifts; Goths, Alani, Roxolani, Sarmatians, Franks, Suebians, Vandals, Germans . . . the Palmyrenes, who had survived, the leading men of the city, and Egyptians too, because of their rebellion." But something even better follows.

Statius' epic fantasy of the mythical Theseus returning to his triumph with an Amazon victim (and bride) in tow was said to have been played out on the streets of Rome in the third century CE: "Ten women were led in the procession, who had been captured fighting in male dress among the Goths after many others had fallen—these, so a placard stated, belonged to the race of Amazons."³⁷ Hardly less exotic is the glimpse of the victory celebrations after the battle of Actium, the culmination of the galaxy of Roman history imagined by Virgil on the famous shield of Aeneas. How far this description draws directly upon the details of Octavian's triumphal ceremony conducted in 29 BCE, how far it is a loaded or glamorous fiction, is a matter of dispute. But fiction or not, it invests heavily in the wide-ranging and exotic origins of the captives on show, "as disparate in their style of dress and weaponry, as in their native tongues." The list includes "the tribe of Nomads and the Africans in their flowing robes, the Leleges and Carians and arrow-bearing Gelonians . . . the Morini, most remote of human kind . . . and the wild Dahae."³⁸

The obvious point is that the triumph and its captives amounted to a physical realization of empire and imperialism. As well as the image of Roman conflicts with monarchy, the procession (or the procession's written versions) instantiated the very idea of Roman territorial expansion, its conquest of the globe. The prisoners' exotic foreignness, at the heart of the imperial capital, put on show to the people watching the procession (or reading of it, or hearing tell of it, later) the most tangible expression you could wish of Rome's world power. It was a much better display of Roman success, as Velleius Paterculus writes of the emperor Tiberius' triumph in which he took part in 12 CE, to have the enemy exhibited in the procession than killed on the field of battle.³⁹

But there is more to it than that. The emphasis on the foreignness of the enemy prisoners goes hand in hand with the equally significant point that Romans themselves belonged only on the winning side of this ceremony. The logic was that the triumph was a celebration of victory over external enemies only; that a triumph in civil war, with Roman citizens dragged along where the exotic barbarian foe should be, was a contradiction in terms. As Lucan has it, at the start of his epic poem on the war between Caesar and Pompey, civil war could, in a sense, be defined as "war that would have no triumphs."⁴⁰ Yet, Lucan's text already hints that this is precisely one of the fault lines of Roman triumphal culture: for, as his readers would have known, victory in the civil war recounted in his poem was, in effect, celebrated in Caesar's triumph in 46 BCE—even if disguised under the convenient rubric of "foreign" wars in Africa and elsewhere.

While none of Caesar's Roman adversaries were themselves on display (the leading ones were dead anyway), paintings of several of them in their last moments were put on parade. According to Appian, Caesar refrained only from exhibiting an image of Pompey, as he was "much missed by all," while for the rest he "took care not to inscribe the names of any Romans," on the grounds that such display of the names of fellow citizens was "unseemly . . . shameful and ill-omened"—a telling detail, given the stress we have already noted on the resonant names of prominent captives.[41]

Cynics might have observed that the roll call of exotic captives in Virgil's version of Octavian's triumph was a loaded cover-up for the fact that there too civil war (against Antony) lay immediately behind the celebrations—just as the hand-picked Jewish prisoners and the Jewish spoils in the triumph of Vespasian and Titus were a useful disguise for the defeat of the Roman enemies in the civil war that put the new Flavian dynasty on the throne in 70 CE.[42]

BEFORE THE CHARIOT?

How exactly the prisoners were displayed in triumphal processions is largely a matter of guesswork and presumably varied over time, according to occasion and to different types of enemy. We find several references to prisoners appearing in chains, while Appian thinks it worthy of note that none of the host of captives in Pompey's triumph in 61 were bound.[43] Some are said to have walked in the parade; others—including some of the enemy generals in Vespasian and Titus' triumph—were carried on biers or floats; yet others, the most elite cadre of captives, rode in wagons or chariots (of different types, finely calibrated to match the precise rank of captive, according to one Roman scholar). But by whatever method the victims traveled, ancient writers are almost unanimous in identifying their place in the procession: *ante currum,* "in front of the

general's chariot." Apart from a rogue line of Lucan that has the prisoners in Caesar's triumph follow the chariot, this phrase, in fact, is repeated
so often that it seems almost the standard term in ancient triumphal jar-
gon—both in literary texts and inscriptions—for leading a victim "in a
triumphal procession."[44]

It is tempting to conclude that the captives, or at least the most celebrated among them, were paraded—as Piloty shows his Thusnelda—directly in front of the triumphing general. And we shall certainly see that
ancient writers sometimes made a good deal of the interplay between
victor and victim that such proximity would imply. But in the only surviving ancient sculpture to represent the overall choreography of a triumphal procession, the layout appears more complex. In the small frieze
that winds its way around the attic storey of the Arch of Trajan at
Beneventum, apparently depicting a procession from the general's chariot to the arrival of the first animals for sacrifice at the Temple of Jupiter
(Fig. 21), several groups of prisoners have been identified. Some walk:
one woman carries a baby, another has a child at her side; in front a placard presumably proclaimed their identity. Others travel in carts and
chariots of different designs: one distinctive pair make their way in a
covered wagon, pulled by oxen; other couples sit chained in horse-
drawn chariots (Fig. 22). All are, in a general sense, "in front of the chariot" (everything in this procession is). But they are not clustered together almost at the victor's feet, as is so often assumed. In fact, in that
position of greatest honor, or humiliation, we find here some rather un-
distinguished attendants carrying booty and what is thought to be one
of the golden crowns often presented to the general.[45]

This is another case of the complex interrelationship between visual
imagery, literary representations, and the procession as it took place on
the streets—just as we saw with the puzzling figure of the slave in the
general's chariot. The temptation to trust its documentary style (Could,
for example, those different types of prisoners' wagons be tied in to
Porphyrio's classification of them?) must always be balanced by the sense
that the sculptors were in the business of recreating a moving, perhaps
messy and disorganized procession as a work of art—and one that was to

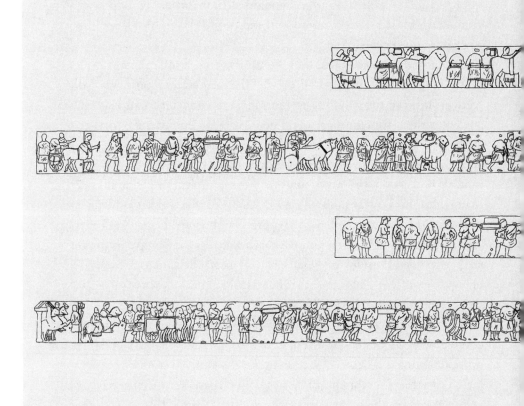

evoke the ceremony around four sides of a monument, in miniature and 12 meters above the ground. In that process, there would have been strong reasons for constructively rearranging any "regular order" that guided the procession and redistributing the prisoners throughout its length.[46]

On the other hand, in literary representations, there were strong imperatives to link closely the general and his chief captive and, in focusing on the relations of the victor and the prisoners "in front of his chariot,"

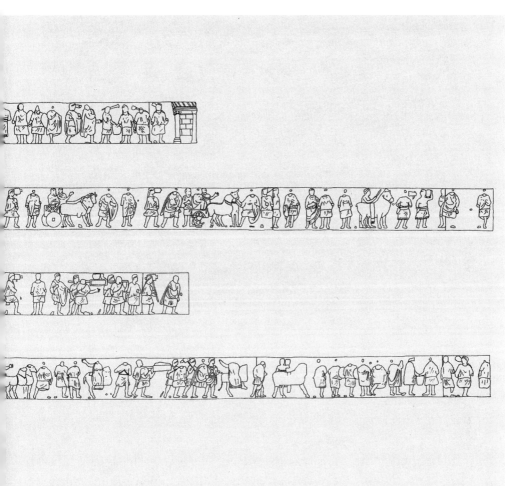

FIGURE 21: The small triumphal frieze of the Arch of Trajan at Beneventum (Fig. 10). The procession runs all around the arch, leading from the group around the general in his char-iot (bottom left, the northwest corner of the monument) to the Temple of Jupiter (top right). Approaching the temple is a series of animals for sacrifice, with their semiclad atten-dants (*victimarii*). Through the rest of the procession the spoils of victory, carried shoulder-high, on *fercula*, and placards are interspersed with prisoners, some riding in carts (detail, Fig. 22), others walking.

FIGURE 22: A pair of prisoners in an ox-drawn cart, from the small frieze of the Arch of Trajan at Beneventum (Fig. 21, center of second register). Both are dressed in barbarian style, with cloaks and hats. One is chained, the other stretches out his hand in supplication—or horror.

to be blind to the diversity of the parade. The bottom line is that different ways of seeing the procession conjured different processional orders.

EXECUTION

We seem to be on much firmer ground with the fate of the captives in the procession. As the triumphal parade was reaching its last lap, passing through the Forum and about to ascend the Capitoline hill, the prisoners—or at least the most prominent, famous, or dastardly among them—were hauled off for execution and worse, probably in the nearby prison *(carcer)*. So Josephus describes the closing stages of the triumph of Vespasian and Titus: "Once they had reached the Temple of Jupiter

Capitolinus, they stopped. For it was ancestral custom to wait at that point for the announcement of the death of the enemy commander. This was Simon, son of Gioras. He had been led in the procession amongst the prisoners of war; then, a noose round his neck, scourged by his guards, he had been taken to that place next to the Forum where Roman law prescribes that condemned criminals be executed. After the announcement came that he had met his end and the universal cheering that followed it, Vespasian and Titus began the sacrifice."[47]

Much the same procedure was mentioned briefly by Dio (to judge at least from a Byzantine paraphrase) in his account of regular triumphal procedure attached to the notice of Camillus' triumph in 396; and more emphatically by Cicero in one of his "speeches for the prosecution" (though never actually delivered in court) against Verres, one-time governor of Sicily. After a flamboyant and implausibly complicated attack on his opponent for having preserved the life of a pirate chief against the interests of the state, Cicero offers a thundering contrast—between Verres' behavior and that of a triumphing general: "Why even those who celebrate a triumph and keep the enemy leaders alive for some time so that the Roman people can enjoy the glorious sight of them being paraded in the triumphal procession and reap the reward of victory—even they, when they start to steer their chariots out of the Forum and up onto the Capitoline, bid their prisoners be taken off to the prison. And the day that ends the authority *(imperium)* of the conqueror also ends the life of the conquered."[48]

This practice of executing the leading captives as the triumphal procession neared its conclusion has launched all kinds of modern theories. Some scholars have seen it as a quasi-judicial punishment. Others have taken it as ritual killing or human sacrifice—and have claimed, through this lens, to glimpse the violent and murky origins of the celebration (perhaps going back to the violent and murky Etruscans).[49] But it will presumably come as no surprise at this point in my account that the "facts" are a much more fragile construction than they are usually made to appear. In this case, we find strikingly few examples of captives (more or less) unequivocally claimed to have been executed during the triumphal procession: apart from Simon in Vespasian and Titus' triumph, the list at its most generous comprises only Caius Pontius, leader of the Samnites in 291 BCE, pirate chiefs in 74, Vercingetorix in Caesar's triumph of 46, and Adiatorix and Alexander in Octavian's celebration of 29.[50]

By and large the more evidence we have on the fate of individual prisoners, the less certain what we might call the "Josephan model" of execution appears to be. Aristoboulus of Judaea, for example, was—according to Appian's confident assertion—the only prisoner put to death in Pompey's triumph of 61, "as had been done at other triumphs." But other writers have him escaping from Rome, making more trouble in the East, being brought back to Rome once more—only to be sent back to the East by Caesar in the civil war to raise support for the Caesarian cause, before being poisoned by Pompeian allies (Pompey may have wished he *had* put him to death in 61).[51] Livy seems to have claimed that Jugurtha also was killed in this way at Marius' triumph in 104 BCE; but Plutarch has him imprisoned after the trial and dying of starvation several days later.[52]

In fact, more often than not, even the most illustrious captives are said to have escaped death. Some were imprisoned, apparently on a long-term basis. King Gentius and his family were put into custody after the triumph of Anicius Gallus in 167. (Livy's story of the senate's decision to have them imprisoned at Spoletum, the objections of the local residents, and their final transfer to Iguvium raises key—if unanswerable—questions about how the practicalities of all this were managed.) Others lived, if not (like Aristoboulus) "to fight another day," then at least to start a new Roman life. One version of Zenobia's story was that she was established—quite the Roman *matrona,* we may perhaps imagine—in a comfortable villa near Tibur.[53]

These uncertainties and contradictions offer a sharp focus on some important aspects of the culture of the Roman triumph; they are not merely regrettable indications of how little we really know. The repeated stories in ancient writers of violence *not* being wreaked on the poor triumphal victims, and their generalizations about normal practice or references to the executions that took place "on other occasions," undoubt-edly served to keep the idea of the death of the captive high on the cultural agenda of the Roman triumph. But that does not necessarily in-dicate that celebrity executions toward the end of the procession were a regular feature of the ceremony. Far from it. The economy of violence and power is extremely complex, and it operated in Rome, as elsewhere, by fantasy, report, threat, and denial as much as it did by the sword or noose itself.

Modern historians, who often have a great deal invested in an image of ancient Rome as an almost uniquely cruel and bloodthirsty society, have generally been reluctant to read the *myths* of Roman violence (whether in the arena, on the battlefield, or in the triumphal procession) as anything other than a direct reflection of the *acts* of violence at which they appear to hint. But often, as here, there is a good case for seeing the bloodshed more as part of a pattern of menacing discourse than of regu-lar practice.

On the evidence we have, the killing of the leading captives was not "ancestral custom" at all. Nor, by and large, was it treated as such by ancient writers. Significantly, in fact, they never appear to give this deathly practice an origin in the distant Roman past, in the triumphs of Romulus and the other legendary heroes of the Republic. That is not to say that victims were never put to death in the course of the proces-sion. It would require some very special pleading to deny that. More likely, a small number of executions, carried out for whatever reason (in the Flavian case perhaps the parade of "tradition" by the new dy-nasty), lay somewhere behind a custom that flourished most of all in the telling and in the retelling—and in the opportunities that it offered for denial and clemency. The clever cultural paradox is that Pompey could become renowned for mercy by *not* doing something that was rarely done anyway.

The exemplary, mythic quality of these executions can be seen in dif-ferent ways in Cicero's reference to the execution of the prisoners "on the day which ends the authority of the conqueror." Pulling this out of con-text, as so often happens, and treating it as a general rule of triumphal practice is to miss the loaded argument that lies behind it—and to fall into the trap that Cicero has set. For Cicero is attempting to make the practice of killing the enemy captives *seem* universal, and thereby turn it into a stick with which to beat Verres for not killing his own pirate prisoner.

But this passage also exposes very clearly how the literary image of the triumph increasingly does duty for the ceremony itself. In a speech in praise of Constantine, dated to 310 CE, the emperor is congratulated for, among other things, his decisive execution of a couple of rebellious Frankish kings. This was heralded as a return to traditional ways: "Emperor *(imperator),* you have renewed that old confidence of the Roman Empire, which used to impose the death penalty on captured enemy leaders. For in those days captive kings added luster to the triumphal chariots from the gates of the city as far as the Forum. Then, as soon as the victorious general *(imperator)* started to steer his chariot up onto the Capitoline, they were taken off to the prison and slaughtered. Perseus alone escaped such a harsh law, when Aemilius Paullus himself, who had received his surrender, made a plea on his behalf."[54] The entirely erroneous claim here that Perseus was the only distinguished captive to be spared the death penalty is striking. Striking too (and a hint at the *modus operandi* of invented traditions) is the way that other forms of execution merge into this particular form of triumphal slaughter. The death of the Frankish kings was not a triumphal punishment in the traditional sense at all; they were thrown to the beasts in the arena.[55]

Even more important is the literary reference. Whatever contact the author of this *Panegyric* had with triumphal practice, the tradition he refers to is drawn not from anything that happened on the streets of Rome but straight from Cicero's text—which is almost directly quoted *(cum de foro in Capitolium currus flectere incipiunt / simul atque in Capitolium currum flectere coeperat).* This is a clear instance of late Roman nostalgia for a "ritual in ink" as much as for the ceremony as performed, and it is very little guide to the triumphal traditions of killing at any period.

VICTIMS AS VICTORS

The tales of prisoners' suicide, true or not, imply that the triumphal parade was deemed to be an overwhelmingly humiliating experience for the once proud kings and other noble captives. Ancient writers, however, lay little stress on the nature of that humiliation. We read in Josephus of Simon being "scourged" before his execution, while the late fourth-century Christian writer John Chrysostom referred (on the basis of what information we do not know) to a triumphal victim as "whipped, insulted and abused." Other texts conjure up a picture of captives as "chained," "hands bound behind their backs," "eyes cast on the ground," or "in tears," and the repertoire of ancient images matches up to these descriptions in some respects at least: chains are much in evidence, faces stare at the ground, hands—not bound behind—stretch out vividly in what is presumably sorrowful supplication (Figs. 23, 24; see also Fig. 22). For the rest, it is not hard to imagine what the victim's experience might have amounted to, as the noisy crowd of spectators took pleasure in feeling that they had at last the upper hand over (in Cicero's words) "those whom they had feared."[56] Jeers, taunts, and, one might guess, the ancient equivalent of eggs and rotten tomatoes.

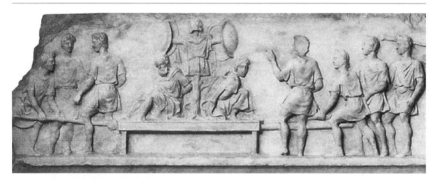

FIGURE 23: Part of a triumphal frieze from the Temple of Apollo Sosianus in Rome, 34–25 BCE. Two prisoners, hands bound behind their backs, sit on a *ferculum* underneath a trophy of victory, which the Roman attendants get ready to lift. This frieze is probably intended to represent the triple triumph of Augustus (Octavian) in 29 BCE.

FIGURE 24: Terracotta relief ("Campana plaque") showing prisoners in a triumphal procession; probably early second century CE. Here the Roman guards control (or harass) their captives with chains attached to their necks.

The degradation of the victims, however, is only one side of the story. There is a competing logic in the display of Roman (or any) victory. The successful general accrues little glory for representing his victory as won by thrashing a mangy band of feeble and unimpressive suppliants. The best conquests are won against tough and worthy opponents, not against those who look as though they could not have put up much of a fight in the first place. As the *Panegyric* of Constantine put it, the captives "added luster to" (almost in the Latin "added dignity," *honestassent*) to the celebration.[57] Hence in part the stress on the high status of the prisoners; hence too the readiness of Pompey to steal some of his Roman rival's most impressive captives.

Indeed, throughout the stories of the triumph, we find—alongside the idea of humiliation—repeated emphasis on the nobility and stature of those "in front of the chariot." In Marius' triumph in 101 BCE, Teutobodus, king of the Teutones, made a splendid sight (or so some said; other writers had him die on the field of battle). A man "of extraordinary height" who was reputed to be able to vault over four, or even six, horses, he "towered over the trophies of his own defeat."[58] It is an image reflected in Tiepolo's eighteenth-century version of Marius' triumph in 104 over the impressive figure of Jugurtha (see Frontispiece). Other monarchs too caught the eye. In Florus' account, Bituitus starred in the procession of Fabius Maximus in 120 BCE, wearing the brightly colored armor and traveling in the silver chariot in which he had fought.[59] Zenobia was said to have been decked out for the triumph of Aurelian in jewels and golden chains so heavy that she needed attendants to carry them.[60]

The image of a regal victim surrounded by attendants carrying her golden ornaments (albeit chains of bondage) cannot help but raise questions about exactly who was the star of the event. Quite simply, glamorous and impressive prisoners were a powerful proof of the splendor of the victory achieved. But at the same time, just like Piloty's vision of Thusnelda, the more impressive they appeared, the more likely they were to steal the show and to upstage the triumphing general himself. On several occasions Roman writers hint at just this scenario, and at a slippage between victor and victim. For Florus (or his source), "nothing stood out more" in Fabius' triumph than the defeated Bituitus.[61] Dio also plays with this paradox when he describes the journey of Tiridates, king of Armenia, to Rome in 66 CE. The idea was that, after the decisive Roman victories under Corbulo, Tiridates was to come to the capital to receive back his crown, as suppliant, from Nero. But with his royal retinue and accompanying army, not to mention his personal appearance and impressive stature, his journey from the Euphrates seemed to resemble more a triumph in his own name than a mark of his defeat.[62]

Ovid had already developed this theme in a poem written about 10 CE from his exile on the Black Sea, imagining the scene back home of a Roman triumph over Germany. It is a tremendous tour de force that makes the most of the literary and representational complexities of the ceremony. In one particularly neat, and gruesome, touch, Ovid pictures (a model of) the river Rhine being carried in the procession—just like the "two-horned Rhine" that Virgil had imagined at the climax of his Actian parade. Ovid's Rhine is a sorry specimen in comparison: he is, frankly, a mess, "covered in green sedge," "stained with his own blood"; his horns have been "smashed." But much of the poet's attention goes to the human victims:

> So all the populace can watch the triumph,
> Read names of generals and captured towns
> See captive kings with necks in chains and marching
> Before the horses in gay laurel crowns
> And note some faces fallen like their fortunes
> And others fierce forgetting how they fare.

Several of the commonplaces of the triumphal procession are deployed here: the victims are kings; they are chained; they cast their eyes to the ground or project a grim absent-mindedness. But Ovid proceeds to insinuate just how difficult it is to keep the captives in their place, as he recounts the words of an imaginary spectator explaining the show—starting from the victims—to his neighbors: "That one," he begins, "who gleams aloft in Sidonian purple was the leader *(dux)* in the war." Where, we are being asked to wonder, does the boundary lie between triumphant general and this proud prisoner? Both are royally clad in purple, aloft in their chariots, leaders *(duces)* of their people. What does it take to tell them apart?[63]

This problem underlies all mass spectacle: how do you control the gaze of the viewer? Is it the emperor in his box who holds our attention in the arena or the slave-gladiator fighting for his life? In the triumphal procession, the grand nobility of the victims can draw the crowds. So also can the pathos of the prisoners on display. The most notorious case of this was the parade in Caesar's triumph of 46 BCE of the young Egyptian princess Arsinoe, carried on a bier (or *ferculum*) like a regular piece of booty. The sight of her in chains, in Dio's account at least, aroused the spectators to pity and prompted them to lament their own misfortunes.[64]

A similar story is told of the triumph of Aemilius Paullus over King Perseus in 167. According to Plutarch, it was the king's children who captured the attention of the crowd: "There were two boys and one girl, too young to be entirely aware of the scale of their misfortunes. Indeed they evoked even more pity—for the very reason that they would in due course lose their innocence—so that Perseus himself walked along almost unnoticed. And so it was out of compassion that the Romans fixed their gaze on the young ones and many ended up crying, and for all of them the spectacle turned out to be a mixture of pleasure and pain until the children had gone by."[65] Of course, we cannot be sure if this is a reliable or well-documented account of reactions on the day itself (we have no reason to believe that Plutarch had, directly or indirectly, an eyewitness source; and he had probably never seen a triumph himself). But even if he is by-passing the available evidence to exploit the rhetorical traditions of pathos, Plutarch's account shows exactly how, in the imagination at least, the pathetic victims could steal the show.

That ambivalence between victor and victim is a theme which informs the accounts of Paullus' triumph of 167 BCE in other respects, too. Perseus—"wearing a dark cloak and distinctively Macedonian boots, struck dumb by the scale of his misfortunes"—may have made a less moving sight than his children, but he rivaled the triumphing general in a different sense.[66] In fact, the ancient cliché about this particular triumph rested on its threat to subvert the hierarchy of victor and victim. For Paullus, at the very height of his glory, was afflicted by a disaster that struck at the heart of his household: out of his four sons, two had already been adopted into other aristocratic families in Rome (a not uncommon practice); the two who remained to carry on his line died over the very period of the triumph, one five days before, the other three days later.[67]

Livy puts a speech into the mouth of Paullus, in which—after contrasting his own misfortunes with the good fortune his campaigns had brought to the state—he compares himself to Perseus: "Both Perseus and I are now on display, as powerful examples of the fate of mortal men. He, who as a prisoner saw his children led before him, prisoners themselves, nevertheless has those children unharmed. I, who triumphed over him, mounted my chariot fresh from the funeral of my one son and, as I returned from the Capitol, found the other almost breathing his last . . . There is no Paullus in my house except one old man." Plutarch imagines the same moment, ending Paullus' speech with a pithier formulation along the same lines: "Fortune makes the victor of the triumph no less clear an example of human weakness than the victim; except that Perseus, though conquered, keeps his children—Aemilius, though conqueror, has lost his."[68] The message is clear. Triumphal glory was a perilous and greasy pole. The victor was always liable to exchange roles with the victim.

This slippage between victim and victor found a place in more general ethical discussions, too. Seneca, for example, exploited it to grind home a moral point—that, in the end, from a philosophical perspective, the triumphal victor and victim *were* indistinguishable. You could, he wrote, show equal virtue whether you were the one who triumphed or the one dragged "in front of the chariot," so long as you were "unconquered in spirit."[69] Elsewhere, in a bold (and disconcerting) anachronism, he puts into the mouth of Socrates a similar point about virtue transcending misfortune, using a triumphal analogy. The sage claims that—even if he was placed on a bier *(ferculum)* and made to "decorate the procession of a proud and fierce victor"—he would be no more humbled when he was driven in front of the triumphal chariot of another than if he was the triumphing general himself.[70] The triumph, in other words, asks you to wonder who the victor really is and so what virtue and heroism consist in.

There is even more to this than a paradox of triumphal ideology, important though that may be. Modern scholarship has, by and large, been committed to a crude view of Roman militarism. Rome, we are repeatedly told, was a culture in which victory and conquest were universally prized. Whether or not this ideology always translated directly into aggressive imperialism is another matter (ideology may have a more complicated relationship to practice than that). But, so the standard argument runs, military prowess was at all periods a guarantee of social glory and political success; and apart from a handful of subversive poets, the Romans were not the sort of people to question the desirability of winning on the field of battle.[71]

Some of this is certainly true. It would be utterly implausible to recast Roman culture in pacifist clothes. But the most militaristic societies can also be—and often are—those that query most energetically the nature and discontents of their own militarism. If we do not spot this aspect in the case of Rome, the chances are that we have turned a blind eye to those Roman debates, or that we have been looking in the wrong place. Literary representations of the triumph, with all their parade of hesitation and ambivalence over the status of victor and victim, are one of the key areas in which the problems as well as the glory of Roman victory were explored.

To take a final vivid example: when in 225 BCE Lucius Aemilius Papus, after his Gallic victory, made the chief captive tribesmen walk in their breastplates up to the Capitol—"because he had heard that they had sworn not to remove their breastplates until they had climbed the Capitol"—he was not only rubbing their noses in their failed ambitions (for they had foolishly imagined that their ascent of the hill would be in their own seizure of Rome). The story also serves to remind the reader of the fragile dividing line between victory and defeat, and their various celebrations.[72]

WHAT HAPPENED NEXT?

Most modern accounts concentrate on the occasion of the triumph as a processional moment, a single day—or at most a few days—of celebration or carnival. This tends to obscure the fact that the triumphal procession is also a single episode in a more extended narrative for victim and general alike. The ceremony should prompt the question "What happened next?" One answer we have already explored. However frequently or infrequently the triumph did in fact end in execution for the leading captives, the often told *story* of execution gives a powerful narrative closure to the victims' part in Roman history. As Cicero summed it up, the triumph was their end. For the less illustrious, the outlook might be no less bleak: Caesar's prisoners of war are said to have become cannon fodder in the arena.[73] But a competing version represents it very differently: not so much as finality but more as a rite of passage. Just as the ceremony itself was no less the beginning of peace than it was the culmination of war, so the victims were both the humiliated and defeated enemies of Rome and at the same time new participants, in whatever role, in the Roman imperial order. The triumph was a key moment in the process by which the enemy became Roman.

This is a theme we have already seen underlying the mythic triumph of Statius' Theseus, whose victim was about to become his wife. Other writers emphasize a similarly domestic outcome for their triumphal victims. Perseus himself may have died, in strange circumstances, in captivity: according to at least one account, he got on the wrong side of his guards, who kept him continually awake until he died of sleep deprivation. One son and his daughter soon died, too, but the other son, the aptly named Alexander, went on to learn metalworking and Latin—so well that he eventually became a secretary to Roman magistrates, an office which (according to Plutarch) he carried out with "skill and elegance."[74] Zenobia, too, in one version, settled down to the life of a middle-aged matron outside Rome. Young Juba, who was carried as a babe in arms in Caesar's triumph of 46, went on to receive Roman citizenship, to write famous historical works and eventually to be reinstated on the throne of Numidia.[75]

At the same time, the progression of captives into Roman status could prompt ribaldry or even insult. Scipio Aemilianus, for example, the natural son of Aemilius Paullus who was adopted into the family of Cornelii Scipiones, is said to have rebuked a rowdy gathering of Romans in the Forum protesting against the murder of Tiberius Gracchus with the taunt: "Let those to whom Italy is a step-mother hold their tongues. You won't make me afraid of those I brought here in chains even now they are freed."[76] This is a taunt that rests on the idea that prisoners had a Roman life after their captivity. So too do some of the jibes made against Julius Caesar for supposedly admitting Gauls to the senate itself. One of the popular verses sung at the time, according to Suetonius, made a direct connection between the appearance of Gallic prisoners in Caesar's triumph and their subsequent appearance in the senate:

> The Gauls our Caesar led to triumph, led them to the
> senate too.
> The Gauls have swapped their breeches for the senate's
> swanky toga.[77]

This aspect of the triumph as *rite de passage* is most vividly encapsulated by the career of Publius Ventidius Bassus, who celebrated a triumph over the Parthians in 38 BCE. In the competitive culture of triumphal glory, this celebration was particularly renowned. It was, as Roman writers insisted, the first triumph the Romans had ever celebrated over the Parthians (who had inflicted such a devastating defeat on Roman forces under Crassus at the battle of Carrhae in 53 BCE). But it was notable for another reason, too—as the same writers insist. For Ventidius Bassus was a native of the Italian town of Picenum and years earlier had been carried as a child victim in the triumph of Pompey's father, Pompeius Strabo, for victories in the Social War. His career was particularly extraordinary, then, as he was the only Roman ever to take part in a triumphal procession as both victor and victim. Or, as Valerius Maximus put it, "The same man, who as a captive had shuddered at the prison, as a victor filled the Capitol with his success." His is the limit case, in other words, of the triumph as a rite of passage into "Romanness"—the clearest example we have of the part the ceremony could play in a narrative of Romanization. Not only that. It is also the limit case of the potential identity of the triumphing general and his victim.[78]

POETIC REVERSAL?

These ironies of the triumph were not lost on Ovid, whom we have identified as our only surviving "voice of the victim." In the second poem of his collection of *Amores* he suffered "in front of the chariot" of Cupid. But not for long. Ovid soon claims for himself the part of the Ventidius Bassus of Love. By the middle of his second book of poems, he has won a notable victory—albeit, as he goes on to confess (or to boast), a bloodless one:

> A wreath for my brows, a wreath of triumphal laurel!
>   Victory—Corinna is here, in my arms
> . . . Thus bloodless conquest
>   Demands a super-triumph. Look at the spoils.[79]

On the erotic battlefield, our erstwhile victim has become a triumphing general.

V

The Art of Representation

IMAGES OF DEFEAT

Cleopatra did not entirely escape display in Octavian's triumphal procession, despite her suicide. For in place of the living queen was a replica staging the moment of her death, probably a three-dimensional model on a couch but perhaps a painting: a *tableau mourant,* as it were, complete with an asp or two. This was one of the star turns of the triumph for ancient viewers and commentators. "It was as if," Dio writes, "in a kind of way she was there with the other prisoners"; and Propertius, who casts himself as an eyewitness of the celebration, claims to have seen "her arms bitten by the sacred snakes and her body drawing in the hidden poison that brought oblivion."[1] It also greatly intrigued Renaissance and later scholars, who assumed that the model had been preserved and expended enormous energy and ingenuity in attempting to track it down. One favorite candidate was the statue we commonly know as the *Sleeping Ariadne* in the Vatican Museums (Fig. 25)—what we now interpret as an armlet being identified as the snakes.[2]

An early sixteenth-century verse monologue by Baldassare Castiglione, written as if spoken by this mute work of art, nicely captures the ambivalent slippage between replica and human prisoner (here in a translation by Alexander Pope):

FIGURE 25: *Sleeping Ariadne.* This sculpture—a Roman version of a third- or second-century BCE Greek work—very likely represents a classic theme of ancient art and myth: Ariadne, abandoned in her sleep by Theseus, whom she had helped to kill the Minotaur. In the Renaissance it was commonly entitled *Cleopatra* and believed to be the model of the Egyptian queen carried in the triumph of 29 BCE.

Whoe're thou art whom this fair statue charms,
These curling aspicks, and these wounded arms,
Who view'st these eyes for ever fixt in death,
Think not unwilling I resign'd my breath.
What, shou'd a *Queen,* so long the boast of fame,
Have stoop'd to serve an haughty *Roman* dame?
Shou'd I have liv'd, in *Caesar's* triumph born,
To grace his conquests and his pomp adorn?[3]

Even as late as 1885 the hunt was still on, when the American artist John Sartain penned a pamphlet to argue that a painting on slate supposedly found at Hadrian's Villa at Tivoli in 1818 and attributed to, among others, Leonardo da Vinci was indeed nothing other than Octavian's replica of Cleopatra. His description is a mixture of art historical dispassion and lascivious interest: "The right arm is bent in a right-angle, the forearm being strongly foreshortened . . . The dark green, yellow-spotted snake has inserted its teeth into the left breast, from which some drops of blood ooze out."[4] Needless to say, the claims of this object to be what was carried in the procession of 29 are about as weak as those of the *Sleeping Ariadne.*

Cleopatra was not the only absent victim to be incorporated into the parade as a painting or model, even if others have not proved to be such compelling topics of modern speculation. So it was, according to Appian, that Mithradates and Tigranes were displayed in Pompey's triumph as paintings. Again in 46 BCE Julius Caesar paraded "on canvas" the deaths of his adversaries in the civil war: Lucius Scipio throwing himself into the sea, Petreius shafting himself at dinner, Cato disemboweling himself "like a wild animal." These humiliating images nearly rebounded on the victor, as the audience groaned at the pathetic sight before settling down to applaud or mock some other less tragic final moments. There was obviously a fine line to be drawn between the impressive vaunting of success and the frankly bad taste of displaying pictures of Roman citizens pulling their own guts out.[5]

But if the place of a live prisoner in the procession could be taken by a mute representation, the further twist is that live victims themselves could sometimes be seen in the guise of images or models. When Dio gestured at the equivalence between the effigy of Cleopatra and the living prisoners ("in a kind of way she was there with the others"), he simultaneously hinted that the equation might be reversed, and living prisoners be likened to mute images. This idea is brought out even more clearly in Josephus' account of the Flavian triumph. He writes of the lavish "floats" that were a conspicuous part of the parade, and on each one he notes an "enemy general was stationed . . . in the very attitude in which he was captured." In a striking inversion, here the prisoners themselves take on the role of actors, miming their moment of defeat on the triumphal stage.[6]

FIGURE 26: Fragment of a triumphal relief, showing captives in eastern dress under a trophy, late second century CE. The small scale of these figures suggests either that the artist was literally cutting the victims down to size, or that what is represented here are sculptures, not live prisoners, being carried in procession.

This blurring of the boundaries of representation is also glimpsed in some of the surviving sculptures of the procession. On several occasions we see apparently "real" captives crouched down next to pieces of booty and carried along shoulder high, as if they themselves were inanimate objects. In fact, sometimes it is hard to tell whether the figures are meant to evoke living captives or their representation or both (Fig. 26; see also Fig. 23). Maybe this is how poor Arsinoe was displayed on her *ferculum* in Caesar's parade.[7]

The procession, in other words, offered many different versions of captives: not only as the walking, talking, live prisoners but also as images representing those who could not appear in the flesh, and as prisoners acting out the part of images and representations. This was one distinctive element in the extravaganza of representation that was the hallmark of Roman triumphal culture more generally—and especially of the triumphal display of spoils, statues, curiosities, booty, gifts, treasures, pictures, and models. Beyond the luxury and the embarrassment of riches, we shall find in the triumph a context in which the potential of the art of representation was exploited to the full, and its dilemmas and ambivalences explored.

THE EMBARRASSMENT OF RICHES

The triumph of Pompey in 61 was one of a series of Roman victory celebrations, from the third century BCE on, whose lavish spectacles of booty and the other paraphernalia of triumphal display were enshrined in the Roman historical imagination. Among these iconic occasions was the procession of Marcus Claudius Marcellus after the capture of the rich Sicilian city of Syracuse in 211 BCE. Marcellus had, in fact, been refused a "full triumph." Political in-fighting with its usual array of objections or *ex post facto* rationalizations (the war in Sicily was not completely finished; it would be invidious to grant him a third triumph; he had conducted his campaign as proconsul not consul; his army was still in Sicily) resulted instead in a triumph on the Alban Mount and an *ovatio* in the city itself.[8] But this did little to dim the reported splendor of the occasion or its lively, and controversial, ancient reputation.

It was, according to Plutarch, the first triumph to display works of art as a spoil of victory: "He transported the greater part and the finest of the objects that in Syracuse had been dedicated to the gods, to be a spectacle for his triumph and an adornment for the city. For before that time Rome neither possessed nor was even aware of these elegant luxuries, nor was there any love in the city for refinement and beauty. Instead it was full of the weapons seized from barbarian enemies and blood-stained booty, and crowned with memorials of triumphs and trophies—

not a pleasant nor a reassuring sight, nor one for faint-hearted spectators or aesthetes."[9]

Exactly how innovative Marcellus' parade really was has been debated. In the ancient world itself, there were other candidates for the introduction of lavish displays into triumphal ceremony: Florus, for example, pinpointed the triumph of Manius Curius Dentatus in 275 BCE, with its "gold and purple, statues and paintings" from Tarentum, as a turning point in luxury: "Up to that time," he wrote, "you would have seen nothing [among the spoils] except the cattle of the Volsci, the flocks of the Sabines, the carts of the Gauls, the broken weapons of the Samnites."[10] Modern writers too have questioned the idea that Marcellus' ovation was such a radical break, listing the works of art said to have been carried in triumphs before his.[11]

Nonetheless, an emphatic ancient tradition does see in this occasion a crucial moment in the cultural revolution that we call the "hellenization" of Rome. As Plutarch goes on to report (and to theorize in terms of political and generational conflict), while some—the rank and file, or *demos*—welcomed the works of art that appeared in Marcellus' ovation as elegant adornments for the city, "older people" objected to his display partly because so many of those wonderful objects were sacred images taken from Syracuse: it was disgraceful that "not only men but also gods were led through the city in triumph as if they were prisoners."[12]

Livy offers a brief catalogue of the booty Marcellus displayed in his procession: "Along with a representation of the captured city of Syracuse, catapults and ballistas and all kinds of other weapons of war were carried in parade, plus the trappings that come with a long period of peace and with royal luxury, a quantity of silver- and bronze-ware, other furnishing and precious fabric and many notable statues with which Syracuse had been adorned on a par with the leading cities of Greece. As a sign that his victory had also been over the Carthaginians eight elephants were in the parade."[13] Hints elsewhere can fill out the picture a little. Cicero writes of a "celestial globe" in the house of Marcellus' grandson—an heirloom that had come down through the family from the spoils of Syracuse. This made a pair with another globe, both the work of the Syracusan scientist Archimedes, which Marcellus dedicated in the Temple of "Honor and Virtue" *(Honos et Virtus)* that he had vowed to the gods in the course of his campaigns. It is a fair assumption that these objects were displayed in the procession, among "the trappings that come with a long period of peace."[14]

Other evidence too sheds light on the final destination of part of the spoils. Whatever we make of Cicero's improbable insistence that, apart from the globe, Marcellus "took nothing else home with him out of the vast quantity of booty," we can tentatively follow some of the statues out of the procession into particular public or sacred contexts in Rome and elsewhere. Two republican statue bases from the city, the statues themselves long lost, carry inscriptions recording the name of Marcellus as the donor. One is specifically a dedication to Mars, and the findspot suggests that it was originally placed in the temple of the god just outside the city, on the Appian Way. Both of the original statues were very likely taken from those paraded in the ovation.[15] Plutarch claims that he also erected statues from his plunder in temples on the island of Samothrace and at Lindos on Rhodes, while Livy points again to the collection in the Temple of Honor and Virtue, as well as offering a nice example of the plunderer receiving a taste of his own medicine. Marcellus' dedications in his temple were once of such high distinction that they were a tourist attraction for foreigners; but by the time Livy was writing, the majority were lost, presumed stolen.[16]

Some of the categories of booty mentioned in Livy's catalogue are found commonly in accounts of earlier celebrations. The display of captured weapons is a recurrent theme in narratives of triumph as far back as the fifth century BCE.[17] Elephants too were part of the literary tradition of earlier celebrations. In fact, both Manius Curius Dentatus in 275 BCE and Lucius Caecilius Metellus in 250 were credited as the first to display these terrifying live war machines as part of their captured spoils.[18] But more significantly, the "menu" of booty in the procession of 211 BCE looks forward to the series of increasingly rich and elaborate triumphs of the succeeding centuries—or at least richly and elaborately written up.

We can almost use Livy's admittedly skeletal register of Marcellus' booty as a basic template for some of the extravagant occasions that followed, the "classic triumphs" of the surviving literary record.

Appian's account of Scipio Africanus' triumphal display in 201, for example, divides into similar categories, including models of captured towns and paintings showing the events of the war, the precious metals (whether as coin, bullion, or art work), and the captured elephants, while adding the "gold crowns" presented, willingly or not, to the victorious general by "allies or the army itself" and put on show in the procession along with the booty.[19] In Livy's description of the triumph of Flamininus over the Macedonians in 194, no captured animals are listed, but many of the other types of booty are highlighted, in enormous quantity and sometimes specific detail. There were "arms and weapons" (Plutarch notes precisely "Greek helmets and Macedonian shields and pikes"), plus statues of marble and bronze, possibly including a statue of Zeus that Cicero claims Flamininus took from Macedonia and dedicated on the Capitol in Rome. Bronze and silver was on show in all shapes and sizes, including 43,270 pounds of silver bullion alone, ten silver shields, and 84,000 Athenian coins known as tetradrachms. In addition, the gold amounted to 3,714 pounds of bullion, one solid gold shield, 14,514 Macedonian gold coins, and 114 gifts of golden crowns. The quantity was such that it took three days to process through the streets of the city—the first three-day triumph.[20]

Even more vivid, extravagant, and exotic are the descriptions of two later celebrations, which almost rival those of Pompey's triumph. The first is the procession, again over three days, celebrating the victory of Aemilius Paullus against King Perseus in 167 BCE—whose overflowing booty, lovingly detailed by Plutarch among others, serves as a piquant contrast with the personal tragedy and "impoverishment," in another sense, of the triumphing general himself. The first day of the show, he writes, "was hardly sufficient for the captive figures, paintings, and colossal statues, carried along in 250 carts." The second day saw impressive wagonloads of enemy weapons, newly polished: masses of helmets, breastplates, greaves, Cretan shields, Thracian body armor, quivers, swords, and bridles, "artfully arranged to look exactly as if they had been piled up indiscriminately, as they fell." They made a horrible sound as they clanked along; and, Plutarch insists, the sight of them was enough to inspire terror, even though they belonged to an enemy who had been conquered.

Behind the weapons came the silver coins, "carried by 3,000 men, in 750 vessels" (each holding some 75 kilos), plus a considerable array of silver bowls, drinking horns, cups, and so on. The gold was not, according to this account, brought out until the final day. This featured 77 further vessels full of gold coins, a vast golden libation bowl inlaid with gems and weighing in at some 250 kilos, which Paullus himself had commissioned from the bullion, some distinctively eastern Mediterranean tableware (bowls known as Antigonids, Seleucids, and Thericleians, the first two named after Hellenistic kings, the third after a Corinthian artist), as well as all the golden vessels from the Macedonian royal dining service. These were followed by Perseus' own chariot, which carried the king's weapons and his royal diadem laid on top. This part, at least, is strongly reminiscent of Livy's brief reference to the "trappings that come with royal luxury."[21]

Other aspects of the story of Flamininus' triumph are echoed in Josephus' account of the procession of booty at the parade of Vespasian and Titus in 71 CE. It was, he trumpets, "impossible to give an adequate description of the extent of those spectacles and their magnificence in every conceivable way—whether as works of art, riches of all sorts, or as rarities of nature. For almost everything that people of good fortune have ever acquired piecemeal, wonderful treasures of diverse origin, all these were on display together on that day and demonstrated the greatness of the Roman Empire." His self-confessed "inadequate" description lists silver, gold, and ivory "flowing like a river"; tapestries and gems (so many that you realized you had been wrong to think them rare); and enormous, precious statues of the Roman gods.

But even these wonders were overshadowed by the moving "floats" or "stages" (the Greek word *pēgmata* means literally any structure "fitted together"), three or four stories high, covered in tapestries around a framework of gold and ivory. Each one depicted an episode from the war—from the devastation of the land of Judaea or the demolition of the Jewish fortifications to the deluge of blood and rivers flowing through a country that was still in flames. It was here that the Jewish generals were stationed, acting out the moment of their capture. The rest of the spoils ("heaps" of them) are passed over quickly, with not even a mention of the "balsam tree" that Pliny implies was one of the notable spectacles of the procession—except for what had been taken from the temple itself.[22] Just as the hostile accounts of Marcellus' ovation emphasize his parade of the sacred images of the enemy, here Josephus, the Jewish turncoat, in a disconcertingly deadpan fashion and offering careful explanations for his non-Jewish readers, lists the sacred objects plundered and on display in the procession: the golden Shewbread Table, the menorah ("a lamp stand made quite differently from that in general use"), and last of all the Jewish Law. His description matches closely the sculptured panel of just this scene on the Arch of Titus (see Fig. 9).[23]

Josephus carefully notes the destination of these objects after the triumph. The majority of the spoils, sacred and other, were in due course transferred to Vespasian's new Temple of Peace (completed in 75 CE and dedicated to a strikingly appropriate—or inappropriate—deity). "Indeed," as Josephus puts it, "into that temple were accumulated and stored all those things which, previously, people had traveled the world over to see, longing to catch a glimpse of them while they were still in their different countries." Only the Jewish Law and the purple hangings from the Temple in Jerusalem were treated differently: these, he explains, were kept in the imperial palace itself.[24]

What happened next, especially to the menorah, has been a subject of modern controversy from at least as far back as the eighteenth century. Various hypotheses have imagined the menorah criss-crossing the Mediterranean in the Middle Ages and falling into the hands of some unlikely owners—moved to Constantinople in 330 at the foundation of the new capital of the Empire and installed in its own shrine in the new imperial palace; robbed from Rome by the Vandal Geiseric in 455 and carted off to Carthage; robbed back by Belisarius and shipped to Constantinople;

returned to Jerusalem but plundered by the Sassanians in 614; stolen from Constantinople by crusaders in 1204; and so on. One particularly picturesque version, based on nothing so dull as plausible historical evidence, has the menorah lost in the Tiber on October 28, 312 CE, falling into the river from the Milvian Bridge during the flight of Maxentius from his victorious rival, Constantine.[25]

An alternative idea, however, persists in Jewish urban legend: that the menorah never left the city of Rome at all, and that it remains stored away in the basement of the Vatican. In 2004, when Israeli chief rabbis visited the ailing Pope John Paul II, they are reported to have considered asking permission to search his storerooms for that and other Jewish artifacts. Only half seriously, no doubt—but it would have been consistent with an official request made the previous year by the president of Israel for a list of all Jewish treasures held by the Vatican, and the demand in 2001 by the Israeli minister of religion for a formal inquiry to determine the menorah's location. These diplomatic negotiations proceeded in the usual way: Israeli claims of "meaningful breakthroughs" and rather more carefully judged optimism on the part of the chief rabbis were balanced by Vatican denials and earnest protestations of commitment to multi-faith understanding and cooperation.[26]

Of course, no thorough search of forgotten cupboards at the Vatican is likely to uncover the lost menorah, any more than the Vatican Museums are likely to hold Octavian's replica of Cleopatra. The treasures of the Jewish Temple much more probably lie at the bottom of the Mediterranean. Yet the continuing conflicts around this single piece of Roman plunder offer vivid testimony to how the moral, religious, and cultural controversies of the triumph and its parade of spoils can continue to matter in our own world, too.

"THE TRIUMPHS OF CAESAR"

These extravagant accounts of late republican and early imperial triumphs, with their emphasis on unimaginable wealth, exotic treasures, and the artifices of display, have determined the modern image—both popular and academic—of the procession of spoils. They lie behind what is probably the most influential visualization of the Roman victory parade ever: Andrea Mantegna's series of nine paintings of the *Triumphs of Caesar,* commissioned by the Gonzaga family of Mantua at the end of the fifteenth century, acquired by King Charles I in 1629, and brought to Hampton Court Palace in England, where they are even now on show.

As a placard displayed on the second canvas clearly proclaims ("To *Imperator* Julius Caesar, for the conquest of Gaul"), the series evokes the Gallic triumph of Julius Caesar, which occupied one day of his quadruple celebration in 46 BCE for victories also over Egypt, the Black Sea kingdom of Pontus, and Africa (victory over King Juba masking what was also a campaign of civil war against his Roman enemies). Ancient writers offer vivid glimpses of these occasions: the effect of Arsinoe on the crowd on the Egyptian day; the distasteful paintings of Caesar's Roman enemies; the broken axle; the inventive songs chanted by the soldiers; the placard in the Pontic triumph with the famous phrase "I came, I saw, I conquered"; the representations (probably three-dimensional) of the Rhine and Rhone, along with a "captive Ocean" in gold; a working model of the Lighthouse of Alexandria, complete with flames.[27] But no detailed narrative survives. Hence, in recreating the parade of plunder and captives, with Caesar himself riding on his triumphal chariot in the ninth and final canvas (Fig. 27), Mantegna has had to look elsewhere. He seems to have used such ancient images as the panels on the Arch of Titus and (filtered no doubt through Renaissance scholarly treatises on the triumph) those accounts we have just been considering—the elaborate descriptions of various notable celebrations by Appian, Josephus, Livy, Plutarch.

The second canvas in the series (Fig. 28), for example, vividly captures a number of the elements detailed in the written versions: colossal statues balanced precariously on carts; models of (presumably) captured towns carried on high; behind them the wooden contraptions belonging to enemy siege engines; then more statues and model towns, some on small wagons, some hoisted by hand; and finally in the background suits

FIGURE 27: A. Mantegna, *Triumphs of Caesar*, 1484–92, Canvas IX: *Caesar on His Triumphal Chariot*. In this final scene the triumphing general is shown seated (not standing, as in a Roman triumph), holding a branch of palm, and being crowned with a wreath by an angelic boy. On top of the arch behind, the captives crouched beneath a trophy are reminiscent of Roman scenes (Figs. 23 and 26).

of armor paraded on poles. The next canvas foregrounds piles of weaponry—shields (including a particularly fine half-moon specimen featuring a centaur carrying a naked woman on his back), greaves, spears, helmets, swords, quivers, and pikes—"artfully arranged," to quote Plutarch, "to look exactly as if they had been piled up indiscriminately." This is followed by a bier *(ferculum),* derived almost certainly from the Arch of Titus, on which are carried "vessels" brimming with coin, as well

FIGURE 28: *Triumphs of Caesar,* Canvas II: *The Bearers of Standards and Siege Equipment.*
Among the loot of victory, statues, models, and military equipment, the placard strikes an
ominous note. The triumph, it explains, was decreed for Caesar's victory over Gaul, "after
envy had been conquered and scorned." It is hard to resist seeing the phrase as a wry reflection on the assassination—whether due to envy or not—that would soon be Caesar's
fate.

as a mixture of classical and decidedly Renaissance-style dining- and
drinking-ware.

The first canvas (Fig. 29) probably aims to show the multi-storey
pēgmata from Josephus' account. Although these are now usually imagined to be "platforms" or "floats," Mantegna has pictured them as two-
tiered paintings or banners, reflecting in one case (bottom right of the

FIGURE 29: *Triumphs of Caesar,* Canvas I: *The Picture-Bearers.* Mantegna launches his triumphal procession with a blast of trumpets and elaborate images of the destructive success of the Roman campaigns, which he seems to have derived from Josephus' account of the triumph of Vespasian and Titus in 71 CE, rather than from any account of Caesar's celebrations in 46 BCE.

second banner) the scenes of devastation that Josephus claims were depicted: here we can just make out the sack of a city and a row of gallows. Throughout the series, the impression is one of lavish display, wealth, and excess.[28]

Mantegna's paintings take a prominent place in modern views of the triumphal procession. Indeed, they are not infrequently reproduced to accompany, and bring to life, even the most technically academic discussions of the procession.²⁹ For these *Triumphs* offer a much more evocative vision of the procession of spoils than any images that survive from antiquity itself, with the exception perhaps of the main relief sculptures from the Arch of Titus. No other ancient image of the procession even hints at the profusion, the dazzling array of treasures, or the seething mass of riches. We are usually faced instead with some frankly rather subdued evocations of the parade of plunder: some modest placards; a few *fercula* bearing nothing more exotic than despondent prisoners, an occasional model of a river god, golden crowns, or a couple of dishes—not a miniature town, siege engine, or statue in sight, still less *pēgmata* or elephants (Fig. 30).³⁰ Admittedly, these representations are often on a relatively small scale or in a subordinate position on an arch or other major building; they were not ever intended to be the center of attention in the way that Mantegna's were. Nonetheless, the contrast is striking.

Whatever other versions of the parade of spoils there were, and however paltry most of the "real life" celebrations may have been compared with what is shown in the *Triumphs of Caesar,* the image of wealth and excess hovers over the ceremony for ancient and modern commentators alike. Ironically, though, there is another, very different sense in which these paintings offer a model for our understanding of the triumph. However vivid and dramatic they may appear when reproduced in modern textbooks, they are in fact a fragile, half-ruined palimpsest of repeated restoration and radical repainting that has gone on since at least the seventeenth century.

The interventions have been drastic, including a wholesale covering of the original egg-tempera with oil paint around 1700, a botched restoration by Roger Fry in the early twentieth century (which, among other things, restored the black face in the first canvas as white), and complete waxing in the 1930s, followed by an only partially successful attempt to get back to the genuine article in the 1960s.³¹ What we now see and admire is in almost no part the original fifteenth-century brushwork of Mantegna. Instead, it is the historical product of centuries of painting and unpainting. As such, it may stand better as a symbol of the complex processes of loss, representation, and reconstruction through which we

FIGURE 30: Part of a triumphal frieze from the Arch of Titus in the Roman Forum. To judge from his appearance and attributes (bearded, naked to the waist, leaning on a vessel from which water flows) the figure on the *ferculum* is a river god: presumably the river Jordan over whom the Romans had been victorious.

must try to understand the triumphal procession than as the vivid evocation of the ancient parade that it is often taken to be.

THE PROFITS OF EMPIRE

The various riches of the triumph have taken a prominent place in the modern academic imagination. Economic historians have used the figures recorded for the coin and bullion paraded through the city to track the growing wealth of Rome, as conquest delivered new imperial territories.[32] Art historians have lingered longingly on the masterpieces captured as booty in the Greek world starting in the late third century BCE and first seen in Rome by a mass audience in triumphal parades. One conservative modern calculation has estimated that by the first century CE fourteen statues by Praxiteles had arrived in Rome, eight by Skopas, four by Lysippos, three each by Euphranor, Myron, and Sthennis, plus two each by Pheidias, Polykleitos, and Strongylion—a good proportion of which would have played their part in some victory parade or other.[33]

Such works of art, it is commonly argued, heralded and catalyzed the "hellenizing" revolution in Roman art and culture of the last centuries of the Republic. It was to be a spiraling effect. Triumphal booty as it was displayed after the ceremony itself changed the visual environment of the city and whetted the Roman appetite for more. Among the triumphal captives were artists and craftsmen who brought with them the artistic expertise of the Hellenistic world, and the cash that was paraded by the wagonload provided the means of acquiring exactly what new taste (or political expediency) demanded.[34]

At the same time, and no less important in the art historical narrative, the other representations on display in the procession—the paintings of the conflict, the models of towns or the defeated enemy—also made a significant contribution to the practice of Roman art and image-making. In part, the usual story runs, these were influenced by the techniques and devices of processional display developed in the Greek world: so that, in a perhaps uncomfortable paradox, the conquered territories provided the artistic inspiration for the celebration of their own defeat. But in part the artistic style adopted in these images of the campaigns was a distinctively "native" tradition, driven by Roman imperatives and their concern for documenting and publicizing their victories. In this sense, the art of the triumph, both in subject matter and style, has been seen as the direct ancestor of that distinctive strand of "documentary realism" in Roman art best known from Trajan's column or the battle panels on the Arch of Septimius Severus.[35]

Other historians, more recently, have moved beyond the specifically financial, visual, or artistic impact of the ceremony to emphasize the wider importance of the triumph in the culture of Roman imperialism and in the imaginative economy of the Romans. Parading the varied profits of conquest—from heaps of coin to statues, trees, and all manner of precious novel bric-à-brac—the procession served as a microcosm of the very processes of imperial expansion; it literally enacted the flow of wealth from the outside into the center of the Empire. The glaring foreignness of some of the spoils of war, along with the various representations of the conquest, delineated a new and expanding image of imperial territory before the eyes of the spectators (or of those who later read of these occasions). As one recent commentator on triumphal culture in the first century CE has put it, the triumph "is an imperial geography"; and he characterizes the ceremony "as a performance of the availability of new territory to Rome . . . train[ing] the gaze on the city of Rome, where new discoveries have been brought in from the edges for theatrical display." Or, as another critic has more succinctly punned, "the triumphal procession . . . brings the *orbs* [world] within the walls of the *urbs* [city]."[36]

These are all important aspects of Rome's triumphal culture, vividly illustrated by ancient discussions of the ceremony. Writers certainly insisted on the vast sums of money sometimes paraded through the streets: Velleius Paterculus, for example, had 600 million sesterces carried in Caesar's quadruple triumph—a colossal sum, equivalent to the minimum subsistence of more than a million families for a year, and outbidding even the biggest estimates of Pompey's war profits. And other eye-opening figures are scattered through notices of triumphs.[37] More to the point, the effects of the influx of wealth that came with lavish triumphs prompted rare economic observations even from ancient writers, who were not usually much concerned with such topics. Famously, Suetonius notes that "the royal treasure of Egypt, brought into the city for Octavian's Alexandrian triumph, caused such growth in the money supply that, as the rate of interest fell, the price of land rose sharply."[38]

Nor can there be any doubt at all that the triumphal procession was one major route through which not only cash but the artistic traditions of the eastern Mediterranean were brought to a Roman audience—a dramatic entrypoint for a whole array of masterpieces amidst the razzmatazz, the cheers, the electricity of a big public occasion. The triumph also provided a highly charged focus around which the conflicts of hellenization (or, as many Romans would have called it, "the growth of luxury") were debated. It was, of course, the preceding conquest—the victory, not the victory parade—that was the main agent in delivering wealth and "luxury" to Rome. Nonetheless, controversy could focus more narrowly on the triumphal display, which was a convenient symbol of the whole process of expansion.

We have already seen how the triumph of Cnaeus Manlius Vulso in

187 BCE was strongly linked to a story of cultural change—the introduction of not only such dangerous luxuries as one-legged tables but also of the whole art of cookery. But other triumphal processions too take their place in a narrative of innovation. Pliny identifies the triumph of Scipio Asiaticus in 189 BCE as a key moment of change, or—curmudgeonly moralizer that he was—decline: "The conquest of Asia first brought luxury to Italy, since Lucius Scipio in his triumph exhibited 1,400 pounds of chased silverware and 1,500 pounds of golden vessels," while the silver statues of Pharnaces and Mithradates displayed in the triumph of Pompey give the lie, Pliny insists, to the idea that such objects were a novelty of the reign of Augustus.[39]

Several ancient discussions of triumphal ceremonies do also highlight the role of the procession in the dramatization of imperialism and the geography of empire. When, for example, Plutarch specifies the different varieties of tableware in the triumph of Aemilius Paullus—Antigonids, Seleucids, and Thericleians—their very names conjured Roman victory over eastern cities and dynasties, prompting readers to think of the triumph as a model of imperial expansion. So too when Plutarch emphasizes the details of the distinctive weaponry of the defeated peoples, or when Pliny reminds us that even exotic trees could be paraded in the triumphal procession on their way to become "tax-paying subjects" of Rome.[40] But some ancient writers make more explicit points about the triumph's role as a model of imperialism.

When Polybius, for example, claims that the procession was a means for generals to bring "right before the eyes of the Roman people a vivid impression of their achievements," he is in essence saying that it re-presented imperial conquest at the center of the Roman world.[41] Josephus goes even further in theorizing the triumph of Vespasian and Titus. He not only defines the objects on parade as a demonstration of "the greatness of the Roman Empire," but by likening the stream of riches flowing into the city to a river, he also emphasizes the naturalness of—he *naturalizes*—the imperial process. If other parts of his description cast the triumph as a magnificent disruption of the natural order (those gems, for example, which in their extraordinary profusion called into question

the very notion of natural rarity), here he offers a glimpse of Roman imperialism, seen in the ritual of the triumph, as unstoppably elemental.[42]
Alternatively, in a rather simpler sense, the parade of riches could be understood as an inducement to further military expansion. Plutarch insists, for example, that it was the sight of all the riches in Lucullus' parade in 63—in particular the royal diadem of Tigranes—that spurred
Crassus to plan his own campaigns in Asia; though, as he further observes, Crassus, who was killed fighting the Parthians, would discover
that there was more to barbarians than spoil and booty.[43]

Yet, important as these aspects are in ancient and modern representations of the triumphal processions, modern enthusiasm for Roman imperialist excess has tended to occlude other ways of seeing the parade of
captured booty and the representational devices that went along with it.

CUTTING THE SPOILS DOWN TO SIZE

How far can we take at face value those lavish accounts of the triumphal
parade? Of course booty did flow in to Rome through the period of its
imperial expansion, sometimes in huge quantities. But how common a
sight were the extravagant displays that form our image of the ceremony? And how far can we trust those sometimes very precise tallies
given by ancient writers? As with the details of the captives, these questions reveal the tantalizing uncertainties about the triumphal ritual as it
was enacted on the streets of Rome. Yet more is at stake here, not least
because of the general modern assumption that—thanks to archives of
various sorts which were available to ancient writers—accurate records
of the content of triumphal display have been transmitted to us.

It goes without saying (though it is perhaps not actually said often
enough) that of the 320 triumphs that Orosius claimed had been celebrated at Rome between Romulus and Vespasian, only a small proportion can have included the parade of lavish booty and all those other accoutrements that we so readily associate with the ceremony. On the
most generous estimate, we are dealing with something in the order of
fifty occasions between the third century BCE and 71 CE; and even that

figure involves both taking on trust some of the overblown descriptions of triumphal riches that we have and assuming a splendid show of magnificence in the case of many triumphs where we have almost no evidence at all, reliable or not, of what was on display. The true total is probably much lower.

Obviously, riches on the scale of the popular image could not possibly have been a feature of early celebrations. Although ancient writers may have filled the gaps in their knowledge by retrojecting the idea of opulence back into their triumphal accounts of the sixth and fifth centuries BCE, Florus cannot be too far from the mark when he writes of cattle, flocks, carts, and broken weapons being the major triumphal spectacle until the increasingly lucrative campaigns of the third century and later. Rome's enemies in the early period simply did not possess the wealth that could have made a showy parade.[44] But even much later not all triumphs can have been loaded with lavish profits of war and expensive props. Occasionally Livy makes a point of mentioning the lack of spoils, as in the case of Cnaeus Octavius in 167 BCE or of Lucius Furius Purpureo, who is said to have triumphed in 200 BCE with no captives, no spoils, and no soldiers (omissions stressed by Livy on this occasion to drive home how little he deserved the celebration).[45]

At other times too we can reasonably infer that the processions were on a modest scale. It is hard, for example, to imagine that Caius Pomptinus put on much of a show in his procession of 54 BCE. He had quashed a revolt of the Gallic tribe of the Allobroges in 62–61 BCE (not so fruitful a source of riches as Eastern monarchies), and he is said to have waited outside Rome for at least four years before he was, controversially, awarded a triumph—which raises the question of where any substantial booty would have been stored in the interim (or, more cynically, whether what was on display in the parade bore much relation to what he brought back with him from Gaul).[46]

In fact, the practical details of the treatment and display of the spoils are predictably murky. We have only the most fleeting hints of how the spoils were handled (such as Appian's claim about the thirty days it took to transfer Mithradates' furniture stores to the Romans); still less on how and where it was kept in Rome in anticipation of the parade, or how it was managed once the parade ended.[47] The idea has been floated that in the procession itself the cash and bullion at least might never have reached the Temple of Jupiter Optimus Maximus but may have been diverted to the treasury en route. There is no ancient evidence for this, merely the convenient location of the treasury building (the Temple of Saturn) near where the road turned up from the Forum to the Capitol (see Plan).[48]

Equally unclear is what proportion of the spoils of war plundered from the enemy cities, palaces, and sanctuaries would have ended up in the parade at all, and in what form. Some were certainly kept by the rank and file soldiers. Some were sold off on the spot and converted into cash. But how those divisions were made, or were expected to be made, we do not know. Aemilius Paullus was famous for cutting a particularly mean deal with his troops, when he left them only a small part of what they had pillaged—albeit a particularly prudent one for state finances. ("Had he given in to his troops' greed," argued Livy, "they would have left nothing to be made over to the treasury.") But how deals of this kind were usually brokered between the soldiers, the general, and the interests of the state is a matter of guesswork.[49]

We do not even fully understand to whom Roman war booty formally belonged—whether it was public property that was to be directed by the general to the public good, or whether all (or part) was entirely at the disposal of the general to do with as he wished. This issue has raised considerable controversy—fueled, as so often, by limited ancient evidence which is itself contradictory, by our own desire to impose consistency and rule on Roman practice, and by apparently technical Latin terms used differently in different contexts. The definitions of two main words for "booty," *manubiae* and *praeda,* were debated in antiquity itself, and modern scholarship has certainly not resolved the question (despite a popular view that *manubiae* were a subsection of the wider *praeda* and one over which the victorious general had a particular interest if not control).[50] In this case, the difficulties and uncertainties may be overstated, since in practice the general seems to have taken the leading role in disposing of the booty, and questions of formal ownership may only have become relevant (and various incompatible theories improvised) when his dispositions were for some reason challenged.

But occasionally such conflicts offer a glimpse of the triumph, too. One vivid example is the puzzling incident connected with the triumph of Manius Acilius Glabrio over King Antiochus in 190 BCE. When he was standing for the office of censorship a couple of years later, his political rivals prosecuted him "on the grounds that he had neither carried in his triumph nor delivered to the treasury an amount of royal money and booty seized in Antiochus' camp." Key witness for the prosecution was Marcus Porcius Cato (also running for the censorship), who claimed that "he had seen some gold and silver vessels amongst the other royal booty when the camp had been captured, but he had not seen them in the triumph." Whatever this says about the legal rights of control over booty (note that Livy does not say exactly what the legal charge against Glabrio was), or about the politics of the early second century CE (the trial was in fact abandoned), it offers a rare pointer to the possible importance of individual pieces of triumphal treasure—and their recognizability. Whether or not we believe Cato's confident testimony (and Livy's account suggests that many Romans did not), it offers an intriguing picture of a Roman notable scanning intensely the items as they passed by on parade, and matching them up with his memory of battlefield plunder. It raises the question, to which we shall return in a slightly different form, that what is on display might not be exactly what it seems.[51]

Less controversial, but hardly any better understood, are the organization and conventions of the display of the spoils and art works in the parade. Minute analysis of the visual images has led to the (not wholly surprising) conclusion that those who carried the objects in the procession and controlled the captives included not only low-grade porters and guards but also more senior officials directing operations.[52] A few brave attempts have also been made to deduce from written accounts of triumphs a standard order of display—to sort out, in other words, the regular processional choreography of the golden crowns, elephants, model rivers, vessels of coins, and so forth—on the assumption that ancient authors more or less accurately reflected the original order of ceremonies.[53] But even if that assumption were correct, unconvincing special pleading is always necessary to iron out the discrepancies or to incorporate the various "exceptions"—as, for example, when the quantity of booty demanded the procession be spread over several days, or when (according to Plutarch) Lucullus chose in 63 BCE to decorate the Circus Flaminius with the captured weapons and siege engines, rather than carry them in procession.[54] Besides, no order suggested in any literary account is remotely compatible with that on the small frieze of Trajan's Arch at Beneventum (see Figs. 10 and 21), where the *fercula* (just six in all) carrying booty and a couple of golden crowns are distributed throughout the procession in front of the general, intermingled with the prisoners.

The bottom line, of course, is that there is always a gap, even in a contemporary eyewitness description, between that messy aggregate of individual movements, displays, stunts, and human beings that make up "the parade" and the literary (or, for that matter, visual) representations that capture it in text (or stone). And for no triumph at all do we possess the full roster of the objects on display. At best, each of the literary versions we have has selected elements from the parade with their own priorities in mind. One obvious case of this is the two descriptions of the triumph of Germanicus in 17 CE: Strabo the geographer concentrates on the various German prisoners, while Tacitus the cynical analyst of imperial power emphasizes the *simulacra* (replicas) of the mountains, rivers, and battle, with the full panoply of imperial (dis)simulation in his sights. At worst (worst, that is, for anyone trying to get back to the procession as it appeared on the streets), those accounts are a confection of exaggeration, misinformation, misunderstandings, and outright falsification.

THE LIMITS OF GULLIBILITY

Occasionally we can spot a story of triumphal spoils that we can be sure is false. Something is certainly wrong with Livy's tale of the gilded shields carried in the triumph of Lucius Papirius Cursor (309 BCE) being divided up "among the proprietors of the banks [or money changers]" and used for decorating the Forum; for there was no coined money to speak of in Rome at that date, still less were there "money changers." And similar doubts have been raised about the denominations—some of them anachronistic or impossible in other ways—in which Livy expresses the coins carried in the processions. He claims, for example, that vast quantities of *cistophori* from Pergamum were displayed in a series of triumphs around 190 BCE, even though these coins are now generally thought not to have been minted until later in the second century. Livy (or his source) may well have been mistakenly retrojecting a currency back into an early triumph—or possibly translating an unfamiliar currency into a more familiar name.[55]

Usually we must rely on first principles and on the limits of our own gullibility in deciding how suspicious to be about any of the objects on display. By and large, modern historians of the triumph (and of other ancient parades and processions) have erred on the side of credulity. Pompey's extravagant display in 61 BCE has not been seriously called into question (even that gold statue of Mithradates eight cubits tall), nor have many of the vast figures for bullion in some implausibly early triumphs, such as the 2,533,000 pounds of bronze supposedly raised from the sale of captives and displayed at the triumph of Lucius Papirius Cursor in 293 BCE.[56] None of this, however, matches the credence generally given to the account (by one Callixeinos of Rhodes, though preserved only as a quotation in a later, second century CE compendium) of a royal procession sponsored by King Ptolemy Philadelphus in Alexandria in the early third century BCE—a hellenistic parade of a type often assumed to have influenced, directly or indirectly, the form, grandeur, and artifice of the Roman triumph.

Maybe we can envisage, as most scholars have wanted to, Callixeinos' "twelve-foot tall statue . . . [which] stood up mechanically without anyone laying a hand on it and sat back down again when it had poured a libation of milk"; given the wealth and sophistication of the city of Alexandria, maybe the vast carts pulled by 600 men, chariots towed by ostriches, or a golden phallos 180 foot long all seem plausible. But surely not a "wine-sack made of leopard skin and holding 3,000 measures" which slowly dribbled its contents onto the parade route. To give some idea of scale, this container made of stitched animal skins and towed through streets of Alexandria is supposed to have had a capacity rather larger than three modern road tankers.[57]

Gullibility? The modern scholarly alibi for trusting the accuracy of both Callixeinos and many of the Roman triumphal accounts is the confidence that they are based on archival records, and that—whatever the strategic omissions or the inevitable gap between the performance and the written record—many of the objects described and listed derive from some form of official documentation. In the case of the Ptolemaic procession, this is hinted only by a brief reference in Callixeinos' account itself to "the records of the five yearly festivals."[58] For the triumph we have rather clearer evidence of an infrastructure of record-keeping associated with the procession and the handling of booty in general.

The key text is a passage from Cicero's attack on Verres where he contrasts his adversary's illicit plundering from Sicily with the properly scrupulous conduct of Publius Servilius, who celebrated a triumph over the Isauri in 74 BCE. According to Cicero, Servilius brought home all kinds of statues and works of art which "he carried in his triumph and had fully registered in the public records at the treasury"; and he goes on to claim that these records contained "not only the number of statues, but also the size of each one, its shape and attitude."[59] Combine this and other hints of such record keeping, with the precise figures sometimes given by ancient writers for the quantity of bullion or coin ("14,732 pounds of silver, 17,023 *denarii*, 119,449 silver coins of Osca") or the amount of statuary on parade ("785 bronze statues, 280 marble") and the idea that a documentary basis underlies the accounts of triumphal booty may seem both appealing and reassuring.[60]

That indeed is what most historians have usually assumed—for want of any obvious argument to the contrary, as well as a strong desire to find for once some firm evidence to build on and a propensity to be more trusting of ancient figures that do not end (when converted to

modern numeration) in 000. In particular they have seen in the austere
and relatively standardized records of triumphal booty given systematically by Livy from 207 BCE until the end of his surviving text in 167 BCE
evidence that derives directly or more likely indirectly (through the earlier historians on whom Livy drew) from an archival record.[61] True, the
argument goes, there may be embellishment at the margins; and true,
ancient numerals are always liable to have been garbled by repeated
copying from one manuscript to the next. So complete trust is not in order. But, in its essentials, the data on Roman triumphal booty that we
read particularly in Livy's later books, but also sometimes in other authors who offer similarly precise lists, are based on some kind of official
archives.

A prime candidate, but not the only one, is some official record or inventory of the Roman treasury. This is suggested both by Cicero's eulogy
of Servilius (though no surviving literary account of any triumph goes
anywhere near to detailing the size or attitudes of the statues as Cicero
claims Servilius did) and also by Livy's common expression in listing the
cash or bullion in the triumph: "The general delivered *to the treasury*
. . ." It may also be reflected in Livy's account of the details of the plunder at the sack of New Carthage, where he claims that a *quaestor* (a junior Roman magistrate, sometimes directly connected with the treasury)
was on hand supervising the weighing out and counting of the coin and
precious metal.[62]

Certainly there were archives at Rome which were concerned in different ways with booty in general and with the triumphal ceremony in
particular, and there is a reasonable chance that some of the data we
have on the objects in the procession (as well as the plunder seized on
the battlefield) goes back ultimately, even if circuitously, to this source.
Yet whether these were themselves sufficiently systematic, accurate, and
accessible to validate the literary accounts is quite another matter. Part
of the problem is that for the great majority of triumphs we are dealing
with information on the display of booty and cash provided by only one
author, most often Livy. It is an uncomfortable truth of modern studies
of the ancient world that we often find it easier to be confident of our

evidence the less of it we have. Nothing can contradict a single account; more often than not two accounts of the same event prove incompatible or at least different in significant details. So it is with ancient descriptions of triumphs, archivally based or not.

We already spotted some flagrant contradictions and awkward divergences in the versions of Pompey's celebration in 61 BCE. Similar issues emerge almost every time that more than one ancient writer gives details of a particular procession. It would be tempting to imagine, for example, that Diodorus Siculus' account of the three-day triumphal display of Aemilius Paullus goes back to an archival inventory. The repertoire for each day is carefully distinguished, and detailed information (albeit tending toward round numbers) is offered: 1,200 wagons full of embossed shields, 12 of bronze shields, 300 carrying other weapons, gold in 220 "loads" or "carriers" (probably the Greek *phorēmata* is a translation of *fercula*), 2,000 elephant tusks, a horse in battle gear, a golden couch with flowered covers, 400 garlands "presented by cities and kings," and so on.[63] But if some archival source does stand behind this, we need to explain why Plutarch's no less full version is so different. He divides the booty up between the three days in a way that directly contradicts Diodorus' account (not armor on the first day but statues and paintings), and throughout he specifies quite different details (77, not 220, "vessels" or "caskets" of gold, for example).[64] And it is not only between different authors that such discrepancies are found: Livy himself offers two different figures for the amount of uncoined silver carried in the ovation of Marcus Fulvius Nobilior (191 BCE) on the two occasions when he mentions it.[65]

Unsettling in a different way are the accounts, in Plutarch and Livy, of the cash and bullion carried in the three-day triumph of Titus Quinctius Flamininus over Macedon in 194 BCE. At first sight they look reassuringly compatible. Plutarch cites the authority of "the followers of Tuditanus" for his specific information on the amount of gold and silver: "3,713 pounds of gold bullion, 43,270 pounds of silver and 14,514 gold 'Philips' [that is, coins bearing the head of King Philip]"; and these figures almost exactly match (but for a single pound of gold bullion) those given by Livy.[66] This has usually been taken to suggest that Livy and Plutarch were dependent on the same historical tradition, which (via the second-century BCE historian Caius Sempronius Tuditanus, whose work has not survived) extended back to a documentary or archival source. Of course, other explanations for the match are possible: that Plutarch took his figures (directly or indirectly) from Livy; that both were dependent on the "information" of an earlier historian, who had nothing to do with any archival tradition.

But it is more complicated than that. In fact, the text of Livy as preserved in the manuscript tradition is significantly different from what we now usually see printed, and it agrees much less closely with Plutarch: while the figures for "Philips" and for gold bullion are the same, Livy's manuscripts have "18,270 pounds of silver," not 43,270. Quite simply the manuscripts have been emended by modern editors of the text to bring Livy's figures into line with Plutarch's. There is a case for doing this: ingenious critics have correctly pointed out that in Roman numerals 43 (XLIII, as in 43,270) is different by only one digit from 18 (XVIII, as in 18,270), so corruption somewhere along the line of transmission is plausible.[67] But at the same time it shows a scholarly incentive to normalize the variant accounts of triumphal processions and their contents that extends to "improving" the Latin texts themselves. It will come as no surprise that the difference between Livy's two figures for Nobilior's silver has often been massaged away by a similar technique.[68]

Where does this leave any modern attempt to reconstruct the displays in the triumphal procession? As so often in the study of ritual occasions in antiquity (or of any other occasions, for that matter), we scratch the surface of what appears to be the clearest evidence and that clarity soon disappears. Accounts of the processions given by Greek and Roman writers almost certainly owe something, sometimes, to archival or official records; they may also derive in part from eyewitness accounts and popular memory (however reliably or unreliably transmitted), as well as being the product of misinformation, wild exaggeration, over-optimistic reinvention, and willful misunderstanding. The problem is that it is now next to impossible to determine the status of any individual piece of "evidence" in the accounts we have: which is a *bona fide* nugget from an official archive, which is a wild flight of fancy, or which is a plucky ancient guess dressed up with spurious precision as if it were one of those archival nuggets? The outright incompatibilities between different accounts alert us to the difficulties. But the overlaps are not necessarily reassuring either: they may indicate a standard authoritative tradition, or they may equally well indicate copying of the same piece of misinformation.

One thing is fairly clear. Seen inevitably, like the triumph itself, through centuries of efforts of reconstruction and repainting, Mantegna's ambitious and influential exercise in recreation is a misleading image to have in mind when we think back to the triumphal procession of, say, Caius Pomptinus as it made its way through the Roman streets in 54 BCE. Mantegna's image is a memorable aggregate of the most flamboyant descriptions of just a handful of the most notoriously extravagant displays of booty, wealth, and artifice in the whole history of the triumph. We should do well to try to call to mind also those occasions where, at most, a few wagonloads of coin and bullion, plus some rather battered captured weapons, were trooped up to the Capitol. We should not allow, in other words, the modest and orderly procession of Trajan's Arch at Beneventum to be entirely swamped by the grandiloquent Renaissance version that plays so powerfully to (and is in part responsible for) our larger-than-life picture of the ceremony.

PROCESSIONAL THEMES

Mantegna's image of the triumphal procession and its riches cannot, of course, be dismissed so easily. When Romans conjured the triumph in their imaginations, one important image in their repertoire was indeed larger than life. It is a fair guess that, by the second century BCE at least, even the most down-beat triumphal ceremony could be reinvented as a blockbuster in the fantasies of the victorious general. Nonetheless, the preoccupations of these ancient literary recreations of the triumph do not match up entirely with the preoccupations of modern historians.

Modern accounts have made much of the individual works of art that flowed into Rome through the triumphal procession: masterpieces by Praxiteles, Pheidias, and other renowned Greek artists that were to revolutionize the visual environment of the city. In fact, there is hardly a surviving ancient account of a triumphal procession that identifies any such work of art. All kinds of precious or curious objects are singled out, and occasionally special mention is made of particularly extravagant statues of notable victims or victors (such as the "six foot" solid gold statue of Mithradates carried in Lucullus' triumph of 63 BCE, overshadowed by the "eight cubit" version paraded by Pompey).[69] In one instance Livy notes that a statue of Jupiter was part of the triumphal booty from the Italian city of Praeneste.[70] But nothing is ever said about any individual masterpiece from the hand of a famous Greek artist. Their presence in the procession we infer by putting together references to wagonloads of statues with notices of particular gifts or dedications of sculpture by famous generals.

It is hard to imagine, for example, that the Athena by Pheidias, which was dedicated according to Pliny by Aemilius Paullus at the Temple of "Today's Good Fortune," was not one of the "captive figures, paintings and colossal statues" that Plutarch imagines "carried along in 250 carts" at Paullus' triumph.[71] But no ancient author actually says so. The main stress in their accounts is on volume and value, not on artistic distinction. This is a very different set of priorities from those of the triumphant procession into Paris in 1798 of Napoleon's haul of masterpieces from Italy, where each of the major works (including such renowned classical pieces as the Laocoön and the Apollo Belvedere) were individually identified, sitting inside their "grandiloquently inscribed packing cases."[72] If Napoleon paraded particularly renowned *chefs d'oeuvre* as the reward of military victory, ancient triumphal culture put the accent on wealth and quantity. This chimes well with repeated stress on monetary value in, for example, Livy's brief notices of triumphs. However accurate they are, these delineate each ceremony, in its essentials, in financial terms: the amount of coin and bullion on display (or transferred to the treasury), the amount of cash given as a donative to the soldiers.[73]

Also prominently in view in ancient triumphal accounts are the displays of weapons and other military equipment captured from the enemy. Of course, not all the detritus of arms and armor from the battlefield arrived in Rome. In fact, we have a series of references to the ceremonial burning of enemy equipment in the war zone.[74] But those that were selected for the parade are often given star billing. This could be as objects of luxury and wonderment in their own right. Lucullus' triumph in 63 BCE apparently featured a marvelous shield "studded with jewels." And among the lists of precious metals in other triumphs we find shields of silver and even gold (parade armor presumably, else the Romans would have had easy victories) rubbing shoulders with the precious drinking cups and dinner plates.[75] At the same time, the distinctive foreign weapons, sometimes explicitly given a national identity ("Cretan shields, Thracian body armor") might serve to highlight—no less than the exotically clad prisoners—the Otherness of Rome's enemies. But such objects evoked the realities of conflict, the bottom line of victory and defeat, too.

In his account of Paullus' triumph, Plutarch lingers for several lines on the display of arms, picking out the various types of equipment, while passing over most of the precious booty in a brisk list. The armory was, he insists, enough to inspire terror—or at least that frisson that comes from looking at the firepower of those whom you have just defeated. Such was the impact surely of the siege engines, ballistas, fighting ships (or their bronze rams), and enemy chariots trundling through the streets of the city. It was the closest you could get to the experience of battle without actually being there—hearing, as Plutarch imagined it, the eerie clanking, or seeing, with Propertius, "the prows of Actium speeding along the Sacred Way" (presumably on wheels, though this is another case where the practical technology of the triumph leaves us guessing).[76] On the other hand, the conversion of the enemy weapons into an object of spectacle on Rome's home territory drew the sting of that fear, as well as adding to the humiliation of the defeated. From military standards to state-of-the-art artillery, their arsenals were now open to the gaze of the conquerors, while—as more than one Roman sculpture portrays it—captives might be made to perch on *fercula* under careful arrangements of their native armor now reappropriated as a trophy of Roman victory (see Figs. 23 and 26).[77]

It is also these weapons, rather than masterpieces of art, whose history, after the triumph itself, ancient writers chose to highlight. In several instances triumphal narratives explicitly give the arms and armor a story that continues after the parade has reached the Capitol. Some are said to have ended up on show in temples and public buildings, both inside and outside Rome.[78] Others, like the rams from ships captured by Pompey, are reported to have adorned the private house of the general himself.[79] In other locations the message must have been rather different. The arms hanging in the Temple of Olympian Zeus in Syracuse, which, according to Livy, were presented to King Hiero by the Roman people, must have been a double-edged gift. They were spoils from Roman conquests in Greece and Illyria, captured from the enemy and presumably (though the connection is not spelled out) paraded in triumph, before being passed to the Syracusans. As such, they both shared with a loyal ally the symbols of Roman victory and offered a warning of what the price of disloyalty might be.[80]

Even more striking, though, are the stories of the reuse—and with it the resignification—of these objects of triumphal display. Spurius Carvilius, for example, in the early third century BCE is supposed to have turned the bronze weapons captured from the Samnites into a statue of Jupiter on the Capitol, "big enough to be seen from the sanctuary of Jupiter Latiaris" (on the Alban Mount); "and from the filings he had a statue of himself made which stands at the feet of the other." True or not, this offers a nice image of captured arms being converted into both a symbol of Roman religious power and a memorial of the glory of the triumphing general.[81]

But even the display of arms in a temple or house was not necessarily the end of their story. Despite Plutarch's assertion that the spoils of war were the only dedications to the gods which were never moved or repaired (echoing Pliny's view of the permanence of the spoils decorating the general's house), weapons from a past triumph could find themselves conveniently recycled.[82] In the desperate stages of Rome's fight against Hannibal, criminals were enlisted and were said to have been armed with the weapons taken from the Gauls and paraded in the triumph of Caius Flaminius seven years earlier.[83] The partisans of the tribune Caius Gracchus in 121 BCE made use of armor on display in the house of Fulvius Flaccus, who had triumphed in 123, in the violent conflicts in which the tribune himself was eventually killed.[84] Indeed, we know of those spoils given to Hiero only because, after the king's death and the assassination of his successor, they were torn down from the temple and put to use by the insurgents.[85]

Some of these stories hint once more at the darker side of the Roman ideology of victory. For it was one thing to appropriate the Gallic spoils as a last ditch weapon against the Carthaginians. It was surely quite another, and a warning of the fragility of power, glory, and political stability, to see triumphal spoils turned against Romans themselves and playing their part in the civil war between Gracchus and his conservative enemies; or for that matter to see the gifts to Hiero used against the supporters of his grandson and successor (albeit under a slogan of "liberty").

We find a hint here too of a more complicated configuration of imperial power than most modern interpretations allow. Certainly the triumphal parade could be seen as a model of the imperial process, a jingoistic display of the profits of empire and the consequences of military victory to the Roman spectator (and reader). But the spoils and booty also gave a glimpse of an altogether bigger narrative of historical change and transfer of power. That is partly the lesson of the recycling of the weapons—and with it the reappearance of the instruments of past conflicts and the symbols of past Roman victories in different hands and under different political and military regimes. This lesson was also stressed by some of the displays of precious booty—a point made particularly clearly by Appian in his account of Scipio Aemilianus' triumph over Carthage in 146 BCE. This was (as so often) "the most splendid triumph of all," partly no doubt because it was "teeming with all the statues and *objets d'art* that the Carthaginians had brought to Africa from all over the world through the long period of their own continuous victories."[86]

What had been the profits of one empire now appeared in the victory parade of another, so that the triumph heralded not simply the Empire of Rome but at the same time the changing pattern of imperial power itself.

Seen in this light, Pompey's reputed use of the cloak of Alexander the Great was not just an instance of a Roman general taking on the mantle of his most famous predecessor, but a larger gesture portraying Rome as the successor of the empire of Macedon. How far this prompted people to wonder, more widely, if Rome also one day would have a successor, we do not know. But for Polybius, at least, the despoiling of Syracuse by the Romans in 211 BCE (the campaign for which Marcellus was awarded an ovation) raised acute issues about the ambivalence and transience of domination: "At any rate," he concluded his reflections, "the point of my remarks is directed to those who succeed to empire in their turn, so that even as they pillage cities they should not suppose that the misfortunes of others are an honor to their own country."[87]

PERFORMANCE ART

Modern historians of Roman art and culture have often been overly enthusiastic in their desire to pinpoint the origin of distinctively "Roman" forms of art in the institutions of the city of Rome and in the social practices of its elite members. It took a very long time indeed for them to give up the idea that the whole genre of portraiture (and particularly the "hyper-realistic" style often known as "verism") could be traced back directly to death masks and the rituals of the aristocratic Roman funeral. The idea clung tenaciously despite an almost total absence of evidence in its favor, and a considerable amount to the contrary.[88]

A similar theory that the traditions of Roman historical painting and some of their most distinctive conventions of narrative representation in sculpture derive from artwork associated with the triumph is still remarkably buoyant—despite having no more to recommend it than the shibboleth about portraiture. For a start, we have very little idea about the artistic idiom of any of the paintings or models carried in the triumphal procession. None survive, *pace* all the optimistic rediscoveries of the image of Cleopatra. And the few tantalizing hints we read about their workmanship—such as Pliny's claim that Paullus asked for an artist from Athens "to decorate his triumph," or the references to the model town in Caesar's triumph in 45 being made of ivory (in contrast to the wooden versions in the procession of his subordinates)—are not enough to give any general impression.[89]

It is little more than a guess to suggest, as art historians often do, that the paintings were rendered in the style of a group of third-century tomb paintings found on the Esquiline hill in Rome, which apparently show scenes from Roman wars with the Samnites.[90] In fact, the vocabulary used by ancient authors to evoke the triumphal representations does not always allow us to be certain whether they have paintings, tapestries, or three-dimensional models in mind—or, for that matter, whether the towns they refer to were miniature replicas or personifications. There are, for example, any number of possibilities for the "representation of the captured city of Syracuse" *(simulacrum captarum Syracusarum)* in Marcellus' ovation. Was it a painting or a sculptural model? A female Syracuse in chains, a map of the city, or the ancient equivalent of a cardboard cutout?

Even more to the point, there is a much bigger gap than is usually supposed between whatever might have been carried in the triumphal parades and the famous series of references, for the most part from Pliny, to early "historical painting" at Rome. These included such works of art as the painting of a battle between the Romans and Carthaginians, erected by Manius Valerius Maximus Messala in the senate house in 263 BCE; the painting in the shape of Sardinia, with "representations of battles" on it, dedicated in 174 BCE by Tiberius Sempronius Gracchus in the Temple of Mater Matuta; and those pictures exhibited in the Forum by Lucius Hostilius Mancinus in 145 BCE showing the "site of Carthage and the various attacks upon it"—beside which Mancinus stood, giving a running commentary on the campaigns and so endearing himself to his audience that, according to Pliny, he won the consulship at the next elections.[91] The usual argument is that these pictures started life as parade objects at their generals' triumphs, that they ended up on permanent display in various locations of the city when the celebration was over, and that they inspired that whole Roman "documentary" tradition in art, which captured historical events using such techniques as bird's-eye perspective and continuous narrative (where different episodes of the same story are depicted within the same overall composition).

In fact, this plausible argument is a decidedly flimsy one. No evidence exists, beyond modern wishful thinking, that the paintings commissioned by Valerius Messala and the rest were ever carried in triumphs before finding a permanent place of display. And that would certainly have been impossible in the case of Mancinus' painting of Carthage, for he never celebrated a triumph at all (despite what is sometimes erroneously claimed for him in modern literature). Besides—although the evidence is admittedly rather thin—the triumphal paintings, as they are very briefly described in ancient accounts, appear to feature significantly different themes from the historical paintings on permanent display.

Where historical paintings seem mostly to focus on the victorious campaigns of the Roman armies and their general, the triumphal images are most often said to depict the defeated enemy and the devastation of the conquered territory. Of course, this could be a matter of the different emphasis, or focalization, of the different accounts: the same painting of a battle can, after all, be described from the point of view of the conquerors or the conquered. But the stark insistence on the fate of the defeated in the references we have to the images carried in the triumph (the disemboweling of Cato, the deluge of blood through Judaea) hardly supports any argument that would link them to those other traditions of historical painting. There is, in fact, very little to be said for putting triumphal painting at the head of the genealogy of the narrative and documentary tradition in Roman art.

Yet there are connections between the ceremony of triumph and Roman arts of representation at a rather more significant level. Just as the traditions of Roman aristocratic funerals and the commemoration of ancestors provided a social context for the development of portraiture, even in the absence of any direct link between the origins of the genre and death masks (or any other sort of mask for that matter), so too triumphal culture as a whole provided a crucial arena within which issues of representation were explored and debated. Ancient authors focus not only on the plunder and the spectacular images in the procession; they return repeatedly to how the display was staged, as if *representation itself*—its conventions, contrivances, and paradoxes—was a central part of the show. The triumph is, in other words, construed as being a ceremony of image-*making* as much as it is one of images. It is the place where, in many written versions, representation (or *mimesis*) reaches its limits, and where the viewer (or reader) is asked to decide what counts as an image or where the boundary between reality and representation is to be drawn.

The poet Ovid explores these issues with particular verve. In one of his poems from exile on the Black Sea (from 8 CE to his death nine or so years later) he conjures up the image of a triumph in Rome, lamenting his own absence from the spectacle and his reliance on his "mind's eye"—in contrast to, in Ovid's words, "the lucky people who will get the real show." Part of the joke, for us at least, is that the triumph he predicts, for the heir-apparent Tiberius to celebrate his victories over the Germans, never actually took place; it was never a "real show" at all. But there is another joke, too, on the idea of reality. For "what exactly," as one critic has recently asked, "is the 'real spectacle' on show? Largely a parade of feignings, images of events and places far off, pictures, tableaux, personifications, imitations which supply the matter for the second-order fictive imitations of the poet." The "real" procession, in other words, is no less fictive than Ovid's "fictive imitations."[92]

In another of his poems from exile, written—we usually assume—to mark the triumph of Tiberius over Illyricum, celebrated in 12 CE, Ovid hints at the problems of triumphal illusion even more economically, in just three words. Here he lists the highlights of mimetic ingenuity featured (he imagines) in the procession, including "barbarian towns, mimicking their sacked walls in silver, with their painted men." *With their painted men (cum pictis viris)?* The question this raises for the reader goes directly to the heart of the representational flux of the (representation of the) triumph. Are these men *painted on the images* of the towns being paraded (like the silver walls)? Or are they *images of painted men*—men smeared with woad or tattooed, after the habit of northern barbarians? Is the paint a means of representation or is it what is represented, the signifier or the signified? And how could the reader tell the difference?[93]

Ovid is not the only writer—determined as he so often is to exploit the lurking ambivalences of Roman culture—who directs our attention to the triumph's representational complexity. Historians too take up these issues. Appian's account of Pompey's triumph of 61, for example— at first sight a relatively straightforward narrative of the procession—in fact leads the reader through a series of reflections on representation and its limits, both in the triumph itself and in its written versions. When he notes that one of the paintings on display depicted the "silence" of the night on which Mithradates fled, he is not only emphasizing the extraordinary realism of this art. By introducing this literary paradox (for only in writing can a painting show sound or its absence) Appian is also pointing to the inevitable mismatch between the visual images and his own written description of the ceremony—and at the same time he is prompting his readers to consider where the mimetic games of the triumph plunge into implausibility, if not absurdity.[94]

A different aspect of the representational paradox follows almost instantly in Appian's account, with the mention of the "images *[eikones]* of the barbarian gods and their native costume." In this case, as with Ovid's "painted men," the very nature of the representation and the mimetic process is elusive. In contrast to Mithradates and his family (whose images took the place of the human beings who, in other circumstances, might have been present in the procession themselves), these gods could appear in no form other than images. The *eikones* here, in other words, were not standing in for captives who were unavoidably absent; they were the "real thing," the captive gods themselves, dressed like the other prisoners in their exotic foreign garb. At least that is the case if we imagine that *eikones* were the statues of these divine figures brought from the East. But we cannot be sure that they were not paintings of those divine images (*eikones* of *eikones*), a second order of representation on painted canvas. In Appian's written representation of the triumph, statues and paintings of statues are impossible to distinguish.[95]

It makes a nice contrast with Josephus' hints on this theme in his account of the triumph of Vespasian and Titus. There the procession is said to have included "images of the Roman gods, of amazing size and skilled workmanship, and all made of some rich material." Roman statues of this kind (such as Pompey's pearl head) may have been a regular presence in triumphal processions, and if so would have contributed to the slippage we have already noted between victor and victim—the treasures of the victors being an object of spectacle no less than those of the vanquished. But they would have been a particularly loaded presence in this case, when, of course, there could have been no images of the Jewish god. His place was taken by representations of a quite different order, the holy objects from the temple and the written text of the Law.[96]

Such mimetic games raised important and difficult questions of interpretation and belief. How did you make sense of what you saw? And could you trust your eyes? Appian directly confronted the problem of belief when he made it absolutely clear that he was none too sure that Pompey really was wearing the genuine cloak of Alexander the Great. But Ovid, again, offers a particularly sophisticated and witty variation on this theme, when he presents the triumphal procession in his *Ars Amatoria (Art of Love)* as a good place for his learner-lover to impress and pick up a girl. The idea is that Ovid's girl (being a girl) cannot work out for herself who or what the personifications of conquered places and peoples are meant to be; and so the boy is advised to play the interpreter and (with confident, if spurious, learning) to produce a plausible set of names to identify the figures, models, and images as they pass.

> . . . "Here comes Euphrates," tell her,
>   "With reed-fringed brow; those dark
> Blue tresses belong to Tigris, I fancy; there go Armenians,
>   That's Persia, and that, h'r'm, was some

Upland Achaemenid city. Both those men are generals."
Give the names if you know them; if not. . .
Invent a likely tale.⁹⁷

The joke in this passage turns on the slipperiness of triumphal imagery. It is partly, of course, on the girl, who cannot make sense of what she sees. But it is on the boy and the narrator, too, as well as on the conventions of the whole charade—and so also on the reader.

After all, just how plausible are the confidently spurious identifications the boy and the narrator between them devise? They may sound reasonable enough to start with, but a moment's thought will surely suggest otherwise. Was it not a dumb decision, for example, to pretend to distinguish so easily the two rivers that are the natural twins of the world's waterways?⁹⁸ Has not the boy just revealed the very superficiality of his own patronizing bravura? Maybe. But any readers who were to take pleasure in their own superiority in this guessing game of interpretation would risk falling into exactly the same trap as the learner-lover. For part of the point of the passage is to insinuate the sheer under-determinacy of the images (kings, rivers, a chieftain or two) that pass by in a triumph. Besides, another question mark hovers here—over the victory itself that is being celebrated. Ovid hints that he has in mind some future triumph of Gaius Caesar (one of Augustus' long series of ill-fated heirs), for a victory over the Parthians. The chances are then that it will be just another one of those diplomatic stitch-ups, passing as military heroics, that characterized most Augustan encounters with that particular enemy. But who cares when the "real" conquest is the girl standing next to you?

In the end, as always, the poet has the last laugh, insinuating a more sinister agenda into this mimetic fun and disrupting the conventional distinction between representation and reality. Suppose we banish the suspicion that these processional images are overblown symbols to bolster bogus heroics and take them straight as memorials of a series of successful Roman massacres in the East. There is then an odd mixture of times and tenses in Ovid's account: "That *is* Persia," "that *was* . . . " At first sight this seems to be tied to the perspective of the boy and girl, as the present tense of what they see now, gives way to a past tense of what has just passed by. But more is hanging on the verbs than that. For "that *was* some upland Achaemenid city" is literally true in another sense. Whatever this nameless town used to be, the chances are that, following our glorious Roman victory, it exists no more: it has only a past. All that is "real" about it now is the brilliant cardboard cutout or painting carried along in the procession. Representation has become the only reality there is.

FAKING IT?

The boundary between models, representations, and replicas on the one hand and fakes and shams on the other is an awkward one—just as Tacitus insinuated in his account of Tiberius' triumph over Germany when he cast the *simulacra* in the procession as an appropriate commemoration for a victory that was itself only a pretense. The final twist in the complicated story of triumphal representation comes with the accounts of the triumphs or projected triumphs of the emperors Caligula and Domitian; here *mimesis* is turned into deception.

Both of these scored hollow military victories and planned, even if they did not celebrate, equally hollow triumphs. But where were the victims or the booty to come from? According to Suetonius, to celebrate his triumph over the Germans, Caligula planned to dress up some Gauls to impersonate *bona fide* German prisoners. They were chosen with the usual desiderata for triumphal captives in mind ("He chose all the tallest of the Gauls")—and, in fact, the emperor is credited with the nice coinage (in Greek) *axiothriambeutos,* or "worth leading in a triumphal procession," to describe the qualities he was looking for. To make the charade more plausible, he was going to get them to dye their hair red, learn the German language, and adopt German names. This is the occasion that the satirist Persius probably refers to when he sends up Caligula's wife for arranging contracts for "kings' cloaks, auburn wigs, chariots *(esseda)* and big models of the Rhine."[99] Much the same story is told of the triumphs of Domitian, but he is credited also with a bright idea for the fake spoils: according to Dio, he raided the palace furniture store, presumably for the kind of royal couches, thrones, and dinner services that featured in accounts of blockbuster triumphs during the late Republic.[100]

True or not, these stories raise crucial questions about the practice of imperial rule, and the nature of that bigger charade that cynical Roman observers saw as the heart of the imperial political system. Here the sham is exposed in the fake victories celebrated with a display of fake victims. But it reflects more specifically on the culture of triumphal representation, too. In Roman imperial ideology, one of the characteristics of monstrous despots is that they literalize the metaphors of cultural politics, to disastrous effect: Elagabalus is said to have responded to the loaded metaphors of ambivalent gendering in his Eastern religion by "really" attempting to give himself a vagina; Commodus is supposed to have sought the charisma of the arena by literally jumping over the barrier to make himself a gladiator.[101] In the stories of despotic triumphs, transgressive rulers play out "for real" the mimetic games of the procession by faking the captives and the spoils that validated the whole show. Despots' triumphs, in other words, literalize triumphal *mimesis* into sheer pretense; the culture of representation is turned into (or is exposed as) the culture of sham.

VI

Playing by the Rules

THE FOG OF WAR

In 51 BCE Cicero—Rome's greatest orator but not, by a long way, its greatest general—began to nurture hopes of being awarded a triumph. He had been appointed, much against his will, to the governorship of the province of Cilicia, a large tract of land in what is now southern Turkey (with the island of Cyprus tacked onto its jurisdiction). For a man of untried military mettle, it was uncomfortably close to the kingdom of Parthia, which had inflicted a devastating defeat on the Roman forces under Crassus just two years earlier. The Parthian victory celebrations had, according to Plutarch, included a parody of a Roman triumph, with a prisoner dressed in women's clothes taking the part of the triumphing Crassus; and they had ended with the general's severed head used as a prop in a performance of Euripides' *Bacchae,* standing in for that of the dismembered king Pentheus.[1]

It was not so much a sense of danger that put Cicero off his overseas posting but rather the enforced absence from the city of Rome. He kept up with the gossip and political in-fighting by letter, giving his friends and colleagues news, in return, of his work in the province. Some of this correspondence survives.[2] It offers the most vivid glimpse we have of Roman provincial government and of the frontline military activity that often went with it. In fact, it represents the only day-to-day first-person account of campaigns to have survived from antiquity. It also sheds important light on the run-up to the celebration of a triumph. In what circumstances might a general decide to seek the honor? How might he best support his case? On this occasion at least, the award (or not) hung on a complex combination of demonstrable military achievement, energetic behind-the-scenes negotiation, and artful persuasion.

In one of these letters, written probably in September 51, a month or so after Cicero had arrived in Cilicia, one of his younger correspondents, the smartly disreputable Marcus Caelius Rufus, trailed the hope that he might secure just enough military success to earn a triumph: "If we could only get the balance right so that a war came along of just the right size for the strength of your forces and we achieved what was needed for glory and a triumph without facing the really dangerous and serious clash—that would be the dream ticket."[3] It was a characteristically naughty piece of subversion on Caelius' part to cast a military victory as merely a useful device in the pursuit of a triumph, rather than seeing a triumph as due honor for military victory; and how seriously Cicero was supposed to take it, we do not know.

But in his reply, sent in mid-November (it could take a couple of months for letters to travel between Rome and Cilicia), he was able to tell Caelius that everything had worked out as he had wanted: "You say that it would suit you if only I could have just enough trouble to earn a sprig of laurel; but you are afraid of the Parthians because you don't have much confidence in my troops. Well that is exactly what has happened." In the face of a Parthian incursion into the neighboring province of Syria, Cicero had moved into the Amanus mountain range, between the two provinces, and terrorized the inhabitants who had long resisted Roman takeover. "Many were captured and slaughtered, the rest scattered. Their strongholds were taken by our surprise attack and torched." Cicero himself was hailed *imperator* by his men, a customary acknowledgment of a significant victory (which went back probably to the late third century BCE) and often seen as a first step in the award of a triumph.[4]

By a happy coincidence, this ceremony took place at Issus, where in 333 the Persian king Darius had been defeated by Alexander the Great— "a not inconsiderably better general than either you or I," as Cicero remarked to Atticus, in a mixture of wry self-deprecation and misplaced self-importance. The campaign culminated in more slash and burn ("stripping and plundering the Amanus") and a long siege of the fortress town of Pindenissum. It was from here that Cicero wrote to Caelius, anticipating the "immense glory" that this success would bring him, "except for the name of the town." No one had heard of it.[5]

The main outlines of Cicero's campaigns in his province are clear enough.[6] But the details—from the structure of command to the identity of the enemy and the significance of Roman victories—are murky and confused now, as they were at the time. The letters often give significantly different stories to different people, not to mention the fact that information was slow to travel and hard to interpret. When Cicero arrived in Cilicia, his predecessor Appius Claudius Pulcher was still in the province and (despite Cicero's arrival, on which he may not have been fully informed) continued to act as governor by holding assize courts in one of its remoter parts. Cicero even suspected that his predecessor was hanging onto three cohorts of the provincial army; at least, Cicero had no clue where these detachments of his forces were.[7]

In the next-door province of Syria, exactly the reverse was the problem. The new governor, Marcus Calpurnius Bibulus, had not arrived before the Parthians had invaded and the response was left to the second in command, Caius Cassius Longinus (best known as one of the assassins of Julius Caesar). One version of the story, as Cicero tells it to Caelius, is that Cassius scored a notable success in driving the Parthians out of Syria. He certainly wrote fulsomely to Cassius himself on these lines, as Cassius left for home late in 51 after Bibulus had at last arrived: "I congratulate you, both for the magnitude of what you achieved and for the timeliness of your success. As you leave your province, its thanks and plaudits speed you on your way."[8]

But other versions circulated, too. Cicero was capable of claiming to Atticus, fairly or not, that the real reason for the Parthian withdrawal had been his own advance into the Amanus and that the senate had been suspicious of Cassius' dispatches announcing his victory. In fact, the whole story of a Parthian incursion into Syria became controversial, as some rumors held that the invaders were not Parthians at all but Arabs "in Parthian kit." Caelius at one stage reports the idea (later to prove unfounded) that Cassius had made it all up: "People were suspecting Cassius of having invented the war so that his own depredations should appear to be the result of enemy devastation—and of letting Arabs into his province and reporting them to the senate as Parthians."[9]

TRIUMPHAL AMBITIONS

In this climate of misinformation, it would have been hard to judge whether any victory was worthy of a triumph. But this did not stop all three of the provincial governors in the region from planning to claim one—and perhaps it even encouraged them. We know almost nothing of Appius Claudius' military activity in Cilicia, but he returned to Rome making no secret of his hopes. Despite Cicero's awkward relations with his predecessor and his low opinion of Appius' government of the province ("It is completely and permanently ruined"), he managed some polite words to Appius himself on the prospect of his "certain and well-deserved" triumphal celebration: "Although it is no more than my own judgment of you . . . nevertheless I was extremely pleased with what your letter had to say about your confident—indeed, assured—expectation of a triumph." Only a casual aside about such a grant enhancing Cicero's own prospects of the honor is noticeably double-edged. In the event, Appius was faced with a legal prosecution and gave up his ambition for a triumph in order to enter the city and fight the case.[10]

Bibulus too, once he had arrived in Syria, was rumored to be on the hunt for triumphal honors and went with his army to the Amanus range looking for an easy victory—or, as Cicero put it, "looking for a sprig of laurel in a wedding cake" (laurel was one of the ingredients in Roman wedding cake and, in that context, was presumably hard to miss). He ended up, as Cicero gloats no less than he regrets, losing a large number of men. More fighting apparently followed in Syria, and it may be from this conflict that Bibulus' hopes of triumphal glory sprang. These hopes were never realized, overtaken—it seems likely—by the outbreak of civil war between Caesar and Pompey in 49 BCE. But not before Cicero had expressed his irritation with Bibulus' ambitions and their (in his view) ludicrous mismatch with the achievements on the ground: "So long as there was a single Parthian in Syria he didn't take a step outside the city gates." And not before their rivalry had spurred Cicero's own triumphal ambitions: "As for me, if it wasn't for the fact that Bibulus was pressing for a triumph . . . I would be quite easy about it."[11]

Cicero's pursuit of a triumph falls into two halves: first the campaign for a *supplicatio,* a ceremony of thanksgiving to the gods voted by the senate, which regularly preceded a triumph; then, once that vote was achieved, the second round of campaigning, ultimately unsuccessful, for another senatorial vote to award a triumph proper.[12] His correspondence documents the intense behind-the-scenes machinations; and in some cases the surviving letters are the frontline weapons in Cicero's bid for triumphal glory, the very medium through which those machinations were carried out. Given that, some favorite themes in modern discussions of the ceremony are striking by their absence. There is no mention at all of any formal rules or qualifications that governed the award of a triumph, except the requirement to remain outside the city before the ceremony. Instead, the letters immerse us in a world of delicate negotiations that center round personal ambition and *amour propre,* bad faith, pay-backs, and rivalry—or alternatively, depending on the correspondent, deny (whether with philosophical *hauteur* or down-to-earth realism) all but a passing interest in such a superficial honor as a triumph.

Cicero claims that he wrote to every member of the senate except for two—one an inveterate enemy, the other the ex-husband of his daughter—to persuade them to vote for his *supplicatio.*[13] That would have meant a total of around six hundred letters, which (even if many followed a standard formula) must have amounted to several days' work for Cicero and his secretaries. Three of these letters survive. Two, probably written within a few weeks of the fall of Pindenissum, were addressed to the consuls of 50, Gaius Claudius Marcellus and Lucius Aemilius Paullus: "So I earnestly beg that you make sure that a decree is passed in the most honorific terms possible concerning my achievements, and as soon as possible too."[14] In neither of these did he restate what those achievements were but referred back to the dispatch he had sent to the senate. By contrast, his long begging letter to Marcus Porcius Cato opens with pages of detail on the military operations.

Cato, whose probity in such matters often verged on curmudgeon, was obviously thought to be a less easy target and, as Bibulus was his son-in-law, he was likely to have received an alternative and no doubt more dismissive account of Cicero's victories. What Cicero offers here is broadly compatible with the narrative he gives in other letters, but it is expertly tailored to impress. He makes no jokes about Alexander the Great (only a pointed reference to his camp being near a place known as "Alexander's Altars"), but he does insinuate that behind his none too infamous opponents lay the much more serious military threat of Parthia: "They were harboring runaways and eagerly awaiting the arrival of the Parthians."

The rest of the letter uses various lines of persuasion to secure Cato's vote for a *supplicatio*. After trading on the history of their mutual admiration ("I have not merely shown tacit admiration for your outstanding qualities [for who doesn't?]; I have extolled you publicly beyond any man we have ever seen or even heard of."), Cicero makes a parade of his own vulnerability and his need for marks of esteem. In his early career, he explains, he could afford to disdain such baubles, but since his period in exile he has been understandably anxious for public honor, "to heal the wound of the injustice against me." He ends by meeting Cato's philosophical pretensions half-way, stressing how his military achievements were backed up by the highest principles in provincial government. It was the case, after all, "that throughout history fewer men were found who could conquer their own desires than could conquer the forces of the enemy." Cicero had been victorious on both fronts.[15]

The senate discussed the request for a *supplicatio* sometime during April or May 50, and Caelius instantly reported back to Cicero, still in his province, that the result was a success, although some hard work had been necessary behind the scenes. Other factors had come into play, particularly the anxiety of the tribune Caius Scribonius Curio that a ceremony of thanksgiving, which could last for days, would occupy some of the time available for legislation and so get in the way of his political aims. In a deal brokered by Caelius, the consul Paullus agreed to circumvent this (Cicero must have felt that his letter had not been in vain), guaranteeing that the *supplicatio* would not actually take place till the next year.

Meanwhile there was potential opposition from one of the two men to whom Cicero had not written. Hirrus threatened to make a long speech, but Caelius and his friends persuaded him not to ("We got to him")—so successfully that he did not even attempt to hold up business by objecting, as he could have, that the meeting was not quorate when the number of animal victims to be sacrificed at the thanksgiving was decided. The vote in the end went Cicero's way, though we do not know how many days of thanksgiving were agreed (the silence suggests that it was rather few), nor indeed whether they were ever held; having been postponed in the deal with Curio, they were presumably lost in the outbreak of civil war early in 49. According to Caelius, the voting pattern was maverick: some voted for the honor without wanting it to succeed (they assumed wrongly that Curio would veto the decision); Cato, by contrast, spoke about Cicero in most honorific terms but voted against.[16]

Cato proceeded to write to Cicero in a letter that has been variously judged by modern readers as "ponderous pedantry," "priggish and crabbed," or "entirely free of rudeness or insult." His main point was to justify his vote on the grounds that a *supplicatio* implied that the responsibility for the victory lay with the gods, whereas he gave the credit to Cicero himself. But he also warned that a triumph did not always follow a thanksgiving—and that, in any case, "much more glorious than a triumph is for the senate to judge that a province has been held and preserved by the governor's mild administration and blameless conduct."[17]

For Cicero and his secretaries, a further flurry of correspondence must have followed. Thank-you letters survive to Marcellus and to his predecessor in Cilicia, Appius Claudius, who had worked for Cicero's thanksgiving as Cicero (whatever the mixed feelings) had worked for his.[18] To Cato, Cicero managed a reply in superficially gracious terms. Nothing, he wrote, could be more complimentary than the speech which Cato had made in the senate in praise of his achievements; in fact, if the world were populated by the likes of Cato, then such an encomium would be worth more than any "triumphal chariot or laurel crown." But, of course, the real world was not run along Catonian lines, and there these honors counted. Cicero concluded with an awkward passage of fence-sitting—and perhaps calculated understatement—about just how important to him the thanksgiving or projected triumph was. It was more a question, he emphasized, of not being averse to it, rather than especially wanting it. A triumph was "not to be unduly coveted," but at the same time it was certainly not to be rejected if offered by the senate. His hope was that the senate would consider him "not unworthy" of such an honor, especially as it was such a common one.[19]

The letters penned over the next few months, during Cicero's final weeks in Cilicia and through the journey back to Rome, return time and again to the possible triumph. In these, too, the themes of ambition and the desire for glory are prominent: how far was it proper actively to want (or to be seen to be wanting) a triumph? Cicero repeatedly stresses that he is not going to do anything that smacks of "eagerness" for the honor—though he could wish, on occasion, that Atticus showed himself a little more "eager" for Cicero to achieve it. He also takes care to blame his ambitions on others—on Caelius who "put the idea in his head" (when in fact a safe return home would be "triumph" enough) or on his friends who "beckon" him back to a triumph.[20]

Nonetheless, the letters also document how energetically he was canvassing for the award, with Pompey and Caesar among others. And when Bibulus was voted a thanksgiving of (probably) twenty days, with Cato this time strongly behind the motion, there was no concealing, from Atticus at least, his eagerness and jealousy: "As far as the triumph is concerned, I wasn't ever at all eager for it until Bibulus sent those outrageous letters which resulted in a thanksgiving on a most lavish scale . . . the fact that I did not win the same honor is a humiliation for you as well as for me."[21]

Inevitably, his ambitions had wider implications. Cicero was anxious about the cost of any triumph, especially in the face of a loan repayment to Caesar: "What I find most annoying is that Caesar's money has to be repaid and the means of my triumph diverted in that direction."[22] He also found that his triumphal aspirations seriously affected his political position in Rome during the run-up to civil war. He tried to use at least one of the constraints to his advantage: the prohibition on a general entering the city before a triumph seemed a convenient excuse for not becoming involved in the dangerous and compromising negotiations that were going on there.[23]

But any such advantages were rare. When Pompey advised him not to attend the senate (presumably meeting outside the city boundary) in case he ended up getting on the wrong side of potential supporters of his honor, we may suspect that Pompey might have had other motives for wanting Cicero well clear of the senatorial debates.[24] Perhaps even worse, far from keeping him out of things, his presence just outside the city, while he still possessed military authority *(imperium)*, made him a sitting target for being sent off to take charge of a region such as Sicily in the looming civil conflict.[25] He himself put the dilemma neatly when he wrote to Atticus: "Two parts that it's impossible to play simultaneously are candidate for a triumph and independent statesman."[26]

The last occasion on which we know that Cicero's prospective triumph was part of public business was on January 7, 49 BCE, at the meeting of the senate which marked the formal outbreak of civil war. Cicero claims that, even at this moment of crisis, "a full senate" demanded a triumph for him, but the consul procrastinated by saying (not unreasonably, given the circumstances) that he would put it to the vote when he had settled the urgent matters of state.[27] But his triumphal ambitions did not fade away at once. He continued to consult Atticus on the matter and—as a consequence of not laying down his office from which he hoped to triumph—to be encumbered by his official attendants (or lictors) with their *fasces,* or rods of office, wreathed in fading laurel. It seems that he did not dismiss these men until 47 and in the process gave up all hope of a triumphal ceremony.[28]

GENERALIZING FROM CICERO?

Cicero's correspondence brings to the surface significant problems in the award of triumphal honors. It is clear, for a start, that lack of reliable information about military achievements in a distant province, and competing versions from different parties, made any decision about granting a triumph a delicate one. Major military success was certainly seen as a basic requirement; but whose story was to be believed? To make matters more complicated, the uncertainty in the chain of command (particularly at the time of transition from governor to governor) was liable to raise questions about whose responsibility any victory was. Suppose that Cassius really had scored a major success against a Parthian invasion before Bibulus had even reached the province of Syria. Would Bibulus, as overall commander (and the holder of *imperium*), have been the candidate for triumph? Or Cassius, despite his subordinate position?

And as the exchange of letters with Cato reveals, in perhaps an unusually extreme form, different parties might hold different ideas about what kind of victory counted as triumph-worthy. Here we find the suggestion that the conduct of the victorious general might count, as well as simple fact of an enemy defeated. But how was that to be assessed? It must partly be because of the gaps in information, and the dilemmas facing anyone who tried to judge competing claims, that the role of personal canvassing was so crucial. Cicero's letters ask for his triumphal claims to be taken seriously on, as Romans might have seen it, the best of all possible grounds: his standing, connections, and friendships.

The letters also expose various ways in which the triumph and its preliminaries could impact on politics more widely. In practical terms, a thanksgiving or triumphal celebration was inevitably an intrusion—welcome or not—into the political business of the city, with consequences (as Curio's anxieties show) for other aspects of public life. Its timing and length were almost bound to be the subject of loaded negotiations and conflicting claims. And for this reason, if for no other, triumphal debates would often be drawn into political wheeling and dealing.

In the wider competition for public status, too, the triumph ranked high. Cicero's insistence on not appearing too "eager" for the honor hints at some of the social ground rules of the competitive culture of the late-republican Roman elite: in this area at least, ambition was veiled as much as it was displayed; and protection from the possible public humiliation of failure might be secured by a contrived *insouciance.* But equally, the triumph was a hugely desirable mark of distinction and crucial in the relative ranking of prestige. When Cicero fulminates at Bibulus' success in achieving a lengthy thanksgiving, it is not merely an indication of personal pique; it shows how the triumph and its associated rituals were a key element in the calibration of glory and status among the elite—and inevitably "political" for that.

Yet Cicero's extraordinarily vivid insider's story on the preliminaries to a triumph has rarely been central to modern studies of the ceremony.[29] Why? Part of the reason must be that Cicero never did achieve his ambition; so, as a noncelebration, this tends to fall through the cracks in the roster of triumphal history and its chronology of awards. Part also, I suspect, is that Cicero's military career as a whole is never treated seriously, as critics tend either to take his own rhetorical self-deprecation literally or alternatively to recoil from the glimpses of pomposity and pride that the correspondence simultaneously offers. Any comparison between Cicero and Alexander the Great does seem, after all, faintly ridiculous; so too does the image of him apparently so desperate for triumphal glory that he spent the first two years of a cataclysmic civil war traipsing around Italy and Greece with a posse of lictors in tow, carrying their laurel-wreathed *fasces.* Equally unappealing is the energetic postal campaign to some six hundred senators urging their support for his *supplicatio*—although in the absence of comparable evidence for other occasions, there is in fact no reason to suppose that this was not a fairly normal procedure: Flamininus, Aemilius Paullus, Mummius, and Pompey may all have tried to ensure a favorable vote in just that way.

An even more significant reason for passing over Cicero's would-be triumph must be the sense that the messy negotiations and trade-offs that the letters expose are a feature of the political collapse of the period, bringing with it a decline in triumphal propriety and order. By this stage, so the argument would go, the honor was a trinket to be squabbled over by generals with only a paltry victory to their name—a far cry from the framework of rules and regulations within which the third- and second-century triumphal debates described by Livy appear to take place, and from the major military successes with which they are concerned. It is to those rules (however highly politicized or partisan their application might sometimes have been) that we should turn if we wish to reconstruct the principles on which the award of a triumph was traditionally made. From this perspective, the simple fact that Cicero and his correspondents seem hardly bothered with any formal qualifications for requesting or granting the honor is a good gauge of how far the system as a whole had sunk into mere in-fighting. Only Cato appears to touch on something remotely like a rule (albeit a negative one) with his assertion that a triumph does not always follow a *supplicatio*—and so, predictably enough, this nugget alone has often been extracted by modern historians from such a rich vein of material.[30]

Such comparisons, however, are hazardous. On the basis of the numbers of triumphs celebrated, it is misleading to claim that the final years of the Republic were a particularly easy time to achieve a triumph as traditional standards broke down: if anything, the early and middle years of the first century BCE show a dearth rather than a bumper crop of celebrations. There is also the question of whether we are comparing like with like. After all, the general's view of the day-to-day negotiations as they progress will inevitably create a different impression from a retrospective historical narrative whose job is to impose order on events as they unfolded, sometimes chaotically. It is perfectly conceivable that Cicero's correspondence took the rules and regulations that framed a triumphal award for granted, without a mention. No less conceivable is it that, had they survived, the private letters of (say) Aemilius Paullus would reveal just as intricate and messy a series of negotiations and uncertainties.

Underlying the whole problem is the issue of what kind of decision-making process we are looking for in the award of a triumph. Starting from Cicero allows us to rethink some of the most hotly debated questions in the history of the ceremony: how, and under what conditions, did a general secure a triumph? This is a very different aspect of the ceremony and its scholarship from the display of wealth and conquest that has been my main theme so far; and it requires attending carefully to contradictory details of principles, procedure, and technicalities, as they are described by ancient writers. Yet the picture that will emerge from this is of a ceremony much less rigidly governed by rules and formal qualifications than has often been assumed. In fact, the triumphal accounts in Livy turn out to be rather more "Ciceronian" in character than is usually recognized.

ARGUING THE CASE

Triumphs were claimed or demanded by a general; they were not usually bestowed on him spontaneously by a grateful senate or people.[31] During the Republic at least (the Empire was very different) the assumption of most surviving accounts is that the initiative lay with the victorious commander. It was always liable to be a politically contentious claim; and all the more so because it is far from clear now—and almost certainly was not much clearer in the ancient world itself—who in the state had the final authority to grant or withhold a general's "right" to celebrate a triumph. Most of the debates on this question that are replayed (or reinvented) in the pages of Roman writers are set in the senate, and the senate is regularly said to allow or refuse the honor. Yet we have notorious examples of men who apparently triumphed in the face of senatorial refusal, with or without the support of the people; and these triumphs, not only those celebrated outside Rome on the Alban Mount, had sufficient official status to appear in the inscribed list in the Forum. An adverse senatorial decision did not in itself, in other words, deny legitimacy to the celebration.[32]

How a triumph was claimed in the earliest period of the Republic is frankly anyone's guess, and the different formulations used by writers such as Livy probably do not bear the weight of speculation placed on them. When he describes an early triumph simply as the commander "returning to Rome in triumph," this may—or may not—imply an archaic version of the ceremony that was little more than a victorious re-entry into the city, without formal regulation.[33] What is clear, however, is that both Livy and Dionysius of Halicarnassus not infrequently envisage political conflict in the triumphal celebrations from the very earliest period.

Dionysius, for example, recounting the triumph of Servilius Priscus in 495, explains that the senate refused authorization for narrowly political reasons and that Servilius took his case instead to the assembly of the people, who enthusiastically endorsed it.[34] Half a century later, Livy elaborates (probably fancifully) on the *supplicatio* and triumph of Valerius Publicola in 449. The thanksgiving of a single day decreed by the senate was thought too mean, and the people spontaneously celebrated an extra one. The senate subsequently refused a triumph, which was granted by an assembly of the people, proposed by a tribune. One objector is supposed to have claimed that, in leading the motion, the tribune was paying back a personal favor, not honoring military success.[35] Fanciful or not, these incidents clearly show that in the Roman historical imagination, political conflicts surrounding the triumph could go back (almost) as far as the institution itself.

Later in the Republic, from at least the end of the third century BCE, we can detect clearer signs of a regular procedure—although, as with most aspects of the triumph, not as fixed as many modern scholars have liked to imagine.[36] There are, indeed, all kinds of diverse tales of how a general might obtain the honor. Pompey's first triumph, for example, was written up by Plutarch as a favor granted by the dictator Sulla. And writing of the confused period after the assassination of Julius Caesar,

Dio casts Mark Antony's wife Fulvia as the power behind the grant of a triumph to Lucius Antonius. He had, according to this account, done little to deserve one, but once Fulvia had given the nod "they voted for it unanimously" (who "they" are is not clear)—"and she gave herself rather more airs than he did, and for a better reason; for to give someone the authority to hold a triumph was a much greater achievement than to celebrate it as the gift of another."[37] But, of course, the fact that Plutarch and Dio pointedly chose to tell the story of these triumphal grants in terms of personal, autocratic, or transgressively female power does not prove that no other public procedures of decision-making took place even in these cases. As Dio's reference to the "unanimous voting" shows, he imagines Fulvia as dominating, rather than replacing, the regular process of triumphal awards.

That process is usually seen—largely on the basis of accounts given by Livy for triumphs of the late third and early second centuries BCE— in two stages. The first took place in the senate, the second before the people. On his return to Rome, if a victorious general wanted to seek a triumph, he would convene the senate outside the *pomerium,* a favorite location being the temple of the appropriately warlike goddess Bellona.[38] This would not be the first the senate knew of the general's ambitions. He would have sent official dispatches from the field of conflict ("laureled letters"—literally, it seems, letters decorated with laurel) or an official envoy, as well as private letters to his friends and colleagues. He might well have emphasized his acclamation as *imperator* by his troops. And very likely he would have already requested and been awarded a thanksgiving: out of some sixty-five republican *supplicationes,* just eleven are known not to have been followed by a triumph, Cicero's and Bibulus' included.[39] Nonetheless, in front of the senators he would put his case for a triumph in a formal address.

The best direct evidence for these communications, whether the speech of the general himself or of his intermediaries, is thought to come not from any historical account but from the late third-century to early second-century BCE comedies of Plautus, which on several occasions appear to parody elements of triumphal celebration. The *Amphitruo,* in particular, which focuses on the tragicomic return home of the victorious Theban general (and cuckolded husband) Amphitruo, makes a point of mimicking triumphal language. Early in the play, Amphitruo's slave messenger Sosia explains to the audience the circumstances of his master's return: "The enemy defeated, the victorious legions are returning home, this mighty conflict brought to an end and the enemy exterminated. A city which brought many casualties to the Theban people has been defeated by the strength and valor of our troops and taken by storm, under the authority and auspices *(imperio atque auspicio)* of my master Amphitruo, especially." The formality of expression and the clipped style echo such traces we have of apparently official records of Roman military achievement, suggesting that Plautus was offering, to those in the know, a wry parody of the traditional language in which requests for triumphs were expressed.[40]

The vote of the senate was vulnerable to objections of all kinds (including outright veto of the decision by one of the ten tribunes, as was threatened by Curio in the case of Cicero's thanksgiving). If the claim went through, the senate then arranged that an assembly of the people should formally grant the triumphing general *imperium* within the sacred boundary of the city for the day of his celebration.[41] According to Roman law, that military authority was normally lost when the *pomerium* was crossed and was only extended by this vote on a special and temporary basis. Hence, until the day of the triumph itself, the general had to wait outside that boundary (or, at least, that was the consistent pattern up to the quadruple triumph of Caesar in 46 BCE). It was perhaps not such a hardship as it might at first seem: by the late Republic, considerable parts of the built-up area of the city fell outside the *pomerium.* All the same, the exclusion of republican triumphal hopefuls from the heart of the city is a striking feature of these preliminary procedures. Sometimes that exclusion could last years. Gaius Pomptinus, who scored a victory in Gaul in 62–61 and probably returned to the city in 58, did not triumph until 54 BCE.

This pattern of decision-making seems, at least, broadly compatible with Cicero's attempts to secure a triumph for himself. But, as we have seen before, such a seamless template for triumphal procedure is also misleading. This is partly, again, because of the scanty evidence behind some of these confident claims of standard practice. The vote of the people to extend the *imperium* of the general is not a regular feature of ancient descriptions of the triumph; it is mentioned on only three occasions, which may or may not be special cases.[42] And this technical issue is further and almost impenetrably complicated by the theory strongly advocated by some modern scholars that *imperium* in itself was not a requirement for a triumph, but more precisely the "military auspices" *(auspicia)*—which regularly, though not always, came with *imperium*.[43]

More practically, the occasional references to "laureled letters" are certainly not enough to prove them a permanent feature of the procedure. (Where, after all, did the laurel come from? Or did every general pack some in his luggage, just in case?)[44] Worryingly too for the idea of a conventional idiom of triumphal requests, Cicero's formal dispatches to the senate bear no especially strong resemblance to the style of the Plautine parodies. But, even more serious problems and inconsistencies underlie the standard account of procedure.

I have already noted that an adverse senatorial vote did not necessarily impede a valid triumph.[45] Why then go through the senate at all? One practical consideration may have been financing. In discussing the distribution of power in the Roman state, Polybius reflects on how the senate exercised control over generals. Triumphs, he argues, were one of the senate's weapons: "For they cannot organize what are known as 'triumphs' in due style, and sometimes they cannot celebrate them at all, unless the senate agrees and provides the funds for the purpose." One "unauthorized" triumph is certainly said, albeit by a much later author, to be held at the general's own expense.[46] Yet financing cannot be the only issue: after all, some of the most successful Roman commanders would have had little trouble raising funds independently, while Cicero was still anxious about the expense of a celebration even when he was anticipating senatorial approval.

More puzzling is how a general could triumph legitimately with the backing of neither the senate nor an assembly of the people. This seems

to have been the position of Appius Claudius Pulcher, who in 143 notoriously rode roughshod over the will of both senate and people in proceeding with the ceremony. The story was that his daughter (or sister)
who was a Vestal Virgin leapt into the triumphal chariot with him, to
give him religious protection against the attack of a hostile tribune.[47] But
how, in these circumstances, without a vote of the people, was the necessary *imperium* extended? We simply do not know. One modern scholar
has ingeniously speculated that Appius Claudius might have used the
good offices of the priestly college of augurs (with which he had strong
family connection) to invest him with the appropriate *auspicia* instead
of relying on the assembly.[48]

In fact, this is only one of many areas where considerable ingenuity
must be deployed to make sense of the supposed triumphal rules on *imperium*. Why, for example, did magistrates who were celebrating triumphs during their year of office (when, according to modern reconstructions of Roman law, they possessed *imperium* within the *pomerium*
anyway) need to go through the formal process of extending their authority? Perhaps they did not. Maybe, as some have argued, this was a
necessary step only for those attempting to triumph after their year of
office had ended (which might help with the Appius Claudius problem,
whose celebration took place during his consulship).[49] Yet, if that were
the case, why did they also need to stay outside the *pomerium* up to the
moment of their celebration? Maybe more than one kind of *imperium*
was at stake here—and what was being granted to the triumphing general was specifically *military* authority within the city, which even serving magistrates did not possess.[50] But, again, why the emphasis on not
crossing the *pomerium*? If there had to be a special grant anyway, why
could it not be made after the general had entered the city?

Perhaps, as others have suggested, this prohibition on crossing Rome's
sacred boundary is not specially connected with *imperium* or the other
aspects of legal authority which that implied, but harked back to different form of "ceremonial inhibition"—the idea perhaps that the triumph
was originally an "entry ritual," which could not properly be celebrated

if the *pomerium* had been crossed and the city already entered.[51] Answers can be devised for all these questions. But as no ancient definition of *imperium* survives, nor any definition of its possibly different varieties (military, domestic, and so on), those answers are inevitably modern constructions.[52]

The varied evidence we have clearly suggests that we should not be thinking only in terms of a fixed and regulated procedure, even in the later Republic. The ceremony of triumph was not merely an extraordinary public mark of honor to an individual commander; it also involved the entry into Rome of a general at the head of his troops. This broke all those key cultural assumptions of Roman life which insisted on the division between the sphere of civilian and military activity, and which underlay many of the legal niceties that grew up around the idea of the *pomerium* or *imperium*. The fundamental question was this: how and in what circumstances could it be deemed legitimate for a successful general to enter the city in triumph?

One answer—and probably the safest—was to obtain the support of the senate and to parade respect for the legal rules which policed the very boundaries that a triumphal celebration would break. That was the answer inscribed in the "traditional procedure" as it is usually painted—though the carping remarks of Cato to Cicero, pointing out that a triumph did not always follow a thanksgiving, shows how the edges of that "tradition" could be blurred even for Romans. Yet, uncongenial as it must seem to the generations of modern scholars who have cast the Romans as legalistic obsessives, this was not the only way of claiming legitimacy for a triumph. To go over the heads of the senate directly to the assembly of the people as arbiters of the distribution of glory was another. Sheer chutzpah was another option, albeit rare. Indeed, though many more triumphs may have been celebrated in the general's head and then rejected as wishful thinking, and others transferred to the Alban Mount in the face of senatorial rejection, we know of no triumphal procession that was ever launched onto the streets of Rome and not subsequently treated as a legitimate ceremony.

MORE RULES AND REGULATIONS

The variants in procedure, then, were numerous. Nonetheless, the senate is usually portrayed as the main arena in which a commander's request for a triumph was debated, endorsed, decried or postponed—and through which, if we are to believe Polybius, his triumph was funded.[53] These senatorial proceedings are vividly recreated by Livy, whose account of the years 211 to 167 (where his surviving text breaks off) includes a series of debates for and against the triumph of individual claimants. In 211, for example, Marcus Claudius Marcellus returned from Sicily and, meeting the senate in the Temple of Bellona, requested a triumph. Livy tells of a long discussion. On one side, some insisted that it would be illogical to deny the general a triumph, when a *supplicatio* for his victories had already been agreed to (not an argument that Cato would have approved). On the other side, some objected that the war could not be regarded as finished if his army had not been brought back to Rome. As a compromise, he was granted an *ovatio,* and he also celebrated a triumph *in Monte Albano.*[54]

A decade later, Lucius Cornelius Lentulus, who had held a special command in Spain, not as a regularly elected magistrate, made a request for a triumph. The senate, Livy tells us, agreed that his achievements were worthy of a triumph but that "no precedent had been handed down from their ancestors for someone to triumph who had not achieved his successes either as dictator or consul or praetor." Again, an *ovatio* was voted as a compromise, but this time in the face of opposition from a tribune, who argued that the lesser award did not solve the problem and, in fact, "was just as out of step with traditional custom."[55]

The arguments and counter-arguments produced in these narratives, combined with a few surviving discussions of "triumphal law" by scholars in antiquity itself, have been largely responsible for one of the most curious academic industries of the last century or so: the repeated attempts to say exactly what criteria the senate applied in deciding whose triumph to ratify and whose not. This industry is fueled, rather than dampened, by the evident contradictions in the decisions described. For example, how do we account for the grant of a triumph to Lucius Furius Purpureo in 200, despite the fact that he had not brought his army home, while that is said to have been the main reason for refusing Marcellus just a decade earlier? Only the occasional voice has ever suggested that these decisions were *ad hoc,* if not arbitrary; most have tried to detect the system, or at least the pattern, underlying the confusing evidence.[56]

One influential view is that a clear set of rules always governed the awards made by the senate, even if they might have been reformed and recast over the course of the Republic, with additional criteria (such as a minimum number of enemy casualties) introduced from time to time—and even if they were sometimes disrupted by all kinds of personal and political interests, favors, and back-scratching. Theodor Mommsen, for example, identified the crucial, nonnegotiable qualification as the possession of the highest form of *imperium* by a serving magistrate; so that no general could properly triumph if, for example, he had won his victory while a second-in-command, or after he had resigned his magistracy. Others, as I have noted, stressed instead the religious qualification of *auspicium,* that is, command and authority seen in terms of the right to conduct relations with the gods on behalf of the state.[57]

This approach is characteristic of that strand of nineteenth-century scholarship which was set on recovering the main principles and details of Roman constitutional law. In reaction to its rigid systematization, more recent critics—while often still stressing the importance of *imperium*—have suggested a much greater degree of improvisation on the part of the senate, especially as they adjusted the traditional rules to the changing circumstances of military leadership and the increasing use by the Romans of generals who were not serving magistrates or held various types of "special commands." The triumphal debates in Livy, for example, have been scrutinized to reveal an increasing willingness to grant triumphs to men who were commanding armies in the, formally, more junior office of praetor rather than consul, while the same evidence has been used to expose the introduction of various other qualifications for an award—such as the stipulation applied to Marcellus that no triumph could be awarded to any commander who had not brought his army back home. But for all the apparent flexibility of this approach ("The actual record demonstrates the Senate had few general principles in this area which it was determined to make stick," as one historian has frankly observed), it still tends to fall back on the language of fixed criteria (even if they were only temporarily fixed). We read, for example, of the "minor *rules*," "certain *requirements*," and "commanders in the field struggling to conform with new *stipulations*."[58]

The truth is that this refreshing emphasis on flexibility does not usually go far enough, nor does it fully reflect the problems of the ancient evidence on which this whole scholarly edifice has been based. It is partly the fact that evidence never quite fits the rules proposed, leading modern scholars to accommodate disjunctions and inconsistencies by postulating some special circumstance, some particular change of policy, or simply disobedience to the law. So, for example, that requirement for a general to bring home his army in order to qualify for a triumph was, we are told, introduced (or at least first heard of) with Marcellus in 211, "dropped" soon after, and "suddenly reappears" in 185. And Mommsen was so confident of the legal framework he had reconstructed for the triumph that he was happy enough to include in it a "rule" that the Romans never strictly enforced.[59] Of course, regulations are not always obeyed, and they may not be systematically applied, but nonetheless there is something decidedly circular about many of these arguments. The whole process is uncomfortably similar to reconstructing the rules of the road from a series of disconnected video-clips of traffic flow and a handful of parking tickets.

There are, however, even more imponderable issues raised by the ancient accounts of triumphal decision-making on which our modern reconstructions of the rules and criteria depend. Livy was writing in the reign of the emperor Augustus, almost two centuries after the major series of triumphal debates he describes. We cannot know whether the different arguments he puts into the mouth of his third- and second-century senators reflect accurately or not the points raised at the time. It would not be impossible for him to have had at least indirect evidence of the tenor and content of such senatorial discussions. But it is much more likely that some element, at least, in his representation of these senatorial sessions derived from his own attempts (or those of his immediate sources) to make sense of the decisions reached.[60]

Like us, Livy may well have been confronted with apparently conflicting and changing practice in the award of triumphs, which he attempted to explain by the arguments from rule, precedent, or political rivalry put into the mouths of his senatorial participants. Why did they decide not to vote a triumph to X? Because he had not brought his army home, because he held an irregular command or fought with an army technically under the control of another . . . and so on. It cannot be irrelevant to this process (and has potentially serious implications for the modern emphasis on *imperium* as the crucial qualification for a triumph) that the period in which Livy was writing was exactly the period when the first emperor was restricting the institution of triumph to include only himself and his family, and may well have been using his own overriding *imperium* as one of the central justifications for that restriction (as we will see in Chapter 9).

Similar problems underlie the attempts of ancient scholars themselves to systematize the triumphal rules. The key text here comes from Valerius Maximus' *Facta et Dicta Memorabilia (Memorable Deeds and Sayings),* a compendium of themed moral and political anecdotes drawn from republican history composed in the reign of the emperor Tiberius. One chapter is concerned specifically with the criteria for celebrating a triumph, including the famous requirement that a minimum of 5,000 of the enemy needed to have been killed in a single battle. This has often been taken as an authoritative guide to "triumphal law."[61] The probability is, however, that Valerius Maximus was operating in much the same way as modern scholars, in extrapolating rules from the various arguments and contradictory practices in republican triumphal history—that he was, in other words, a Mommsen *avant la lettre*. The more we scratch the surface of his rules and regulations, the more fragile they seem.

Valerius' chapter starts with two "laws" *(leges)*. The first is the 5,000-

dead rule. The second, "passed by Lucius Mar[c?]ius and Marcus Cato when they were tribunes," penalized generals who lied about enemy casualties or Roman losses and demanded that "as soon as they enter the city they take an oath before the city quaestors that their dispatches to the senate had been truthful in both these respects." In fact, neither rule is ever explicitly referred to in any account of triumphal debates by any surviving classical author whatsoever. We have no idea at what date the first law, such a favorite of modern discussions, is supposed to have been passed, but its existence is hinted at only once in any other writer. The Christian historian Orosius, discussing in the early fifth century CE the contested triumph of Appius Claudius Pulcher in 143 BCE, claims that he first lost 5,000 of his own men, then killed 5,000 of the enemy. This claim has all the appearance of those favorite (and imaginary) Roman legal conundrums (what do you do about the man who has killed 5,000 of the enemy but has lost exactly the same number of his own men?) and is more likely dependent on Valerius Maximus rather than independent confirmation of his "facts."[62]

The second law certainly reflects the general concern about false reporting evident in the discussions at the time of Cicero's thanksgiving. But it is entirely unattested anywhere else, never appealed to, and raises a host of tricky questions. Where was this swearing supposed to take place, inside or outside the *pomerium?* And if it was a law passed by Cato, is it not strange that neither he nor Cicero made even passing allusion to it in their exchanges over Cicero's triumph?[63]

The rest of Valerius Maximus' chapter is mostly taken up with cases of disputed triumphs and hardly inspires confidence in a clear and agreed upon framework of triumphal law—or, at least, not as he reconstructed it. The first case focuses on the dispute between praetor Quintus Valerius Falto and consul Caius Lutatius Catulus after a naval victory in 242 BCE. Falto had destroyed a Carthaginian fleet off Sicily while Catulus had been resting up, lame, in his litter; and for his success Falto claimed a triumph. Valerius describes a complex (and distinctly implausible) process of legal adjudication, ending up with the decision that Catulus, not Falto, should triumph because he was in overall command. In fact, the list in the Forum attributes a triumph to both generals.[64]

In another case, Valerius Maximus explains the failure of two commanders to secure triumphs for quashing revolts against Rome by reference to a regulation that such honors were awarded only "for adding to the Empire, not for recovering what had been lost." This is "definitely mistaken," as one historian has recently put in, reflecting on the scores of triumphs which, by no stretch of the imagination, celebrated an increase of Roman territory.[65] In yet another example, stressing how "well-guarded" triumphal law was, he examines the refusal of triumphs to Publius Cornelius Scipio Africanus in 206 and Marcus Claudius Marcellus in 211. Strikingly, in explaining the senate's decision to grant Marcellus no more than an ovation, he appeals to a quite different regulation from Livy: while Livy cited the argument that Marcellus had failed to bring his army back home, Valerius put it down to the fact that "he had been sent to conduct operations holding no magistracy."[66]

These contradictions and "mistakes" do not, of course, show that arguments from precedent and "rule" would have played no part in senatorial discussions on the award of triumphs, or that these were not sometimes couched, and perceived by participants at the time, in legal or quasi-legal terms. Unless Livy and Valerius Maximus were writing entirely against the grain of Roman assumptions in their *ex post facto* rationalizing explanations, their appeals to established (or invented) precedent were all very likely the weapons of choice in the contested process of deciding who was, or was not, to triumph—not to mention claims of fair reward for success and the occasional call to adjust tradition to new circumstances.

This was necessarily a shifting set of precedents and arguments. For the senate's job was not to adjudicate whether any particular commander *qualified* for a triumph against a clear framework of prescriptive legal rules. The question before it was whether he should or should not celebrate one on this occasion, in the light of his request, the achievements he reported, and all the particular circumstances. The stakes were high, and there was a repertoire—as time went by, a widening repertoire—of potentially conflicting factors that might steer the senate toward a decision. Precedents could be remembered or forgotten, rules defended, invented, adjusted, or discarded, and political partisanship dressed up as principle. This is a far cry from the systematization of "triumphal law" imagined by the majority of modern scholars.[67]

Even more important, perhaps, is that fact that Livy (especially) suggests a much more varied set of criteria and a wider range of dilemmas facing the senate than is usually recognized—and indeed closer to some of the issues prominent in the triumphal correspondence of Cicero. Much as they have replayed Cato's sound-bite on the relationship of the triumph and thanksgiving, modern legally inclined historians have tended to lay enormous emphasis on the occasional claims in Livy's triumphal debates that might pass as a rule or firm principle: "It was established that up to that time no one had triumphed whose successes had been achieved without a magistracy," or "The reason for refusing him a triumph was that he had fought under another person's auspices, in another person's province."[68] In doing so, they have often failed to pay attention to the more general texture of Livy's discussions and to those less obviously "legal" issues that he presents as central to the debates and decision-making.

The first of these is the question of responsibility and achievement. The priority of Livy's senate is to reward the man responsible for scoring a decisive success on behalf of Rome, or—where appropriate—to divide the honor of a triumph fairly between two commanders.[69] The dilemma it repeatedly faces is how to make a decision on those terms, particularly in the complicated, messy, and unprecedented situations that war threw up. True, the technical issue of *imperium* is relevant here. It was one potential guarantee of where ultimate command lay, and it ensured that the victory was achieved by an official acting for the Roman state (the triumph was not intended to reward private brigandage, however many barbarians might have been killed). In fact, the majority of Roman commanders in major military engagements during the Republic did possess *imperium*—and so, therefore, did the majority of those who triumphed.

But Livy also depicts his senators grappling with more practical and awkward considerations. For example, when they decided to award a triumph to the praetor Lucius Furius Purpureo in 200, despite the fact that he had not brought his army back home and that, in any case, the army was technically under the command of an absent consul, one of the factors they were said to have borne in mind was simply "what he had achieved." That was just the argument Livy later put into the mouth of Cnaeus Manlius Vulso, who triumphed in 187. While his opponents accused him of illegal war-mongering, he rested his (successful) defense on the idea of military necessity and the outstanding results of his actions.[70] Who was actually in command could be a more pressing and complicated question than asking who had formal authority.[71]

Likewise the question of what counted as a decisive Roman success could be trickier than either simply counting up the casualties or checking that war had been properly declared. Livy himself gives us a glimpse of one of the surprising limit cases here, when he records what he calls the first triumph awarded "without a war being fought." The consuls Marcus Baebius Tamphilus and Publius Cornelius Cethegus had in 180 marched against the Ligurians, who had promptly surrendered; and the whole population of about 40,000 men (plus women and children) was resettled away from their mountain strongholds, thus bringing the war to an end.[72] Livy does not on this occasion script any senatorial debate on the consuls' triumph, but Cato's stress on the "principles of government" rather than brute conquest would surely have been one of the relevant considerations here.

More striking still is Livy's portrayal of the senate's concern with obtaining proof of the victory claimed, and their repeated anxiety over how competing claims might be adjudicated. In the case of Purpureo's triumph, he reports that some senior senators wished to postpone a decision until the consul returned to Rome, since "when they had heard the consul and praetor debating face to face, they would be able to judge the issue more accurately." And indeed, he claims, when the consul did finally return to Rome, he protested that they had heard only one side of the case, as even the soldiers (as "witnesses of the achievements") had been absent.[73] Just three years later, in 197 BCE, a triumph was refused to

Quintus Minucius Rufus, who had reputedly fabricated the surrender of a few towns and villages "with no proof."[74]

In 193 Livy stages a much more elaborate dispute over a celebration claimed by Lucius Cornelius Merula. The senatorial vote was postponed because of a clash of evidence: Merula's dispatches were contradicted by the account of his military campaigns in letters written "to a large proportion of the senators" by Marcus Claudius Marcellus, an ex-consul, serving as one of Merula's legates, and it was felt that the disagreements ought to be resolved with both men present.[75] To be sure, we have no means of knowing how far these issues presented by Livy accurately reflected the concerns of the senatorial debates at the time. Yet accurate or not, it is arresting to look beyond Livy's nuggets of apparent legalism and to find his senators facing very similar issues to those faced by Cicero's colleagues—stories about military victories that were not entirely trustworthy and a flood of letters from one of the interested parties.[76]

ON WANTING OR NON-WANTING A TRIUMPH

There is, however, a twist in the stories of the victorious commander's campaign for a triumph—a campaign that Livy once archly insinuated might be the cause of "greater strife than the war itself." Many of the moral lessons pointed by Roman writers at the eager general do indeed stress the dangers of wanting a triumph too much and the virtue of a certain reluctance to grab the honor. "The prospect of a triumph" (*spes triumphi*) was one thing; and indeed "trying out the prospect of a triumph" was a regular way of expressing the general's proper petition to the senate. Being seen to be too eager for the honor was quite another. Cicero was not the only one who criticized *cupiditas triumphi*. Livy, for example, scripts a tribune in 191 BCE objecting to an immediate triumphal celebration for Publius Cornelius Scipio Nasica on the grounds that "in his rush for a triumph" he had lost sight of his military priorities. The desire for true glory was, in other words, different from a hankering after its baubles.[77]

The impact of such triumph-hunting, and of the senate's desire to curb it, on what we might now call Roman "foreign policy" is clear enough. On the one hand, there was a repeated pressure to pick up easy victories wherever they might be found, so further driving Roman conquest. On the other, it is a fair guess that one of the factors that lay behind the senate's decision to offer alliances to various peoples in the mid to late Republic was—if not to protect them from their own generals on the look out for a triumph—at least to attempt to limit the excesses of such triumph-hunting. Not necessarily successfully: Roman generals were perfectly capable of attacking those who were not Rome's enemies, or those who had come to terms with Rome.[78]

But at the same time, on the individual level, there were dangers in being seen *not* to want a triumph. In Rome no less than other societies, the rejection of such marks of honor might not only signal high-minded disinterest in the insubstantial trinkets of public acclaim; it might also imply a disdain for the system of values and priorities that those "trinkets" legitimated. To put it another way, if true honor goes to those who have turned down a triumph, where does that leave those who have celebrated one? This dilemma is nicely captured by two very different tales of triumphs refused told by, again, Livy and Valerius Maximus.

The first is the story of the consul Marcus Fabius Vibulanus, who supposedly turned down a triumph that was spontaneously offered to him by the senate after a victory in 480 BCE, because both the other consul and his own brother had been lost in the fighting. "He would not, he said, accept laurel blighted with public and private grief. No triumph ever celebrated was more renowned than this triumph refused."[79] The opposite lesson is drawn by Valerius Maximus in another case history in his chapter on "triumphal law." It concerns one Cnaeus Fulvius Flaccus, who "spurned and rejected the honor of a triumph, so sought after by others, when it was decreed to him by the senate for his successes." We know nothing else of this incident, nor can we plausibly identify or date the commander concerned. But Valerius insists that he was suitably punished for his disdain of the prize: "In his refusal he anticipated no more than what actually came about. For when he entered the city, he was instantly convicted in a public trial and punished with exile. So, if he broke the religious law by his arrogance, he expiated the offence with the penalty."[80]

This theme is explored at much greater length and complexity in Cicero's speech *In Pisonem (Against Piso),* the written up and no doubt reworked version of his attack on Lucius Calpurnius Piso delivered in the senate in August 55 BCE. From Cicero's point of view, Piso's main claim to infamy lay in the fact that he had been consul in 58, the year in which Cicero had been sent into exile, but the speech, as published, is a comprehensive attack on Piso's character, his Epicurean philosophical interests, and his political career—including his governorship of the province of Macedonia, from where he had only just returned. This province was, in Cicero's bald phrase, more "triumphable" *(triumphalis)* than any other, implying a ranking of imperial territory according to how likely (or not) it was to produce a triumph for its elite Roman masters.[81]

So far as we can tell through the dense fog of Cicero's oratory, Piso had had a very successful tenure: he had secured a considerable victory against Thracian tribesmen, and had been hailed "Imperator" by his troops.[82] Cicero, of course, denigrates. After a litany of typically baroque, if unspecific, accusations of sacrilege, murder, extortion, and robbery, he claims that Piso was not even present at the crucial battle (another case where the senate might have found assigning responsibility tricky).[83] But even more venom is reserved for Piso's return to Italy, a pointed contrast with Cicero's own return home from exile. Whereas Cicero came back to what was almost, even if he does not use the word itself, a triumph or "a sort of immortality," Piso did not even ask for a triumph, despite his supposed victory and acclamation as *imperator.* Over what is now several pages of written invective, Cicero pokes fun and spite at that refusal, exposing in the process some crucial tensions in the idea of "triumph-seeking."[84]

At one point Cicero ventriloquizes Piso's objections to triumphal honors. It is, of course, a nasty parody and rests on a crude misrepresentation of Epicurean views on the undesirability of worldly glory and fame, and on the importance of physical pleasure.[85] But it is nevertheless the only glimpse we have of what the views of a triumphal *refusenik* might be (as well as being—although this has almost never been recognized—the only republican summary of the ceremony that we have):

> What is the use of that chariot? What of the generals in chains before the chariot? What of the model towns? What of the gold? What of the silver? What of the lieutenants on horseback and the tribunes? What of the cheering of the soldiers? What of the whole ostentatious parade? It is mere vanity, I assure you, the trifling pleasure one might almost say of children, to hunt applause, to drive through the city, to want to be noticed. In none of this is there anything substantial to get hold of, nothing you can associate with bodily pleasure.[86]

But no less striking is Cicero's framing of the opposite side of the argument. Far from distancing himself from "triumphal eagerness," he in fact elevates *cupiditas triumphi* to a leading principle of Roman public life. In fact, more than that—a triumph is the single most approved driving force in a man's career, the acceptable face of other less acceptable ambitions:

> I have often noticed that those who seemed to me and others to be rather too keen on being assigned a province tend to conceal and cloak their desire under the pretext of wanting a triumph. This is exactly what Decius Silanus used to say in the senate, even what my colleague used to say. In fact, it is impossible for anyone to desire an army command and openly canvas for it, without using eagerness for a triumph as a pretext.[87]

And he goes on to praise Lucius Crassus, who "went through the Alps with a magnifying glass" looking for a triumph-worthy conflict where there was no enemy, and Gaius Cotta, who "burned with similar desires" although he also was unable to find a proper opponent. But irony is an even sharper weapon. Poor old Pompey, "He really has made a mistake," he sighs at one point. "He never had the appetite for your sort of philosophy. The fool has already triumphed three times." As for "the likes of Camillus, Curius, Fabricius, Calatinus, Scipio, Marcellus, Maximus," he thunders, listing an honorable clutch of famous triumphing generals, "Fools the lot of you!"[88]

Different circumstances inevitably call for different arguments. No doubt Cicero could have been equally, but quite differently, devastating if the target of his invective had been a man who was lingering outside the *pomerium,* plus army and lictors with their fading laurel, just waiting for the senate to say yes. But the cultural logic of Cicero's case against Piso is nevertheless striking. Why was Piso's disdain for triumph-seeking a powerful rhetorical weapon? Why the insistence here on *cupiditas triumphi* as a positive force? There were presumably immediate rhetorical factors to be considered. Cicero was playing to the assumptions about triumphal ambitions among his listeners, and later readers. If the majority of the senate shared aspirations for triumphal glory, to mock someone who did not share those aspirations would have been as distancing of Piso as it was bonding for the collectivity. Who did Cicero wish to seem more ridiculous? Those keen characters who hoped that even an unlikely backwater of the Alps might allow them to follow in the triumphal footsteps of the heroes of the past? Or the triumphal *refusenik,* Piso? Piso, of course.

Yet this hints a broader structural point too. What Cicero implies by his attack on Piso is that the desire for a triumph played an important role in the structural cohesion of the Roman political and military elite. For all the elegant denial of excessive desire for such rewards that Cicero and others might on occasion display, the shared goal of triumphal glory was one of the mechanisms through which the ambitions of the elite were framed and regulated. A rash of trivial triumph-hunting was much less dangerous to the collectivity than a rash of men choosing to disdain the traditional goals and the procedures through which they were policed. It is, in fact, a powerful marker of the end of the competitive politics of the Republic that the first emperor, Augustus, is able not only to monopolize triumphal glory to himself and his family but also to turn repeated triumphal refusal into a positive political stance.

Playing God

TRIUMPHATOR?

Some years before the fragments of the triumphal *Fasti* were excavated from the Roman Forum and installed in the Palazzo dei Conservatori on the Capitoline hill, another major triumphal monument had been put on display in the same building. This was a large marble sculptured panel, measuring three and a half by almost two and a half meters, depicting the second-century emperor Marcus Aurelius, attended by a figure of Victory, in a triumphal chariot drawn by four horses (Fig. 31). It was usually assumed to represent his triumph of 176 CE. Long part of the decoration of the small church of Santa Martina at the northwestern end of the Forum, it was removed in 1515 to the courtyard of the Palazzo dei Conservatori, along with two other matching panels, one depicting the emperor receiving the submission of barbarians, the other showing him performing sacrifice. In 1572 all three were installed indoors, on the landing of the monumental staircase, where they remain to this day.[1]

They are an intensely controversial group of sculptures. Debates have raged for well over a hundred years on many aspects of their history and archaeology: from the precise identification of the events depicted, to the style and location of the monument from which they came.[2] But the

FIGURE 31: The triumph of Marcus Aurelius, one of a series of panels from a lost monument in honor of the emperor, 176–80 CE. The vacant space in front of Marcus was once occupied by his son Commodus, who was erased after his assassination in 192 (and the lower left-hand corner of the temple in the background awkwardly extended).

sense in which this triumphal panel captured the idea of "triumph" is clear enough. In contrast to those few surviving ancient representations that attempted to encompass the procession as a whole, this image trades on an emblematic shorthand for the ceremony that is still familiar from many sculptures and literally thousands of Roman coins—and in antiquity would have been even more, perhaps oppressively, familiar as the standard theme of the free-standing sculptural groups that once stood on top of commemorative arches, dominating the imperial cityscape.[3] This is the triumph seen without the paraphernalia of prisoners, booty, paintings, and models but instead pared down to the figure of the triumphing general, aloft on his chariot, accompanied by only his closest entourage, divine and human. The image more or less conflates the ceremony of triumph with the triumphing general himself; or—to use for once the favored modern term, which I have otherwise deliberately avoided (largely because it is not attested in surviving Latin before the second century CE)—the image conflates the triumph with the *triumphator*.[4]

A BUMPY RIDE

In this scene, the triumphant emperor stands against a background of a temple and an awkwardly attenuated arch. Various attempts have been made to identify these buildings and so, of course, to support different theories on the triumphal route.[5] But to attempt to read this visual evocation of triumphal topography literally is probably to miss the point. The image itself hints otherwise—with its team of horses that simultaneously turns through and swerves away from the arch, the *fasces* that signify magisterial authority not carried, as they would have been, at the ceremony itself but etched into the pillar of the arch, and the magnificent trumpet which, impossibly, fills the whole passageway.

The viewer is being prompted to remember this ceremony as one embedded in the cityscape, rather than to pinpoint any particular stage of the procession, and—no less important—to recapture the sounds of its musical accompaniment. We cannot know how musicians were deployed through the parade (and they are certainly not so prominent in the sculptures of the complete procession as they are here). But ancient writers do sometimes imagine trumpets "leading the way" or "blaring around" the general, and Appian refers to a "a chorus of lyre players and pipers" in the parade.[6] In fact, a rare republican representation of a triumphal procession—a little-known and frankly unprepossessing fragment of relief sculpture from Pesaro—depicts a trio of two pipers and a lyre player in front of what appears to be a group of barbarian prisoners (hence the identification as a triumph).[7]

On the Capitoline panel, Marcus Aurelius rides in a lavishly decorated chariot—the figures have been identified as Neptune, Minerva, and the divine personification of Rome—beneath a pair of Victories holding a shield that is largely hidden behind the horse. As usual, the practical details are as elusive as they are intriguing. Most representations of a triumph depict a chariot of very much this design: two large wheels, high suspension, tall sides, with a curved front and open back, often richly ornamented. This tallies well enough with Dio's claim, as reported at least in Byzantine paraphrase, that it was "like a round tower." Dio also insists that the triumphal chariot proper did not resemble the version used in warfare or in games.

If he is correct (by Dio's time chariots had played no part in regular Roman warfare for centuries), it is far from clear when the chariot took on its recognizable form and distinctively ceremonial character, and what the implications of that were for its manufacture and possible reuse.[8] Were triumphal chariots in Rome stored away, ready to be brought out again next time? Or if they were made specially for each occasion, what happened to them when the ceremony was over? One of the few hints we have comes from accounts of Nero's quasi-triumph in 67 CE for his athletic and artistic victories on the Greek festival circuit: both Suetonius and Dio claim that he rode in the very triumphal chariot that Augustus had used to celebrate his military victories.[9]

What is clear is that these chariots must have offered the general an uncomfortable ride. This did not escape the notice of J. C. Ginzrot, the author—some two centuries ago—of one of the most thorough studies ever of ancient chariots, who used his rare practical expertise as "Inspector of Carriage-Building at the Bavarian Court" to throw light on the Roman traditions. It would have been very difficult, he pointed out, after a careful study of the surviving images, to keep upright all day in such a means of transport: whatever the upholstery, the passenger would be standing directly over the axle and, without the possibility of sitting down, "the jolting would have been almost intolerable for the elderly."[10] Ginzrot was in part echoing the sentiments of Vespasian after his triumph of 71. According to Suetonius, the emperor, "exhausted by the slow and tiresome procession," made one of his famous down-to-earth quips: "I've got my come-uppance for being so stupid as to long for a triumph in my old age."[11]

Yet this bumpy vehicle was one of the most richly symbolic of all the triumphing general's accessories. However cheap, everyday, or do-it-yourself the reality may often have been, in their mind's eye ancient writers as well as artists repeatedly imagined the triumphal chariot in extravagant terms. It was not only Ovid's triumphant Cupid who was said to ride in a chariot of gold. Other poets and historians play up the exquisite decoration and precious materials: Pompey's chariot in 61, for example, was pictured as "studded with gems"; Aemilius Paullus was said to have ridden "in an astonishing chariot of ivory"; Livy's roster of the honors associated with a triumph includes a "gilded chariot" (or perhaps "inlaid with gold").[12] In fact, second only to "laurel," the word "chariot" *(currus)* was often used as a shorthand for the ceremony as a whole, and the honor it implied. "What good did the *chariots* of my ancestors do me?" asks the shade of Cornelia from beyond the grave, in one of Propertius' poems—meaning "What good did their *triumphs* do?" as they could not save her from death.[13]

But more than that, the physical image of the chariot was itself conscripted into those Roman ethical debates on the nature of triumphal glory and the conditions of true triumphal honor. In a particularly memorable passage at the start of his *Facta et Dicta Memorabilia (Memorable Deeds and Sayings)*, Valerius Maximus tells the story of the flight of the Vestal Virgins from Rome in 390 BCE, when the city had been captured by the Gauls. Weighed down with all the sacred objects they were rescuing from the enemy, the Virgins were given a lift to safety in the town of Caere by a local farmer, who ("as public religion was more important to him than private affection") had turfed his wife and daughter out of his wagon to make room for the priestesses and their precious cargo. So it came about that the "rustic cart of theirs, dirty as it

was . . . equaled or even surpassed the glory of the most brilliant triumphal chariot you could imagine."[14] Again, as so often in triumphal culture, we are being asked to reflect on the different forms that honor and
glory might take.

However difficult the ride may have been, there is something even
more decidedly awkward about the pose of the passengers in Marcus
Aurelius' triumphal chariot. The winged Victory, who in visual images
usually took the place of the slave that is such a favorite of modern
scholars, was originally holding a garland above the emperor's head—as
the trace of a ribbon still hanging from her left hand shows. But she
is precariously balanced, not to say uncomfortably squashed, behind
the emperor, despite the fact that there is plenty of space in front of
him. This is because, as other marks on the stone (and the unsatisfac-
tory reworking of the lower left-hand side of the temple) indicate, another, smaller passenger once stood in the chariot whose figure has been
erased.[15]

It seems to have been, or become, the custom that the general's
young children should travel in the chariot with him, or, if they were
older, to ride horses alongside. We have already seen Germanicus sharing his chariot in 17 CE with five offspring. Appian claims that Scipio
in 201 BCE was accompanied by "boys and girls," while Livy laments
the fact that in 167 BCE Aemilius Paullus' young sons could not—
through death or sickness—travel with him, "planning similar triumphs for themselves" (a nice interpretation of the ceremony as a
prompt to ambition and a spur to the continuation of family glory).[16]
Notably, the newly discovered monument from the battlesite of Actium depicting the triumph of 29 BCE shows two children, a boy and
a girl, beside the figure of Octavian (Augustus). The excavator is determined to see in these figures the two children of Cleopatra by Mark
Antony, Cleopatra Selene and Alexander Helios.[17] But Roman tradition would strongly suggest that they were the children or young relatives of the triumphing general himself. If, as Suetonius claims, Tiberius and Marcellus rode alongside Octavian's chariot on horseback,
then the slightly younger Julia and Drusus (the offspring respectively of

Octavian and Livia from their first marriages) are the most likely candidates.[18]

On the Aurelian panel, the erased figure must have been Marcus Aurelius' son, the future emperor Commodus (aged fifteen in 176 and hailed *imperator* for victories over the Germans and Sarmatians along with his father). Coins and medallions show him sharing the chariot.[19] Here, he was presumably deleted after his assassination in 192 CE. This is a pointed reminder not only of the uncertainties in the transmission of triumphal glory but also of the risks that might lurk in the permanent memorialization of such a dynastic triumph. In this image, the awkwardly vacant chariot acts as a continuing reminder of the figure which had been obliterated.

DRESSED DIVINE?

The triumphant emperor here cuts a sober figure. He looks studiously ahead, dressed, so far as we can see, in a simple toga. Though a military ceremony in many respects, there is no sign that the general ever appeared in military garb. Quite the reverse: his war was over. What Marcus Aurelius originally held in his hands on this panel we cannot know. The right hand with its short staff is a much later restoration, and the left has lost whatever it once contained—so giving perhaps a misleadingly plain, uncluttered impression of his accessories. More significantly, however, there is no indication whatsoever of the flamboyant colors and idiosyncrasies of the general's clothes and "make-up" that were noted by ancient writers and have been the subject of intense modern interest.

Of course, the plain marble of the sculpture would not have been the best medium to capture any gaudy display. Paint might have compensated; but if it was ever applied to this stone, no trace of it remains. In fact, this is another case where we find a striking disjunction between visual and literary evidence for the ceremony. In no surviving image of a triumphal procession (unless we fancy that some barely detectable patterning on Tiberius' toga on the Boscoreale cup is meant to indicate the elaborate *toga picta*) do we see anything like the fancy dress that the general is supposed to have sported.[20]

We would certainly never guess from this particular sculpture that the general's costume had been the crucial factor in launching certainly the most dramatic and probably the most influential theory in the whole of modern triumphal scholarship: namely, that the victorious commander impersonated the god Jupiter Optimus Maximus himself, and that for his triumph he became (or at least was dressed as) "god for a day." We have already noted the implications of divinity in the words whispered by the slave. Even clearer signs of super-human status have been detected in the general's outfit. The red-painted face, mentioned by Pliny, is supposed to have echoed the face of the terracotta cult statue of Jupiter in his Capitoline temple (which was periodically coated with red cinnabar). What is more, Livy on one occasion expressly states that the triumphing general ascended to the Capitol "adorned in the clothes of Jupiter Optimus Maximus."[21]

Unsurprisingly, this view was enthusiastically promoted by the founding father of anthropology, J. G. Frazer, who saw in the figure of the general welcome confirmation of his own theory of primitive divine kingship. Once you have recognized that the general was the direct descendant of the early Italic kings, he argued, then it was obvious (to Frazer, at least) that those kings had been in Frazerian terms "gods."[22] But radical recent theorists of religious representation have also stressed the godlike aspects of the costume and have seen in the general a characteristically Roman attempt to conceptualize the divine. As one argument runs, the general oscillated between divine and human status through the course of the procession; he constituted both a living image of the god himself and, simultaneously, a negation of the divine presence (hence the slave's words).[23]

These arguments have not been without their critics. The early years of the twentieth century saw some fierce (even if not entirely persuasive) challenges to the whole idea of the divine general. Sheer absurdity was one objection—even though absurdity in not necessarily a significant stumbling block in matters of religious truth. If the general was really seen as the god Jupiter, it was argued, why on earth would he ride in procession to his own temple to make offerings to himself? Another was a perceived discrepancy between the general's attributes and the god's. Why, in particular, did he have no thunderbolt, when that was the defining symbol of Jupiter? One partisan even went so far as to throw down a challenge: "If anyone can produce a coin or other work of art on which he [the general] is represented as holding the thunderbolt, I should at once reconsider the whole question." No one could. And there was also a rival explanation for the costume waiting in the wings—the symbolism and dress associated with early Etruscan kings of Rome. Dionysius of Halicarnassus, for example, refers to the marks of sovereignty said to have been offered by ambassadors from Etruria to King Tarquin: "a gold crown . . . an eagle-topped scepter, a purple tunic sewn with gold, an embroidered purple robe." These not only include several elements with an obvious triumphal resonance; but he goes on explicitly to note the continued use of such objects by those "deemed worthy of a triumph."[24]

The current orthodoxy has been reached by combining these two positions. In his 1970 study, *Triumphus,* H. S. Versnel, by an elegant theoretical maneuver (or clever sleight of hand, depending on your point of view), argued that the general represented *both* god *and* king. In any case, as he pointed out, the iconography of Jupiter was inextricable from (and partly derived from) the insignia of the early Etruscan monarchy, and vice versa. Versnel was drawing on the then fashionable scholarly ideas of "ambivalence" and "interstitiality" and, partly for that reason, found a ready and appreciative audience among specialists. At almost exactly the same moment, L. Bonfante Warren reached a not wholly dissimilar conclusion by a different route. She too accepted that the figure of the general showed characteristics both of the Etruscan kings and of super-human divinity (after the model of Jupiter himself). But she explained these different aspects by the historical development of the ceremony itself. The insignia of the Etruscan kings could be traced back to the Etruscan period of the triumph's history; the idea of divinity, she argued, entered under Greek influence at a later period, perhaps around the third century BCE. Thereafter they coexisted.[25]

Most modern studies, whatever other influences or historical developments they detect and whatever explanation they offer, have supported the basic idea that the triumphing general shared divine characteristics. I too shall be returning to the links between the general and the gods, but not before taking a harder look at the evidence for this famous costume. For its character and appearance, never mind its interpretation, turn out to be more elusive than is usually supposed.

For Romans, triumphal costume certainly conjured up an image in purple and gold. These colors are consistently stressed in ancient accounts of the ceremony and are so closely linked with the figure of the general that writers can describe him simply as "purple," "golden," or "purple-and-gold."[26] We also find a clear assumption in ancient authors that the general's ceremonial dress did represent a distinctive, special, and recognizable ensemble. Marius, for example, caused offense by wearing his *triumphalis vestis* (triumphal clothes) in the senate; and, as we shall see, there are several references to specific elements of this constume such as the *toga picta*.[27] But how far there was ever a fixed triumphal uniform, let alone how it changed over time, is a much more debatable point. As with our own wedding dress, a basic template can allow, and even encourage, significant variations. Pompey, after all, was reputed to have worn the cloak of Alexander the Great at his triumph in 61—which can hardly have been part of the traditional garb.

The truth is that, despite our own fascination with the topic, ancient writers do not often pay more than passing attention to what the general wore, and we have no detailed description (reliable or not) of any individual general's outfit as a whole, still less of any regular, prescribed costume; and the surviving images are for the most part as unspecific as the Aurelian panel.[28] The modern textbook reconstruction of the general's ceremonial kit—*toga picta* and *tunica palmata* ("a tunic embroidered with palms"), the variety of wreaths, the amulet round his neck, plus iron ring, red face, eagle-topped scepter, armlets, laurel, and palm branches—is another of those optimistic compilations.[29] Take a more careful look and you find glaring contradictions or, at the very least, a suspiciously overdressed general.

So, for example, the only way to come close to deriving a coherent picture out of the different crowns and wreaths associated with the triumph is to have the general wear not one but two: a heavy gold crown held above his head by the slave and a laurel wreath worn directly on his head beneath it (although this is certainly not how visual images normally depict him, and even in this reconstruction the term *corona triumphalis,* "triumphal crown," must refer on different occasions to different types of headgear).[30]

Similar problems arise with the ceremonial toga. Leaving aside Festus' brave attempt to trace a historical development from a plain purple garment to an embroidered *(picta)* one, the regular modern pairing of a *tunica palmata* under a *toga picta* is not quite as regular in ancient writing as we might be tempted to assume. Both Martial and Apuleius, for example, refer to a *toga* (not a *tunica) palmata.* Was it simply, as one careful modern critic is driven to conclude, that "in the principate the terminology became less precise"?[31] And what did these "palmed" garments look like anyway? Festus does not make it any easier when he asserts that "the *tunica palmata* used to be so termed from the breadth of the stripes [presumably a palm's breadth], but is now called after the type of decoration [palms]."[32]

The exact nature of his divine costume also proves puzzling. It is true that Livy refers to "the clothes of Jupiter Optimus Maximus," and a few other writers, albeit less directly, appear to chime in.[33] But what would this mean? Clothes like those worn by Jupiter? Clothes kept in the Temple of Jupiter? Or the very clothes worn by (the statue of) Jupiter in his temple on the Capitoline? This most extreme option appears to be supported by one piece of evidence: a very puzzling passage in a tract of Tertullian that briefly discusses "Etruscan crowns," the name Pliny gave to the gold wreath held over the triumphing general's head. The text of the original Latin is far from certain, but it is often taken to mean something like: "This is the name given to those famous crowns, made with precious stones and golden oak leaves, *which they take from Jupiter,* along with togas embroidered with palms, for conducting the procession to the games." Tertullian is not talking about a triumph here, but on the assumption that the practice at the games was more or less the same as at the triumph, this might confirm the view that the general's crown and toga were taken directly from (the statue of) Jupiter—that, in other words, the general literally dressed up in the god's clothes.[34]

It does nothing of the sort. Even supposing that Tertullian knew what he was talking about, he was almost certainly not intending to suggest that the costume was lifted from Jupiter's statue; his Latin much more plausibly means that the crowns were "famous because of their connection with Jupiter." In any case, the idea that the general donned Jupiter's kit causes far more practical difficulties than it solves. Never mind the one-size-fits-all model of triumphal outfitting, or the problems that would have been caused by two generals (such as Titus and Vespasian in 71) triumphing simultaneously. Even harder to accept is the unlikely idea, which direct borrowing from the statue necessarily implies, that all the various cult images of Jupiter that replaced one another over the long and eventful history of the Capitoline temple were constructed on a human scale.[35]

There is also the problem of the wider use of triumphal dress. If the general's costume was properly returned to the god's statue at the end of the parade, then what did Marius wear to give offense in the senate? What was it that was worn by those who impersonated their triumphal ancestors in funeral parades? What were the triumphal togas that Lucan imagined were consumed on Pompey's funeral pyre?[36] Perhaps these were all "copies" of the original garments (as some have been forced to argue); but that itself would dilute the idea of a single set of triumphal clothes and insignia belonging to Jupiter's statue, or even lodged in his temple. Precise questions of how the general's costume was commissioned, chosen, made, stored, handed down, or reused are now impossible to answer. But there is certainly no good reason to think of it as literally borrowed from Jupiter—nor any evidence that Livy's phrase *ornatus Iovis* or "clothes of Jupiter" (though widely used as a technical term in modern studies of the triumph) was ever regularly used for triumphal costume in Latin.[37]

The same is true of other features that are taken to link the general's appearance to the gods. One particularly seductive false lead is the general's red-painted face. Our main information on this custom comes, as so often, from the elder Pliny, apparently backed up by a handful of late antique writers—who might all, in fact, be directly or indirectly dependent on Pliny himself. The passage in question is at the start of his discussion of the uses of red lead or cinnabar, and he offers an unusually guarded, self-confessedly third-hand account, explicitly derived from reports in an earlier first-century antiquarian writer, Verrius Flaccus:

> Verrius gives a list of authorities—and trust them we must—who state that on festival days it used to be the custom for the face of the statue of Jupiter to be coated with cinnabar, so too the bodies of those in triumph. They also state that Camillus triumphed in this way, and that it was according to the same observance that even in their day it was added to the unguents at a triumphal banquet and that one of the first responsibilities of the censors was to place the contract for coloring Jupiter with cinnabar. The origin of this custom, I must say, baffles me.[38]

Pliny does not vouch for this practice himself, nor claim that it took place in his day, or even in Verrius'. But this has not stopped (indeed, it has encouraged) generations of modern critics from basing extravagant theories on it—partly in the belief, no doubt, that Pliny's sources are taking us back to the raw primitive heart of triumphal practice, or somewhere near it.

For many, the key lies in the equivalence that may be hinted in Pliny's text between the cult image of Jupiter and the general. At its strongest, this has been taken to indicate that the general did not so much impersonate a god as impersonate a statue (so launching theories that link the origin of the triumph with the origin of commemorative statuary).[39] For others, the color itself has prompted a variety of (sub-)anthropological speculations: that, for example, the face-painting was an apotropaic device to frighten off the spirits of the conquered dead; or that it was an

imitation of blood—and indeed that "it was not red paint at all originally, but blood" intended to transfer the *mana* ("life force" or "power"
in Austronesian terms) of the enemy to the victorious general.[40]

In fact, the tenuous evidence we have hardly supports the idea that
the triumphing general's face, or body for that matter, was regularly
colored red, or that there was a well-established association between
the general and the statue of Jupiter (or the statue of anyone else). In
fact, the cult image on the Capitoline can hardly have been made of
terracotta after 83 BCE, when the archaic temple was completely destroyed, and so would not then have required the treatment with cinnabar that Pliny describes. At the very most, from the early first century,
the general would have been imitating a previous version of the cult
statue that no longer existed.[41]

Of course, we always run the risk of normalizing the Romans, of
too readily erasing behavior that seems, in our terms, impossibly weird
or archaic. Painted faces may perhaps have been a standard feature of
early triumphs, and we cannot definitively rule out the practice at any
point. Nonetheless, my guess is that there is no particular need to see red
on the face of any of the late republican or early imperial generals.
Aemilius Paullus, Pompey, and Octavian did not necessarily ride in triumph smeared with cinnabar.

The problem we are confronting here is not just the fragility of the
evidence, or its over-enthusiastic interpretation, though that is part of it.
It is equally a question, as the various interpretations of the red face vividly illustrate, of the fixation of modern scholars with explaining the individual elements in the ceremony by reference to the customs and symbols of primitive Rome. Few historians of the triumph have been able to
resist the attraction of the obscure origins of the ceremony—whether
that means detecting in the general a hangover of the god-kings of
"Frazer-land," a descendant of the rulers of the early Etruscan city, or
even an embodiment of primitive conceptualizations of the divine. The
rarely stated truth is that we have no reliable evidence at all for what
early triumphing generals wore and not much more for the costume of
the Etruscan kings of the city.

The Romans themselves were equally ill-informed. True, "Etruscan origins" were one of the most convenient recourses they had when explaining puzzling features of their own culture. But we certainly should not assume that they were correct. What is more, at least from the period of Julius Caesar on (as we shall explore in the next chapter), they were busy confusing such issues even further by seeking precedents and models for the increasingly dynastic attire of their political leaders not just in triumphal costume but also in their imaginative reconstruction of early regal outfits. The confident statements of Dionysius of Halicarnassus and others about Etruscan symbols of monarchy may possibly be a product of some archaeological knowledge; but they are much more likely to be the outcome of this politically loaded combination of antiquarian fantasy and invented tradition.[42]

For the most part, long as its history is, the triumph does not give us a clear window onto the primitive customs of Rome—nor, conversely, can its features simply be explained by retreating to the religious and political culture of the early city.

MAN OR GOD?

By contrast, what we do know is that there were strong links between the triumphing general and those contested ideas of deity and deification that were so high on the cultural and political agenda of the late Republic and early Empire. These connections are often passed over, if not lost, in the preoccupation with the ritual's prehistory, but they offer us a much surer point of entry to the intriguing evidence we have.

The power of late republican dynasts and of the early imperial family was often represented in divine terms. Human success and its accompanying glory could push a mortal toward and even across the permeable boundary which, for the Romans, separated men from gods. This was seen in many different ways—from metaphors of power that implicitly identified the individual with the gods to, eventually, the institutional structure of cult and worship that delivered more or less explicit divine honors to both dead and living emperors. So far as we can tell, Roman thinkers and writers took the idea of deification (that is, of a human being literally becoming a god) with no greater equanimity than we do ourselves. The nature of the "divine human" was constantly debated, recalibrated, negotiated, and ridiculed. Emperors drew back from claiming the role and privileges of gods as enthusiastically as they basked in divine worship. The dividing line between mortality and immortality could be as carefully respected as it was triumphantly crossed. Nonetheless, divine power and status were a measure against which to judge its human equivalents, and a potential goal and ambition for the super-successful.[43]

These debates offer the best context for understanding the special status of the triumphing general. Whatever Livy's phrase *ornatus Iovis* tells us of the regular costume adopted in the ceremony (less than we might hope, as I have already suggested), it certainly shows that Livy could imagine the general in divine terms. But the nuances and implications of that connection with the gods come out more clearly if we look at another element in his retinue—the horses who pulled the triumphal chariot. Again, the appearance of these animals on the Aurelian panel hardly gives the modern viewer any hint of the controversy that has surrounded them, or any hint of what they might imply about the status of the general whom they transport. But ancient literary discussions occasionally lay great emphasis on the different types of beast that might appear in this role and their significance.[44]

All kinds of variants are in fact recorded (the most extravagantly baroque being the mention of stags that supposedly drew the chariot of the emperor Aurelian and then did double duty as sacrificial victims when they reached the Capitol).[45] Modern interest has concentrated, however, on the four white horses which, according to Dio, were decreed to Caesar for his triumphal celebrations of 46 BCE.[46] The fact that chariots drawn by white horses were regularly associated with Jupiter or Sol (the divine Sun) has strongly suggested that Caesar was attempting to claim some such divine status for himself.

Dio does not offer an explanation, nor does he record any reactions to Caesar's team. But there is a striking parallel in accounts of the triumph of Camillus over the Gauls in 396 BCE, where Livy claims that the general aroused considerable popular indignation: "He himself was the most conspicuous object in the procession riding through the city on a chariot harnessed with white horses—an act that seemed not only too autocratic, but also inappropriate for any mortal man. For they took it as sacrilege that the horses put the dictator on a level with Jupiter and Sol, and it was really for this single reason that his triumph was more famous than it was popular." This sentiment is echoed by Plutarch, who asserts (with constructive amnesia, apparently, of Caesar's triumph) that "he harnessed a team of four white horses, mounted the chariot and drove through the city, a thing which no commander has ever done before or since." This story may or may not contain a germ of a "genuine" tradition about Camillus. Who knows? But it is usually assumed that Livy's version was elaborated, if not invented, to provide a precedent for Caesar's actions.[47]

Picking up the cue from Livy and Plutarch, modern writers have tended confidently to assume that "the horses used [in the triumph] were usually dark" and that white animals were therefore a daring innovation. Yet it is not quite so straightforward. For, we have no ancient evidence at all to suggest that a dark color was ever the norm.[48] The only color ever explicitly ascribed to the triumphal horses is white. Propertius, for example, retrojected "four white horses" onto the triumph of Romulus, and Ovid did the same for the triumph of Aulus Postumius Tubertus in 431 BCE. Tibullus too seems to have envisaged his patron Messalla's triumphal chariot in 27 BCE being drawn by "dazzling white horses" (though "sleek" would also be a possible translation), while the younger Pliny implies that white horses were part of the ceremony's standard repertoire.[49] At the same time, these animals clearly did have powerful divine associations—dramatically evidenced when, according to Suetonius, the father of the future emperor Augustus dreamt of his son carried in a triumphal chariot drawn by twelve white horses, wielding the thunderbolt of Jupiter.[50] It is clear too that, as in the stories of Camillus, they could offer a pointed hint of the unacceptable face of (excessive) triumphal glory.

These contradictory indications fit together in a more interesting way than is often recognized. Whatever happened in the early days of triumphal history (and we shall, of course, never know what kind of animals pulled Camillus' chariot, let alone how or why he selected them), from the end of the first century BCE Roman imagination envisaged the general's chariot pulled by white horses. Writers interpreted this both as an embedded part of triumphal tradition stretching back as far as the ceremony itself and as a radical innovation reeking of divine power. By the first century BCE at least the triumph was an institution in which breaking the normal rules of human moderation (and mortal status) could be cast simultaneously as dangerous *and* traditional.

A similar argument may apply to the association of elephants with the general's chariot.[51] We have already reflected on the moral of Pompey's reported failure to squeeze his elephants through one of the gates along his route; it was a piquant warning of the dangers of divine self-aggrandizement. Yet a triumphal chariot pulled by elephants is attested as the theme of the statuary perched on the top of more than one imperial commemorative arch in Rome. The Arch of Titus, for example, appears to have supported one such group (to judge from the bronze elephants apparently found nearby, and restored, in the sixth century CE); the Arch of Domitian celebrated by Martial was capped by another two ("twin chariots numbering many an elephant," as Martial put it); and elephant chariots almost certainly adorned some arches erected in the reign of Augustus (see Fig. 18).[52]

Maybe Roman culture became increasingly tolerant of the blatant use of such extravagant honors; so that what was unacceptable for Pompey was a perfectly acceptable element of display in public monuments less than a century later. But, awkwardly for that view, it is imperial authors, writing more than a century after Pompey's triumph, who transmit to us the carping tales of his ignominy.[53] Much more likely, we are glimpsing again the ambivalence of triumphal glory, which—in the imagination at least—always threatened to undermine the general through the very honors that celebrated him. To contemplate a triumphal chariot drawn by elephants was simultaneously an idea legitimated by the public state monuments of the city of Rome and a step too far.

FIGURE 32: Sculptured panel from vault of the Arch of Titus, early 80s CE, showing the emperor transported to heaven on the back of an eagle. Walking through the arch and looking up, the viewer saw this image of the underbelly of the bird and of Titus, its passenger, peering down to earth. A hint of the association of the triumph with death and deification.

The most astonishing link between the triumph and deification has nothing to do with the costume of the general. It is a rarely noticed sculpture in the vault of the passageway of the Arch of Titus, visible to a spectator who stops between the famous scenes of the triumph over the Jews (see Figs. 8 and 9) and looks up. There you can still just make out from the ground a very strange image (Fig. 32). The eagle of Jupiter is seen as from below, tummy facing us; and peeping over the bird's "shoulders," looking down to earth, is the distinctive face of its passenger. That passenger is Titus himself, whom we must imagine being lifted to heaven after death by the eagle, soaring to join the ranks of the gods. It is, in other words, an image of the process of deification itself. There have been all kinds of interpretations of this: one ingenious (if incorrect) idea was that Titus' cremated remains were in fact laid to rest in the arch's attic, directly above. But most striking of all is the proximity of this image of deification and the triumphal panels themselves; it cannot help but underline the structural connection between the ceremony of triumph and the divine status of the general.[54]

The key fact here is the powerful connection in the late Republic and early Empire between triumphal and divine glory. In various forms and media, the extraordinary public honor granted to the general in a triumph—like other honors at this period—was represented, contested, and debated in divine terms. It may have been, in the case of the triumph, that this exploited and reinterpreted an association between general and Jupiter that stretched back centuries. Yet it is crucial to remember (as we shall see at the end of this chapter) that the earliest evidence to suggest an identification between general and god is an early second-century BCE play of Plautus; and that even those few antiquarian details that survive about his traditional costume and various accoutrements are mediated through—and necessarily to some extent reinterpreted by— the concerns of the late Republic and early Empire. Whatever his primitive origins may have been, the divine general we can still glimpse is essentially a late republican creation.

THE WIDER PICTURE

The general was not on his own among the prisoners and the booty— however splendid his isolation in so many triumphal images. Even in a procession that featured a most impressive array of the conquered enemy, the home team always far outnumbered their adversaries. The triumph was overwhelmingly a Roman show, of Romans to Romans.

We have already glimpsed some of the porters, attendants, musicians, guards, and other officials who carried the spoils, led the animals, played the trumpets, or conducted the prisoners.[55] Around and behind the triumphal chariot (at least as the choreography of the procession is conventionally imagined) were many more, perhaps thousands. In the group most closely linked to the general, ancient writers mention lictors (carrying the *fasces*), military officers, magistrates, even "the whole senate," as well as Roman citizens freed from slavery by whatever successful campaign was being celebrated. On one occasion we read of an adult woman (not merely the young daughters of the general) taking a prominent place in this company: according to Suetonius, at the triumph of the emperor Claudius over Britain in 44 CE, his wife Messalina followed his chariot, riding in a *carpentum* (a covered carriage).[56]

As usual, modern scholars have tended to systematize and to impose a regular pattern onto this group. But there is even less sign here of any rigid template, either of personnel or order, than elsewhere in the procession. A group of Roman citizens rescued from slavery might have been the star feature, in Plutarch's view, of the triumph of Titus Quinctius Flamininus in 194 BCE; but a commander could only rarely have produced such specimens. (Even Flamininus had at first decided not to upset the property rights of their owners, until the Greeks offered to ransom them for a good price.)[57]

There are also awkward contradictions in our evidence. Those, for example, who would infer from some accounts that by the late Republic the city's magistrates or the senate as a group were a standard element in the general's immediate entourage need to explain how this fits with an incident reported for one of Julius Caesar's triumphs: when he was riding past the tribunes' benches, one of them—Pontius Aquila—did not get to his feet; Caesar took it as an insult and is supposed to have shouted "Take the Republic back from me then, Aquila, you tribune!"[58] Tribunes could not have been both sitting on their benches in the Forum and accompanying the procession. Either they were not included in that regular group of magistrates who went with the general or, more likely, they sometimes accompanied the general, sometimes watched the proceedings from their official seats—and sometimes (to be realistic) some of them would have had nothing to do with the show at all. An appropriate entourage for the triumphant commander was most likely assembled on each occasion, as the particular combination of circumstances and tradition demanded.

As the story of the tribune hints, many of these accounts share a concern with the complexities and antagonism of calibrating honor and relative superiority, and with the ambiguities of status and glory between the general and those most closely accompanying him. Sometimes the message is clear, as when Dio emphasizes the crowd's displeasure at the number of lictors attending Caesar in his triumph of 46, and (presumably) at the implications of that for Caesar's position in the state. In Dio's reconstruction at least, Caesar overstepped the mark by parading too many of these human symbols of authority. "On account of their numbers the lictors made an offensive crowd, since never before had they seen so many altogether." It was, he suggests, a triumphal *faux pas* that ranked with Caesar's display of poor Arsinoe, which prompted such lamentation among the Roman spectators.[59]

But sometimes the signals are, for us, much harder to read. Dio again highlights an innovation in the triumph of Octavian (Augustus) in 29 BCE: although, he writes, magistrates usually walked in front of the triumphal chariot, while those senators who had participated in the victory walked behind, Octavian "allowed his fellow consul and the other magistrates to follow him." Modern commentators, predictably enough, see this as a reflection of Octavian's dominance: "The deference to Octavian is patent." In fact, in saying that he *allowed* them to follow, Dio more obviously implies the reverse—that it was an honor to walk behind, rather than in front of, the chariot. Whether Dio understood what he was talking about is a moot point. But if he was correct about traditional practice, the space *ante currum* would sometimes have held an interesting, if not uncomfortable, *melée* of consuls and barbarian queens. Nevertheless, we are probably catching a glimpse here of the loaded etiquette of "who walked where" and of the significance that an avid scrutineer, if not the more casual observer, might detect (or invent) in the different placements around the triumphal chariot.[60]

Other stories focus on the rivalry, implicit or explicit, between the general and different members of his group. One famous occasion was the celebration in 207 BCE of Marcus Livius Salinator and Caius Claudius Nero, who were both granted a triumph for victory over Hasdrubal. They shared the same procession, but only Salinator rode in the chariot (the battle had been fought in his province, Livy explains, and he had held the auspices on the crucial day); Nero accompanied him on horseback. In fact, the victory was well known to have been much more Nero's doing, and the reaction of the spectators was to overturn the hierarchy implied in the difference between horse and chariot: "The real triumphal procession was the one conducted on a single horse," and the modesty of Nero in settling for that added to his glory; as Valerius Maximus put it, "In the case of Salinator, victory alone was being celebrated; in Nero's case, moderation too."[61]

A variation on this theme is found in the story of Lucius Siccius Dentatus in the fifth century BCE. A hugely successful and much decorated soldier of almost mythic (not to say parodic) renown, "he fought in 120 battles, blazoning 45 scars on his front and none on his back," and he walked behind the triumphal chariot in no fewer than nine triumphs. With his dazzling array of military awards, from the eight gold crowns to the 160 armlets, "enough for a legion," "he turned the eyes of the whole state onto himself"—and presumably away from those nine generals "who triumphed thanks to him."[62] It was not only glamorous captives who might upstage the commander in the Roman imagination. There was the lurking question of who was really responsible for the victory being celebrated. The man in the chariot, or one of those who were merely walking or riding in the procession? And at the same time the other moral qualities on display might always challenge the military heroics that appear to underpin the ceremony. Moderation might trump victory.

It is a reasonable guess that the majority of participants in the triumphal procession were the rank-and-file soldiery who followed the general's chariot. These men are invisible in the many visual representations of the triumph, which focus on the general or—if more widely—on the captives, spoils, and occasionally animal victims destined for slaughter on the Capitol. It is, in fact, a striking testimony to the selective gaze of Roman visual culture that there is no surviving ancient image of the celebration that depicts the mass of soldiers. Literary representations, however, do sometimes bring them strongly into the frame. The triumph could be presented as a celebration that belonged to the troops as much as to the general. In the dispute over Aemilius Paullus' celebration in 167 BCE, for example, Livy puts into the mouth of an elderly war hero a speech that stresses the centrality of the soldiers themselves: "In fact the triumph is the business of the soldiers . . . If ever the troops are not brought back from the field of campaigning to the triumph, they complain. Yet even when they are absent, they believe that they are part of the triumph, since the victory was won by their hands. If someone were to ask you, soldiers, for what purpose you were brought back to Italy and were not demobbed as soon as your mission was done . . . what would you say, except that you wished to be seen triumphing?"[63]

This is a tendentious piece of rhetoric, intended to encourage the troops to vote for the triumph of their general. But the idea of the triumph as a prize and a spectacle (note the emphasis on "be *seen* triumphing") in which the soldiers had as much stake as their commander is found elsewhere, too. A revealing case is an incident, reported by Appian, when the threat to deprive them of their role in a triumph is successfully used as a weapon against mutinous soldiers. In 47 BCE, when Julius Caesar's troops complained that they had not been paid their promised donatives (in effect, cash bonuses) and demanded to be discharged, Caesar is said to have responded shrewdly: he agreed to their discharge and said, "I shall give you everything I have promised when I triumph with other troops." In Appian's reconstruction, it was in part the thought that "others would triumph instead of themselves" that brought them to beg Caesar to take them back into the army.[64]

This anecdote points also to the importance of the donative associated with the triumph. From the late third century, when Livy's account regularly includes a record of the total amount added to the treasury by the triumphing general, it also includes a note of the bonuses given to the troops and how this was scaled by rank (it was usual practice with handouts in the ancient world that the higher status you held the more cash you received). The figures given here and elsewhere vary plausibly, with an underlying inflationary tendency up to the massive handouts of Pompey in 61 and later Caesar.[65] But their reliability is as uncertain as any, and the apparently standard rule that centurions received twice as much as rank-and-file foot soldiers—and elite equestrian officers three times as much—is partly a product of scholarly emendations (right or wrong) of the numerals in ancient texts, to bring them into line with these "standard" proportions.[66]

Whatever the exact amounts, the interests of the soldiers in this element of triumphal tradition are easy to understand. From the general's point of view, it must have been a useful bait to bring his soldiers back to Rome for the procession. On some, if not many occasions the troops would have returned to their homes during that period of waiting before a triumph was granted or celebrated; beyond the symbolic value of the triumph itself, the cash would have been a powerful incentive to turn up on the day.[67] How old the tradition was, how the cash was distributed to the men, or at what precise point in the proceedings we do not know. It is one of the penumbra of rituals associated with the triumph that are almost completely lost to us.

Donatives could, however, backfire. The enthusiasm of the soldiers certainly played its part in ensuring that a triumph was granted. For example, the hailing of the general as *imperator* on the battlefield after his victory might be (as in Cicero's case) an important first step in his campaign for triumphal honors. But conversely, disgruntled troops could always attempt to wreck their commander's aspirations or at least spoil his show. Pompey's first triumph was almost ruined by the soldiers who threatened to mutiny or help themselves to the booty on display, if they were not given a bigger bonus.

Even more notorious was the reaction of the troops to the senatorial approval given to Aemilius Paullus' triumph in 167 BCE. For the soldiers, angered by his meanness with the donative and smarting under his rigid "old-fashioned discipline," were stirred up by one of their junior officers and a personal enemy of Paullus to try to hijack the assembly specially convened to assign him *imperium* on the day of his triumph and so prevent his procession: "Avenge yourselves on that domineering and stingy commander by voting down the proposal about his triumph." Only the intervention of the elderly war hero with his emphasis on the importance of the triumph for the soldiers (and accompanied by a public display of war wounds) saved the day for Paullus.[68] The rights and wrongs of this conflict are impossible to determine—especially given the tendency of officer-class historians (ancient as well as modern) to present the demands of the rank and file as impertinent greed, and stinginess on the part of the general as admirable prudence. But it makes clear how the soldiers themselves could be seen as a force to be reckoned with in the planning and voting of a triumph—even if we know of no case where the ambitions of a general were in fact blocked by his men.

On the day itself the soldiers brought up the rear of the procession, marching, according to some accounts, in proper military order (one cannot help but suspect that the reality was often less disciplined). Unlike the general, they wore military dress and displayed their various military decorations—armlets, crowns of various shapes and sizes, presentation spears, and the ancient equivalents of campaign medals (albeit not usually in the quantity paraded by Siccius Dentatus). This was the only time that regular soldiers under arms legitimately entered Rome and an extraordinary, almost aggressive reversal of the usual norm that the city itself was a demilitarized zone.[69]

SOLDIERS' KIT

Three features of the soldiers' dress or behavior have played a particular role in modern accounts of the triumph. The first is their characteristic chant, as they went through the streets: "Io triumpe." The second is the laurel wreaths, which they—like other participants—are said to have worn. Third is their singing directed at the general, part in praise, part in ribaldry. Each one of these has usually been explained by reference to the deepest prehistory and primitive meaning of the ceremony; and each in turn has been conscripted as evidence into some particular theory of triumphal origins. But once again, there are major stumbling blocks with this approach—and other more telling interpretations.

In the case of "Io triumpe," many critics have eagerly fallen on Varro's tentative explanation in his treatise *De Lingua Latina (On the Latin language):* the whole ceremony, he claims, owes its name to the chant (not vice versa), which "could be derived from the word *thriambos* and the Greek title of Liber [or Bacchus/Dionysus]." Not only does Varro appear to suggest a Bacchic origin for the ceremony. But, according to one significant variant of this argument, his etymology of the Latin *triumpe* from the Greek *thriambos* is only linguistically possible if we imagine an intermediate Etruscan phase—a predictably attractive idea to those who would like to see the ceremony as an import to Rome from Etruria. Others have linked the soldiers' chant with the refrain *triumpe triumpe triumpe triumpe* in a surviving (and deeply obscure) archaic hymn, and concluded that the word was an appeal for divine epiphany—and so a convenient support for the idea that the triumphing general in some way represented a god.[70]

All this is guesswork. We have no idea if Varro is right. We have no clue even about the grammatical form of *io triumpe* (a vocative, an imperative, a primitive exclamation, or an Etruscan nominative have all been suggested). And the latest linguist to look at the question, without starting from a *parti pris* on the history of the triumph, has concluded that the history of the word may have included an Etruscan phase but did not necessarily do so.[71]

What gets passed over is the significance of the phrase for those who shouted it out, listened to it, or committed it to writing in the historical period. For some, it may have evoked the archaic religious world. Some may have shared Varro's speculation on the Dionysiac roots of the chant. But the overwhelming impression must have been that the participants in the procession were repeatedly hailing the very ceremony they were enacting ("Triumph, Triumph, Triumph")—or, as Livy puts it, that the soldiers "called on triumph by name."[72] There is no need to translate this as "calling on the *spirit* of Triumph," as if Livy had some kind of tutelary deity of the ceremony in mind.[73] It is easier to see this as a powerful example of a characteristic kind of ritual solipsism—whereby the ritual turns itself into the object of ritual, the triumph celebrates the triumph.

Ancient writers themselves were more interested in the wearing of laurel than in the triumphal chant. Some Roman etymologists could not resist the obvious temptation to explain its use in the ceremony by deriving the word *laurus* (laurel) from *laus* (praise).[74] Pliny, however, in a long discussion of various species of the plant, trails a whole series of different lines of approach. Modern scholars who have their eye on explaining the origins of the triumph as a purification of the troops from the blood guilt of war have often homed in on the suggestion he reports (from the pen of the first-century CE Masurius Sabinus, and echoed in Festus' dictionary) that would connect its role in the ceremony with its purificatory properties.[75] What they do not usually emphasize is that this idea is explicitly rejected by Pliny, who prefers three different explanations of the connection of laurel with the triumph: that it was a plant dear to Apollo at Delphi; that "laurel-bearing ground" at Delphi had been kissed by Lucius Junius Brutus (later first consul of the Republic), in response to a famous oracle offering power *(imperium)* at Rome to him who first kissed his "mother"; or that it was the only cultivated plant never struck by lightning.

Our evidence, beyond this, for the early significance of laurel and for how it might have related to the primitive function of the triumph is very slight. It is possible—who knows?—that in stressing the role of purification Masurius and Festus (or their sources) had picked up a theme in the ceremony that did stretch back to the distant Roman past.[76] Certainly the problems of pollution seem more plausible to us now than Pliny's daft theories about Delphi and lightning. But in passing these over, we are in danger again of turning a blind eye to the history of the triumph in favor of its imagined prehistory. No one would think for moment that Pliny was "right" on why laurel was originally used in a triumphal procession. But his explanations are important in gesturing toward the different ways in which the plant (and the ceremony as a whole) was understood in the multicultural world of the first century BCE and later. Delphic laurel underpins such ideas as the "triumph of poetry" (as we have seen already in Horace and Propertius) and the "triumph of love" (in the myth of Apollo and Daphne—turned, as she was, into laurel). In a sense, Pliny is offering not so much an explanation of why laurel was used in the first place as a legitimating aetiology for the widest interpretation of "triumphal culture."[77]

A third characteristic of the soldiers in the procession that has recently captured the most scholarly attention is their songs. These are regularly referred to by Livy as *carmina incondita,* which might mean anything from "spontaneous" to "artless" or "rude."[78] The best known, and some of the very few directly quoted by ancient writers, are those sung at the triumph of Caesar in 46 BCE—including some predictable potshots at the commander's sexual exploits:

Romans, watch your wives, see the bald adulterer's back home.
You fucked away in Gaul the gold you borrowed here in Rome[79]

Caesar screwed the lands of Gaul, Nicomedes screwed our Caesar,
Look Caesar now is triumphing, the one who screwed the Gauls
No Nicomedes triumphs though, the one who screwed our Caesar[80]

But there were also some more narrowly political darts. Dio reports some clear references to Caesar's desire to become king and the illegalities that entailed. In an unusually acute piece of analysis (born, one imagines, of a lifetime's experience of autocratic rule), Dio claims that Caesar was rather flattered by most of this, as the troops' boldness to speak their mind ultimately reflected well on himself. Most autocrats, after all, like to be seen to be able to take a joke—up to a point. That point, for Caesar, was (again, according to Dio) the insinuations about his affair with Nicomedes, the king of Bithynia, in which the Latin of the verse clearly paints him as the passive partner ("screwed" *subegit* is literally "subjugated" or "subdued"). According to Dio, Caesar "tried to defend himself and denied the affair on oath, and so brought more ridicule on himself."[81]

The other references to this tradition suggest that the singing, whether ribald or eulogistic, often homed in on—and so marked out—the "real" star of the show, which was not always the general himself. At the triumph of Salinator and Nero in 207, the fact that more of the songs were directed at Nero was one of the things, according to Livy, which indicated that the greater honor was Nero's (despite Salinator's riding in the triumphal chariot).[82] In 295 BCE one of the chief subjects of the verses was in fact dead. Although Quintus Fabius Maximus was triumphing after the Roman victory at the battle of Sentinum, the success was thought to be largely due to the self-sacrifice of his fellow consul Publius Decius Mus—and this "glorious death" no less than the achievements of Fabius was celebrated in the "rough and ready verses of the soldiers." It was as if the soldiers' songs gave a presence in the triumph to the man truly responsible for the Roman victory despite (and because of) his death.[83]

The standard modern view sees these verses as "apotropaic," their apparently insulting tone designed to protect the general and his moment of overweening glory from the dangers of "the evil eye."[84] It cannot be as simple as that. For a start, despite our own fascination with more ribald variety of these verses, they were not all of that type; some are explicitly said to have eulogistic.[85] Nor, as we have seen, were they always directed at the general. Besides, once again—as the very terms "apotropaic" and "evil eye" indicate—the modern frame of analysis points us back to a primitivizing form of explanation, with its seductive but often misleading gravitational pull toward the archaic. Yet we have repeatedly seen how the triumph raises questions about the perilous status of the honor it bestows. What risks are entailed in triumphal glory? What limits are there to that glory? Where does the "real" honor of the ceremony lie? There is no need to retreat to the obscure world of primitive Rome to see that the soldiers' songs—lauding the general, as well as taking him down a peg or two, while also bringing other objects or targets into their frame—contribute to those questions, and to their answers.[86]

CLIMAX OR ANTICLIMAX?

The high point of any complicated ritual or ceremony depends on your point of view: although the liturgical climax of a Christian wedding is the moment when the couple exchange their vows, many spectators will remember much more vividly the walk down the aisle or the showers of confetti. In the case of the triumph, artists and writers dwelt on the procession as it made its way through the streets; they barely recorded in any form, literary or visual, what happened when it reached its destination. The result is that we know very little about the final proceedings. For some participants, these were perhaps the most impressive, moving, or memorable part of the show. For others—whose position along the route would have given them no chance to witness what went on at the finale—these events may have been more of an anticlimax. That is certainly what the general silence would tentatively suggest.

The procession ended with the ascent of the Capitoline hill up to the Temple of Jupiter Optimus Maximus. Julius Caesar is reputed to have "climbed the stairs on the Capitol on his knees" in a gesture of humility that was apparently later copied by the emperor Claudius. Although this is sometimes imagined as a lengthy progress up the hill itself (with all the complications of managing the elaborate toga in a kneeling crawl), it presumably refers only to the steps of the temple itself. Once the general had arrived at the temple, we assume that he presided over the sacrifice of the animals that had been led in the parade.[87] But was that all? The notion that he ran around the building three times has proved so unpalatable to most modern critics that it has usually been ignored; primitivism is one thing, farce quite another. Yet the reference to climbing the steps suggests that on some occasions at least the general went inside the temple. This was not for the animal sacrifice, which would have happened in the open air. It is usually assumed that he went to offer his "laurel" (wreath or branch?) to Jupiter, even to lay it on the lap of the statue.[88]

A slightly different procedure is suggested by that second set of inscribed triumphal records, the *Fasti Barberiniani:* each entry concludes with the words "he dedicated his palm." Whether this was a synonym or a substitute for the laurel, or whether we should imagine palm as well as laurel regularly carried by the general we do not know. But the phrase does give a glimpse of the different priorities that different sections of the triumph's audience or its participants might have had. Whoever commissioned this record (and there has been some optimistic speculation, partly on the basis of its possible findspot nearby, that it was connected with the Temple of Jupiter itself), they saw the defining event of the triumph as this (to us mysterious) "dedication of the palm."[89]

The choreography of this final stage of the procession is even more baffling to us than the rest. How many of the parade's participants made the ascent to the Capitoline, how the prisoners and soldiers were deployed while the sacrifice took place, whether there was a popular audience for this part of the show, and how all the people, the booty, and the various models and paintings were safely dispersed afterward (the "exit strategy," in other words), we have no idea at all. It is easy enough perhaps to visualize the scene for the majority of relatively modest celebrations, but how the blockbuster shows were organized and controlled at this point is quite another matter. It is even less clear with those processions that stretched over two or three days. The implication of some of the surviving descriptions is that the general himself appeared only on the last day.[90] If so, on the previous days did the procession simply go up to the Capitoline, unload, and disperse without any particular ceremony? How was all that precious loot kept safe from thieving hands? True to type, no ancient writer is interested in the practical infrastructure.

However anticlimactic the finale of the ceremony might seem to us or to its original audience, most modern scholars have agreed that for the general in the Roman Republic (the dynamics of the imperial celebration was, as we shall see in Chapter 9, rather different) the triumph as a whole represented the pinnacle of ambition achieved. It was both a marker and guarantor of his success within the competitive culture of the Roman elite; it was the ceremony that an ambitious young Roman would dream of. That is certainly one side of the ancient story, as we have already seen. The triumph and its trappings operated both symbolically and practically to elevate the general, to secure his status, and to transmit it down the generations.

Notable commemorative statues, such as that of Publius Scipio Africanus in the Temple of Jupiter, depicted their subjects in triumphal dress—as if that captured the very moment of their highest renown.[91] The adjective *triumphalis* ("triumphal") could be used to distinguish those who had triumphed, and even to mark out their children. On a grossly overblown early imperial family tomb at Tivoli, for example, one epitaph blazoned the man commemorated as *triumphalis filius* ("son of a triumpher" or "triumphal son"), in place of the usual Roman formula of filiation ("son of Marcus"); his father, whose epitaph was alongside, had been awarded "triumphal ornaments" under Augustus.[92] In the race for more direct political rewards, there is some evidence of a link between the celebration of a triumph and future success. Livy occasionally refers to the impact of a celebration on up-coming elections, and Cicero linked the splendid triumph celebrated by the father of his client Lucius Licinius Murena to Murena junior's subsequent election to the consulship.[93]

Modern scholars have made some attempts to look beyond individual cases. Tracking the careers of those men of praetorian rank who secured triumphs seems to show that this group had particular success in securing a consulship. Between 227 and 79 the unusually high proportion of fifteen out of nineteen triumphing praetorians went on to the higher office; and of the remaining four who did not, some may have died before they had a chance to stand for election. It is hard of course to isolate the significant variable here: the victory itself may have been a more important factor than its celebration. Nonetheless, statistics such as these have helped to entrench the modern view that triumph signaled success.[94]

But as I have repeatedly shown, triumph could signal failure too—

and not only for those generals who, despite what they themselves regarded as a triumph-worthy victory, were refused a celebration. Time and again, ancient writers told the story of triumphs that went wrong for all kinds of reasons. Humiliating incidents might occur in mid-procession, as when Pompey's elephants became jammed in the archway or when Caesar's axle broke. Or the spectacular highlights might misfire, as when Caesar's paintings of his dying enemies called forth more revulsion than admiration among the gawping crowd, or the tragic prisoner Arsinoe reduced them to tears. A poor show might go down badly. Scipio Aemilianus' triumph over Numantia in 132 BCE was noticeably austere. The Roman destruction of the city had been so complete that not a single captive nor any booty could be put on display: "It was a triumph over a name only," as Florus put it disapprovingly, reflecting on the absence of spectacle and also no doubt on the brutality that accounted for it.[95] But, on the other side, there was always a fine line between splendor and morally questionable excess, a line which, in Pliny's eyes at least, Pompey ominously crossed with his portrait head made out of pearls.

Even if nothing of this sort was drastically awry, the general in his chariot still risked being upstaged by any number of other participants in the parade. What could he do, standing helpless in the chariot, if he realized that the eyes of the spectators were being drawn increasingly to the glamorous prisoners or to the valiant battle-scarred soldier walking behind him? And what could he do about the negative spin that might always be put on his finest hour? We cannot be sure how many of the piquant jibes on triumphal celebrations that we find in the written record went back directly to contemporary reactions and to the street talk that no doubt accompanied the show itself. But plenty of evidence suggests that even (or especially) the most splendid triumphs could come to be seen more as an own-goal than as a glorious reflection of success. However mythologized it may have been, Camillus' extravaganza in 396 BCE is usually presented as the catalyst for political opposition to the general.

Significantly, too, the triumph is an important rhetorical theme in Livy's story of Scipio Africanus' fall from favor. After a brief backward glance to Scipio's triumphal celebration over Syphax in 201 BCE, Livy re-counts the debates at Scipio's trial a decade or so later. For his oppo-nents, he was a tyrant who had robbed Romans of their liberty and had (in a phrase that makes a more shocking paradox in Latin than in Eng-lish translation) "triumphed over the Roman people"; his accusers were accused in return of "seeking spoils from a triumph over Africanus." One implication here is that his triumph cast a dark shadow, rather than glorious luster, over the succeeding years.[96]

Extraordinary marks of honor always entail high risk. For the tri-umphing general himself, the pride, excitement, and sense of richly de-served glory must regularly have gone hand in hand with fear and appre-hension for the occasion itself and for the future. More things, after all, could go wrong than could go right with a triumph.

ACTING UP?

The figure of the general also raises issues of representation and *mimesis,* similar to those raised by the prisoners and the spoils. But in his case they have an extra dimension, which brings us back, in a different way, to his divine status—raising the question not merely of *what* he repre-sents but *how* he represents, and of his role in the wider hermeneutics of the parade. If the models and tableaux could be read as both brilliant artifice and treacherous sham, could the general be seen as both the di-vine double and ludicrous actor?

I mean "ludicrous actor" quite literally. For one of the most potent ancient explorations of the figure of the triumphing general is found in Plautus' comedy *Amphitruo,* a piece of theater that is framed by and ex-poses the mimetic conventions of the triumph and the general's role within those. The action of this play leads up to the birth of Hercules, by way of an intricate tale of adultery, disguise, and mistaken identity. Amphitruo himself is a Theban general, just returned from a heroically successful campaign against the "Teleboans." Geographical precision would place this people in Acarnania, in western Greece, but the Greek would literally mean that they are "a far cry" *(tele boe)* from where we are. While Amphitruo has been away, Jupiter has taken a fancy to his wife, Alcmena, and has been making love to her, cunningly disguised as her husband. The return of the real Amphitruo causes the predictable confusion, archly complicated by the god Mercury—also in disguise as Amphitruo's slave Sosia. The ensuing slapstick and carnival sadism (part of which is lost in a gap in our text) finally ends with a resolution in which divine unction is poured on the proceedings: Alcmena bears twins—Hercules, son of Jupiter, and Iphicles, son of the cuckold Amphitruo (Fig. 33).

The comedies of Plautus are derived and adapted from Greek antecedents (hence Thebes and the Teleboans) and for that reason have often played a marginal role in modern studies of Roman culture and society. Sometimes the precise Greek model used by the Roman playwright is well known; in this case we know next to nothing about it. What is clear, though, is the extent to which any earlier version of the plot has been thoroughly Romanized—so comprehensively, in fact, that much of the story as we have it would make no sense outside Rome or Rome's cultural orbit. A good deal of this Roman flavor is provided by the character of Amphitruo himself and by the clear hints in the text that we should see him not just as a returning victor but more specifically as a triumphing general. We have already noted, for example, that (the real) Sosia's account of his master's military successes almost certainly mimics the official language of triumphal petitions, and includes characteristic technical Roman rubric *(suo auspicio, suo imperio)*.[97]

These triumphal echoes have prompted critics to try to pinpoint some particular celebration that Plautus had in mind. Is this supposed to be a comic glance at the triumph of Marcus Fulvius Nobilior in 187 BCE (and so was the play possibly first performed at the games celebrating his victory in 186)? Or perhaps rather the triumphant return of Livius Salinator or of Lucius Scipio?[98] This desperate search for a specific historical referent for Amphitruo's victory has tended to occlude other, more important aspects of the play. A few critics have lifted their eyes above the geopolitics of the early second century to discuss *Amphitruo* as a play in which the representational games of the stage are themselves on parade: the divine doubling, mistaken identities, and impersonations of-

FIGURE 33: The next episode in the story of Amphitruo, in a painting from the House of
the Vettii, Pompeii, 62–79 CE. Jupiter's wife Hera, jealous of his affair, sends a pair of
snakes to attack baby Hercules, but he proves his strength and gives a sign of his future
prowess by strangling them. Here Alcmena backs away from the scene, while Amphitruo—
in a costume strikingly reminiscent of Jupiter—looks on thoughtfully. This hints at an alternative version of the story in which Amphitruo himself sends the snakes, to discover
which son was really his.

fer reflections on the very nature of theater, and beyond that on human
subjectivity and the very idea of a unitary personality. One recent study
has also focused more directly on triumphal convention, seeing the play
as a whole in the tradition of the "apotropaic" songs sung by the soldiers
in procession.[99]

But even these approaches have by-passed what seems to me to be the central (Roman) joke around which the play is structured. If the triumphal celebration staged the general as—in some sense at least—a look-alike god for the day, then Plautus cunningly reverses those mimetic conventions: his play stages Jupiter as a look-alike general, acting human for the day (or, more exactly, for the one night on which the play's action takes place).[100]

The question at stake here is one which, in different forms and with different nuances, runs through much of the triumphal procession and its images—and which must trump narrower questions of what the general represented. How do you tell the difference between representation and reality? What distinguishes the man who is "being," "playing," or "acting" god?

The Boundaries of the Ritual

MAKING A MEAL OUT OF A VICTORY

In 89 CE the emperor Domitian hosted a particularly imaginative (or menacing) dinner party for Roman senators and knights. The dining room was entirely black, with black couches, crockery, and food; even the naked serving-boys were painted in the same color. Each guest's name was inscribed on a slab shaped like a tombstone, while the emperor himself held forth on the topic of death to the silent and fearful company, who were convinced that their last hour had come. In fact, it was to be nothing of the sort. They were all sent home, and the ominous knock at the door that followed shortly after their return heralded not arrest and murder but a display of imperial generosity: Domitian had sent each guest as a present their name-slab (made of silver), the precious black dishes from which they had been served, and their individual serving-boy, now well scrubbed and nicely dressed. Or so at least Dio (as his Byzantine excerptors have preserved his text) tells the story.[1]

This has become a notorious and controversial incident in modern attempts to configure the relations between the emperor and the Roman elite. Some see it as a classic case of imperial sadism, showing that scare tactics in the form of humiliation and terror were as effective a means of control as violence itself. Others suspect that Dio, in his eagerness to cast Domitian as a full-blown tyrant, has missed the point of the dinner, and missed the joke. For lurking under Dio's outrage, they detect an elegant parade of imperial wit (and expensive fancy dress), or alternatively a philosophical fantasy in keeping with the other-worldly themes found elsewhere in the dining culture of the early Empire.[2]

What no one has spotted, to my knowledge, is that this occasion was not merely *any* banquet hosted by the emperor, but the banquet laid on to follow the emperor's triumph over the Germans and Dacians.[3] Even in its mangled state, Dio's text makes it clear that we are dealing with the triumphal celebrations of 89, which were followed both by a dinner at public expense for the people at large "lasting all night" and by this elegant, or somber, occasion for a more select group of the elite.

In fact, various forms of eating and drinking are referred to as an accompaniment to triumphs. We have already seen, in Josephus' account, that in 71 CE the soldiers were served with "the traditional breakfast" (or "lunch," depending on how we choose to translate the Greek *ariston*) before the procession itself started out, while Vespasian and Titus had a bite to eat, privately, elsewhere. In a triumph, no less than on campaign, the army marched on its stomach. It also needed a drink. An aside in a play of Plautus—that "the soldiers will be entertained with honeyed wine," even if there is no triumph—strongly hints (though we might have guessed it anyway) that the celebrating troops did not necessarily remain sober all day.[4]

More striking are the retrospective fictions that offer a different vision of how the soldiers were plied with food in some of the earliest Roman triumphs. Dionysius of Halicarnassus, in his account of the founding celebration of Romulus, imagines the ceremony consisting simply of the homecoming of the victorious troops, met outside the town by their wives and children and other citizens. As they enter this proto-Rome, they find that outside the most distinguished houses tables have been laid with food and wine from which, as they pass in procession, they can eat their fill. The image is repeated in Dionysius' account of Publicola's triumph in 509, the first year of the newly founded Republic, and in Livy's story of the triumph of Cincinnatus in 458 BCE. Here, he pictures tables spread out before all the houses and "the soldiers, feasting as they went, to the accompaniment of the triumphal chant; and the usual ribald songs followed the chariot like revelers."[5]

These are more complex stories than at first they may appear, with an interlocking set of historical explanations and originary myths at play. On the one hand, the triumph is being used as an imaginary frame for a distinctively primitive form of banqueting: what is being conjured here is the "degree zero" of Roman dining, unencumbered by the rules and rituals of commensality, something as close to *just eating* as you can get within organized society. On the other hand, this practice of eating on the part of the soldiers—retrojected by Dionysius to the very first triumph of all and to the first triumph of the Republic—is itself being used, mythically, as a way of recreating and explaining the origins of the ceremony of triumph. Livy's language points clearly in that direction. When he writes that the soldiers were "like revelers," the Latin word he uses is *comisor (modo comisantium),* which echoes, even if it does not directly derive from, the Greek word *kōmos*—the procession of drunken revelers associated, for example, with marriages, some religious rituals, or with the celebrations for victorious athletes. Livy is asking his readers to imagine the early triumph on the model of a Greek *kōmos,* a soldiers' *kōmos.*

Most ancient writers, however, are not particularly concerned with the soldiers' fare but focus on the post-triumphal festivities for the other participants and spectators, both people and elite. The classic case is the banqueting provided by Julius Caesar after his triumphs in 46 and 45 BCE. The general impression of lavishness is backed up by some ostensibly specific detail. Plutarch, for example, claims that in 46 the people feasted at 22,000 *triclinia*—which, according to the usual understanding that a *triclinium* comprises three couches with three diners each, means a grand total of 198,000 diners. The elder Pliny fills in some of the culinary information. In discussing different varieties of wine, he notes that Caesar provided Chian and Falernian for his triumphal guests. Elsewhere, in the context of lamprey ponds, he notes that Gaius Lucilius Hirrus—second-rate politician, erstwhile ally of Pompey, and highly successful fish breeder—gave Caesar 6,000 lampreys "as a loan" for one of his triumphal banquets. It was a generous and politically expedient gesture, no doubt, though, as the largest lamprey hardly exceeds a meter in length, if divided equally they would have provided a meager helping for 198,000 diners.[6]

This mass public dining has captured the scholarly imagination. Modern historians of ancient food and foodways have seen in such triumphal banquets the "greatest occasions" of public feasting at Rome. More than that, they have made the feast—rather than the sacrifice on the Capitol, or the dedication of the laurel or palm—the culminating moment of the whole triumphal ceremony. The public feast, as one historian recently suggested, was "ritually the capstone of triumphs."[7] Even poor Aemilius Paullus has been wheeled out to support such claims. "The organization of a feast and the giving of games is the business of a man who knows how to win wars," he is supposed to have once remarked—as if to imply that, as soon as the war was won, the general had to devote himself to organizing a (triumphal) banquet for the people and laying on games. But it is an over-optimistic translation. The sense is more correctly: "It takes the same talent to organize a feast, to give games, and to marshal troops like a general to face the enemy."[8] A significantly different observation.

In fact, the idea that mass eating, on the Caesarian model, was the regular culmination of the triumph is a typical example of the kind of generalization we have repeatedly seen in modern reconstructions of the ceremony. It is not that we have no further evidence for it at all. Athenaeus, for example, in his second-century CE compendium *Deipnosophistae (Sophists at Dinner)* refers to skins of "gorgons," sheep-like creatures with deadly eyes sent from Africa by Marius to hang "in the Temple of Hercules where commanders celebrating their triumphs give a banquet to the citizens." And elsewhere he quotes the early first-century BCE Stoic philosopher Poseidonius, who wrote of the banquets held "in the precinct of Hercules, when a man who at that time is celebrating a triumph is giving dinner."[9] There are also the observations of Varro on the agricultural profits to be made from supplying "a triumph and a banquet."[10] Yet it is hard to pin down precise occasions of any such mass feasting.

The only case mentioned before Caesar is that of Lucullus' triumph in 63 BCE, when according to Plutarch a banquet was given both in the city and in surrounding villages.[11] Otherwise, the few examples of large-scale dining are all of early imperial date: a banquet to celebrate Tiberius' ovation in 9 BCE (dinner for "some" on the Capitol, for others "all over the place," while Livia and Julia entertained the women); the entertainment following the triumph of Vespasian and Titus ("some" eating at the imperial table, others in their own homes); and Domitian's dinners in 89 CE.[12] Nowhere in Livy's notices of republican triumphs do we find any reference to any form of post-triumphal entertainment on a large scale.

Equally hard to pin down are the practical details of such occasions. Athenaeus does not specify which "precinct of Hercules" he means, but there was none in Rome that could possibly hold 198,000 diners. The most likely location for Caesar's banquet would be the Forum itself; and precedents do indeed exist for its transformation into an open-air dining area. Livy, for example, tells a vivid story of a funeral feast taking place there in 183 BCE, when it was so windy that the diners were forced to erect little tents or windbreaks around their tables.[13] But the accounts we have hint that formal communal banquets may regularly have been offered to the elite alone, the mass of the people having food (or even cash equivalent) provided for private or local consumption—on the model of the "take-away" mentioned by Josephus at the triumph of 71 CE, or the widely dispersed dining ("all over the place") following Tiberius' ovation.[14] As for the menu, much of the information we have may well refer, again, to the elite rather than the popular version of the feast. Those 6,000 lampreys, or Varro's aunt's 5,000 thrushes, would have made a handsome contribution to the "top-table" party of perhaps senators and knights.

Unlike the mass dining of the people, there is considerable evidence for triumphal feasting by the elite (still, to be sure, on a large scale), as well as for ancient scholarly interest in the particular customs and social oddities that characterized it. In addition to the occasions we have just noted (where the "some" dining on the Capitol or at the imperial table almost certainly indicates the upper echelons of Roman society), Appian refers to Scipio entertaining his friends "at the temple, as was customary" at the conclusion of his triumph in 201 BCE, just as Dionysius envisages Publicola in 509 "feasting the most distinguished of the citizens" at the end of his own procession and Dio reports a banquet for senators on the Capitol at the triumph of Tiberius in 7 BCE.[15]

Livy, too, though silent on popular triumphal dining, mentions this elite custom in the context of Aemilius Paullus' triumph in 167. In the course of the triumphal debate, Paullus' champion (as Livy scripts his words) lists the "senate's feast" as one of the religious elements of the ceremony: "What about that feast of the senate that is held neither on private property, nor on unconsecrated public land, but on the Capitol? Does this take place for the pleasure of mortal men or to honor the gods?"[16] In other words, it seems that once the general had arrived at the Temple of Jupiter and the sacrifices had been performed, he did not necessarily make his weary way home: a banquet for the senate or maybe a wider group of the elite often followed, in the Capitoline temple itself or perhaps at a Temple of Hercules.

Puzzling to ancient scholars were the rules of precedence at these dinners. Both Valerius Maximus and Plutarch refer to the "customary" banquet. Why, they ask, was it the tradition for the consuls to be invited to this occasion and then to be sent a message that they should not turn up? The answer, they each suggest in slightly different formulations, is to ensure that the triumphant commander is not upstaged: "So that, on the day on which he triumphs, no one of greater *imperium* should be present at the same dinner party."[17] This nicely indicates that more was at stake in this banquet than the standard Roman practice of sharing the sacrificial meat between priests, officials, and key participants—the "religious" function hinted at by Livy.[18] More too than the reintegration of the general into the society of his elite peers after his day on the borderline of divinity. We have already seen how written recreations of the triumph repeatedly harp on the fragility of triumphal success, on the

competitive calibration of triumphal glory, and on the dangers of humiliation that went along with the temporary elevation of the general. Exactly those issues are reflected in this ancient explanation of the strange
"rule" about the invitation and disinvitation of the consuls, with its implied recognition of the threats to the general's status.

Those issues are reflected, too, in Domitian's black dinner party.
Though the fact that emperor and triumphing general were here one
and the same inevitably complicates the story, an important underlying
theme remains the jockeying for preeminence between the general and
other participants in (or observers of) the triumph. The intricate games
of power, humiliation, and control implied by the ceremony are in this
case both won and lost by Domitian: the emperor-general retains the
upper hand, but only at the cost of revealing his own sadistic tyranny
(or, on the other interpretation, at the cost of history forever missing
his joke!).

RITUAL BOUNDARIES

Triumphal feasting, in whatever form, raises larger questions about
where we choose to draw the boundary of this (or any) ritual—how we
decide what is to count as part of the ritual process and what to be taken
as merely ancillary. To put it simply, should we see the banqueting as an
integral element, perhaps even the highlight, of the triumph, or as a
common sequel to it—one of the "post-triumphal" festivities, as I have
already put it. And what difference does our choice make?

Feasting is only one aspect of the wider diffusion of the triumph beyond the procession itself. As Pompey's triumph in 61 vividly illustrated,
the ceremony and its impact extended in a variety of different ways. Notably, temples funded by the profits of victory that had been paraded
through the streets and housing the most precious objects of triumphal
booty might serve to memorialize the occasion for centuries. The performance of plays and the various displays at the games *(ludi)* associated
with military victory might fulfill a similar function. There is no clear
evidence for games formally attached to a triumphal procession (the so-

called *Ludi Triumphales* were a fourth-century commemoration of Constantine's victory over his rival Licinius in 324 CE), still less for dramatic performances in a strictly triumphal context.[19] Yet the games sometimes vowed by the general in the heat of battle, and celebrated in the event of victory when he returned home, or those that might be held at the dedication of "manubial" temples, could be linked in various more or less direct ways to triumphal celebrations. So, for example, the "prisoners of war" who featured in the arena at the games to mark the dedication of Julius Caesar's Temple of Venus Genetrix were, in all likelihood, those who had earlier been paraded in his triumphal procession.[20] And I speculated earlier that the triumphal scenes in the plays performed at the inauguration of Pompey's vast building complex, on the anniversary of his triumph, might have showcased some of the booty that had already been on display in the triumphal procession itself.

More generally, games of this kind offer a very plausible context for the production of those Roman historical dramas, *fabulae praetextae,* which sometimes focused on particular military victories.[21] The *Ambracia* of Ennius, for example, took as its theme the defeat of the city of Ambracia in northwest Greece, for which Ennius' patron Marcus Fulvius Nobilior celebrated a triumph in 187 BCE. We do not know exactly when it was first performed, but either the lavish ten-day games held in fulfillment of the vow Nobilior made in battle (and funded out of the triumphal booty) or the celebrations that would have accompanied the dedication of Nobilior's Temple of Hercules of the Muses seem very likely occasions.[22] Whether or not Ennius took *Ambracia's* story down as far as the triumph of Nobilior, so reenacting it on stage, we cannot infer from the few fragments and scattered references to it that have been preserved. But 150 years later, Horace had some sharp words for the vulgar visual spectacle of plays which, he claimed, re-presented triumphal processions on stage, with captive kings, chariots, and spoils of ivory and bronze.[23]

So where does the triumph stop? There is no single right answer to the question of where to draw its boundaries, and whether or not to include the feasting or these dramatic replays and anniversary performances. The fact is that the Roman triumph, like all rituals, was a po-rous set of practices and ideas, embedded in the day-to-day political, social, and cultural world of Rome, with innumerable links and associa-tions, both personal and institutional, to other ceremonies, customs, events, and traditions. For modern scholars there is an inevitable trade-off between a restrictively narrow approach and an impossibly all-em-bracing one. To limit what we understand as "the ritual" simply to the procession itself, and so to exclude from view the (maybe no less "ritual-ized") preparations or the different forms in which the triumph pro-longed its impact in further spectacles and celebration would amount to a very blinkered view of the occasion and its significance. Conversely, to include every aspect of the memorialization and representation of the triumph (or even of victory) as part of the ritual itself risks diluting and decentering the ceremony beyond what is either plausible or useful.

That is not merely a modern dilemma. Romans too were involved in the process—a contested, loaded, changing, and inevitably provisional one—of "fixing" the ritual *as ritual,* defining, policing, and also trans-gressing the boundaries that marked it off from the everyday nonritual world, and drawing a line between the triumph and all those other cere-monies that were *not* to count as triumph. This is part of what the dy-namics of "ritualization" are all about. We have already seen one side of this, and its potential complexity, in the various subcategories of the tri-umphal ceremony as they are defined by Roman writers. Both the *ovatio* and triumph *in monte Albano* were carefully distanced from the triumph "proper" by a series of precise distinctions and calibrations: the general traveling on foot or horseback, for example, not in a chariot; a myrtle, not a laurel, wreath; a standard senatorial toga, rather than the *toga picta;* or simply a changed location.

Such calibrations could matter. Why else would Marcus Licinius Crassus have chosen to wear a laurel, not a myrtle, wreath at his ovation for victory over a slave rebellion in 71 BCE, if not to make it seem more like a full triumph?[24] Yet in other contexts and circumstances those dis-tinctions could be overlooked, so as to treat all the variants as *bona fide* triumphs. This was strikingly the case in the inscribed triumphal record in the Forum, where all were listed together. The ovation and ceremony on the Alban Mount, in other words, both were and were not triumphs. The rest of this chapter explores the contested margins of the ceremony of triumph itself, and the ways that various forms of triumphal symbolism extended more generally into other areas of public life. It is concerned with the triumph outside the triumph.

WHEN WAS A TRIUMPH NOT A TRIUMPH?

Roman history and history writing are full of triumphlike occasions. Outside the roster of official triumphs, the ceremony gave the general a model of how to celebrate his victory at other times and places, just as it offered ancient writers a model for describing and representing other celebrations. Plutarch, for example, notes the magnificent arrival of Aemilius Paullus back into Italy after his victory over Perseus, "like the spectacle of triumphal procession, for the Romans to enjoy in advance," while Flamininus and his troops are said by Livy to have passed through Italy in 194 BCE "in a virtual triumph." A more striking phrase—which is most likely a clever coinage by Livy, but just conceivably an otherwise unattested piece of technical triumphal vocabulary—describes a "campsite triumph" *(castrensis triumphus)* for a junior officer who had successfully rescued the Romans from a bad military blunder on the part of his commander: "Decius had a campsite triumph, making his way through the midst of the camp with his troops under arms, and all eyes turned upon him."[25]

Proceedings even more reminiscent of the particularities of the Roman triumph may well lie behind Josephus' account of Titus' circuitous journey back to Italy, after the fall of Jerusalem in 70 CE. Traveling through Syria, "he exhibited costly spectacles in all the towns through which he passed, and he used his Jewish captives to act out their own destruction." This sounds very similar to the "floats" in the Jewish triumph itself, each one featuring "an enemy general in the very attitude in which he was captured"—prompting one recent critic to suggest that more was at stake here than just an ostentatious victory tour: Titus was offering to the eastern cities a lesson in a distinctively Roman form of triumphal celebration, "with its pageantry and ideologically charged images of conqueror and conquered."[26]

None of these celebrations is known to have provoked controversy or to have been seen as a challenge to the ritual of triumph itself. On other occasions, however, triumphlike ceremonies did raise questions (as they still do) about exactly where the ritual boundaries of the ceremony lay, what counted as a timely adaptation of the traditional rituals, and what was a potentially dangerous subversion. The advent of autocracy, from Julius Caesar on, heralded a whole range of extensions of triumphal ceremonial that were likely to have been, at the very least, the subject of delicate negotiation or packaging. Caesar's hybrid celebration in 44 BCE, referred to in the inscribed *Fasti* as an ovation *ex monte Albano* is a case in point. So too is the return of Octavian and Mark Antony to Rome after temporarily patching up their differences in 40 BCE. Dio refers to them coming "into the city, mounted on horses *as if* at some triumph." The *Fasti,* by contrast, show no such hesitation, including the ceremony twice, once for Octavian and once for Antony, each time with the addition of *ovans;* and in place of the usual information on the defeated enemy, it includes the explanation "because he made peace with Mark Antony/with Imperator Caesar" (to give Octavian his Roman title). The justification might run that the restoration of good will between these two was as militarily significant, and as worthy of an ovation, as any victory in war.[27]

But two notorious incidents particularly stand out. The first was, in Dio's words, "a sort of triumph" over the Armenian king Artavasdes celebrated by Antony in 34 BCE—but in the Egyptian capital of Alexandria, not in Rome. Among the several accounts of this event, Plutarch's is the most open, and acerbic, on the triumphal character and implications of this ceremony. "Antony captured Artavasdes, took him in chains to Alexandria, and led him in triumph [*ethriambeusen,* a standard Greek term for the Roman ritual]. In this he gave particular offense to the Romans, because for the sake of Cleopatra he bestowed on the Egyptians the honorable and solemn ceremonies of his own country." Others are less direct but still focus on various elements of the show that echo triumphal ritual and symbolism: Antony driving in a chariot, the royal prisoners paraded through the city, even in some accounts bound (like Zenobia) in golden chains. In place of the distaste felt for the occasion by Plutarch's Romans, Dio projects resistance onto the prisoners themselves, who refused to do obeisance to Cleopatra despite being pressed to—and suffering for it later.[28]

The second case, a bizarre triumphal ceremony of Nero in 67 CE, is recounted even more vividly, in this case by Suetonius and Dio (in a passage known to us in his Byzantine excerption).[29] The occasion in question is the return of the emperor from his notorious tour of Greece, where he had achieved victory—or had it engineered for him—in all the major Greek games. In Suetonius' version, Nero enjoyed a ceremonial progress through Italy, entering the cities he visited on white horses through a breach in their defenses, which was the traditional way that Greek victors themselves had reentered their home towns after such success. He did the same at Rome, but there he also rode in a chariot, "the very one that Augustus had once used in his triumphs," and he wore a costume that combined triumphal and decidedly Greek elements: a purple robe with a Greek cloak *(chlamys)* decorated with golden stars; the characteristic olive wreath of Olympic victors on his head; the laurel wreath of the Pythian games as well as of the triumph in his hand. In front of his chariot, placards were carried, blazoning the names and places of the athletic and artistic contests he had won and the themes of his songs and plays. Behind came his claque of cheerleaders, shouting his praises and proclaiming among other thing that they were "the soldiers at his triumph."

The whole procession made its way from the Circus Maximus, through the Velabrum and the Forum, but then to the Temple of Apollo on the Palatine, not to the Temple of Jupiter on the Capitol—with victims slain along the route, saffron sprinkled over the streets, and birds, ribbons, and sweets showered on the emperor as he passed. Dio's account is very similar and was probably drawn from the same source. He adds the detail that one of Nero's defeated rivals, Diodorus the lyre player, traveled with him in the chariot, perhaps on the model of the triumphant general's son; and he offers a variant on the route which inserts the Capitol as a stop on the way, before the procession reached the Palatine (or "Palace," both being possible translations of the Greek).

Modern scholars have debated at length the significance and intent of these ceremonies. Plutarch explicitly claims that the Romans were offended at Antony's performance as a usurpation of the triumph, which could properly take place only in Rome itself. But is that what Antony was aiming at? While not disputing the basic "logic of place" that would underlie the popular disquiet (much of the ritual, ceremony, and myth of the Roman state was indeed closely tied to the topography of the city), recent critics have tended to suspect a rather more complicated explanation. Antony, in this view, was probably launching a specifically Dionysiac celebration, as is suggested in the account of Velleius ("at Alexandria he had ridden in a chariot like Father Liber [that is, Dionysus or Bacchus], kitted out in buskins and holding a thyrsus"). It was Octavian's propaganda that chose to represent this as a triumph and so to hint that if Antony were victorious he would effectively transfer Rome to Egypt.[30]

Even more ingenious attempts have been made to extract from the hostile accounts of Suetonius and Dio the significance of Nero's much more explicitly triumphlike ceremony. To be sure, some recent interpretations have closely followed Dio in casting the whole affair as a direct subversion, or parody, of the traditional ritual and the values that went with it. This antimilitary triumph is an apt conclusion to Dio's story of the whole Greek tour, which starts out with a barbed comparison between Nero's retinue and an invading army—"big enough to have conquered the Parthians and all other nations" except that the weapons they carried were "lyres and plectra, masks and stage-shoes."[31] The occasion was conceived, as one of Nero's modern biographers has put it, as an "answer to a Roman triumph"—"his greatest insult," as another critic concludes, "to the Roman military tradition."[32]

But others have detected different sides to this Neronian extravaganza. It has, for example, been interpreted as part of a more constructive merging of the customary rituals of triumph and the homecoming of Greek victors: Vitruvius, after all, already in the reign of Augustus had described that Greek ceremony in decidedly triumphal terminology. It has also been seen as a reformulation of the ritual into an essentially theatrical performance (the sprinkling of saffron was a distinctive feature of the Roman theater). Others have seen it as a sincere attempt to extend triumphlike ceremonies to honor achievement of a nonmilitary kind, a further step perhaps down the path heralded by the ovation that celebrated the peaceful reconciliation of Octavian and Antony.[33]

One particularly ambitious recent analysis homes in on the Augustan features of this parade: Nero's use of Augustus' triumphal chariot and the procession's final destination at the Temple of Apollo on the Palatine, which was not only built by Augustus but also featured in the *Aeneid* as the culmination of Virgil's imaginary recreation of Octavian's triple triumph of 29 BCE (which, in real life, would have ended on the Capitoline). According to this argument, Nero was attempting to act out that Virgilian scene and so to outdo his predecessor by creating a triumph that was more "Augustan" than Octavian's own.[34]

It is, of course, impossible now to recover the original form of Antony's or Nero's displays, let alone the intention behind them. What is clear enough, however, is that the triumph, as a cultural category as well as a ritual, had shifting and potentially controversial boundaries. The Neronian spectacular, in its literary representations, both was and was not a triumph. It used some of the same paraphernalia, replayed some of the same ritual tropes (the companion in the chariot), and celebrated the emperor's victory; it would be easy to imagine that it could be talked of as Nero's "triumph." Yet there is no sign whatsoever that it was formally treated on a par with the usual ceremony. It did not celebrate the military success that had consistently justified a triumph (even if occasionally rather tenuously), and it flagrantly diverged from some of the standard triumphal practices. The issue is not so much whether Nero's victory parade is to be thought of as a "triumph" or as a "parody of a triumph" but—much more generally—at what point a parody becomes the real thing. For us, in other words, it raises the question of just how triumph*like* a ceremony has to be before it counts as a triumph.

In these accounts, as elsewhere, triumphs and their various subversions were being used by writers as a vivid index of political and military worth. The role of the emperor or, in the case of Antony, the leading dynast is a crucial factor here. As triumphs became exclusively associated with the single ruler and his closest family, so too they became convenient markers of his qualities, propriety, and legitimacy. In its simplest terms, "good emperors" held proper triumphs for proper victories, while "bad emperors" held sham ceremonies for empty victories. For example, it was put down to Tiberius' credit—not exactly a "good emperor" but apparently a no-nonsense traditionalist in many respects—that, when some fawning sycophant of a senator proposed that he celebrate an ovation on returning to Rome from Campania, he robustly turned the suggestion down. "He was not, he declared, so lacking in glory that, after subduing the fiercest nations, and after receiving or declining so many triumphs in his youth, he would now at his age seek an empty honor conferred merely for a trip in the country."[35] Claudius, by contrast, was reported to be happy to accept "triumphal *insignia*" for a war that had finished before he had even come to the throne.[36]

So Roman rhetorical skills came to be expertly deployed in coloring different celebrations with subtly different triumphal nuances: from the accounts of Caligula's mad procession across a bridge over the sea near Baiae (with the emperor in Alexander the Great's breastplate, so it was claimed, and some mock prisoners in tow), to Tacitus' insinuation of a triumphal style in Nero's return to Rome after the murder of his mother Agrippina (with the people watching from tiers of seats, "as they do at triumphs," and offerings on the Capitol by the "victor").[37]

A particularly pointed example is the triumphal language used to highlight the ambivalences of Rome's so-called "victory" over the Parthians under Nero and the installation of Tiridates, a Parthian prince, as king of Armenia. Tiridates was in fact the Parthian nominee for the Armenian throne. But after a disastrous Roman attempt to replace him with one of their own puppets, followed by some military successes in the region scored by Cnaeus Domitius Corbulo, a compromise was hammered out: Tiridates would formally accept his crown from the Romans.[38] He deposited his diadem in front of a statue of the emperor in a legionary camp on the eastern frontier, not to wear it again until he had received it from Nero's hands in Rome.

Tacitus clearly casts Tiridates as more or less a captive at this point (an "object of spectacle," as he insists). But Dio—at least in the words of his excerptor—pointedly reverses the roles: for he hints at the awkward balance of power between Romans and Parthians (who had, after all, got their own way) by presenting Tiridates' journey to Rome from the Euphrates as itself "like a triumphal procession."[39] Finally, once he reaches the capital, a magnificent show is staged, out of all proportion to the military victory secured: the emperor, we are told, was dressed in triumphal costume; celebrations were held in that most triumphal of monuments, the theater of Pompey; and a laurel wreath was deposited in the Temple of Jupiter.[40] Triumph or triumphlike? For most modern observers, triumphlike. But, strikingly, both Pliny (who lived through it) and Dio call it, straightforwardly, a "triumph."[41]

These stories are a nice indication of the two faces of triumphal ceremony and discourse. On the one hand, no doubt, it was a mark of autocratic power that emperors could, and did, extend or subvert the traditional norms of the triumph. On the other, writers exploited the vocabulary of triumphal subversion to symbolize the emperor's misconduct or to calibrate his impropriety. Which face we are seeing on any individual occasion, or what combination of the two, is almost impossible to determine.

DRESSING THE PART

One of the most powerful ways of extending the resonance of the triumph outside the brief hours of the ceremony did not involve vast memorial building schemes nor the launching of look-alike processions with their expensive chariots and stand-in prisoners or soldiers. Much more simply and economically, it involved the wider use of the costume worn by triumphing generals. By adopting all or part of the characteristic triumphal dress on certain occasions after his triumph, a man might publicly call to mind past successes and prolong his triumphal glory. Even for those who had themselves never celebrated a triumph, this might offer a way of appropriating some of the power, glory, and status associated with the ceremony.

From at least the mid-second century BCE to the final years of the Republic, we find a handful of dramatic instances of triumphal dressing outside the procession itself. These went far beyond the wearing of laurel, which generals who had once triumphed may have been regularly allowed to do on certain public occasions.[42] According to one later Roman biographer, after his procession in 167 BCE Aemilius Paullus was given the right "by the people and by the senate" to wear his triumphal costume at circus games. Pompey too is said to have been voted that honor, while Marius—immediately following his first triumph in 104—reputedly called the senate into session, still dressed in his triumphal outfit. Metellus Pius, on the other hand, a Roman commander in Spain in the 70s BCE, used the same technique to anticipate rather than to extend triumphal honors: the story was that after a victory against the Roman rebel Sertorius he was hailed *imperator* by his troops and took to wearing triumphal garb (specifically *palmata vestis,* "palm-embroidered costume") at dinners.[43]

Strikingly, almost every one of these incidents is recounted with more or less explicit disapproval.[44] In Metellus' case, the triumphal aspect of his dress is seen as part and parcel of his disgracefully extravagant behavior in Spain. Pompey is said to have used his right to wear triumphal dress only once, "and that was once too often." Marius quickly saw the unfavorable reaction of the other senators and went out to change. These were, in other words, exemplary anecdotes, marking out this kind of formal extension of triumphal glory beyond the procession itself as unacceptable, at least in a republican context. In fact, if we follow Polybius' claim that the cortège of an aristocratic Roman funeral paraded men impersonating the ancestors of the deceased, with costume to match (if they had celebrated a triumph, "a purple toga embroidered with gold"), it was only the dead who could safely put on their triumphal robes again.[45]

The single possible exception is found in the "diplomatic presentation sets" that were offered occasionally to friendly foreign kings in recognition of their services or loyalty to Rome. These are not, in fact, quite as "triumphal" as modern scholars tend to make them out to be.[46] In only one of the four reported republican instances do the gifts include anything undeniably reminiscent of the triumph or explicitly likened to it; that occasion was in 203 BCE, when the Numidian leader Massinissa was said by Livy to have been presented with the distinctive combination of *toga picta* and *tunica palmata,* as well as a gold crown, scepter, and official "curule" chair.[47] Yet in the Empire, Tacitus looks back to republican precedent when he refers to the "revival" of an ancient custom in 24 CE, with the presentation to King Ptolemy of "an ivory scepter and *toga picta,* the traditional gifts offered by the senate."

Tacitus' interest is, of course, more than antiquarianism. Once again, he is presenting the use and misuse of triumphal symbolism as a means of measuring the use and misuse of imperial power more generally. Here, the triumphal trappings given to Ptolemy, who had done nothing more than remain loyal during Rome's war in North Africa, are contrasted with the emperor's refusal (reported just a few lines earlier) to grant triumphal *insignia* to Publius Cornelius Dolabella, who had actually secured the Roman victory.[48]

These *insignia* or *ornamenta* were all that was awarded to successful generals in the Principate, once the ceremony of triumph itself had been monopolized by the imperial family. Tacitus' hint of an equivalence between them and the package of honors offered to foreign kings explains some of the disproportionate modern interest in these diplomatic presents. For one seductive idea is that they offered a model and an origin for the triumphal ornaments of the later period.[49] In fact, that connection is very fragile. In part this is because the accounts we have of explicitly triumphal gifts to friendly kings may themselves be based on the imperial custom; Livy, in other words, may have concocted the award to

Massinissa out of the later practice of bestowing triumphal *insignia* (rather than vice versa).[50] But even more to the point, it is very uncertain what the ornaments themselves consisted in, beyond the fact that their grant was commemorated with a statue in the Forum of Augustus. They did not even necessarily, or regularly, include the *toga picta* and *tunica palmata*.[51]

What is clear is that, in glaring contrast to the republican pattern, aspects of triumphal dress in the Principate did regularly appear outside the context of the triumphal procession. The prime example of this is in the dress of the emperor himself. For not only was the ceremony of triumph monopolized by the imperial family, but its conventions and symbols were deployed as ways of marking, defining, and conceptualizing the emperor's power. The imperial title *imperator* echoed the acclamation that had often in the late Republic preceded the grant of a triumph.[52] And significant elements of the emperor's costume, on certain ceremonial occasions at least, were identical to those of the triumphing general (or they were presented as such by Roman writers).[53] In other words, the blazoning of power implied by the more-than-temporary adoption of triumphal dress that was so unacceptable to the political culture of republican Rome found its inverse correlate in the Empire. One-man rule could be expressed as a more or less permanent triumphal status.

The stages in this transition are now practically irrecoverable. True, Roman writers note a perplexing series of individual grants awarding Caesar and Octavian the right to specific elements of triumphal dress on particular occasions. In his account of 45, for example, Dio records that "by decree Caesar wore triumphal dress at all festivals and dressed up with a laurel wreath wherever and whenever" (though, implying that republican anxieties were still a factor, he goes on to explain that Caesar's excuse was that it covered up his baldness); and he adds (in his account of 44) that he was given the right "always to ride around in the city itself dressed in triumphal garb." Appian meanwhile notes that he was given the right to wear triumphal dress when he sacrificed.[54] And similar decrees are recorded for Octavian (later Augustus). Separate grants recorded on 40, 36, and 29 gave him the right to wear laurel wreaths or a crown of victory. In 25 he was awarded both crown and triumphal dress on the first day of the year—which means that, had he himself been in Rome when Tiberius triumphed on January 1, 7 BCE, there would have been the bizarre coincidence of both emperor and general in traditional triumphal costume.[55]

Yet a host of problems arises in trying to understand what is going on in any detail. Were the honors granted really so minutely calibrated? Or have the later historians on whom we must rely introduced some of these repetitions and complexities? When Dio, for example, refers to the decision in 44 that Caesar should have the right to ride around the city in "triumphal dress," is that significantly separate from the grant he records in the same year of "the costume used by the kings"? Or has Dio been confused by differently worded accounts of the same decree?[56] It is, in fact, in that particular distinction between "triumphal" and "regal" costume that the most intense confusion lies—and where we seem to find the most flagrant conflicts in ancient accounts. So, for example, in describing the famous incident at which Antony offered Caesar a crown during the festival of the Lupercalia, Plutarch has Caesar sitting on a dais "dressed in triumphal clothes"; Dio has him "in regal costume."[57]

Modern scholars have made ingenious attempts to sort out these different strands and to determine what kind of outfit was being worn when: "Plutarch's 'triumphal costume' seems a mistake," as one recent commentator corrects him, "Caesar was wearing . . . 'regal', rather than triumphal, dress."[58] This is to miss the point. At this early period of the new Roman autocracy, precedents were sought and invented in a variety of different registers of power: triumphal, regal, divine. No one in the first century BCE (still less in the third century CE when Dio was writing) had any accurate knowledge about what the early Roman kings had actually worn. Instead, power brokers, observers, and critics were appealing to different reconstructions of that in their various analyses of the autocracy and its symbols, and in their various attempts to find ways of presenting (and dressing up—literally) one-man rule. And, of course, soon enough the circular nature of this process would have meant that the costume of Caesar and his successors helped to legitimate particular reconstructions of primitive Roman dress. This nexus of first-century debate no doubt lies behind many of the "confusions" about triumphal and regal outfits, as well as behind the conflicting attempts to relate the triumphing general to (or to distinguish him from) the early monarchs.

That said, the key fact is that triumphal dress did become a significant element in the symbolic armory of the Roman emperor. Suetonius refers to Caligula "frequently" wearing the garb of a triumphing general, as does Dio, who contrasts this (favorably, by implication) with his more explicitly divine attire.[59] Republican anxieties were not entirely lost. The right given Domitian to wear triumphal dress whenever he entered the senate house is listed by Dio among that emperor's excesses. And Claudius is praised for not wearing it throughout a whole celebration but only when he was actually sacrificing; the rest of the occasion (after what must have been a nifty costume change) he directed in a *toga praetexta*.[60] But the equivalence between emperor and triumphing general—in title as much as dress—was firmly established. If the triumphal procession through the streets of Rome became a rarer event when the ceremony was restricted to the imperial family itself, the same could not be said for the image of the triumphing general—or at least his double.

THE TRIUMPH OF THE CONSULSHIP

This symbolic language of triumphal power extended further than the imperial house. In particular, triumphal dress was associated with what came to be known as the *processus consularis,* the "consular procession"— the ceremony held at the inauguration of new consuls. The best known literary representations of this are found in works of the fourth century CE and later: *Panegyrics* of the poet Claudian, celebrating consulships of the emperor Honorius in 398 in Milan, and in 404 in Rome; and the fourth book of Corippus' *In Laudem Iustini Minoris (Panegyric of Justin II),* which hypes that emperor's entry into the consulship in 566, in the Christian city of Constantinople, or "New Rome."[61]

How far either of these accounts can be taken as a reasonably faithful description of the ceremony is a moot point. (One of Corippus' recent commentators tends to understate the problem when she observes: "The exercise of the imagination in such descriptive passages is not ruled out.")[62] But both evoke its triumphal aspects, Corippus especially strongly: he describes the decorations of "triumphal laurel," the emperor being carried along shoulder-high "for his great triumph" *(in magnum triumphum),* while also echoing the traditional vocabulary of the occasion (Justin is described as *ovans*). What is more, some ceremonial images of consuls from this period depict them wearing what has been taken to be a version of the *toga picta.*[63]

Of course, these texts are much later in date than most of what we have been concerned with so far; they have as their subject the emperor himself as consul, which might explain some of the triumphal imagery; and in the case of Honorius' sixth consulship the ceremony was also celebrating his military victory over the Goths.[64] Yet we have evidence of a procession to the Capitoline at the inauguration of consuls at least as far back as the first century BCE.[65] By the end of the first century CE there are signs that this was—or at least could be—invested with triumphal character, even for consuls who were not part of the imperial family. Martial writing in the 90s hints at the connection of (triumphal) laurel and the beginning of a consul's office.[66]

But the most aggressive statement of these links is to be found slightly later and in visual form on the Monument of Philopappos, still a well-known landmark in Athens (Fig. 34). This is the tomb of Caius Julius Antiochus Epiphanes Philopappos, descendant of the royal house of Commagene (in Syria), honorary citizen of Athens and Roman consul in 109 CE. Part of its sculptural decoration appears to show Philopappos in triumph, in a scene that is closely modeled on the famous panel from the Arch of Titus. Philopappos certainly never celebrated a triumph. Assuming that this is not a dangerous fantasy, depicting its honorand usurping the triumphal privileges of the imperial house, then it must be a visual reference to one of the highlights of his career: his consulship at Rome. Whether it is to be seen as a documentary depiction of his inaugural procession or as a bold "literalization" of the symbolic triumphal

FIGURE 34: The façade of the Monument of Philopappos, Athens, 114–116 CE, as restored in the third volume of Stuart and Revett's *Antiquities of Athens* (1794). Beneath the central seated portrait of Philopappos is the triumphal scene of his inauguration as consul in 109 CE.

aspects of the inauguration has been much debated. But whichever approach we take, Philopappos' monument casts the consular ceremony in a form almost indistinguishable from a triumph "proper."[67]

This representation—and the idea of the *processus consularis* in general—raises sharply again the question of the boundaries between triumphal ceremony and its imitators, parodies, and look-alikes. Scholars have struggled in trying to define the relationship between the consular inauguration and the traditional triumphal procession. They have written vaguely about the "increasing coalescence" between such ceremonies toward the late Empire and the "merging of the associations" of consulship and triumph. "Any imperial ceremony," it has been said, "could take on the overtones of a triumph."[68] This gives the impression of some kind of ritual melting pot, in which traditional distinctions gradually broke down and everything seeped together into some undifferentiated late antique ceremonial. Better, in general, to think of triumphal symbolism as providing a way of conceptualizing other forms of Roman political and social power, and being used selectively to that end.

In this case, it is important in particular to be alert to a longstanding convergence between triumph and consulship that is often overlooked. For in the late Republic we know of a series of generals who, in a striking union of different forms of glory, celebrated their triumph on the very day of their entry into the consulship, or immediately before: Marius in 104 BCE, probably Pompey in 71 (the day before his consulship started in 70), and a decided clutch in the Caesarian and triumviral periods, including Marcus Aemilius Lepidus in 43 (the eve of his consulship in 42), Lucius Antonius in 41, Lucius Marcius Censorinus in 39, and possibly Quintus Fabius Maximus in 45.[69] What this suggests is that something more than a merging of different forms of ceremonial is at stake in the imperial *processus consularis*. The connection—however it was originally formed—between the triumph and the consulship went back into the Republic. It points to the Januslike face of the ceremony, not only a backward-looking commemoration of past success but an inaugural moment in the political order. In the next chapter we shall see the most extreme (mythical) example of this, when the triumph of Romulus coincided with the first day of the Roman state itself.

THE TRIUMPH OF DEATH

The most notorious instance of the use of triumphal costume and symbolism outside the procession is also one of the most alluring cul de sacs in modern scholarship on the triumph. In his tenth *Satire* (adapted by Samuel Johnson as *The Vanity of Human Wishes*), Juvenal mocks the pomposity of the magistrate who presides over the games *(ludi)*—that characteristic Roman combination of religious ritual and popular entertainment that involved a variety of spectacles from horse or chariot racing in the Circus Maximus to theatrical performances *(ludi scaenici)*. The president is dressed up, writes Juvenal, "in the tunic of Jupiter, carrying the purple swathes of his embroidered toga on his shoulders and a vast crown so huge that no neck could bear the weight." It would be an extraordinary ego trip for this Roman bigwig, but for the fact that, as the satirist gleefully points out, he must share the ride with a sweaty slave who stands with him in the chariot to take the weight of the crown.[70]

Again, this is a more complicated passage than it at first seems. There is no indication which of the several different cycles of games celebrated in Rome by the late first century CE Juvenal had in mind (if indeed he intended any such precise reference). And the puzzle is complicated by the fact that within just six lines he calls the presiding magistrate both "praetor" and "consul."[71] Nonetheless, the overall implication that the president of the games was kitted out like a triumphing general (right down to the presence of that elusive slave) has launched a galaxy of theories on the links between the games and the triumph—in particular between the procession that opened the circus games *(pompa circensis)* and the triumphal equivalent.[72]

Most of these theories look back once more to the earliest phases of the city's history. Attention has focused on the so-called Roman Games or Great Games *(ludi Romani* or *magni/maximi)* which are widely believed to have been the earliest of this form of celebration and to have provided a model for the later versions. Mommsen, for example, argued a century and a half ago (in a claim often repeated even in modern accounts) that these *ludi* were originally, under the early Etruscan kings of Rome, an integral part of the ceremony of triumph itself; but they were progressively separated from it until they became an independent and regular festival in the Roman calendar in the fourth century BCE. Hence—insofar as the *pompa circensis* was in effect a "triumphal proces-

sion minus the triumph"—the distinctive outfit of the presiding magistrate.[73] Versnel, by contrast, has tried to explain the shared symbolism of
triumph and *ludi* by tracing both ceremonies back to a common ancestor in an eastern New Year festival, whose distinctive attributes were preserved even as its Roman "spin-offs" diverged.[74]

Much of this is learned and ingenious fantasy. The problem is, in
part, that the early history of the games is even murkier than that of the
triumph, and hot scholarly dispute has raged over almost every single aspect. Were the Great Games and the Roman Games always synony-
mous, or was there once a distinction between the two? What was their
original purpose—to celebrate victory or, as a primitive plebeian festival,
to promote agricultural success? And just how far back in time can we
trace the rituals that later writers associate with the games?

This last question is frustratingly complicated by our one extended
literary account of a circus procession: the description by Dionysius
of Halicarnassus, writing under Augustus, of *ludi* vowed in 499 BCE.
Dionysius explicitly claims that he has drawn on an earlier version by
the late third-century BCE "father of Roman history" Fabius Pictor—
who may, or may not, have had reliable information on the fifth century.
But he has also certainly been influenced (how substantially influenced
is again hotly disputed) by his own pet theory that Rome was in origin a
Greek city and by his determination to find Greek elements in the most
hoary Roman traditions.[75] Leaving that controversial text aside, big arguments have necessarily been built on the tiniest scraps of evidence.
Much of the discussion of Mommsen's hypothesis has centered on the
placing of a single comma in a passage of Livy.[76]

The fact is that we have no evidence at all for seeing the costume of
the president of the games as distinctively triumphal before the Empire—and even for that period there is very little. The key text is that
one passage of Juvenal, plus a jibe about the Megalesian Games (connected with the cult of Cybele) in the *Satire* that follows: "There sits the
praetor, like a triumph, the booty *(praeda)* of the gee-gees." Losing his
money in betting, in other words, the presiding magistrate has become
the "booty" of the horses: so not only is he dressed as for a triumph, but

CIRCI·ET·LVDICRI·CIRCENSIS·ANTIQVOM·MARMOREVM·FRVSTVM·QVOD·IN·AEDIBVS·MAFEIORVM·ROMAE·AD·THERMAS·AGRIPPÍNAS·EXT/

FIGURE 35: The panel of a lost sarcophagus (shown here in an engraving by E. Dupérac, d. 1604) depicts the Circus Maximus in Rome and some of its distinctive monuments, including the obelisk, which stood on the center-line, or *spina*, of the racetrack. To the right, the figure riding in the triumphal-style chariot (though drawn by only two horses) and being crowned from behind is presumably the presiding magistrate of the games.

he has become victim of that classic triumphal paradox that always threatens to make a victim out of the celebrating general.[77] Juvenal apart, the only unambiguous evidence identifying the two forms of ceremonial dress is the statement by both Tacitus and Dio that at the games established in honor of Augustus at his death in 14 CE, the tribunes who presided were to wear triumphal costume but not to have the use of a chariot *(currus)*. Dionysius, significantly or not, does not mention the magistrate's clothing.[78]

The visual evidence is not much clearer. One evocative image from Rome appears to show the president of the games driving through the Circus Maximus, a slave behind him holding his crown—just as described by Juvenal (Fig. 35). But as bad luck would have it, the sculpture itself has been lost and is recorded only in Renaissance drawings and a single engraving, none of which allows us to say much about its original form or date (beyond that it appears to belong somewhere in the mid to late Empire).[79] Otherwise, vaguely triumphal-style figures in imperial art tend to be claimed (according to the enthusiasm of the archaeologist concerned) for the circus games, the *processus consularis,* or the triumph proper. Or to put it another way, one consequence of the spread of triumphal symbolism outside the triumph is that it is necessarily hard to pin a definite label onto any individual "triumphal" scene.[80] But—suspiciously, one might almost think—nothing survives that combines the iconography of circus and triumph so clearly as the lost piece.

This evidence is, of course, not incompatible with the idea that from time immemorial the leader of the games (or at least of some particular cycles of *ludi*) was dressed in triumphal costume—however we might choose to explain that. What we can document for the first time in the first century CE might go back much earlier than that; and those who hold that Roman religious practice was rigidly conservative and almost unchanging would presumably argue that it almost certainly did. But a less primitivizing reconstruction is more plausible. The evidence we have fits much more easily with the idea that the extension of triumphal symbolism to the circus president was part and parcel of a wider use of triumphal dress from the start of the Principate to mark out positions of honor and power more generally. Proof is impossible either way; but the circus president's triumphal garb probably owes more to the emperor Augustus than to old King Tarquin or (on Versnel's view) some eastern god-king.

An obsession with the connection between the triumph and the games has tended to obscure the links between the triumph and another great ceremonial procession in Roman culture—known by convenient, if misleading, shorthand as the aristocratic funeral. I am not here referring to particular overlaps in ritual. Certainly, some elements of triumphal practice have been found in funeral processions. Dionysius of Halicarnassus himself observed, in his account of the *pompa circensis,* that a strand of ribaldry and satire was shared by all three of the circus, funeral, and triumphal parades: men dressed as satyrs or Sileni, dancing and jesting, in both circus procession and funeral, the satiric songs of the soldiers in the triumph.[81] Some have tried to argue from this for a common ancestry for all three *pompae:* Greek roots, as Dionysius himself would predictably have it, or an Etruscan inheritance, as some of his modern successors would prefer?[82]

What makes one ritual seem similar to another is just as complicated as what makes them different. And the significance of similarities is often hard to see. Or more precisely, in this case, it has proved difficult to decide which of the many perceived similarities (the use of torches, the final banquet) might be important indicators for the history of the ritu-als.[83] At the same time it has proved all too tempting to discover ritual borrowings where none exist. Recently, for example, it has been con-fidently asserted that the floats, painting, and spoils displayed in trium-phal processions were "re-used at funeral processions." If so, this would make a compelling visual link between the two occasions. But in fact there is no clear evidence for this practice at all.[84]

My concern is not so much with these overlaps between the two pro-cessions but with their interrelationship at a broader cultural and ideo-logical level. We have already noted the links between imperial triumph and apotheosis, monumentalized in the Arch of Titus with its echoes be-tween the more-than-human status of the triumphing general and the deification of the emperor on his death. The logic of that connection had an even bigger impact on early imperial ritual culture. This is strik-ingly evident not only in the strange story of Trajan's posthumous tri-umph (when an effigy of the already deified emperor was said to have processed in the triumphal chariot) but also in the arrangements made for the funeral of Augustus.

On that occasion, one proposal was that the cortège should pass through the *porta triumphalis;* another, that the statue of Victory from the senate house should be carried at the head of the procession; an-other, that placards blazoning the titles of laws Augustus had sponsored and peoples he had conquered should be paraded, too. Dio, reflecting the logic even if not the more sober facts, claims that the cortège did in-deed pass through the triumphal gate, that the emperor was laid out on his bier in triumphal costume, and that elsewhere in the procession there was an image of him in a triumphal chariot.[85] The triumph here was providing a language for representing (even if not performing) an imperial funeral and the apotheosis that the funeral might simulta-neously entail.[86]

There was, however, a bleaker side to this—and one that chimes in with the theme of the ambivalence and fragility of triumphal glory. True, the funeral may have been an occasion in which triumphal splen-dor could be called to mind and, in part, recreated long after the day of the triumph itself had passed, as with the impersonation of the ancestors of the dead man—dressed, if appropriate, in their triumphal robes. But at the same time the funeral might point to the final destruction of triumphal glory: Pompey's triumphal toga was consigned to what passed for his funeral pyre; and at the culmination of Caesar's funeral the "musicians and actors took off the clothes that they taken from the equipment *(instrumentum)* of his triumphs and put on for the occasion, tore them to shreds and threw them into the blaze."[87]

The triumph was repeatedly linked with death in other ways, too. Aemilius Paullus famously starred in his triumphal procession amidst the funerals of his sons. But on the most poignant occasions the two rituals could be presented as almost interchangeable: if death in battle robbed the victor of the triumphal ceremony he deserved, then the funeral might have to substitute. This is a theme eloquently developed by Seneca in an essay on grief, mourning, and the acceptance of the necessity of death, *Ad Marciam, de consolatione (To Marcia, On Consolation)*. One of the examples he takes is the death in 9 BCE of Drusus, Augustus' stepson, during successful campaigns in Germany. His body was brought back home in a procession through Italy; and crowds poured out from towns along the route to escort it to the city: "a funeral procession very like a triumph."[88]

The cultural resonance of this connection is nicely illustrated by Plutarch, when he projects a similar idea onto the Greek world in his description of the death of the Achaean general Philopoemen in 182 BCE. After he had been poisoned by the Messenians, his compatriots in Megalopolis launched an expedition to recover his body, cremate it, and bring it home. It was, Plutarch explains, an impressive and orderly procession that returned to Megalopolis, "combining a triumphal procession and a funeral."[89]

These connections—with their reminder that, for better or worse, death always courted glory—give an added point to the story of Domitian's strange banquet with which I started this chapter. It was in Roman terms magnificently appropriate that when the emperor was looking for a theme for his triumphal dinner party, he should take such a funerary turn.

IX

The Triumph of History

IMPERIAL LAURELS

Toward the end of his long account of laurel and its various uses, Pliny tells the story of an unusual laurel grove at the imperial villa known as "The Hennery" *(Ad Gallinas),* just outside Rome. It had been planted from the sprig of laurel held in the beak of a white hen that had been dropped by an eagle into the lap of the unsuspecting Livia, just after her betrothal to Octavian. It was obviously an omen of their future greatness. So the soothsayers *(haruspices)* ordered that the bird and any future brood should be carefully preserved—hence the name of the villa—and that the laurel should be planted. It successfully took root, and when Octavian triumphed in 29 BCE he wore a wreath and carried in his hand a branch, both taken from that burgeoning tree. "And all the ruling Caesars *(imperatores Caesares)* did likewise." In fact, the custom grew up of them planting the branch after the triumphal ceremony and calling the resulting trees by the name of the emperor or prince concerned. A veritable Julio-Claudian memorial grove.[1]

Suetonius reports a rather more sinister version. At the beginning of his *Life* of Galba, Nero's successor, he explains that as the death of each emperor approached, his own particular tree withered. At the end of Nero's reign, "the whole grove died from the root up" (as well as all the hens that were the descendants of that original laurel bringer). This heralded the advent of a new dynasty.[2]

Unsurprisingly perhaps, these stories do not quite add up. How do we reconcile the thriving grove described by Pliny with Suetonius' picture of blight at the end of Rome's first imperial dynasty? Either Pliny was writing this part of his great encyclopedia before 68 CE, or—more likely—reliable information about the state of the trees at "The Hennery" was limited. Besides, we find a troubling inconsistency even within Suetonius' account. If all the imperial laurels died out at the death of their own particular emperor, what exactly was left to wither and so make way for Galba?

But the importance of the story does not lie in those practical details. For it offers a political genealogy—literally, a family tree—of the new-style imperial triumph. It provides a founding myth for a ceremony that since the reign of Augustus had been restricted to the ruling house itself. Dio's narrative makes this very nearly explicit. His version of the tale is not told with quite the verve of Pliny or Suetonius (though his interpretation of the original omen as partly a dreadful presage of the future power of Livia over Augustus is a nice touch). But, unlike them, he locates the story at a precise moment in the unfolding historical narrative. Pinpointing it to 37 BCE, Dio makes it follow shortly after his account of the refusal of a triumph by Marcus Vipsanius Agrippa, Octavian's aide and at that time consul.

According to Dio, Octavian had not had such military success, and Agrippa was unwilling to "puff himself up" with the honor in case (so the implication is) he thereby showed up Octavian in contrast. This is the first of a series of triumphal refusals by Agrippa, which lead in Dio's narrative to the development of triumphal *insignia,* rather than the full triumph, as the standard reward for successful generals outside the imperial family. The close link here between Agrippa's declining a triumph and the depositing of the laurel in the imperial lap points strongly to the importance of the story as the charter myth of the restricted triumph and as a marker of historical change.[3]

HISTORY AND RITUAL

This chapter is concerned with the ways in which we, as well as the ancients themselves, identify, describe, and explain this and other developments in the ceremony of triumph. I emphasized at the start of this book that the triumph was one of the few Roman rituals with a "history." By that, I meant that—notwithstanding all the uncertainties I have repeatedly pointed to—we could trace a series of individual triumphs, their dates, their cast of characters, and sometimes their particular circumstances across a millennium or so of Roman time. To move from there to "history" in the stronger sense, delineating and accounting for change in the ritual as it was performed, is a much more difficult issue. Ancients and moderns alike have tended to resort to big assertions. Some of these are true but self-evident; others are based on little more than conjecture. Often they are tinged with that nostalgia for the noble simplicity of early Rome that modern historiography shares with (or borrows from) its ancient counterpart.

One theme has been the increasing "hellenization" of the original ceremony.[4] But this apparently technical term does not necessarily deliver more than the obviously correct observation that Rome's growing contact with cultures of the Eastern Mediterranean catalyzed new forms of triumphal display—while at the same time the lucrative process of conquest provided the wherewithal with which to sponsor ever more lavish spectacle. Other themes headline various forms of deterioration or corruption in the ceremony. Modern writers echo Dionysius' lament that by his day (the reign of Augustus) triumphs had become a "histrionic show," far removed from "the ancient tradition of frugality," or Dio's view that "cliques and factions" had "changed" the ceremony for the worse. It is commonly now claimed that, at the very least, a shift of emphasis can be traced over the ritual's history from a primitive religious significance to political power-play and self-advertising spectacular display.[5]

This again may be partly true. Certainly the terms in which the triumph was discussed and debated must have changed radically over the centuries. The sometimes cynical quips or philosophical *bons mots* from Seneca and his like about its functions and ambiguities are inconceivable in the early city. But it would be romantic nostalgia to imagine that the Romans of, say, the fifth or fourth centuries BCE, whose words are lost to us, were unfailingly pious; that they never quarreled about the ceremony, never saw it as an opportunity for self advancement; or, for that matter, that they never wrote the whole thing off as a waste of time. It is always an easy way out to project innocent simplicity onto periods for which we have no evidence. But we should remember that the very earliest extended meditation on triumphal culture that we do have, Plautus' *Amphitruo* of the early second century BCE, is already highly sophisticated and ironizing about the ritual and its participants. As for later Roman commentators themselves, if one of their gambits was to proclaim the increasing politicization of the triumph over time, another (as we have seen) was to retroject many of the later disputes and in-fighting back into its earliest phases.

On a smaller scale, the triumphal chronology does reveal some striking changes in the pattern of celebration. The triumph on the Alban Mount, for example, is first attested in 231 BCE, is celebrated four times over the next sixty years, and is not heard of again after 172. The pattern of the twenty-one known ovations, between the first in 503 BCE and the dictatorship of Caesar, is even more complicated: there is a clutch in the early years of the Republic, then a long gap (none, or perhaps one, celebrated between 360 and Marcellus' ovation in 211), followed by a rash of seven between 200 and 174, then a lull again until three were celebrated in the late second and early first centuries BCE—each for victories in slave wars.

Even in the Empire, when the absence of any systematic record, such as the Forum inscription, means that we are much less certain of dates and type of celebration (and indeed when a number of triumphal ceremonies may be entirely lost to us), some patterns are clear. Ovations are not heard of after 47 CE, when—in a gesture of no doubt self-conscious archaism on the emperor's part—Aulus Plautius was given the honor for his achievements in Britain by Claudius. The award of triumphal *insig-nia,* by contrast, was a relatively regular event in the early Empire. In fact, it became rather too regular in the eyes of some historians, who sneered at its award to the undeserving, even on occasion to children. But it too seems to have fallen into abeyance after the reign of Hadrian, in the mid-second century.[6]

Something more than the changing patterns of Roman military success must surely underlie these changes in the pattern of celebration. But exactly *what* more remains a matter of inference or guesswork. One scholar, for example, has recently conjectured that the low social status of the last man to triumph on the Alban Mount, in 172, was one factor that "doom[ed] the institution in perpetuity."[7] This is a perfectly reasonable guess on the basis of the evidence we have—yet a single *declassé* honorand seems hardly sufficient to kill off an institution unless other factors were at work, too. Others have suggested that it was the increasing emphasis on triumphal dress as a mark of the emperor's power that caused the demise of triumphal *insignia* for "ordinary" generals.[8] Again, this is a reasonable guess, but no more than that.

As for the peaks and troughs in the history of ovations, it does seem that the ceremony—whatever its origin—came to be used as a way of adjusting triumphal honors to different occasions, circumstances, or types of victory. The seven ovations clustered in the early second century BCE are, as one modern commentator has emphasized, all for "non-consular commanders returning from Spain"; and it has been tempting to see the ceremony as a way of handling the demands of lower-status generals, in the context of new and wider spheres of warfare.[9] Later, the *ovatio* apparently proved useful as a means of rewarding those who had defeated enemies of lower status, namely, slaves. The development of the ceremony under Caesar and Octavian (when, as we have seen, it was used to celebrate such "victories" as the pact made between Antony and Octavian in 40 BCE) would also fit this improvisatory pattern. So far, so good. But it is hard to see what prompts the improvisation on some occasions and not others, and why the experiments are so short-lived.

But the underlying problem in any attempt to reconstruct the development of the triumph in traditional historical terms is the complex relationship between the ceremony as performed and the ceremony as written. Or, to put it more positively, the history of the triumph is a marvelously instructive example of the dynamic relationship between ritual practice and "rituals in ink"—a relationship that cannot be reduced to a simple story of development and change and that, indeed, often directly subverts the very idea of a linear narrative.

This is partly a question of the so-called invention of tradition. One of the ways in which change is legitimated in any culture is by the construction of precedent. New rituals are given authority not by their novelty but by claims that they mark a return to the rituals of old. Sometimes these claims may be true; sometimes they are flagrant fictions, whether consciously invented or not; more often, no doubt, they lie somewhere on the spectrum between truth and fiction. But, whichever precise variant we are dealing with, the key point is that innovations can be dressed up as tradition and projected back into the past so successfully that it is almost impossible—whether for the modern historian or even for members of the culture concerned—to distinguish the "truly" ancient rituals from the retrojections. After all, how many people in twentieth-first-century Britain are aware that most so-called traditional royal pageantry is a brilliant confection cooked up in the late nineteenth century, rather than a precious inheritance from "Merrie England" and the Middle Ages?[10] Societies that make repeated use of this means of cultural legitimation are often characterized, like ancient Rome, as "conservative"; but they do not so much resist change as justify sometimes very radical innovation by the denial that it is innovation at all.[11]

We have already noted some individual elements of the triumph that have been understood in this way—for example, the role of Camillus as an invented precedent for Julius Caesar. The potential impact of such inventions on our understanding of the triumph's history as a whole is vividly encapsulated by the confusion that surrounds the "subtriumphal" ritual of the dedication of the *spolia opima* ("the spoils of honor"). It is an honor usually assumed to have been granted only to those Romans who had killed the enemy commander in single combat—and who then, we are told, carried the spoils taken from the body to dedicate them on the Capitoline at the Temple of Jupiter "Feretrius" (Romans debated whether the title came from *carrying* the spoils *(ferre)* or *smiting (ferire)* the enemy).[12]

According to the orthodox account, this happened only three times in the whole of Roman history: first when Romulus killed the king of the Caeninenses; second in the late fifth century BCE when Aulus Cornelius Cossus killed the king of Veii; and in 222 when Marcus Claudius Marcellus combined dedicating the *spolia* of King Viridomarus with his triumph proper.[13] One deviant tradition—particularly striking given the chorus of writers who insist on just the trio of celebrations, and usually dismissed as wrong—has Scipio Aemilianus also dedicating the *spolia opima* thanks to a victory in single combat in Spain some fifty years after Marcellus.[14]

Taking their cue from the association with Romulus, some modern scholars see in the *spolia opima* a primitive proto-triumph, the most ancient version of Roman victory parade.[15] But the evidence we have is equally compatible with exactly the opposite position. Indeed, one recent study has claimed that the only historical celebration of the dedication of these spoils was that by Marcellus in 222 BCE—an innovation that was legitimated by the invention, or (less pejoratively) the imaginative rediscovery, of the two earlier dedications.[16] If this is the case, it offers a marvelous example of the inextricable inter-relationship of "history" and "invented tradition." For, as Livy notes, the emperor Augustus himself claimed to have seen the spoils of Cossus in the Temple of Jupiter Feretrius, as well as his linen corselet (which carried an inscription proving that Cossus was consul at the time of his dedication, not a mere military tribune). Cossus' dedication may have been an imaginative fiction. But even if he had dedicated his spoils in the 430s or 420s, the linen corselet can have been at best the product of loving restoration over four centuries, at worst an outright fake.

Nonetheless, invention or not, the object itself, what was inscribed upon it, and the ritual believed to lie behind it held an established place in Roman literary tradition and historical investigations—and it *mat-*

tered to Livy and Augustus himself. Modern writers have often inferred (though there is no explicit evidence for it in any ancient text) that Augustus was particularly interested in the corselet because, by proving Cossus' high rank, it offered him ammunition against one of his generals, Marcus Licinius Crassus, whom he wanted to prevent from dedicating the *spolia* after killing an enemy king in 29 BCE. That may (or may not) be the background to Dio's claim that Crassus would have performed the ritual "if he had been supreme commander."[17]

The lesson of this one small part of triumphal tradition is not that there is no "history" here, but that it is not the linear narrative of change and development we so often try to reconstruct. The "history" of the *spolia opima* is embedded in invention and reinvention, and in competing (and often loaded) ancient narratives, explanations, and reconstructions. Much the same goes for the triumph itself. But here the stark chronological disjunction between triumphal practice and its written traces even more strongly challenges the simplicity of a linear chronology and pushes issues of discourse to center stage.

Most of the detailed surviving accounts of the triumph and its customs were written in the imperial period. The issue is not simply that these were sometimes composed centuries after the ceremonial they purport to describe, and that the earliest triumphs are always therefore seen through the filter of later interests and prejudices. This is the case for every aspect of early Rome; and it is now a truism that the history of the early kings of the city was indelibly marked by the concerns and preoccupations of the age of the emperors. The extra issue with the triumph is that most accounts come from that period when the ritual itself had been dramatically restricted to relatively rare celebrations by the imperial family. By the first century CE, in other words, the triumph in writing, in images, and in cultural memory largely replaced the triumph in the sense of a victory parade through the streets.

This fact throws into particularly high relief the competing chronologies that to some extent underlie all history. If one chronology of this ritual is the familiar chronology of performance (ordering triumphs, as in the Forum inscription, by date of celebration), another is the chronology of writing (based on the order in which they were described, not performed). To put this at its simplest, Ovid's imagined triumphs of the early Empire are both later and earlier than the celebration of Aemilius Paullus in 167 BCE as told by Plutarch in the late first or early second century CE.

The rest of this chapter explores these competing chronologies and complex histories of the triumph by focusing on the narratives (ancient and modern) of three key moments in the triumphal story. First, it looks at the changes in triumphal symbol and practice under Augustus. Then it turns to the beginning and end of the history of the triumph, with an eye not only on the various narratives used to open or close the story of the ritual but also on the bigger question of what we mean by the origin or end of a ceremony such as this. My aim is to celebrate, rather than to straighten out or compress, the historical intricacies and the sheer "thickness" of the triumph's history.

THE AUGUSTAN REVOLUTION

The reign of the first Roman emperor was a pivotal moment in triumphal history, and the bare bones of the story are worth repeating. Triumphal symbolism appears to have been given more emphasis at this period than ever before, setting the style for later imperial image-making. The Forum of Augustus, in many ways the programmatic monument of the whole regime, celebrated the triumph at every turn—from the assembled statues of the great men of the Republic, each one, according to Suetonius, "in triumphal dress," through the four-horse chariot in the center of the piazza, to that famous painting featuring Alexander "in his triumphal chariot" (later cannily retouched on Claudius' instructions to depict Augustus himself).

Coins across the Empire featured miniature images of distinctive chariots, figures of Victory, and laurels. Commemorative arches in Rome and elsewhere were topped by bronze sculptures of the emperor in his triumphal *quadriga*. And of course, in the Forum itself stood the inscribed list of triumphs—perhaps displayed on an arch surmounted by the triumphant emperor, in what would be a powerful juxtaposition. The symbols and ritual of the imperial house also exploited the triumphal theme. Augustus was almost certainly the first Roman to use *imperator*, with all its triumphal associations, as a regular part of his title ("Imperator Caesar Augustus"), almost as if it were a first name, while in addition accumulating—exactly when, how, and for what reason we do not know—no fewer than twenty-one separate acclamations as *imperator* on more or less the republican model.

Many of the new public and dynastic rituals of the period also drew on triumphal customs. Dio, for example, records the occasion in 13 BCE when Augustus returned to the city from Germany, went up to the Capitol, and, with a clear triumphal resonance, laid the laurel from around his *fasces* "on the knees of Jupiter" (this was, so Dio says, before giving the people free baths and barbers for a day). Five years later, no doubt with the *spolia opima* in mind, he deposited his laurel in the Temple of Jupiter Feretrius. Augustan poets chimed in too. Reflecting (and reinforcing) the topicality of the triumph, they treated it to praise and irony, hype and subversion in almost equal measure—while exploiting its metaphorical power in writing of love and longing, power and poetry itself. This was the age of the triumph.[18]

Or so it was, in all senses but one. For, on the other hand, the reign of Augustus is well known to mark a dramatic limitation in the actual performance of the ritual—as the story of the laurel grove that opened this chapter illustrated. Not in the early years of the reign: the emperor's own extravagant triple triumph of 29 BCE (which was certainly the inspiration behind some of the triumphal poetry and visual images) was followed through the 20s by a number of more "ordinary" triumphs, six in all, for victories in Spain, Gaul, Africa, and Thrace. But after the triumph of Cornelius Balbus in 19, for the rest of Roman history there was no further celebration except by the emperor and his immediate family, unless we count the isolated ovation for Aulus Plautius.

In practice, triumphs were now dynastic events, seemingly used either to showcase chosen heirs (as in the triumph of Tiberius in 12 CE) or to celebrate the beginning of reigns, almost as a coronation ritual. In a sense, that was already one function of the triple triumph of 29; and the triumph over the Jews in 71 marked the start of the reign of Vespasian and the new Flavian dynasty, while the posthumous triumph of Trajan opened the reign of his successor, Hadrian, in 118. Those outside the imperial family (and sometimes those within it) had to be content with triumphal *insignia*.

The change is nicely encapsulated in the poetry books of the Augustan poet Tibullus. The focal poem of his first book celebrates the triumph in 27 of his patron Marcus Valerius Messalla Corvinus for a victory over the Aquitanians. In the second book, he predicts a future triumph for Messalla's son, Marcus Valerius Messalla Messalinus. This triumph never took place. Instead, decades later and long after the death of Tibullus himself, Messalinus was awarded triumphal *insignia* for successes in Illyricum and walked in the triumphal procession of Tiberius in 12.[19]

Modern scholars offer two types of historical explanation for this change. First, they commonly argue that the redirection of the triumph was a crucial part of Augustus' tactics for politically and militarily emasculating the Roman elite. To deprive other senators (and potential rivals) of the traditional marks of glory and the symbolic rewards of victory was part and parcel of his own monopoly of power, and of his insistence that military success lay in his hands alone, and that he and no one else commanded the loyalty of the troops. Or to put it the other way round, the extraordinary prominence that a triumph gave to the successful general was too much for the canny emperor to risk sharing widely.[20]

A second reason given for the change, by both ancient and modern writers, concerns the technical qualifications for celebrating a triumph and the legal status of most military commanders under Augustus. If triumphs could be held only by those who had commanded troops with *imperium* and "under their own auspices," then many commanders would not qualify. For under the new structures of provincial command devised by Augustus, those who governed in the so-called "imperial" provinces (where most of the legions were stationed and where most se-

rious fighting took place) were technically "legates" of the emperor himself, acting under his auspices. Either this meant that traditional triumphal practice ruled out the ceremony for all but the emperor, or this
technicality provided Augustus with a convenient alibi for depriving the
rest of the aristocracy of the opportunity to triumph.[21]

This characterization of the Augustan triumphal revolution is not
wrong—far from it. But the changes under Augustus, the reasons for
them, and how they were understood in antiquity itself are more complicated (and more interesting) than is usually supposed. Once again the
legal technicalities are not clear cut. True, ancient authors, both explicitly and implicitly, relate the apparent exclusion of victors outside
the imperial house to the superior legal and constitutional position of
the emperor. Velleius, for example, in explaining why in 9 CE Marcus
Aemilius Lepidus only received triumphal ornaments, states that "if he
had been fighting under his own auspices, he ought to have celebrated a
triumph." And in his *Res Gestae (Achievements)*, Augustus himself notes
that *supplicationes* were voted to him "either for successes won by myself
or through my legates acting under my auspices."[22] Yet, even so, these
technicalities do not provide a clear guide to who triumphed and who
did not.

Looking back, for example, to the period between 45 BCE and the
final victory of Octavian in the civil wars after Caesar's assassination,
triumphs were certainly then celebrated by those who were legates and
subordinates of the supreme commanders.[23] And after 19 CE those who
scored military victories as proconsuls of senatorial provinces (according, more or less, to the old model of provincial command) did not celebrate triumphs, even if they had been acclaimed *imperator,* which would
normally indicate the possibility, at least, of a subsequent triumphal
celebration.[24] Germanicus, by contrast, was awarded a triumph even
though he was fighting "under the auspices of Tiberius."[25]

The only way to inject consistency into this conflicting evidence is to
turn a blind eye to material that does not fit, or to ingeniously explain it
away. Were legates at this period, for example, entitled to be hailed "imperator"? Some scholars have argued that they were—in the face of

strong contrary implications in Dio; others would regard those acclamations for which we have evidence largely in inscriptions as entirely unofficial, or the action of those who did not understand what the rules really were. How easy would it be to explain to the soldiers that, however enthusiastic about their general's achievements they might have been, he did not actually "qualify" for an acclamation? The truth is that, far from being able to decide who was entitled to what honor, we often do not know what constitutional authority a general possessed. We do not understand, for example, who fought "under their own auspices" at this crucial period of change and who did not; and, according to one recent commentator, neither did Livy ("Livy indeed may not have realized that promagistrates lacked the auspices").

Perhaps even more to the point, we do not know how far to trust Dio, who provides the only detailed narrative of the period. Writing in the third century CE, by which time it may well have been taken for granted that only those fully invested with *imperium* could triumph, he repeatedly attempts to use this "rule" as the key to making sense of the evidence of the triumviral and Augustan periods—even though it sometimes ended in entirely implausible reconstructions of events.[26]

There is no simple way to delineate the legal or constitutional basis of the changes in triumphal celebrations at the start of the Principate. But the conclusions reached in Chapter 6 about how improvisatory triumphal practice was suggest that, once again, we should not necessarily be thinking of identifying fixed rules. Much more likely we are dealing with a rapid period of change, uncertainties in the structures of command, and a series of *ad hoc* triumphal decisions, combined with attempts both at the time and later to justify and explain the principles by which those decisions were reached or might be defended.

But other factors too suggest that we are missing the point if we concentrate on the legal restrictions which might lie behind the change in triumphal practice. If the first emperor had wished to share triumphal celebrations widely, he would not have been prevented from doing so by a narrow application of the rules. To imagine an apologetic courtier explaining to Augustus that the law did not allow him to grant a triumph to a general who had not, say, fought "under his own auspices" is completely incompatible with our understanding of the power structures of the Empire more generally. At most, the appeal to restrictive legislation can only have been a way of packaging or conceptualizing the change, not its cause.

Also, the idea that the major development in triumphal practice initiated under Augustus was the exclusion from the ritual of those outside the imperial family does not completely capture the nature of the change. That is certainly one aspect of it. But hardly less striking is the fact that even the emperor and his family triumphed very rarely. After the triple triumph of 29, Augustus never triumphed again. The rest of his reign is characterized not by triumphal celebrations (after Balbus, there were only two triumphs, in 7 BCE and 12 CE, and an ovation in 9 BCE—all by Tiberius) but by a series of offers of triumphs to himself or to members of his family that were refused. For example, Augustus was offered a triumph in 25 BCE, but he refused it, as he probably did again in 19. In 12 BCE after the senate voted a triumph to Tiberius, Augustus disallowed it, granting only triumphal *insignia*. In 8 Augustus again turned down a triumph for himself. In fact, this practice of turning down triumphs is blazoned in his *Res Gestae (Achievements):* "The senate decreed more triumphs to me, all of which I passed over."[27]

Dio's account takes this as a key theme. For if one of his explanations for the new Augustan culture of the triumph focuses on legal rules, another offers a genealogy of this style of triumphal refusal—centering on the figure of Agrippa. We already noted that in Dio the founding myth of the triumphal laurel grove was closely linked to Agrippa's refusal of a triumph in 37, when he was consul. In his discussion of the events of the year 19 BCE, Dio does not mention the triumph of Balbus but gives full coverage instead to another refusal by Agrippa, now Augustus' son-in-law and probably his intended heir. On this occasion, the refusal came after the senate, at the emperor's own request, had offered him a triumph for victories in Spain. "Other men," wrote Dio, "went after triumphs and got them, not only for exploits not comparable to Agrippa's but merely for arresting robbers . . . For at the beginning at least Augus-

tus was happy to bestow this kind of reward lavishly, and he also honored many with public funerals. The result was that these men glowed
with distinction." But Agrippa, so Dio's message is, gained more out of
refusal than the others did out of acceptance. For "he was promoted to
supreme power, you might say."[28]

Dio, in other words, is identifying here a crucial moment of triumphal change, when a signal of power within the state can be seen in the
refusal rather than acceptance of a triumph. Agrippa's third refusal in 14
BCE finally defines the pattern. In a passage that, significantly perhaps,
just precedes his account of the ill-fated opening of Balbus' theater (the
Tiber was in flood and Balbus could only enter the new building by
boat), Dio explains that Agrippa turned down the triumph offered for
victories in the East—and it was because of this refusal, "at least in my
opinion, that no one else of his peers was permitted to triumph in future
but enjoyed only the distinction of triumphal *insignia*."[29]

How far we should follow Dio's hunch in seeing Agrippa's example as
the catalyst to change is a moot point. The bigger question that Dio's
narrative raises is how to explain the new culture of triumphal refusal in
general. It is understandable enough that Augustus should be keen to
keep potentially rival aristocrats off the triumphal stage. But why also
have his own family triumph so rarely? I am tempted to imagine that he
was canny enough to realize the ambivalence of the triumph, and wise
enough to see that these ceremonials courted humiliation and danger as
much as glory and success. It was safer to keep triumphal performance
on the streets to a minimum, while monumentalizing the ritual in marble, bronze, and ink.

But even this explanation does not capture the striking variety of ancient accounts of Augustan triumphal culture, which modern views of a
more or less radical restriction of the celebration tend to pass over.
Suetonius is possibly a maverick when he portrays Augustus' reign as a
bumper period for performance of the ritual, claiming that Augustus
had "regular triumphs" *(iusti triumphi)* voted for more than thirty generals.[30] No commentator has convincingly explained this total—and, even
with the most generous definition of a "regular triumph" I can reach that

number only by starting to count immediately after the murder of Caesar and including the whole of the triumviral period.

But ancient writers' treatment of what has become famous in modern scholarship as the "last traditional triumph," Balbus' celebration of 19 BCE, is almost as surprising. True, this is where the list on the Forum inscription decisively ends, as if it were trying to indicate closure of the republican tradition. But there is no surviving ancient writer who takes the same line, or even mentions that Balbus was the last from outside the imperial family to triumph. As we have seen, Dio—interested as he is in the ritual's history—is entirely silent on this particular procession. Others, far from making him the last in any triumphal line, treat him as a unique innovator; for as a native of Gades in Spain he was, according to Pliny, the only foreigner to triumph at Rome.[31]

But this final section of the Forum inscription itself repays further attention, particularly seen together with the only other surviving fragment of triumphal chronology from the city of Rome, the *Fasti Barberiniani* (Figs. 36, 37). Close inspection reveals all kinds of interesting details. For example, the description of Octavian at his ovation in 40 BCE appears on the Forum inscription as "Imperator Caesar, son of a god, son of Caius . . . " This apparently refers to his descent by adoption from Julius Caesar both in his divine aspect ("son of a god") and in his human aspect ("son of Caius"—unless that is meant to point us to Octavian's natural father, also called Caius). But, curiously, a closer look at the stone reveals here, as in the entry for his ovation in 36, that the phrase "son of Caius" (*C.f*) has been carved over some previous wording that was erased. We do not know what that previous wording was. But the general rule was that generals (apart from a handful of the early kings with murky or mythical ancestry, and the "foreigner" Balbus) appear in this list with the name of their father and grandfather. Whatever the exact history here, and however the awkward issue of Octavian's paternity was hammered out, the erasure and the second thoughts it implies gives us a hint of the problems of dealing with "normal" patterns in human descent at the start of the new world of deification and (constructed) divine ancestry.

FIGURE 36: The final section of the inscribed register of triumphing generals from the Roman Forum, listing triumphs between 28 and 19 BCE. Each entry normally includes the same standard information: the name of the general, with that of his father and grandfather; the office he held at the time of the victory; the year of the victory (expressed in years since the foundation of the city); the place or people over which the victory was won; the date of the triumph. So the final entry for Balbus reads: Lucius Cornelius Balbus, son of Publius, proconsul, in the year 734, over Africa, on the sixth day before the Kalends of April (that is, March 27). The omission of his grandfather reflects Balbus' status as a new citizen.

No less revealing is the entry in the *Fasti Barberiniani* for Octavian's triple triumph in 29 BCE (which does not survive in the Forum list). Here the three separate celebrations—the first for victory over Dalmatia and Illyricum, the second for victory at the battle of Actium, the third for victory over Egypt—appear as just two: for Dalmatia and Egypt, apparently separated by a day. This has been put down to sloppy stone carving.[32] But a more political explanation is also possible. Actium had been a victory in a *civil* war, without even a euphemistic foreign label such as Julius Caesar had pinned onto his own victories over Roman citizens. It is tempting to imagine that whoever composed or commis-

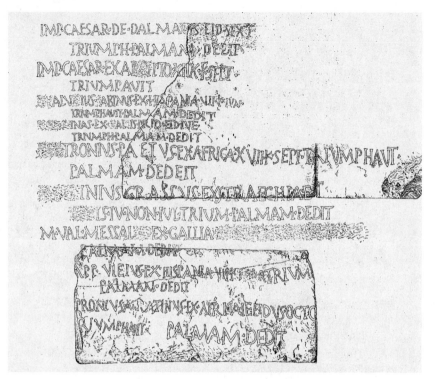

FIGURE 37: The final section of the *Fasti Barberiniani* (with missing sections completed from an earlier manuscript copy), listing triumphs from 29 to 21. The first four lines list two out of the three triumphs celebrated by Octavian in 29 BCE. The contrast with the Forum list (Fig. 36) is striking. The standard formula is different. There is no dating by year, and no mention of the father or grandfather's name or the office held. Instead we find the formula *triumphavit palmam dedit* ("triumphed, dedicated his palm"). No less different is the style and consistency of presentation. Here spellings are not uniform (usually, for example, *dedit*, but once *dedeit*). And there are numerous other variants which may be significant or merely careless: *palmam dedit*, for example, is omitted for Octavian's second triumph, line 4—a mistake, or maybe he did not on that occasion "dedicate his palm."

sioned this particular triumphal list was attempting to "clean up" triumphal history by finessing Actium out of the picture.

But the end of the *Barberiniani* springs the biggest historical surprise. For the last triumph to be recorded here is not that of Balbus but of Lucius Sempronius Atratinus for another African victory in 21 BCE. It is possible, of course, that there was originally another slab (in which case—unless we are to imagine his as the only name on the next installment—the list would almost certainly have continued beyond Balbus). But the way the inscription trails off, in what must count as a shoddy piece of the stone carver's art (hence perhaps the idea of a mere error over the Actian entry), might suggest that the list was here trailing to its close. At least, the degeneration of the text seems neatly to capture the end of the traditional celebration, albeit one triumph too soon.[33]

If the Forum text had been lost and we had only the *Fasti Barberiniani,* we would tell a rather different version of the Augustan changes, or at least of their chronology. But all the different narratives we have been looking at lead to a more significant point: that no single history of this ritual ever existed; that ancient writers told the story of the triumph and explained its development and changes in more—and more varied—ways than modern orthodoxy would allow.

THE MYTH OF ORIGINS

The origin of the triumph continues to be one of the fetishes of modern scholarship. This is not just a question of the "primitive turn" in many historians' attempts to explain individual elements of ceremony (the ribald songs, for example, or the phallos under the chariot). There is also a scholarly preoccupation with the history of the very earliest phases of the triumph more generally, which has produced volumes of learned discussion and ingenious speculation. In this context, it may seem, at first sight, to be going against the grain—even cavalier—to have postponed the particular topic of triumphal origins to the end of this book and to deal with it (as I shall) so briefly. The pages that follow aim to redefine this search for a beginning and, at the same time, to justify the amount of attention I have chosen to give it.

So when and where, on the conventional view, did the whole thing start? Unsurprisingly perhaps, a number of competing theories have been proposed—and for most of them there is no firm evidence at all. One common view is that the triumph was not the earliest victory celebration at Rome; that the dedication of the *spolia opima,* and perhaps the *ovatio* too, were "native Roman" pretriumphal celebrations; and that at some point in Roman history these were overlaid by the triumph proper. Exactly which point is a matter of further and greater dispute. One bold recent contribution to the debate, in linking the ceremony of triumph to the practice of erecting commemorative statues to successful generals (who, with their red-painted faces, played the part of the statue itself in the procession), argues that the form of the "classical triumph" was not established until the late fourth century BCE.[34] Others have stressed the direct Greek input into the form of the ceremony (a neat fit if you imagine that the Latin cry *Io triumpe*—and so the word *triumphus* itself—comes straight from the Greek *thriambos*).[35]

It is, however, the idea of Etruscan influence (or Greek and/or Near Eastern influence mediated through Etruria) that commands the widest support. This is backed up not only by various statements in ancient writers who traced specific aspects of the triumph back to the Etruscans but also by the ritual's destination at the Temple of Jupiter Optimus Maximus on the Capitoline, which was, according to tradition, founded in the sixth century BCE by the Tarquins, the Etruscan kings of Rome. How could you have a triumph before you had a temple for the procession to aim for?[36] In addition, traces have been found in Etruria that seem to reflect a ceremony similar enough to the Roman triumph to count as its ancestor. A few Etruscan paintings, stone sculptures, and terracotta reliefs have been taken to depict Etruscan triumphal paraphernalia or ceremonies. For example, a precursor of the *toga picta* has often been spotted in a well-known painting from the François Tomb at Vulci: it shows a man (named, in Etruscan, Vel Saties) draped in an elaborately decorated purple cloak, reminiscent of a triumphing general (Fig. 38).[37]

But, beyond that, a series of sculptures are claimed to offer some glimpse of the Etruscan triumphal ritual itself. A little known funerary piece, probably of the early sixth century BCE and probably from the Cerveteri, is supposed to show an Etruscan triumphing general in his chariot, carrying a scepter and with a crown held over his head from be-

FIGURE 38: Vel Saties from the François Tomb, Vulci. The interpretation of this scene is very puzzling. The small figure in front of Vel Saties may be his son, or a servant. The bird may be a plaything, or connected with divination. And what is the relationship, if any, between this magnificent purple cloak and the *toga picta* of the triumphing general? The date is no less uncertain. The tomb was originally constructed in the fifth century BCE, but the paintings have been dated variously between the fourth and first centuries BCE.

FIGURE 39: Front panel of a sarcophagus from Sperandio necropolis, Perugia, late sixth century BCE. The procession includes animals, armed men, and (on the right) prisoners bound at the neck. A homecoming from war?

hind (as in some Roman triumphal images); and a slightly later sixth-century sarcophagus from Perugia depicts a triumphal procession of bound prisoners and booty (Fig. 39). Other archaeological material has been pressed to deliver even more dramatic conclusions. At the town of Praeneste, for example, a group of sixth- or fifth-century terracottas (Fig. 40), produced during a period of Etruscan influence, have been taken to evoke not just a triumphal procession but the ideology of the ceremony more specifically: the claim is that the design depicts the apotheosis of the triumphant general who has just left his mortal chariot (on the right) to join his divine transport, with its winged horses and goddess as driver (on the left).

These terracottas have in turn been linked to the reconstruction of a whole "triumphal route" through the city, leading up to the (perhaps significantly named) Temple of Jupiter Imperator. In Rome itself, meanwhile, material excavated from the earliest phases of occupation on the Capitoline hill has been attributed to the complex around Romulus' original Temple of Jupiter Feretrius; and reconstruction drawings have been produced that depict the very oak tree on which the spoils he won from the king of the Caeninenses can be seen hanging![38]

Some difficulties with these lines of argument should be obvious straightaway. We have already seen that the surviving evidence for the dedication of the *spolia opima* is just as compatible with its being a relatively late, invented tradition as with its being a primitive relic of pretriumphal Rome. (Needless to say the archaeological traces that lie behind the confident reconstructions are flimsy in the extreme.) The ovation too might equally well have postdated as predated the triumph proper. There is no good evidence (beyond hunch and first principles) for establishing the priority of one over the other.

But what of the specific arguments for the Etruscan ancestry of the ceremony? The Roman literary evidence is frankly flimsy. We cannot assume that any particular feature of the triumph originated in Etruria simply because some ancient scholar asserted that it did. They may well have been just as much at a loss as we are, and Etruria offered a convenient explanation for puzzling features of Roman cultural and religious practice. Besides, although individual aspects of triumphal custom are credited with an Etruscan origin, it is only Florus who goes so far as to hint that the ceremony as a whole was an Etruscan phenomenon.[39]

The material traces of the supposed Etruscan triumph are no more secure. In fact, not a single one of the "triumphal" depictions I have noted stands up to much hard-nosed scrutiny. Most collapse almost instantly. A

FIGURE 40: One of a series of architectural terracottas (roof edgings) from Praeneste, with scenes of chariots and riders (sixth or fifth century BCE). The idea that the warrior on the left is mounting a divine chariot, drawn by winged horses, has in turn suggested links with the Roman triumph, and the divine associations of the successful general.

purple cloak (and it is a cloak, not a toga) does not necessarily mean a triumph, even if Vel Saties is wearing a wreath of some sort.[40] But the sculptural evidence is equally flimsy. The "triumphing general" on the sixth-century funerary relief from Cerveteri certainly did not leap to the notice of the author of the only extensive publication of the sculpture—who identified the figure in the chariot (which is, in any case, sitting down rather than standing up) as a woman, and in place of the attendant with a crown saw a female servant with a fan![41] The sarcophagus from Perugia clearly depicts four figures, bound at the neck and so presumably slaves or prisoners, followed by men and women leading, among other things, some heavily laden pack animals. This may (or may not) represent a procession of spoils of war. But there is no sign whatsoever of any of the key distinguishing features of a triumph, such as the general in his chariot.[42]

The reliefs from Praeneste do at least include chariots. But, despite the determination to find a narrative of triumphal apotheosis, there is no good reason to assume that the man mounting the left-hand chariot has just dismounted from the chariot on the right—or, if he has, that his action alludes to the ideology of the triumph. There is in fact nothing to rule out some mythological story.[43] And as for the "triumphal route," this is another case of an imaginative joining of the dots. Two of the fixed points on the route are provided by the temples to which these (possibly triumphal, more possibly not) archaic reliefs were once fixed. The supposed *porta triumphalis* is identified from nothing more than the findspot of the second-century CE relief from Praeneste (see Fig. 17) depicting the triumph of the emperor Trajan. It is a very fragile construction indeed.[44]

From the second century BCE we do have, to be sure, a series of funerary urns, especially from the area around the Etruscan city of Volterra, showing a scene that seems much closer to the Roman triumph than any of those earlier examples: a toga-clad figure in the distinctively shaped (triumphal) chariot, drawn by four horses, and preceded by lictors (Fig. 41). These urns may have been intended to depict a triumphal ceremony; they may have appropriated the symbolism of the tri-

FIGURE 41: Etruscan funerary urn, from Volterra, second century BCE. This scene—with its toga-clad figure riding in a *quadriga*, and the bundles of *fasces* carried in front—is strikingly reminiscent of the Roman triumph. But is this a sign of Roman influence on Etruria, rather than *vice versa*?

umph for a funerary message; or possibly, to be honest, we may have imposed a "triumphal" reading on a more less specific rendering of a man in a chariot. We cannot be certain. But even if we opt to see a clear reference to the triumph here, we still have not found powerful evidence for an early Etruscan triumphal ceremony. In this case the date is the crucial factor. For these urns are from a period well after the Roman conquest of Etruria. If their iconography includes a triumph, it is almost certainly a Roman triumph, and the influence is from Rome to Etruria, not *vice versa*.[45]

Of course, we should not rule out the possibility of all kinds of mutual interdependence and cultural interaction between "Etruscan" and "Roman" culture. To suggest that early Rome existed in a vacuum, immune from the influence of its neighbors, would be simply wrong. But we have no clearly decisive evidence at all for the favorite modern theory of an Etruscan genealogy of the Roman ceremony. None of the much-cited material objects can bear the weight of argument regularly placed on them. Again, as so often is the case in the game of cultural "matching," the criteria that distinguish *significant* or *telling* similarities are elusive: one person's "man holding a crown" is another's "woman with a fan"; one person's proto-triumphing general sporting an early version of triumphal regalia is for others just a man in a purple cloak.

Yet these intriguing ambiguities of the evidence are only one side of the problems that any search for the origins of the triumph must raise. It is not just that the surviving material fails to deliver a clear answer to the question of where the triumph came from, and when. In a fundamental respect, that question is wrongly posed. The simple point is that there was no such thing in a literal sense as the "first" or "earliest" triumph. The "origin" of any ceremonial institution or ritual—"invented tradition" or not—is almost always a form of historical retrojection. It is not (or only in the rarest of circumstances) a moment "in the present tense" when we can imagine the primitive community coming together, devising and performing for the first time a ceremony that they intend to make customary. It is almost always the product of a retrospective ideological collusion to identify one moment, or one influence, rather than another as the start and foundation of traditional practice. As a term of description and analysis, it acts—and acted—as a tool in the construction of a cultural genealogy: in the case of the triumph, a culturally agreed (and culturally debated) ordering device intended to historicize the messy, divergent, and changing ritual improvisations that from time immemorial had no doubt ceremonialized the end of fighting.[46]

The "origin of the triumph" is, in other words, a cultural trope. Its job is to draw a line between, on the one hand, the kind of occasion when the lads rolled home in a jolly mood, victorious with their loot and captives and, on the other, a Roman *institution* with a history. There is no objectively correct time or place to locate the triumph's origin; instead, we are faced with choices, of potential inclusions and exclusions, each investing the ritual with a different history, character, authority, and legitimacy. To put it another way, any decision to identify, say, the fourth century BCE as the birth of the triumph is about more than chronology. Such decisions are always already about what the triumph is thought to be *for*, and what is or is not to count in the institution's history.

This inevitably focuses our attention once again on discursive aspects of the triumphal story, on how the ritual's origins were defined and debated by the Romans themselves, and with what implications for our understanding of it. Here too we find a much wider range of "origin accounts" than the cherry-picking practiced by modern scholars usually admits. Ancient claims about the Etruscan origins of the *toga picta,* the golden crown, or the eagle-topped scepter are enthusiastically repeated; so too, as we have noted, is Varro's tentative derivation of the word *triumphus* ultimately from a Greek epithet of the god Dionysus. A blind eye, however, has fairly consistently been turned to those ancient theories that sit less comfortably with modern ideas. The claim by one late commentary that Pliny and the Augustan historian Pompeius Trogus (whose work is largely lost to us) both believed that the triumph was invented by the Africans hardly makes it to even the most learned footnotes. Likewise swept under the carpet for the most part is the derivation of *triumphus* suggested by Suetonius (at least as Isidore in the seventh century reports him), which puts the accent on the *tri*partite honor that a grant of a triumph represents—being dependent on the decision of the army, senate, and Roman people.[47]

The issue, of course, is not whether these theories are correct (whatever being "correct" would mean in this context). It is rather how such curious speculations and false etymologies reflect different ways of conceptualizing the triumph, bringing different aspects of it into our view. Suetonius' etymology appears to assert the centrality of the institution within the Roman polity and its delicate balance of power. More often, though, ancient theorizing broaches a cluster of issues that underlie so much of Roman cultural debate more generally: What was Roman about this characteristically Roman institution? Do the roots of Roman cultural practice lie outside the city? How far is traditional Roman culture always by definition "foreign"? These themes are familiar from the conflicting stories told of the origins of the Roman state as a whole, where the idea of a native Italic identity (in the shape of the Romulus myth) is held in tension with the competing version (in the shape of the Aeneas myth) that derives the Roman state from distant Troy. They are familiar too from the more self-consciously intellectualizing version of Dionysius of Halicarnassus, the aim of whose *Antiquitates Romanae (Roman Antiquities)* was to prove that Rome had been in origin a Greek city.

In the range of often fantastic explanations of the triumph, its customs, and its terminology, we find the "Romanness" of that ceremony also keenly scrutinized and debated. On the one hand are attempts to locate its origins externally, even (to follow the wild card of Pliny and Pompeius Trogus) outside the nexus of Greek and Etruscan myth and culture and inside Africa. On the other hand are the claims that the triumph is inextricably bound up with Rome itself.

These claims are seen most vividly in the Forum inscription. We have already explored the implications of the last triumph recorded here. The first triumph recorded is no less loaded. That honor is ascribed to Romulus on the "Kalends of March" (March 1) in the first year of the city. This date is much more resonant than it might appear at first sight. For it was a common assumption among ancient scholars that the Roman year had originally begun not in January but in March.[48] The first of March in year 1 would have counted as the first day in the existence of Rome. Leaving aside the chronological paradoxes that this raises (How does it relate to the famous birthday of the city celebrated on April 21? How was Romulus' victory secured before Roman time had begun?), it amounts to a very strong assertion indeed that the triumph was coterminous with Rome itself. The inscription presents a complete series of celebrations from 753 to 19 BCE, with a beginning and an end defined by the physical limits of its marble frame, as if there was no need to look for triumphal history beyond or before that. The message is clear: Rome was a triumphal city from its very birth; there was no Rome without the triumph, no triumph without Rome.[49]

Strikingly similar debates are replayed in discussions of the origins of the *ovatio,* which Romans also argued over, albeit with less intensity. The issue was not, as in modern scholarship, its possible priority to the triumph proper but the cultural and ethnic identity revealed by the title of the ceremony. Two main views were canvassed. On the one hand were those who saw the name as straightforwardly Greek, derived from the

Greek word *euasmos*—which refers to the shout of *eua!* characteristic of Greek rituals and apparently also of the *ovatio*. This was predictably the line taken by Dionysius, but he claimed that many "native histories" also supported that derivation.[50] Plutarch certainly gives the impression that he felt himself in the minority in rejecting that explanation (partly because "they use that cry in triumphs too") and in seeing the origin of the word in the type of sacrifice offered at the *ovatio*. "For at the major triumph it was the custom for generals to sacrifice an ox, but at this ceremony they used to sacrifice a sheep. The Roman name for sheep is *oba* (Latin *ovis*). And so they call the lesser triumph *oba (ovatio)*."[51]

Desperately unconvincing it may be, but it is also found in Servius' fourth-century commentary on the *Aeneid*: "The man who earns an *ovatio* . . . sacrifices sheep *(oves)*. Hence the name *ovatio*."[52] This surely takes us back to the pastoral world of early Italy and its religious rules, rather than to the rituals of Greece. Indeed, Plutarch makes a point of saying that religious procedure at Sparta was the reverse: a lesser victor sacrificed an ox.

The shout of *eua* introduces yet another, boldly mythical, version of triumphal origins that I have already had cause to note on various occasions. For, as Plutarch states, it was especially associated with the Greek god Dionysus. And Dionysus—or his Latin counterpart, Liber—is also credited with the invention of the triumph. This turns out to be a story that illustrates not only the multicultural complexities of such myths of origin but also how active a part in ritual practice itself these stories can play. As we shall see, the story of Dionysus does not simply explain the origins of the ritual of triumph, it also reconfigures and reshapes its performance.

When Pliny claims that Liber invented the triumph, he is evoking a story that we have come to know (thanks in part to its place of honor in Renaissance painting) as "The Triumph of Bacchus."[53] This was the story of the victorious military campaigns of the god Bacchus (or Dionysus) against the Indians and his triumphal progress back to Greece amidst a band of satyrs, maenads, and assorted drunks. We find hints of a story of Dionysus' journey from the Far East as early as the opening of Euripides' *Bacchae*.[54] But whatever the earliest versions of the myth, it was clearly drastically resignified following the eastern campaigns of Alexander the Great. At that point the tale of Bacchus' exploits in India was vastly elaborated and taken as the model for Alexander in his role as the new Dionysus. There is, as many modern students of myth have seen, a series of double bluffs here. For the truth is that the god's exploits were modeled on Alexander's, not the other way round; and that it is an entirely second-order reworking of the story to suggest that Alexander saw himself in terms of the god (rather that the god being presented as Alexander).[55] But whatever the processes were by which it developed, there are numerous traces in the Hellenistic Greek world of this newly elaborated "Return of Bacchus" from India. These include one of the main floats in the third-century procession of Ptolemy Philadelpus in Alexandria, which supposedly carried a tableau of Dionysus' return—including, so Callixeinos would have us believe, an eighteen-foot statue of the god, followed by his Bacchic troops and Indian prisoners.

How exactly, and when, this myth was appropriated by Roman theorists as the origin of their own ceremony of triumph we do not know. The theory is almost certainly bound up with Varro's etymology of the word *triumphus* from the Dionysiac *thriambos;* but whether that etymology launched, legitimated, or followed the identification of Dionysus as the "first to triumph" is lost to us. What is clear, however, is that at least by the first century BCE the "Return of Dionysus" from the East (as Callixeinos puts it) had been translated into the "Triumph of Dionysus/ Bacchus" and repackaged in explicitly Roman triumphal terms. Even if the conventional title for the myth, at any period, is now "The *Triumph* of Bacchus," the god's return could not have been thought of as a "triumph" in a technical sense until the Romans had seen in it the founding moment of their own triumphal ceremony (which, incidentally perhaps, had the added advantage of translating Alexander the Great too into Roman cultural and religious vocabulary).[56]

But the chain of connections does not stop there. First, within Roman representations, the story of Bacchus' triumph became increasingly

FIGURE 42: *The Triumph of Bacchus* on a Roman sarcophagus, mid-second century CE. For all its elements of Bacchic extravagance (the exotic animals, the cupids), this divine procession bears a decided resemblance to a triumph—in, for example, the pathetic group of prisoners to the right.

assimilated into a triumph in the most specifically Roman sense of the word. It is a not-uncommon theme on imperial sarcophagi, for example; and it can be presented in a strikingly official triumphal guise. A sarcophagus from Rome illustrates this point nicely (Fig. 42). True, there are some decidedly Bacchic elements here: the elephants pulling the chariot, with cupids as their drivers; the lions and tigers carrying participants in the procession; the thyrsus in the "general's" hands. But the chariot is close enough to a triumphal shape; the crew of prisoners is reminiscent of a Roman triumphal procession; and there may even be that elusive slave pictured standing behind the god (reminding him that he was only a man?). Other sarcophagi of this type depict carts showing off booty, with chained prisoners crouching beside, as on official Roman representations of the procession.[57]

But just as the Triumph of Bacchus came to be seen in increasingly Roman terms, so the reverse was also true: the Roman triumphal ceremony itself could be seen afresh in Bacchic terms. The classic case of this is the first triumph of Pompey, at which the commander attempted to have his chariot drawn by elephants rather than horses. We cannot now reconstruct Pompey's motivations in launching this extravagant— and ultimately failed—gesture. Very likely he was reformulating the ceremony in the light of the return of Dionysus. But whether that was Pompey's intention or not, Roman observers and commentators saw it in that way. Pliny, for example, specifically relates the story of Pompey's elephants to the "Triumph of Liber."⁵⁸ In other words, the story of triumphal origins becomes acted out (or, at least, is seen to be acted out) in a significantly new form of triumph. It takes a determining as well as an explanatory role.

Irrecoverable—nonexistent, perhaps—as the historical origin of the triumph must be, the myth of its origin is nevertheless a dynamic constituent of that nexus of Roman actions and representations that make up "the ritual."⁵⁹

THE END OF THE TRIUMPH?

In the sixth century CE the historian Procopius described the victory celebrations of the general Belisarius, who had scored a notable success over the Vandals in Africa and returned to celebrate a "triumph" in 534. Procopius underlines the significance of the event: "He was deemed worthy to receive the honors which in earlier times had been granted to those generals of the Romans who had won the greatest and most noteworthy victories. A period of around six hundred years had gone by since anyone had achieved these honors, except for Titus and Trajan, and the other emperors who had won campaigns against the barbarians."

We find all kinds of traditional triumphal features in Procopius' account of this ceremony. Belisarius, he explains, had brought back for display the Vandal king Gelimer, who behaved with the dignity associated with the most noble captives and who rose above the occasion far enough to have muttered repeatedly the words "Vanity of vanities, all is vanity" at the climax of the parade. (He was later granted land by the emperor and lived out his days with his family.) There was an array of prisoners, too, chosen for their striking appearance—"tall and physically beautiful." Most impressive of all, though, were the spoils, including the holy treasure from the Temple of Jerusalem which had first been looted by Vespasian and Titus, then in this version of the story taken off to Africa by the Vandals in the mid-fifth century CE, and finally recaptured by Belisarius. What had been paraded through in the triumph of Vespasian and Titus in 71 CE was here put on display again in a triumph 450 years later.[60]

This celebration has often captured the imagination. According to Procopius it was commemorated in a mosaic in the imperial palace, which brilliantly evoked the joyful spirit of the occasion. More recently it has been dramatically restaged in, for example, Donizetti's opera *Belisario* and makes a marvelous set piece in Robert Graves' novel *Count Belisarius*. For Graves, as for a number of scholars, Belisarius was "the last to be awarded a triumph."[61] This was, in other words, the "last Roman triumph."

If so, it was significantly different from the triumphs we have been exploring. This ceremony was taking place not in Rome but in Constantinople, a city with its own well-established traditions of victory celebration and commemoration.[62] It involved a procession on foot, not in a chariot, and to the Hippodrome, not to the Capitoline. And in the Christian city, no sacrifices were offered to Jupiter. Instead, both Gelimer and Belisarius prostrated themselves in front of the emperor Justinian; and the rhetoric is so far from being pagan that the moralizing slogan muttered by the king was actually a quotation from Ecclesiastes. Besides, however Procopius construes this as a triumph of Belisarius (and so a return to pre-Augustan practice), the principal honorand is more often seen as the emperor himself. According to Procopius' own account, this was the message behind the design of the palace mosaic, with Justinian and the empress Theodora at center-stage, honored by both captives and general. Other accounts also focus on Justinian, sometimes not counting the celebration as a "triumph" at all, still less a triumph of Belisarius.[63]

Procopius' own version, in fact, highlights some ambivalences about just how traditional (or "traditional" in what sense) this ceremony could be made out to be. True, he launches his account by stressing the return to ancient practice after six hundred years. But that length of time itself, as well as his careful explanation of "what the Romans call a 'triumph,'" raises the question of how far we should take this as a self-conscious revival of an ancient institution rather than a seamless part of ancestral custom. He is also quite straightforward about the fact that what took place was "not *in the ancient manner*" at all—for several of the reasons just noted (Belisarius was on foot, following a different route in a different city).

But even more revealing of the chronological and narrative complexities, Procopius goes on to remark that "a little later the triumph was also celebrated by Belisarius *in the ancient manner.*" By this he means not that he celebrated a regular triumph, but that he entered into his consulship in January 535 with what had become, by that date, the traditional "triumphal" ceremonial. Confusingly for us, and for Procopius' original readers also no doubt, two different versions of the "ancient manner" were in competition here: on the one hand, the "ancient manner" of the Roman victory procession (to which the triumphal ceremonial in the Hippodrome had not quite matched up); on the other, the "ancient manner" of the consular inauguration in triumphal style (by the sixth century CE a venerably old-fashioned institution).

In short, Procopius' account shows how complicated the traditions of the triumph and its different chronologies had become after more than a millennium of triumphal history. It also hints at some of the dilemmas that we face in trying to fix an endpoint for the ceremony's history. Unlike some rituals (such as animal sacrifice, for example), we know of no legislation that outlawed its performance. And ceremonies harked back to ancient triumphal symbolism or claimed specifically to imitate or revive it through the Middle Ages and Renaissance, right into the twentieth century. The question has been where to draw the dividing line between the Roman ceremony and later imitations or revivals—between the life and the afterlife of the triumph. This raises issues of intellectual policing similar to those that surrounded the question of triumphal origins. Unsurprisingly, the "Triumph of Belisarius" is only one of a handful of candidates for the accolade of "last Roman triumph." Others are much more closely connected—in place, religion, and ritual practice—to the ceremony that has been the subject of this book than the Christian spectacle in 534. But all the different choices expose different views about what counts as the irreducible core of the ceremony, about what allows a ritual to qualify as a "Roman triumph."

The period from the middle of the second century CE through the third is, for the modern observer at least, a very low point in the history of the triumph. Between the triumph of Marcus Aurelius over the Parthians in 166 and the victory celebrations of the co-emperors Diocletian and Maximian in 303, we can document fewer than ten triumphs—and most of these are not the subject of any lavish description, reliable or not.[64] An exception is the triumph celebrated by the emperor Aurelian in 274 over enemies in the East and West (including that ersatz Cleopatra, Queen Zenobia) and extravagantly evoked in that puzzling—and often flagrantly fantastical—collection of late Roman imperial biographies known as the *Historia Augusta (Augustan History)*. The description of this triumph lives up to the reputation of the work as a whole. It features a glittering array of captured royal chariots, in one of which Aurelian himself rode, drawn by stags that were to be sacrificed on the Capitol. Other exotic animals, from elephants to elks, are said to have joined in the procession; as well as a glamorous troupe of foreign captives, including a little posse of Amazons and Zenobia herself (bound with those golden chains so heavy that they had to be carried for her).[65]

Most discussions of this account have been concerned with proving its inaccuracy or working out what the writer must have misunderstood in order to have come up with this rubbish.[66] Certainly, to imagine that it was an accurate reflection of what was on show in the procession would be naive. But the fantasy of the *Historia Augusta* is here more an exaggeration of traditional triumphal concerns than sheer invention. The stress on the exotic, on royal prisoners in particular, and on the potential rivalry between triumphing general and the star victim all echo major themes in triumphal culture that we have already identified. Similar echoes are found in other descriptions of third-century triumphs. On one occasion, the *Historia Augusta* offers a notable variation on that favorite triumphal theme of representation and reality. In his speech to the senate after his triumph of 233, the emperor Severus Alexander is imagined listing the various spoils of the battlefield that he either did, or did not, parade in his procession. This includes 1,800 scythed chariots captured from the enemy: "Of these we could have put on display two hundred chariots, their animals killed; but because that could be faked, we passed up the opportunity of doing so."[67] Strangely inverted as the quip may be, it closely chimes in with all those anxieties about fake triumphs for fake victories.

In some other respects, however, even in the relatively sparse notices of triumphs in this period, we can glimpse the characteristic style of later "triumphal" celebrations of the fourth century and beyond. We find, for example, a greater emphasis on shows and games connected with the procession—as if they were now a much more integral part of the triumphal celebration than they appear to have been in earlier periods. Likewise the surviving descriptions increasingly blur the boundaries between triumphal victory celebration and other forms of dynastic or imperial display. In 202, for example, celebrations took place in Rome in honor of the emperor Septimius Severus and his son Caracalla. Septimius had secured victories in the East (as are commemorated on his famous arch in the Forum). But did he celebrate a triumph? Our various accounts appear to be agreed that he did not, but each with a different nuance.

The *Historia Augusta* states that the senate offered both the emperor and Caracalla a triumph. Septimius himself declined on the grounds (echoing Vespasian's earlier complaint) that "he could not stand up in the chariot because of his arthritis." He did, however, give permission for his son to triumph. Both Dio and Herodian suggest a different configuration of ceremonial, without either of them mentioning a triumph. Dio, who was a contemporary and even eyewitness, refers to a dazzling concatenation of festivities. These included the celebration of the emperor's tenth anniversary on the throne; the wedding of Caracalla (Dio, a guest, claims that the menu was partly in "royal" and partly in "barbaric" style, with not only cooked meat on the menu but also "uncooked and even live animals," or so the Byzantine paraphrase has it); and magnificent shows in the amphitheater in honor of Septimius' return to the city, his anniversary, and his victories. Herodian, another contemporary, refers instead to the emperor's reception on his return to Rome "as a victor," and to sacrifices, spectacles, handouts, and games.[68]

This combination of ceremonial fits with the picture we have of triumphal celebrations in late antiquity. We explored in the last chapter the extension of triumphal symbolism and the way in which, by the second century CE at least, the inauguration of consuls was represented in triumphal terms (for Procopius, "the ancient manner"); and we have noted in this chapter the connection between triumphs and imperial accession and other dynastic events from as far back as the reign of Augustus. These trends are usually taken to have become yet more pronounced with time, as triumphal symbols came to serve as the markers of imperial monarchy itself across the Empire as a whole and the triumph became less directly connected with specific individual victories and more associated with the emperor's military power in general and his dynastic anniversaries. It was at this period that the word *triumphator* entered common use—as part of the emperor's title blazoned on inscriptions and coins. Various imperial rituals too came to be expressed in a triumphal idiom, and not necessarily only in Rome (a city that later Roman emperors visited only rarely).

This is most clearly the case with the ceremony of the emperor's *adventus,* his formal "arrival" in Rome, Constantinople, or other cities of the Empire. This involved a ceremonial greeting of the emperor, his procession through the streets traveling in a chariot or carriage, and often also the celebration of his victories.[69] One vivid case is the famous entry of Constantius II into Rome in 357 CE, his first visit to the city. In what has become a *locus classicus* of the supposedly hieratic ceremonial of late antiquity, he sat in his carriage absolutely still, looking neither to left or to right, "as if he were a statue." Several years earlier he had defeated Magnentius, his rival to the throne, and Ammianus Marcellinus describes his arrival in Rome as "an attempt to hold a triumph over Roman blood."[70]

Showing scruples about celebrations of victories in civil war that would have been more at home in the first century BCE (for by now

many triumphal ceremonies were unashamedly rooted in conflicts between Roman and Roman), Ammianus continues, disapprovingly and
still in a decidedly triumphal vein: "For he did not conquer under his
own command any foreign people who were making war, nor did he
know of any such people who had been vanquished by the valor of his
generals. He did not add anything to the Empire either; nor in times
of crisis was he ever seen to be the leader or amongst the leaders. But
he was keen to show off to a people living in complete peace—who neither hoped nor wished to see this or anything of the sort—a vastly overblown procession, banners stiff with threads of gold, and an array of
retainers."[71]

Accounts of this type lie behind the claim that by the end of the
fourth century the triumph was "in effect transformed into *adventus*."[72]
This is not the only way of understanding the realignment of ritual
practice, or necessarily the best. One could equally well argue that *adventus* had been transformed into triumph, or better (as I suggested in
the context of consular inauguration) that the symbolic language of the
triumph provided an apt way of representing this ceremonial form of
imperial entrance. Nor is it clear that the overlap between *adventus* and
triumph is as distinctive of this later period as is sometimes assumed. For
in some sense the triumph always had been, in essence, the arrival of the
successful general and his re-entry into the city—and it was certainly
cast in those terms by writers of the Augustan period, looking back to
the ritual's early history.[73] Nonetheless, the "seepage" of triumphal forms
into other rituals does seem to be a particular marker of the ceremonial
from the fourth, or even the third, century on. One could almost say
that the adjective tends to replace the noun: we now deal as much with
ceremonies that are "triumphal" or "like a triumph" as with triumphs
themselves.

That said, a group of notable triumphs or triumphal occasions between the fourth and sixth centuries have been taken as turning points
in the history of the ritual, or possible candidates for being "the last Roman triumph." Modern fingers have often pointed at the triumph of
Diocletian and Maximian in 303, which joined together celebrations of

the twentieth anniversary of Diocletian's reign with those for victories won by the co-rulers in both East and West, some of them many years earlier. (One surviving speech in praise of Maximian turns this delay to the emperor's advantage: "You put off triumphal processions themselves by further conquering.") The evidence for this occasion is murkier than many of the confident statements about it would encourage one to think. Not only are there some troubling—though probably not compelling—doubts about whether this is anything more than a figment of unreliable historical imagination. But the repeated view that the procession incorporated paintings or models of the defeated, in the traditional way, is no more than a rationalization of the awkward conflict of different assertions in different literary accounts: that the relatives of the Persian king Narses were on display in the procession, that they had been restored to him according to the peace treaty after the war with the Persians, and that the whole family was put on display in the temples of Rome. Nonetheless, the description offered by Eutropius, a fourth-century pagan historian, has been felt to be reassuringly familiar and "in the ancient manner": he refers to the "wonderful procession of floats *(fercula)*" and to the victims being led "before the chariot *(ante currum)*."[74]

A clear break is often detected between this and the triumphal entry of Constantine after his defeat of his rival Maxentius at the battle of the Milvian Bridge in 312. There is no question here of anything so refined as a model of the defeated being on display. In contrast to those occasions in the earlier history of the triumph when the crowd was reported to be upset by the mere sight of paintings of the dying, Maxentius' severed head itself was paraded for mockery before the people (a not uncommon element in these later ceremonies). One writer of a speech in praise of Constantine, moreover, plays with the idea that this was the most illustrious triumph ever, precisely because it used and subverted triumphal traditions: no chained enemy generals were hauled *ante currum,* but the Roman nobility marched there "free at last"; "barbarians were not thrown into prison, but ex-consuls were thrown out"; and so on.

But the key idea for most modern commentators has been an omission of a different kind. It is widely assumed that this was the first occasion when the emperor broke with tradition and, under the influence of Christianity, chose not to end the procession with honor paid to the pagan gods. Or so we infer from the fact that no ancient account mentions Constantine performing sacrifice on the Capitoline (there is no firmer or more positive evidence than that).[75] Almost a hundred years later in 404, the triumph-cum-consular-inauguration of the emperor Honorius may represent another turning point. Written up in aggressively traditional idiom by Claudian—with images of white horses (though only two, not four), praise for triumphs over foreign rather than Roman enemies, and a reference to the once significant boundary of the *pomerium*—this is the last triumph we know to have been celebrated by an emperor in Rome.[76]

The significance of any of these turning points depends on how we interpret the triumph more generally. There is no right answer to the teasing question of when the traditional Roman triumph grinds to a halt. For those who see the culminating sacrifice on the Capitoline as an essential part of the institution, the triumph of Diocletian and Maximian will be the end of the road. A Christian triumph will be a contradiction in terms, or at best a new ceremony imitating the old. Those, by contrast, who emphasize physical location as an integral part of the ritual—and so regard a triumph outside the topography of the city of Rome, or the Alban Mount, as an impossible hybrid—might take the history of the ceremony as far of 404 but no further. In those terms, a triumph in Constantinople could be only a copy. The case for extending our reach as far as Justinian and Belisarius in the sixth century would depend on taking literally Procopius' claims to place it (notwithstanding all its radically new elements) in the tradition of triumphs stretching back even before the advent of the Roman Empire. In the end, it probably does not matter very much where we choose to stop, so long as we realize that different choices offer different views not only of the history but also of the character of the institution.

Here too, however, there are also big issues of discursive as well as more strictly ritual practice. As we have seen repeatedly, ceremonies such as the triumph are defined not only by the actions of the participants, the costume, the choreography, and the paraphernalia. No less important are the terms in which they are described, represented, and understood by their ancient observers. In part, it was the description or representation of a ritual *as a triumph* that made it one. Greek and Roman writers, no less than we ourselves, made rhetorical choices about which ceremonies to cast in triumphal terms and which not. Some writers, from the fourth to the sixth century, and especially those who saw themselves in the lineage of the "pagan" classics, were heavily invested in portraying a range of ceremonies in traditionally triumphal terms, even at the cost of some tension between image and practice.

It has often been noticed, for example, that the triumphant emperor was still said to have traveled in the traditional *currus,* even when there is clear evidence that the regular vehicle was now a cart or carriage in which (as we saw in the case of Constantius) he sat down. In another speech in praise of Constantine, the mockery of the head of Maxentius, and of the man who had the misfortune to be carrying it in the procession, is seen in terms of the ribaldry *(ioci triumphales)* of the traditional triumphal ceremony. And there are many examples of the parade of illustrious Roman triumphal forbears: Belisarius' ceremony is, for examples, seen alongside the triumphs of Titus and Trajan, as well as the heroes of the Republic; the poet Priscian likens the triumphal ceremony of the emperor Anastasius in 498 to the triumph of Aemilius Paullus.[77] The ideological choices that underlie these triumphal portrayals are clear if we compare other accounts of the same events. In discussing what is elsewhere treated as the (pagan) "triumph" of Constantine, Eusebius and Lactantius, both committed to seeing Constantine in the lineage of specifically Christian history, take a different approach. Lactantius merely refers to great rejoicing at the emperor's victory; Eusebius conscripts the incident into the story of the triumph of Christianity.

Yet we should hesitate before we conclude that the ancient triumph lasted as long as anyone was prepared to describe ceremonies in triumphal terms. This was, after all, contested territory. And at a certain point the gap between the triumphal rhetoric and the ritual action must have become so wide as to be implausible. The "ritual in ink," in other words, had lost touch with ritual practice. It must have seemed either a brilliant literary game, a frankly desperate gambit in defense of old Roman traditions, or hopeless blindness to see Aemilius Paullus as a meaningful ancestor for the emperors of the fifth century CE. When that "certain point" *was* is almost impossible to determine, but the parameters for the end of the "traditional Roman triumph" are clear enough, albeit wide.

If one boundary is the triumphal ceremony in Constantinople in 534, whose ambivalences were so nicely exposed by Procopius, the earlier limit must be set several centuries before. Subversive suggestion though it is, a case could even be made for seeing the celebration of Vespasian and Titus in 71, with Josephus' insistent rhetoric of precedent and procedure (while the whole thing ended up at a temple that was in fact in ruins), as the first triumph that was more of a "revival" than living tradition, more afterlife than life.

POSTSCRIPT: ABYSSINIA 1916

The contemporary world continues to debate the ways in which victory should be celebrated. In the United Kingdom, the Church has several times over the past few decades spoken out explicitly against "triumphalism"—in response to a government that wishes to honor (as well as to magnify) the country's military success. Parades through the streets are less controversial when they involve winning football teams than when they feature winning armies. Even when such processions are sanctioned, they are usually a display of the well-choreographed surviving soldiers and the victorious military hardware. They do not now include those distinctive elements of the Roman triumph, spoils and prisoners. Admiral Dewey may have had a triumphal arch on Madison Avenue, but no exotic captives were on display. If the idea of the triumph is still very much with us, the details of its practice are not.

The last great triumphal display of looted works of art in Europe must have been the procession of the masterpieces of Italy paraded through the streets of Paris after Napoleon's conquests. Modern western warfare does not aim for spoils in the same way. Oil does not make a particularly picturesque show. And although cultural treasures are often stolen and still constitute a significant profit (or loss) of warfare, this is more often under cover than in full view. A classic example is the prehistoric gold from Troy discovered by Heinrich Schliemann, taken from Berlin by the Soviets in 1945, and not officially rediscovered, in a Moscow museum, until the 1980s. The closest the Soviets came to parading their booty was in the 1945 Victory Parade in Moscow, when German flags and military standards were thrown at the foot of Lenin's tomb.

The display of prisoners of war is also officially off the agenda in a post–Geneva Convention world. This not to say that there are no opportunities for voyeurism (provided by television and especially the Internet, or occasionally by the apparently spontaneous public humiliation of enemy prisoners); but there could be no thought of marching captives through the streets with the victorious army in an official display. The crowd-pulling exotic elements are now more commonly provided by the home team. In the 1945 Victory Parade in London, it was the Commonwealth troops and the Greek soldiers in their ceremonial kit that provided the color.

Yet some of these triumphal practices may not be so remote as we imagine. One of the very first memories of the explorer and writer Wilfred Thesiger was witnessing in Abyssinia in 1916 the parade to celebrate the victory of the troops of Ras Tafari (later Haile Selassi) over the rebel Negus Mikael. It is described at length in a letter from Thesiger's father, who was head of the British Legation in Addis Ababa.[78] First the "minstrel" from the victorious army marched past the ruling empress. Some of the men "tore off their mantles and threw them before the Empress" and asked for better clothes. "On these occasions," Thesiger senior noted, "every freedom of speech is allowed." Then came the cavalry ("round the horses' necks were hung the bloodstained cloaks and trophies of the men each rider had killed"), followed by the foot soldiers—and eventually Ras Tafari himself, followed by the "banners and icons of the two principal churches which had sent their Arks to be present at the battle." Finally it was the prisoners' turn: "Negus Mikael was brought in. He came on foot and in chains, an old, fine-looking man dressed in the usual black silk cloak with a white cloth wound round his head, stern and very dignified . . . One felt sorry for him; he had fought like a man . . . Only a month before Mikael had been the proudest chief in Abyssinia and it must have been a bitter moment for him to be led in triumph before the hated Shoans."

"It was," he concluded, "the most wonderful sight I have ever seen, wild and barbaric to the last degree and the whole thing so wonderfully staged and orderly." His son's memories chime in. "Even now, nearly seventy years later, I can recall almost every detail: the embroidered caps of the drummers decorated with cowries; a man falling off his horse as he charged by; a small boy carried past in triumph—he had killed two men though he seemed little older than myself . . . I believe that day implanted in me a life-long craving for barbaric splendour, for savagery and colour and the throb of drums, and that it gave me a lasting veneration for long-established custom and ritual." The echoes with the Roman triumph seem uncanny: the freedom of speech, the impact of the noble captive, the memorable mishaps. And the deep impression that the whole occasion made on both the Thesigers perhaps gives us some hint of how the triumph, too, lasted in Roman memory.

Yet there is a sting in the tail. Before we become too carried away with ideas of the universality of the triumph, we should remember that these observers had been educated in elite British schools, with all their emphasis on Latin, Greek, and ancient culture. They must both have known well some of the classic accounts of the Roman ceremony. Almost certainly they were seeing the Abyssinian occasion through Roman eyes; no less than the classicizing writers of late antiquity, they were re-creating a *triumph in ink*.

Rome, May 2006

During the final stages of writing this book, I visited the Roman Forum. It was a very hot day in early summer, but I chose to make the climb up to the Capitoline hill along the route of the ancient road. It was this way that triumphing generals must have traveled on the last stretch of the procession that would end at the Temple of Jupiter. All sorts of images came into my mind: the porters heaving up the treasures of conquest; the noisy animals on their way to sacrificial death; the frightened or proudly unrepentant captives; the puzzled, hot, but enthusiastic spectators; the lurid paintings of enemy casualties; the jeering troops; the general himself, aching though he must have been by this point, basking in his finest moment of glory—or, alternatively, disguising his embarrassment at the low turn-out, the frankly unimpressive haul of booty, the sauciness of the soldiers' songs, or that humiliating *impasse* with the elephants.

As I climbed higher rather more subversive thoughts took over. The gradient seemed very steep; the paving slabs (even if not the original, then a close match) were slippery, uneven, and treacherous. Could we really imagine the procession of Pompey in 61 BCE safety negotiating its way up this, or something like it? At the very least the chariot would need some burly men lending a shoulder to prevent it (or the general) falling catastrophically backwards. And why do we never hear of those piles of precious tableware simply falling off the *fercula* on which they were being carted? Why are there no stories of the captured trophies ending up in the gutter? That, after all, is what notoriously happened in the sedate streets of London to part of the ceremonial crown balanced on the coffin of George V at his funeral in 1936. Why not in Rome? Perhaps, I reflected, the sternest test for those of us who want to understand antiquity is to learn how to resist taking literally the imaginative constructions and reconstructions of ancient writers themselves—while still remaining alert to what they are saying about their world.

As I came back down the hill into the Forum, I passed a party of English schoolchildren listening, surprisingly attentively, to a tourist guide. She was telling them about the triumphal procession and how it had passed by just where they were standing. She conjured up with tremendous verve the extravagance and excitement and oddity of the occasion, before explaining that it had a very serious purpose indeed. For when the Roman armies came home from their great victories, they were polluted with "blood guilt" from the deaths they had caused, and they had to be purified. That is what the triumph was *for*. The children appeared very happy with this nicely gory and slightly exotic story, and moved on to inspect the Temple of Saturn. My own reactions were more ambivalent.

I too had begun my encounter with the triumph wanting to know, to put it at its simplest, what it was *for*. Why on earth did the Romans do it? Why did they invest such time, energy, and expense in this ceremony? *Why?* Theories abound, ancient and modern, ingenious and banal. A celebration of, or thank-offering for, victory. A reincorporation of the general and his troops back into the civilian community. A spectacular demonstration (and justification) of Rome's imperialist enterprise. A reaffirmation of Roman militaristic values. A religious fulfillment of the vows made to the gods at the start of the campaign. A complex negotiation of "symbolic capital" between successful general and the senate. The theory of purification, with a pedigree that goes back to Festus and Masurius Sabinus, is just one among many.

Almost ten years on, I am far from convinced that the "Why?" question is the most useful one to ask. My anxieties partly reflect the objections often raised to purposive or functional explanations of ritual or cultural practice. They fail to engage with the complicated, multifarious, personal, and partisan agendas that underlie any mass celebration. The triumph could be no more or less accurately defined as a ritual of purification than Christmas could be defined as a celebration of the birth of Jesus (leaving out the gift exchange, the reindeers, the snow, the conspicuous consumption, the trees). They also risk turning some general cultural truth into a specific explanation. The triumph, for example, may well have had a role in the complicated trade-offs in Rome between individual prestige and the interests of the communality. But was not that the case with almost every form of public ritual?

More to the point, I have come to read the Roman triumph in a sense that goes far beyond its role as a procession through the streets. Of course it was that. But it was also a cultural idea, a "ritual in ink," a trope of power, a metaphor of love, a thorn in the side, a world view, a dangerous hyperbole, a marker of time, of change, and continuity. "Why?" questions do not reach the heart of those issues. It is more pressing to understand *how* those meanings, connections, and reformulations are generated and sustained.

I could not blame the children for lapping up so eagerly the explanation of their guide. But as I watched and listened, I fancied intervening to tell them that it was not so simple: that there was much more to a triumph than a ceremony of purification; that we do not really know if "blood guilt" ever worried the Romans at all (and if it did, how was it dealt with when a triumph was not celebrated?); that complex ritual and social institutions could not really be reduced to such a simple formula.

In the event, I did not spoil their day. I have inscribed the case as powerfully as I can in this book.

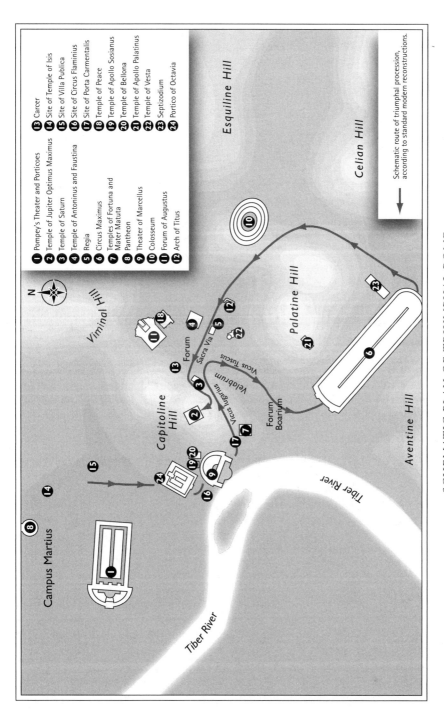

Legend:

1. Pompey's Theater and Porticoes
2. Temple of Jupiter Optimus Maximus
3. Temple of Saturn
4. Temple of Antoninus and Faustina
5. Regia
6. Circus Maximus
7. Temples of Fortuna and Mater Matuta
8. Pantheon
9. Theater of Marcellus
10. Colosseum
11. Forum of Augustus
12. Arch of Titus
13. Carcer
14. Site of Temple of Isis
15. Site of Villa Publica
16. Site of Circus Flaminius
17. Site of Porta Carmentalis
18. Temple of Peace
19. Temple of Apollo Sosianus
20. Temple of Bellona
21. Temple of Apollo Palatinus
22. Temple of Vesta
23. Septizodium
24. Portico of Octavia

Schematic route of triumphal procession, according to standard modern reconstructions.

Campus Martius

Tiber River

Capitoline Hill

Viminal Hill

Esquiline Hill

Celian Hill

Palatine Hill

Aventine Hill

Forum

Sacra Via

Vicus Tuscus

Velabrum

Vicus Jugarius

Forum Boarium

SCHEMATIC PLAN OF TRIUMPHAL ROME

Abbreviations

Abbreviations of journal titles in the notes and bibliography are those used by the annual bibliography of classical studies, *L'Année Philologique*. The following abbreviations of standard reference works are also used.

ANRW:	Temporini, H., et al., eds. 1972–. *Aufstieg und Niedergang der römischen Welt*. Berlin and New York.
BMCRE:	Mattingly, H., et al., eds. 1923–. *Coins of the Roman Empire in the British Museum*. London.
BMCRR:	Grueber, H. A., ed. 1910. *Coins of the Roman Republic in the British Museum*. London.
CIL:	Mommsen, T., et al., eds. 1863–. *Corpus Inscriptionum Latinarum*. Berlin.
Degrassi, *Inscr. It.* XIII. 1, 2, 3:	1947, 1963, 1937. Degrassi, A. *Inscriptiones Italiae* XIII, vols. 1, 2, 3. Rome.
ESAR:	Frank, T. 1933–40. *An Economic Survey of Ancient Rome*. Baltimore.
FGrH:	Jacoby, F., et al., eds. 1923–. *Fragmente der griechischen Historiker*. Berlin and Leiden.
IGUR:	Moretti, L., ed. 1968–79. *Inscriptiones Graecae Urbis Romae*. Rome.
ILLRP:	Degrassi, A., ed. 1957–63. *Inscriptiones Latinae Liberae Rei Publicae*. Florence.
ILS:	Dessau, H., ed. 1892–1916. *Inscriptiones Latinae Selectae*. Berlin.
Keil, *Grammatici Latini*:	Keil, H. 1855–1923. *Grammatici Latini*. Leipzig.
LTUR:	Steinby, E. M., ed. 1993–2000. *Lexicon Topographicum Urbis Romae*. Rome.

MGH:	Mommsen, T., et al., eds. 1877–1919. *Monumenta Germaniae Historica*. Berlin.
New Pauly:	Cancik, H., and H. Schneider, eds. 2002–. *Brill's Encyclopaedia of the Ancient World, New Pauly*. Leiden and Boston.
ORF:	Malcovati, H., ed. 1953–79. *Oratorum Romanorum Fragmenta: liberae reipublicae,* 3rd ed. Turin.
RE:	Pauly, A., G. Wissowa, and W. Kroll, eds. 1893–. *Real-Encyclopädie der klassischen Altertumswissenschaft*. Stuttgart.
RIC:	Mattingly, H., E. A. Sydenham, et al., eds. 1923–1994. *Roman Imperial Coinage*. London. Vol. I, rev. ed., ed. C. H. V. Sutherland and R. A. G. Carson, 1984.
Richardson, *Dictionary:*	Richardson, L., Jr. 1992. *A New Topographical Dictionary of Ancient Rome*. Baltimore and London.
ROL:	Warmington, E. H., ed. 1935–40. *Remains of Old Latin*. Cambridge, MA, and London (with later revisions).
RRC:	Crawford, M. H., ed. 1974. *Roman Republican Coinage*. Cambridge.
ThesCRA:	*Thesaurus Cultus et Rituum Antiquorum*. 2004–. Los Angeles.

Notes

The titles of ancient works cited are regularly abbreviated, in most cases following the conventions of the *Oxford Latin Dictionary* (Oxford, 1968–1982) and Liddell and Scott's *Greek-English Lexicon,* 9th rev. edition., ed. H. S. Jones (Oxford, 1940). I have sometimes lengthened these for clarity (so "*Aen.*" rather than "*A.*" for Vergil's *Aeneid*); and I have replaced the hopelessly purist *Anc.* as a reference to the emperor Augustus' *Res Gestae (Achievements)* with *RG*. Where only one work by an author survives, I have referred to it by the author's name alone. All quotations from ancient texts are given in English translation (my own unless stated otherwise). Reliable translations of almost every work I cite can be found in the Loeb Classical Library (parallel texts in Latin/Greek and English, published by Harvard University Press). Increasingly, translations are available online. "Perseus" or "Lacus Curtius" are good places to start: http://www.perseus.tufts.edu/ and http://penelope.uchicago.edu/Thayer/E/Roman/home.html. On all details about the classical world, from authors to battles, the *Oxford Classical Dictionary,* 3rd ed. (Oxford, 1996), is an excellent source of reliable information and pointers to further reading.

PROLOGUE: THE QUESTION OF TRIUMPH

1. Seneca, *Ep.* 87, 23.
2. A convenient compendium of Renaissance triumphal ceremonial: Mulryne, Watanabe-O'Kelly, and Shewring (2004). Napoleon: Haskell and Penny (1981) 108–16; McClellan (1994) 121–3. Dewey: Malamud (forthcoming). "Triumphal" parades in modern politics and culture: Kimpel and Werckmeister (2001).
3. I follow the dating of Sperling (1992).

4. L. Schneider (1973).

5. Hopkins (1983) 1; Kelly (2006) 4.

1. POMPEY'S FINEST HOUR?

1. Overview: Greenhalgh (1980) 168–76 and Mattingly (1936–7), a perceptive fictionalizing account.

2. Campaigns: Greenhalgh (1980) 72–167; Seager (2002) 40–62. Furniture store: Appian, *Mith.* 115.

3. Suetonius, *Jul.* 51.

4. Plutarch, *Luc.* 37, 4 (63 BCE).

5. Plutarch, *Pomp.* 45, 1; Pliny, *Nat.* 37, 14 (the object which directly prompted this fulmination was the portrait in pearls).

6. Appian, *Mith.* 116. The annual Roman tax revenue is an estimate, based on figures given by Plutarch (*Pomp.* 45, 3) who states that before Pompey's conquests the annual tax revenue amounted to 50 million drachmae (the equivalent of the Roman *denarius*); after Pompey it increased to 85 million. We might well distrust the reliability of these figures; but most economic historians have—in the absence of anything better—chosen to believe that they represent roughly the right order of magnitude. Subsistence food bill: Hopkins (1978) 38–40.

7. Appian, *Mith.* 116; with Pliny, *Nat.* 33, 151 (silver statues of Mithradates and Pharnaces).

8. Pliny, *Nat.* 37, 13–4; and 18 (agate).

9. Pliny, *Nat.* 37, 14. Eastern landscapes: Kuttner (1999) 345.

10. Dio Cassius 37, 21, 2. The idea of the "whole world" in Pompey's celebrations: Nicolet (1991) 31–3.

11. The work of Jacopo Ripanda: Ebert-Schifferer (1988).

12. Musei Capitolini, inv. 1068; Stuart Jones (1926) 175; Helbig (1966) 2, no. 1453. The chances are that it came from the villa of the emperor Nero at Anzio.

13. Pliny, *Nat.* 12, 111 (trees in general); 12, 20 (ebony); 25, 7 (the library). Others (e.g. Kuttner [1999] 345) have imagined that balsam trees were included in the procession, but Pliny (12, 111) is clear that these belonged to the triumph of Vespasian and Titus in 71 CE.

14. Battlefield spoils: Appian *Mith.* 116.

15. Placards: Plutarch, *Pomp.* 45, 2; Appian, *Mith.* 117.

16. Appian, *Mith.* 116–7; Plutarch, *Pomp.* 45, 4 offers a different selection of resonant names.

17. Dio Cassius 36, 19. Metellus' triumph took place in 62 BCE.

18. Appian, *Mith.* 104–6, 111.

19. Appian, *Mith.* 117. The word *eikones* could indicate three- or two-dimensional images; but in referring to the picture of the daughters of Mithradates, Appian writes explicitly of "painting" (Greek: *para-zōgrapheō*).

20. Appian, *Mith.* 117. Beard (2003a) 35 wrongly suggested that this Cleopatra was the sister of Alexander and so implied a slightly different history for the cloak.

21. Appian, *Mith.* 117. A different ancient tradition has not even Aristoboulus put to death (p. 130).

22. Lucan 8, 553–4; 9, 599–600; also Propertius 3, 11, 35; Manilius 1, 793–4; Deutsch (1924).

23. Dio Cassius 42, 18, 3. Trophies: Picard (1957).

24. Plutarch, *Pomp.* 45, 5.

25. Valerius Maximus 6, 2, 8.

26. Plutarch, *Pomp.* 11–2. The campaigns: Greenhalgh (1980) 12–29; Seager (2002) 25–9.

27. Plutarch, *Pomp.* 14, 1–3; also *Mor.* 203E (=*Apophthegmata Pompei* 5); Zonaras, *Epitome* 10, 2.

28. Date (between 82 and 79): Eutropius 5, 9; Livy, *Periochae.* 89; Granius Licinianus 36, 1–2; *De Viris Illustribus* 77; Badian (1955), (1961); Greenhalgh (1980) 235. Lack of status: Plutarch, *Sert.* 18, 2; Cicero, *Man.* 61; also Pliny, *Nat.* 7, 95; Valerius Maximus 8, 15, 8.

29. Below, p. 315–8.

30. Granius Licinianus 36, 3–4; Pliny, *Nat.* 8, 4; Plutarch, *Pomp.* 14, 4. Stage-management: Hölscher (2004) esp. 83–5.

31. Plutarch, *Pomp.* 14, 5; *Mor.* 203 F (=*Apophthegmata Pompei* 5); Frontinus, *Str.* 4, 5, 1.

32. Pliny, *Nat.* 37, 16; Appian, *Mith.* 116; Plutarch, *Pomp.* 45, 3. 6,000 sesterces would have been enough to support a peasant family at basic subsistence for twelve years: above, n. 6.

33. Pinelli (1985) 320–1.

34. Memorial monuments: Hölscher (2006) esp. 39–45.

35. *RRC* no. 402. The dating problems are irresolvable. Different views: *BMCRR* II, 464–5; Mattingly (1963) 51–2; *RRC* 83.

36. *RRC* no. 426.

37. Globe: Nicolet (1991) 37.

38. "Manubial" temples (so-called from their funding from *manubiae*, "spoils"): Aberson (1994); Orlin (1996) 116–40, *passim*.

39. Pliny, *Nat.* 7, 97. The title *imperator* was often bestowed on a victorious general as a preliminary to a triumph. The temple itself and its possible location: *LTUR*, s.v. Minerva, delubrum; Palmer (1990) esp. 13.

40. Vitruvius 3, 3, 5; Pliny, *Nat.* 34, 57; *RRC* no. 426, 4.

41. *RRC* no. 426, 3.

42. The basement of Ristorante da Pancrazio, Piazza del Biscione, offers a convenient glimpse of one small section of the buried foundations. The influence of the ancient structures on later topography: Capoferro Cencetti (1979).

43. *LTUR* and Richardson, *Dictionary* s.v. Porticus Pompei, Theatrum Pompei, Venus Victrix, aedes; Beacham (1999) 61–72; Gagliardo and Packer (2006). This section of the Marble Plan (known in part from a renaissance manuscript copy, Cod. Vat. Lat 3439 fol. 23r): Rodriquez Almeida (1982) pl. 28 and 32.

44. Aulus Gellius 10, 1, 7, quoting, or paraphrasing, a letter of Cicero's ex-slave Tiro (whether the mistake was Tiro's, or in the transmission of Gellius, we do not know). Coarelli (1997) 568–9 defends Gellius' accuracy, by suggesting that he was referring to one of the smaller shrines in Pompey's complex which *may* have been dedicated to Victoria (Fasti Allif. ad 12 Aug. in Degrassi *Inscr. It.* XIII.2, 180–1); but Gellius seems clearly to be referring to the main temple.

45. Pliny, *Nat.* 36, 115; the fourth-century *Regionary Catalogues* give a much lower figure of 17,580 *loca* (Valentini and Zucchetti [1940] 122–3).

46. Theater-temples: Hanson (1959). Mytilene: Plutarch, *Pomp.* 42, 4—though excavations there have not produced an obvious model (Evangelides [1958], L. Richardson [1987]). A combined inspiration is presumably the most likely (as in the second-century BCE theater-temple at Praeneste, where an Italic sanctuary and "native" architectural forms are developed in a strikingly Hellenizing idiom). Tacitus, *Ann.* 14, 20 indirectly reports some unfavorable reactions to Pompey's innovations in Rome; however, the often-repeated charge of Tertullian (*De Spectaculis* 10) that the Temple of Venus (with its convenient steps) was merely a cunning device to disguise the existence of the theater is almost certainly a willful (or, at best, inadvertent) Christian misunderstanding of pagan architecture, culture, and religion.

47. Gleason (1990). Location of Caesar's murder: Plutarch, *Caes.* 66; *Brut.* 17. Quote: Shakespeare, *Julius Caesar,* Act 3, sc. ii.

48. Pliny *Nat.* 7, 34 (Alcippe); 35, 114 (Cadmus and Europa); 35, 59 ("shield-bearer").

49. Muses: Fuchs (1982). Seated figure: Helbig (1966) 2, no. 1789. Statue

bases: *IGUR* I, no. 210–212; Coarelli (1971–72) 100–3. The statue bases are almost certainly later than the original development (perhaps Augustan replacements of earlier bases); some of the surviving sculpture *may* be mid-first century BCE.

50. Tatian, *Ad Graecos* 33–4. The speculation was initiated by Coarelli (1971–72), who saw that a Greek statue-base found in the area of the Pompeian porticoes, recording the statue of "Mystis" by one "Aristodot[os]" (*IGUR* I, no. 212), matched a statue in Tatian's list (and indeed confirmed the manuscript reading of "Mystis," which had generally been emended to "Nossis"). Two other statues in the list ("Glaucippe" and "Panteuchis") seemed more or less to match a pair assigned to Pompey's complex by Pliny (*Nat.* 7, 34, "Alcippe" and "Eutychis"). So far, so good. But Tatian's list includes over twenty works of art, three of which (as Coarelli acknowledges) were definitely to be found elsewhere in Rome. There is no good reason for assuming that all those sculptures whose locations are unknown to us were in fact part of Pompey's scheme.

51. Poetesses and courtesans: Coarelli (1971–72). "Quintessentially Roman formulation": Kuttner (1999) (quotes p. 348), who fails to convince me that several of Antipater's epigrams evoke works of art from Pompey's scheme. Varro: Sauron (1987) and (1994) 280–97 (even more decidedly unconvincing).

52. Gleason (1990) 10; (1994) 19; Beacham (1999) 70.

53. Pliny, *Nat.* 35, 132 (Alexander); 36, 41 *(nationes)*. The manuscripts read simply "circa Pompeium"; editors have suggested "circa Pompei/ Pompei theatrum"; the precise arrangement of the statues must remain unclear.

54. *Nationes:* Plutarch, *Pomp.* 45, 2; Pliny, *Nat.* 7, 98. Nero: Suetonius, *Nero* 46, 1. Nero's "subtriumphal" show in 66, formally restoring Tiradates to the Armenian throne, took place in Pompey's theater, specially gilded for the day (Pliny, *Nat.* 33.54; Dio Cassius 63, 1–6).

55. The post-antique history of the statue and possible Domitianic date: Faccenna (1956). First century BCE: Coarelli (1971–72) 117–21 (though he misrepresents Faccenna's reasoning). The findspot in the Piazza della Cancelleria is at the opposite end of the whole complex from the senate house; the statue was, however, moved by Augustus to an arch opposite the main entrance of the theater when he closed off the site of his adoptive father's murder (Suetonius, *Aug.* 31, 5; Dio Cassius 47, 19, 1).

56. Coarelli (1971–72) 99–100. The speech *In Pisonem* is not itself independently dated, its timing deduced from references to Caesar's activities in

Gaul included in it (esp. *Pis.* 81). Coarelli argues for the end of September; Nisbet (1961) 199–202 allows a date between July and September.

57. Cicero, *Fam.* 7, 1, 2–3; Champlin (2003a) 297–8. The sparse surviving fragments of these plays are collected in *ROL* 2.

58. Greenhalgh (1980) 202–17; (1981) 47–63; Seager (2002) 133–51.

59. "Dyspeptic": Champlin (2003a) 298, on *Fam.* 7, 1. Elephants: Pliny, *Nat.* 8, 20–1; Dio Cassius 39, 38 (both locating the wildbeast hunts in the Circus, not in Pompey's complex itself).

60. Suetonius, *Jul.* 50, 1; Champlin (2003a) 298–9.

61. Pliny, *Nat.* 35, 7 (*aeternae* ["for ever"] is Mayhoff's plausible emendation of the implausible text of the manuscripts); Suetonius, *Nero* 38, 2 (on the destruction of such memorials in the Great Fire of Rome).

62. Cicero, *Phil.* 2, 64–70 (esp. 68). The (disputed) later history of the house: Suetonius, *Tib.* 15, 1; SHA, *Gordians* 3; Guilhembet (1992) 810–6; *LTUR* s.v. Domus Pompeiorum.

63. Velleius Paterculus 2, 40, 4; Dio Cassius 37, 21, 3–4.

64. Cicero, *Att.* 1, 18, 6. The Latin diminutive *togula picta* ("dinky little triumphal toga") refers, slightingly, to the embroidered toga (*toga picta*) characteristic of triumphal dress.

65. *C'est la deduction du somptueux ordre . . . Roy de France, Henry second* (Rouen, 1551) O, 4v (with McGowan [1973] 38–44; [2000] 332). Pompey is also depicted on one of the arches erected to celebrate Louis XIII's triumphant entry to Paris in 1628 (Mulryne, Watanabe-O'Kelly, and Shewring [2004] 2, 157).

66. Polybius 6, 15, 8. My translation (slightly) oversimplifies and elides the marked language of vision and artistry: *enargeia* ("vivid impression") is a highly loaded rhetorical term, involving the *power* to conjure up presence, or to make an audience *see* what is being represented in words (Hardie [2002] 5–6).

67. Pliny, *Nat.* 7, 99; repeated by Florus, *Epit.* 1, 40 (3, 5, 31). A better pun on paper than orally, for *media* has a short "e," *Media* a long "e."

68. Dio Cassius 36, 19, 3; Plutarch, *Pomp.* 29, 4–5 (with Plutarch, *Luc.* 35, 7 for another tale of Pompey preempting a rival's triumphal glory). The similarity between Pompey's triumphal *aureus* (*RRC* no. 402 = Fig. 3) and Sulla's of 82 BCE (*RRC* no. 367) and the issue commemorating Marius' (*RRC* no. 326 = Fig. 19) clearly suggests that in this medium too triumphing generals and/or their friends and subordinates were looking over their shoulders at earlier triumphs (though the homage of imitation is necessarily hard to distinguish from attempts to outbid).

69. Quotation: Beard (2003a) 25, paraphrasing the standard view.

70. Suetonius, *Jul.* 37, 2; Dio Cassius 43, 21, 1.

71. Pliny, *Nat.* 37, 14–6, with Hölscher (2004) 95–6. Caesar's tears: Dio Cassius 42, 8, 1; Valerius Maximus 5, 1, 10 (also stressing the head "without the rest of his body"); Plutarch, *Pomp.* 80, 5; *Caes.* 48, 2 (making the signet ring the prompt for weeping, the head being too upsetting for Caesar even to look at); Lucan 9, 1035–43 (explicitly "crocodile" tears).

72. Lucan 1, 12.

73. Lucan 2, 726–8.

74. Lucan 9, 175–9; cf Cicero, *Att.* 1, 18, 6. "Thrice seen by Jupiter" refers to his three triumphal processions culminating at the Temple of Jupiter. Triumphal accoutrements thrown also on the pyre of Caesar: Suetonius, *Jul.* 84, 4.

75. Lucan 7, 7–27 (conflating the first and second triumphs, implying his first triumph was over Spain, rather than Africa). The dream: Plutarch, *Pomp.* 68, 2; Florus, *Epit.* 2, 13 (4, 2, 45); H. J. Rose (1958); Walde (2001) 399–414. The tragedy of Pompey's triumph as a theme of Renaissance literature: McGowan (2002) 280.

76. Dio Cassius 42, 5; Velleius Paterculus 2, 53, 3; Plutarch, *Pomp.* 79, 4 (putting his death on the day after his birthday). The attempts of Bayet (1940) and Bonneau (1961) to place the "real" date of his death in August do not undermine the significance of the "traditional" chronology of Pompey's life.

77. Itgenshorst (2005) esp. 13–41 stresses the role of literary accounts in memorializing the ceremony (rather than as documentary descriptions).

78. Theophanes: Peter (1865) 114–7; Anderson (1963) 35–41; Anastasiadis and Souris (1992); he was certainly in Rome in April 59 BCE, but we do not know for how long before that (Cicero, *Att.* 2, 5, 1). Asinius Pollio: Gabba (1956) 79–88; Pollio could well have been present and had a personal investment in the triumph, having triumphed himself in 39, but his histories are known to have started in 60 BCE, so any account of Pompey's parade would have been, at most, a flashback.

79. Pliny's list (*Nat.* 7, 98) includes Crete and the Basternae not mentioned by Plutarch (*Pomp.* 45, 2) who includes instead Mesopotamia, Arabia, and "the area of Phoenicia and Palestine." Colchis and Media in Plutarch's list are likely to be the equivalents of the Scythians and Asia in Pliny's. Even so the arithmetic is precarious and depends on including the pirates in Pliny to make it up to the required fourteen. Other lists are given by Appian, *Mith.* 116; Diodorus Siculus 40, 4. The inscribed list of triumphs

from the Roman Forum, fragmentary at this point, record only [Paphla]gonia, Cappadoc(ia), [Alb]ania and the pirates (Degrassi, *Inscr. It.* XIII. 1, 84, frag. XXXIX). Recent discussion: Girardet (1991), Bellemore (2000).

80. Diodorus Siculus 40, 4 quoted in Constantine Porphyrogenitus, *Excerpta* 4, pp. 405–6 (Boissevain). Venus Victrix: Pais (1920) 256–7. The Greek East: Vogel-Weidemann (1985). A compilation: Bellemore (2000) 110–8.

81. "Fictional figures": Scheidel (1996).

82. Dreizehnter (1975) 226–30, though his main point is to try to show that many are "figures of art," arranged to make clever number games, and bear little or no relation to "real" numbers.

83. Brunt (1971) 459–60 is the most judicious, and honest, attempt to move from the figures for the donative to the number of troops. Economic theorizing deploying Plutarch's estimates of revenue: Duncan-Jones (1990) 43; (1994) 253.

84. Pliny, *Nat.* 37, 16; Plutarch, *Pomp.* 45, 3.

85. Hopkins (1980) 109–12.

86. McGowan (2002); Watanabe-O'Kelly (2002).

2. THE IMPACT OF THE TRIUMPH

1. SHA, *Hadrian* 6, 1–4; Dio Cassius 69, 2, 3; *BMCRE* III, Hadrian, no. 47. Ceremony: Richard (1966). Dating: Kierdorf (1986); Birley (1997) 99–100; Bennett (1997) 204.

2. Silius Italicus 17, 625–54. The clearest ancient evidence for the triumph in the fifteenth book of the *Annales* (which was later extended to eighteen books) is *De Viris Illustribus* 52 (with Skutsch [1985] 104 and 553); otherwise the Ennian triumph is a (not implausible) reconstruction from echoes in later poetry. The triumphal aspects of Ennius in general: Hardie (forthcoming).

3. Statius, *Theb.* 12, 519–39; Braund (1996) 12–3.

4. Künzl (1988) 19–24; Pfanner (1983) 13–90.

5. *Ex manubiis:* Augustus, *RG* 21, 1. *Quadriga* now lost: Augustus, *RG* 35, 1; Hickson (1991) 134. Possibly empty: Rich (1998) 115–25; Barchiesi (2002) 22. Bronze foot: Ungaro and Milella (1995) 50, cat. no. 15; La Rocca (1995) 75–6; Tufi (2002) 179–81 (envisaging a different location in the Forum for the Victory). Heroes of the Republic: Suetonius, *Aug.* 31, 5 (although the surviving fragments of sculpture do not obviously bear his description out: Ungaro and Milella (1995) 52–80, cat. nos. 16–28; Degrassi, *Inscr. It.*

XIII. 3, 1–8). Paintings: Pliny *Nat.* 35, 27 and 93–4; Servius (auct.), *Aen.* 1, 294; Daut (1984). Other triumphal associations: Suetonius, *Aug.* 29, 2; Velleius Paterculus 2, 39, 2; Spannagel (1999) 79–85. Reconstructions of the whole iconographic scheme: Zanker (1968); Galinsky (1996) 197–213.

6. History of the site, rams: Murray and Petsas (1989). Triumphal sculpture: Murray (2004). Function of triumph: Polybius 6, 15, 7–8. A relief sculpture now in Spain, also almost certainly depicting the Actian triumph: Trunk (2002) 250–4.

7. *Arcus triumphalis:* Ammianus Marcellinus 21, 16, 15; *ILS* 2933 = *CIL* VIII, 7094–8; *CIL* VIII, 1314 = 14817, 8321, 14728 (all inscriptions from North Africa); the Arch of Constantine in Rome (*ILS* 694 = *CIL* VI, 1139) uses the term *arcus triumphis insignis* ("arch noted for its triumphs/of triumphal renown"). Function, history and nomenclature: F. S. Kleiner (1989); Wallace-Hadrill (1990). Arches for Germanicus: Tacitus, *Ann.* 2, 83; Crawford *et al.* (1996) 1, no. 37, 9–29; Lebek (1987), (1991). Beneventum: Rotili (1972); Künzl (1988) 25–9.

8. Kuttner (1995) 143–206, though she tries to argue that this miniature representation is, in fact, a copy of a large public relief sculpture.

9. Dio Cassius 39, 65.

10. Ovid, *Ars* 1, 217–22 (trans. P. Green).

11. *ILS* 5088 = *CIL* VI, 10194.

12. Varro, *RR* 3, 2, 15–6; repeated by Columella 8, 10, 6 (Varro wrongly refers to Scipio Metellus).

13. Gladiator: Seneca, *Dial.* 1 *(De Providentia),* 4, 4. Town: Pliny, *Nat.* 3, 10. Password: Vegetius 3, 5. Infants: Livy 21, 62, 2; 24, 10, 10; Valerius Maximus 1, 6, 5. "Prodigious" is meant literally: these were "prodigies" in the Roman religious sense of signs from the gods.

14. Slaves: e.g. Plautus, *Bac.* 1068–75; Itgenshorst (2005) 50–5. Clemency, etc: Seneca, *Cl.* 1, 21, 3; *Ep.* 71, 22. Christian triumph: 2 Corinthians 2, 14; Colossians 2, 15; Tertullian, *Apologeticus* 50, 1–4; Egan (1977) (a skeptical review of key passages in the New Testament); Schmidt (1995).

15. Horace, *Carm.* 3, 30 (cf Horace's use of *deducere/deduxisse* in a strictly triumphal context, *Carm.* 1, 37, 31). Putnam (1973) explores these and other (triumphal) subtleties of the poem. Poet as triumphant general in Virgil's *Georgics:* Buchheit (1972) 101–3. In Ennius: Hardie (forthcoming).

16. Propertius 3, 1, 9–12.

17. Eisenbichler and Iannucci (1990); A. Miller (2001) 52–6. English translation: Wilkins (1962).

18. Ovid, *Am.* 1, 2 (quote ll. 27–30; trans. P. Green).

19. Romulus: Plutarch, *Rom.* 16, 5–8. Bacchus/Liber: Pliny, *Nat.* 7, 191; derivation of *triumphus:* Varro, *LL* 6, 68; Isidore *Orig.* 18, 2, 3 (claiming to quote Suetonius).

20. Pliny, *Nat.* 15, 133–5 (quoting Masurius); Festus (Paulus) p. 104L.

21. Valerius Maximus 2, 8; Aulus Gellius 5, 6, 20–3.

22. Porphyrio *ad* Horace, *Ep.* 2, 1, 192 (with Ps. Acro *ad loc.* a text which may derive in part from earlier commentators).

23. Mantegna: Martindale (1979). Petrarch's *Africa:* Bernardo (1962); Suerbaum (1972); Colilli (1990); Hardie (1993) 299–300; A. Miller (2001) 51–2.

24. Panvinio (1558), with McCuaig (1991), A. Miller (2001) 47–51 and Stenhouse (2005) 1–20, 103–12.

25. Gibbon (1796) 2, 361–401 (with English translation).

26. Renaissance discussion of the triumph: A. Miller (2001) 38–61. Christian triumphalism: Biondo (1459). Charles V's triumph: Jacquot (1956–75) 2, 206, 368 and esp. 431, 488–9; Madonna (1980); Chastel (1983), 209–15.

27. Classically different positions on "triumphal law": Mommsen (1887) 1, 126–36 and Laqueur (1909).

28. J. S. Richardson (1975); Develin (1978); Auliard (2001).

29. North (1976).

30. Frazer (1911) 174–8; Versnel (1970) esp. 201–303. The early focus of *Triumphus* is now nicely conceded in Versnel (2006) 291–2: "The addition of the word 'early' in the title would have prevented much uproar."

31. Women: Flory (1998). Christian triumph: McCormick (1986). Funerals: Brelich (1938); Richard (1966). Iconography: Andreae (1979); Angelicoussis (1984); Brilliant (1999). Poetry: Galinsky (1969); Taisne (1973). Social semiotics: Flaig (2003a) 32–40; (2003b). Elite control and conflict resolution: Hölkeskamp (1987) 236–8; Itgenshorst (2005) 193–209. Individual triumphs: J. S. Richardson (1983) (Metellus Scipio); Weinstock (1971) 71–5 (Camillus); Östenberg (1999) (Octavian); Sumi (2002) (Sulla); Beard (2003b) (Vespasian and Titus).

32. McCormick (1986) 11 notes "the dearth of thorough studies" of the development under the Principate. Barini (1952) is little more than a discursive list of military victories and triumphs reign by reign. Payne (1962) is a popular work which takes the later triumphs seriously. Particularly useful for the character of the procession in the late Republic and early Empire: Östenberg (2003).

33. Bell (1992); Humphrey and Laidlaw (1994). My summary here is, of course, a strategically useful but drastic oversimplification of the argu-

ments of these books, both of which include much more that enlightens the study of ancient ritual. I have been struck, for example, by Humphrey and Laidlaw's stress on "non-intentionality": actions performed as "ritual actions" do not depend for their significance on the individual intentions of those carrying them out; their performance is understood both by participants and observers as following a pre-stipulated pattern; and, in that respect, those who perform ritual are not, in the ordinary everyday sense, the "authors of their actions." Such nonintentionality can help to distinguish the "celebration" of even the most modest triumph from any other journey up to the Capitol in a chariot—or, for that matter, the "ritual" preparation of a turkey at Thanksgiving or Christmas from everyday domestic drudgery.

34. Barchiesi (2000); Barchiesi, Rüpke, and Stephens (2004).

35. This is a necessarily unfair summary of the apparently rich strand of recent work on public ritual; but not as unfair as one might hope. Even the most acute students of the ancient world, widely read in cultural anthropology and studies of other historical periods, tend to offer bland conclusions, sometimes little more than tautologies, on the role of processions and ceremonial: "the state festival . . . glorify[ing] the state" (Goldhill [1987] 61); "the careful regulations for participation in the processions are also important expressions of civic ideology" (Price [1984] 111); "the leader . . . often uses tribal structures, processions, or festivals to articulate community values and emerging consensuses about state policy . . . His success derives . . . in [sic] his attunement to civic needs and aspirations, and his ability to give them form and expression" (Connor [1987] 50); processions "locate the society's center and affirm its connection with transcendant things by stamping a territory with ritual signs of dominance" (Stewart [1993] 254, quoting Geertz [1983] 125). Nonetheless—for all my doubts—like almost any other study of ceremonial culture ancient or modern, this book cannot fail to be indebted to such much-cited and no doubt much-read classics as Geertz (1973), especially the famous essay on the Balinese cockfight, Le Roy Ladurie (1979) and Muir (1981).

36. The reformulation of the Parilia (originally, it seems, concerned with flocks and herds) as the "birthday of Rome" is a case in point: Beard (1987).

37. Plutarch, *Caes.* 61 (with Weinstock (1971) 331–40); Herodian 1, 10.

38. Livy 9, 43, 22 (306 BCE); 7, 16, 6 (357 BCE).

39. Complete text and story of rediscovery: Degrassi, *Inscr. It.* XIII. 1, 1–142, 346–571. Display and reconstruction: Degrassi (1943); Beard (2003c).

40. Cerco's triumph: Degrassi, *Inscr. It.* XIII. 1, 549.

41. Itgenshorst (2004) 443–8; (2005) 219–23 would see these inclusions as a highly loaded Augustan innovation, designed in part to mask the irregularity of Octavian's ovations in 40 and 36. The fact that ovations appear also on the independent *Fasti Barberiniani* does not support her case.

42. Aulus Gellius 5, 6, 21–23. "Lesser triumph": Pliny, *Nat.* 15, 19; Dionysius of Halicarnassus, *Ant.* 5, 47, 2–4; 8, 67, 10. Consolation prize: Livy 26, 21, 1–6 (Marcus Claudius Marcellus in 211).

43. Brennan (1996). The *Fasti* explicitly note the triumph of Caius Papirius Maso in 231 as "the first *in Monte Albano*."

44. Suetonius, *Gram.* 17. Panvinio (1558) Introduction ("A quibus tabulae . . . ") b. He was following an earlier emendation by Gabriele Faerno: Stenhouse (2005) 9.

45. The problem is that it is impossible to coordinate convincingly the surviving archaeological remains, ancient literary references to various structures in the Forum, and Renaissance accounts of what was found where. The flamboyant reconstructions in Coarelli (1985) 258–308 have been influential, and have attracted more credence than they deserve. Recent conjectures and critiques: Simpson (1993); Nedergaard (1994–5); Chioffi (1996) 22–6; C. B. Rose (2005) 30–3.

46. The triumphal lists must have been inscribed after 19 BCE (the date of the last in what is clearly a series of entries inscribed at a single time); though Spannagel (1999) 249 suggests a first conception of this list which culminated in the triple triumph of Octavian in 29 BCE (so rhyming the three triumph of Romulus at the start). Dating arguments have largely centered on the patterns of erasure in the different lists. The names of Mark Antony and his grandfather were erased and later restored in the list of consuls but remained intact on the triumphal list. If the erasures followed the cancellation of Antony's honors in Sept./Oct. 30 BCE, then the consular list must have been inscribed before then; a later date is possible if the erasure followed the downfall of Antony's son Iullus in 2 BCE. Detailed discussion: Taylor (1946); (1950); (1951).

47. Braccesi (1981) 39–55. Atticus' chronology: Nepos, *Att.* 18, 1–4.

48. Degrassi, *Inscr. It.* XIII. 1, 338–47; Moretti (1925). The fact that the *Fasti Urbisalvienses* are inscribed on Greek marble, not regularly exploited in northern Italy until the Augustan period, effectively scotches the idea that they are earlier than the *Capitolini*.

49. Florus, *Epit.* 1, 5 (1, 11, 6). Invention or not, this is a characteristically sharp observation by an author far less vapid than modern scholars often assume.

50. Valerius Maximus 4, 4, 5. Apuleius, *Apol.* 17 (Apuleius is defending himself against the charge that he had too few slaves).

51. Dionysius of Halicarnassus, *Ant.* 2, 34, 3.

52. Zonaras, *Epitome* 7, 21.

53. Livy 39, 6–7 (echoed almost verbatim by Augustine, *De Civitate Dei* 3, 21); Pliny, *Nat.* 34, 14.

54. Balbus' victories: Pliny, *Nat.* 5, 36–7; Strabo 3, 5, 3; Velleius Paterculus 2, 51, 3. The final slab ends with Balbus' triumph, then a roughly finished "tongue" where it was presumably inserted into its frame; I am at a loss to understand why T. Hölscher and others think this to be an element of deliberate archaizing, with the implication that there was space for further names (Spannagel [1999] 250; Itgenshorst [2004] 449).

55. Suetonius, *Cl.* 24, 3.

56. Campbell (1984) 136.

57. Boyce (1942); Maxfield (1981) 105–9; Campbell (1984) 358–62; Eck (1999). The key passage, Suetonius, *Cl.* 17, 3, reads (literally): "Those who had received triumphal ornaments in the same war followed [the chariot], but the rest went on foot wearing a *toga praetexta,* Marcus Crassus Frugi on a horse with full trappings and a palmed outfit *(vestis palmata),* because he had received the honor twice." The problem is: does this suggest that the usual dress associated with triumphal *insignia* was the *toga praetexta?* Or that it was the *toga praetexta* only when on parade in the full triumphal procession of someone else? Opposing views: Marquardt (1884) 591–2 and Boyce (1942) 131–2 *(toga picta* etc.); Mommsen (1887) 1, 412 and Taylor (1936) 170 *(praetexta).*

58. Dio Cassius 55, 10, 3, with Swan (2004) 97.

59. Eck (1984) 138; (2003) 60–2.

60. Suetonius, *Aug.* 38, 1.

61. E.g., Velleius Paterculus 2, 115, 3; Dio Cassius 54, 24, 7–8.

62. Östenberg (2003) esp. 14 attempts to draw a clear distinction between Roman and Greek imperial writers on the triumph. I am not convinced that this is as crucial as she suggests. In fact, leaving Livy on one side, the majority of the lengthy triumphal accounts are written in Greek—but that is no clear indicator of the writer's familiarity with Roman culture (Dio was after all a senator).

3. CONSTRUCTIONS AND RECONSTRUCTIONS

1. Romulus' triumph(s): Degrassi, *Inscr. It.* XIII. 1, 534 (triumph alone); Dionysius of Halicarnassus, *Ant.* 2, 34 (triumph and *spolia opima*); 2, 54,

2; 2, 55, 5 (also Plutarch, *Rom.* 16, 5–8 [triumph and *spolia opima*]; 25, 5). *Spolia opima* alone: Livy 1, 10, 5–7 (also Propertius 4, 10, 5–22; Valerius Maximus 3, 2, 3; Plutarch, *Marc.* 8, 3).

2. Dionysius may well have been writing after the display of the inscribed *Fasti* (*Ant.* 1, 7, 2 implies that he was composing his preface c. 8 BCE). The first five books of Livy are dated on internal evidence to the early 20s BCE; Ogilvie (1965) 2 and Luce (1965) suggest slightly different chronologies within that period. But, as we shall explore in Chapter 9, there is more to these discrepancies than simple chronology.

3. Generally optimistic: Cornell (1986); Drummond (1989) 173–6; Oakley (1997) 38–72, 100–4. More skeptical: Beloch (1926) (the classically super-skeptical account); Wiseman (1995) 103–7; Forsythe (2005) 59–77. Among the vast bibliography dicussing the early priestly record, later published as the *Annales Maximi* and believed by some (for example, Oakley [1997] 24–7, relying on the remarks of Servius (auct.), *Aen.* 1, 373 and Sempronius Asellio frag. 1–2 = Aulus Gellius 5, 18, 8–9) to have in-cluded notices of triumphs: Crake (1940), an "optimistic" view; Fraccaro (1957), skeptical; Rawson (1971), who doubts that they were much used in history writing, against whom Frier (1979) 22 would see their "discernible imprint" in Roman history writing.

4. Cicero, *Brut.* 62, a passage which is the starting point for Ridley (1983).

5. Caesius Bassus, *De Saturnio Versu* (in Keil, *Grammatici Latini* 6, 265).

6. *Ver.* 2.1, 57.

7. Livy 41, 28, 8–10.

8. Quoted by Pliny, *Nat.* 18, 17.

9. Livy 8, 40; Beloch (1926) 86–92; Ridley (1983) 375–8; Oakley (1997) 56–7.

10. The exact date is lost in the inscribed text, but can be deduced from Plu-tarch, *Publ.* 9, 5. Richard (1994) 414 argues that the dating to March 1, 509, goes back to the attempts of the early first-century historian Valerius Antias to associate his own ancestor with Romulus. But whether this specific type of family loyalty is at issue, or a more general attempt to align the or-igin of the city and the origin of the Republic (or both), is irrecoverable.

11. The other triumphs on the first of March marked on the surviving por-tions of the *Fasti:* 329 BCE (two celebrations), 275, 241, 222, 174. The tri-umph of 222 included Marcus Claudius Marcellus' dedication of the *spolia opima* (matching the tradition of Romulus' dedication on the same day). Perceived significance of triumphal anniversaries: Livy 40, 59, 3 (though Livy himself attributes the coincidence of dating to "chance"). Brennan (1996) 322 discusses evidence for the apparently conscious choice of significant dates (and anniversaries) for triumphs.

12. Livy 7, 15, 9; 9, 24; 10, 10, 1–5. Detailed disussion of the fit between the *Fasti Triumphales* and Livy 5–10: Oakley (2005b) 487–9.

13. 504: Livy 2, 16, 6; Dionysius of Halicarnassus, *Ant.* 5, 53, 2. 502: Livy 2, 17, 7. 495: Dionysius of Halicarnassus, *Ant.* 6, 30, 2–3. 264: Silius Italicus 6, 660–2, a tradition reflected also in Eutropius 2, 18, 2.

14. Invented not ignored: Oakley (2005a) 343. Omission of Actian triumph: *CIL* I, 1, 78 (2nd ed.) and below, pp. 302–4.

15. Three further triumphs in 33 and 28 noted on the *Fasti Barberiniani* (where the *Fasti Capitolini* do not survive) are also otherwise unknown.

16. Polybius 11, 33, 7; Livy 28, 38, 4–5. Appian, *Hisp.* 38 also notes a triumph, while Valerius Maximus 2, 8, 5 and Dio Cassius 17, frag. 57, 56 refer to the refusal of a ceremony (though according to Dio he was allowed to sacrifice 100 white oxen). There is a lacuna in the inscribed *Fasti* at this point.

17. Livy 39, 6–7; Florus, *Epit.* 1, 27 (2, 11, 3).

18. The text from the Forum is deduced from a copy found at Arezzo: Degrassi, *Inscr. It.* XIII. 3, 57; 59–60.

19. Degrassi, *Inscr. It.* XIII. 3, 50–1; *LTUR* s.v. Fornix Fabianus. The embellishment of the arch is inferred from Cicero, *Vat.* 28. The family concerned is descended from Paullus through a natural son of his first marriage, adopted into the Fabian family.

20. Velleius Paterculus 1, 9, 3. Coins (*RRC* no. 415—minted in 62 BCE by L. Aemilius Lepidus Paullus to highlight his "spurious claim to descent from L. Aemilius Paullus") also blazon the slogan *TER* ("three times"), which may reflect again a family tradition of three triumphs—or possibly that he was acclaimed *imperator* by his victorious troops on three occasions. Other aspects of the inconsistent evidence: Morgan (1973) 228–9; Ridley (1983) 375.

21. Though note the disputed 3 or 4 triumphs of Manius Curius Dentatus in the early third century BCE: J. S. Richardson (1975) 54.

22. Beard, North, and Price (1998) 2, 119–24 (Lupercalia); 116–9 (Parilia); 87–8, 151–2 (Arvals).

23. The broad lines of this reconstruction are based on Ehlers, *RE* 2. VIIA, 1, 493–511, Hopkins (1978) 26–7 and Champlin (2003b) 210–5, though most scholars tell the same story.

24. "Un-garbling": Henderson (2002) 42–8, on the similar process lying behind our reconstructions of the history and procedures of the circus games.

25. Livy 10, 37, 10–2; the reason for his speed was to forestall opposition.

26. Pliny, *Nat.* 28, 39. "Slung": Hopkins (1978) 27; Champlin (2003b) 214 ("large phallos").

27. Stars: Appian, *Pun.* 66 (though Suetonius refers to golden stars on a cloak worn by Nero at a "triumph" held to commemorate his musical and athletic victories, *Nero* 25, 1). Development of toga: Festus p. 228L (using chronological development to account for divergent evidence). Painted body: Pliny, *Nat.* 33, 111 (though the face may specifically have been referred to by Dio, to judge from Tzetzes, *Epistulae* 107); Servius (auct.), *Ecl.* 6, 22; 10, 27; Isidore *Orig.* 18, 2, 6.

28. Tzetzes, *Epistulae* 107.

29. Doubts on the tradition of "bell and whip": Reid (1916) 181, n. 3 ("not credible, for the earlier time at least"). The "economical" solution: Champlin (2003b) 214. Versnel (1970) 56 also envisages a chariot laden with both phallos and bell and whip, but does not speculate on the precise arrangement.

30. Tertullian, *Apologeticus* 33; Jerome, *Epistulae* 39, 2, 8.

31. Arrian, *Epict.* 3, 24, 85; Philostratus, *VS* 488; Whitmarsh (2001) 241–2. Aelian's story (*VH* 8, 15) of Philip of Macedon keeping a slave to remind him three times a day, "you are a man" may also be a fictionalizing retrojection from the triumph.

32. Zonaras, *Epitome* 7, 21; Tzetzes, *Epistulae* 107; Juvenal, 10, 41–2; Pliny, *Nat.* 33, 11; 28, 39; Isidore, *Orig.* 18, 2, 6. Köves-Zulauf (1972) 122–49 starts from Pliny and proposes a different reading of his now corrupt text—but ends up with an interpretation of the role of the slave not very far different from that most of scholars.

33. Triumphal imagery extends more widely through this section of the *Apologeticus,* which is concerned with the subordination of the emperor to the Christian God (see, for example, *Apologeticus* 30, 2: "Let the emperor carry heaven captive in his triumph . . . He cannot."). Even so, Barnes (1971) 243–5 convincingly disposes of the argument that Tertullian can be shown to have witnessed a triumph himself.

34. Kuttner (1995) 143–54; Musso (1987); Agnoli (2002) 222–34.

35. Plaque: Klein (1889) 85 (also Favro [1994] 154). Sarcophagus: Rodenwaldt (1940) 24–6.

36. Images of Victory: Hölscher (1967) 68–97.

37. Forum of Augustus: above, pp. 43–4. Coin: *BMCRE,* I, Augustus, no. 432–4 (Spanish *aureus* and *denarii* of 17–16 BCE) = Fig. 18.

38. *RRC* no. 367, 402.

39. *RRC* no. 326 (= Fig. 19). Exactly what counts as the first "historical" representation of a triumph is of course a moot point, and there is a fuzzy boundary between representations that appear to show Jupiter with a Victory in a *quadriga* (so-called *quadrigati* types of the third century BCE,

RRC no. 28–34) and those that show the triumphal general in similar pose. The date of this particular coin has been disputed; its common assignment to 101 BCE rests largely on the assumption that it is a commemoration of Marius' triumph. Literary tradition projected the image of Victory crowning the successful general back to the very beginning of Roman time: Plutarch, *Rom.* 24, 3.

40. Hölscher (1967) 84.

41. Kuttner (1995) 148–52 explains the slave on the Boscoreale cup (and on the major Augustan state monument of which she believes it to be a copy) as a feature of Tiberius' subservience to Augustus, emphasizing that the triumphing general was here not yet supreme. Hölscher (1967) 84 similarly refers to Tiberius' "strong rejection of emperor-worship."

42. Musso (1987) 23–4; Agnoli (2002) 229.

43. Connection of procession and cityscape: Favro (1996) 236–43. Greek processions: Price (1984) 110–2; Connor (1987); and—stressing the key role of processions in linking the center and periphery of a state's territory—Jost (1994) 228–30; Polignac (1995) 32–88. The importance of a circular route: Coarelli (1992) 388, with Pliny, *Nat.* 15, 133–5 and Festus (Paulus) p. 104 L.

44. Josephus, *BJ* 7, 123–57 (quoted 123–31).

45. Itgenshorst (2005) 24–9 is sharply aware of the gap which separates Josephus' text from physical and ritual "reality." Millar (2005) 103–7 offers a level-headed overview of some of the main topographical problems.

46. Tacitus, *Hist.* 3, 74; Suetonius, *Dom.* 1, 2; the temple burned down in 80 and was restored by Domitian, see *LTUR* s.v. Iseum et Serapeum in Campo Martio.

47. Beard (2003b) 555–8.

48. Makin (1921) 26–8; Coarelli (1968) 59 (function to accommodate generals); Künzl (1988) 32; Champlin (2003b) 212 (waiting to apply).

49. Cicero, *Pis.* 55; Tacitus *Ann.* 1, 8; Suetonius, *Aug.* 100, 2; Dio Cassius 56, 42, 1. Apuleius' feeble joke (*Apol.* 17) about "a single gate" associated with the triumph may also be a reference to the *porta triumphalis.* Discussion: Lyngby (1954) 107–22.

50. Versnel (1970) 132–63; Künzl (1988) 42–4; Rüpke (1990) 228–9; though what exactly Hölkeskamp (2006) 484 means by calling it "a sort of virtual gate" I am not sure.

51. Morpurgo (1908).

52. Modern theories: *LTUR* s.v. Porta Triumphalis (Murus Servii Tullii: Mura Repubblicane: portae). Renaissance theories, especially those of Biondo (1459): Martindale (1979) 60–3.

53. The popularity of this view is largely due to the enthusiastic arguments of Coarelli in Coarelli (1968), revised in (1992) 363–414 and repeated in his various contributions to *LTUR;* very similar arguments were put forward in the early nineteenth century (Nibby [1821] 131–4). The theory treated as "fact": Champlin (2003b) 212. A useful corrective: Haselberger (2002) s.v. Porta Carmentalis, Porta Triumphalis.

54. The commentary *(scholion)* is quoted by Lyngby (1954) 108–9 and by Coarelli (1992) 368–9, who asserts that it is in fact ancient and then attempts to tie down the Porta Catularia in a convenient place for his overall theory. Others have not been convinced; Richardson, *Dictionary* s.v. Porta Catularia shows just how murky the evidence is.

55. Livy 2, 49, 8; Ovid, *Fast.* 2, 201–4 (with Festus p. 450L; Servius, *Aen.* 8, 337). The *porta triumphalis* as the right-hand passage-way, *as you left the city*—also known as the Porta Scelerata (the "Accursed Gate"): Coarelli (1992) 370–2. The right-hand, *as you returned:* Bonfante Warren (1974) 578, drawing on Coarelli (1968); Richardson, *Dictionary* s.v. Porta Carmentalis. Clear analysis of the difficulties: Haselberger (2002) s.v. Porta Carmentalis.

56. Martial 8, 65, fully discussed by Schöffel (2002) 541–53. The connection of the poem with the *porta triumphalis* is encouraged by Martial's reference to the arch as "gate" *(porta).* But that is not to claim that this is the *porta triumphalis* in any technical sense—and Domitian's fondness for constructing arches (Suetonius, *Dom.* 13, 2) implies that there are many other candidates. Martial's phrase "open space"—*felix area* (literally, "lucky space")—may also be a play on the name of the divinity concerned.

57. Domitianic coin: *BMCRE,* II, Domitian, no. 303. The elephant-topped arch has also been identified on the Aurelian panels inserted in the Arch of Constantine (ill. Coarelli [1992] 376–7); possibly (though minus the elephants!) on the triumphal relief of Marcus Aurelius (Fig. 31). A different attempt to visualize the *porta triumphalis* (this time in a mid-sixteenth century manuscript illustrating a lost Roman relief sculpture): Pfanner (1980); F. S. Kleiner (1989) 201–4. As yet, despite occasional claims to the contrary, no archaeological traces of either the *porta triumphalis,* Carmentalis, or Catularia have been found.

58. A way out might be found in the precise sense of Josephus' Greek. "Anachōreō" (common in some parts of his writing, rare in others, a pattern perhaps derived from his sources) can mean "withdraw" as well as "go back" in the sense of "retracing steps"; but where motion is implied it regularly indicates, literally, back-tracking (e.g. *BJ* 2, 13; *AJ* 10, 17).

59. Makin (1921) 29–31; Sjöqvist (1946) 117.

60. Coarelli (1992) 368.

61. *LTUR* s.v. Iuppiter Optimus Maximus Capitolinus, aedes (fasi tardo-repubblicane e di età imperiale). Earlier triumphs had, of course, taken place against the background of a ruined temple: notably in the period after the fire on the Capitoline in 83 BCE and before the restoration of the Temple of Jupiter was completed in 69.

62. The triumph probably took place in June 71. Vespasian had returned to Rome in early autumn, probably October, of 70 (Chilver and Townend [1985] 83); it is hardly conceivable that in the intervening months the new emperor had not crossed the *pomerium*. Titus may have obeyed the traditional rules: according to Josephus (*BJ* 7, 121) only a few days elapsed between his return from the East and the triumph. Caesar's crossing of the *pomerium:* Weinstock (1971) 61–2.

63. *LTUR* s.v. Via Triumphalis (1), citing "the persuasive suggestion" that the name derives from the tradition of Camillus' triumph over Veii. Possible connections between this and further "triumphal porticoes" lining the established route (the prototype of "triumphal porticoes" attested in villas outside Rome [e.g. *CIL* VI, 29776; probably XIV, 3695a]: Coarelli (1992) 394–8. Sanest account: Haselberger (2002) s.v. Via Triumphalis, Porticus: Forum Holitorium.

64. Statue of Hercules: Pliny, *Nat.* 34, 33. Aemilius Paullus: Plutarch, *Aem.* 32, 1 (a spurious modern orthodoxy has the whole procession starting from the Circus Flaminius; though, in fact, none of the three ancient references cited by Coarelli [1992] 365 to prove that this circus was "certainly" the starting point says anything of the sort). Circus Maximus: Wiseman (forthcoming). Nero's "triumph" in 67, though with a different start and finish, also took in the Circus Maximus: Suetonius, *Nero* 25; Dio Cassius 62, 20–1 (with Champlin [2003b] 229–34, J. F. Miller [2000]).

65. Tribunes: Suetonius, *Jul.* 79, 2. Prisoners: Josephus, *BJ* 7, 153–4; Cicero, *Ver.* 2. 5, 77. Summary of debates on Sacra Via: Haselberger (2002) s.v. Sacra Via.

66. Künzl (1988) 66–7. Aemilius Paullus: Diodorus Siculus 31, 8, 10, from the Byzantine excerption of Georgius Syncellus (a variant reading might reduce the figure to a mere 1500!).

67. Suetonius, *Jul.* 37.2; Dio Cassius 43, 21, 1 (who refers to the temple in Greek as *Tuchaion*).

68. Morpurgo (1908) 135–7; Makin (1921) 34–5.

69. Coarelli (1992) 365–6, 384–5.

70. Coarelli (1992) 384.

71. Further confirmation of the Velabrum loop is thought to be found in Livy 27, 37, 11–15 on a religious procession of 207 BCE, which traveled from the Porta Carmentalis down the Vicus Iugarius to the Forum (where 27 maidens performed a dance) then back up the Vicus Tuscus to the Aventine. But the final destination (on the Aventine) makes this a much more logical itinerary, not obviously comparable with the triumph.

72. Ammerman (2006) 305–7.

73. Skirting, avoiding: Suetonius, *Aug.* 98, 2; Cicero, *Cael.* 51.

74. Wiseman (forthcoming) reaches a similar conclusion, by a different route: that the word "Velabrum" does not refer to a whole area but to a specific location near the Forum Boarium.

4. CAPTIVES ON PARADE

1. Lankheit (1984) 5–7; Baumstark and Büttner (2003) 318–49 (both citing Pecht [1873] 54–7). The painting is now in the Neue Pinakothek, Munich (WAF 771); a smaller version is in the Metropolitan Museum, New York (Inv. 87.2).

2. Campaigns and celebration: Timpe (1968); Seager (2005) 61–74; Levick (1976) 143–7.

3. Velleius Paterculus 2, 129, 2. Calendar: Fasti Amiternini s.v. 26 May (= Degrassi, *Inscr. It.* XIII. 2, 186–7 (a very fragmentary entry in which, if the restorations are correct, the Latin for "was borne," *invectus,* was creatively mispelled as *invictus,* "unconquered." Coins: *RIC* I (rev. ed.), Gaius, 57. One (optimistic) reconstruction sees a fragment of an inscription (*CIL* VI, 906c = 31575c) reading "RECIP" (perhaps part of the Latin for "recovered") as part of an arch commemorating the victory at the west end of the Forum; *LTUR* s.v. Arcus Tiberii (Forum).

4. Strabo 7, 1, 4.

5. Tacitus, *Ann.* 1, 55.

6. Vatinius *apud* Cicero, *Fam.* 5, 10a, 3 offers one (not particularly auspicious) precedent.

7. Tacitus, *Ann.* 2, 41.

8. Ovid, *Am.* 1, 2, 19–52 (trans. P. Green).

9. Ovid, *Am.* 1, 9, 1.

10. Dicussion of the poem: Galinsky (1969) 92–5 (pointing to echoes of Virgil's opening of the third *Georgic,* with its claims to triumphal status for the poet); F. D. Harvey (1983) (seeing the relationship of Cupid and Au-

gustus in the context of Augustus' restriction of the triumph to members of his own family); McKeown (1987–) 1, 31–59; Buchan (1995) 56–66; Athanassaki (1992); J. F. Miller (1995); Habinek (2002) 47–9. In the reference to "Conscience, hands bound behind her, and Modesty" several writers see a parodic allusion to the painting of Apelles in the Forum of Augustus (p. 44).

11. Horace, *Carm.* 1, 37, 29–32 (trans. D. West).

12. Plutarch, *Ant.* 84; Florus, *Epit.* 2, 21 (4, 11, 10–11); Dio Cassius 51, 13–4; Shakespeare, *Antony and Cleopatra* Act 4, sc. 15; Porphyrio *ad* Horace, *Carm.* 1, 37.

13. Pelling (1988) 319.

14. Different options: Pelling (1988) 318–20; Nisbet and Hubbard (1970) 407–11; Whitehorne (1994) 186–202.

15. Appian, *Mith* 111.

16. Livy 26, 13, 15.

17. SHA, *Aurelian* 34, 3; *Tyranni XXX (Thirty Pretenders)* 30, 4–12 and 24–7; Zosimus, 1, 59. Other candidates for taking the option of suicide rather than (triumphal) captivity might include: the Carthaginian Sophonisba, who supposedly took poison in 203 BCE rather than fall into Roman hands, although there is no specific mention of plans for a triumph (Livy 30, 15, 1–8; Zonaras, *Epitome* 9, 13); the Aetolian leader Damocritus, who is said to have escaped from prison a few nights before the triumph of Manius Acilius Glabrio in 190 BCE and stabbed himself when rearrested (Livy 37, 46, 5).

18. SHA, *Tyranni XXX (Thirty Pretenders)* 30, 2 and 19.

19. Plutarch, *Aem.* 34, 2; *Mor.* 198b (*Apophthegmata Paulli* 7); Cicero, *Tusc.* 5, 118.

20. Wyke (2002) 240.

21. Brunt (1971) 694–7; Oakley (1998) 189–90; Scheidel (1996).

22. Eutropius 2, 5, 2; Dionysius of Halicarnassus, *Ant.* 6, 17, 2; Livy 7, 27, 8–9 (even Livy has doubts here, noting disagreements about whether they were captured soldiers or slaves—either way, the high figure is hard to reconcile with the demography or economy of early Italy).

23. Livy 45, 42, 2.

24. E.g., Livy 10, 46, 5 refers to 2,533,000 pounds of bronze carried in the triumph of Papirius Cursor in 293 BCE, said to have come from the sale of prisoners.

25. Josephus, *BJ* 6, 416–9; Appian, *Hisp.* 98.

26. Sardi Venales: Festus p. 428–30L (ascribing this explanation to the second century BCE grammarian, Sinnius Capito); *De Viris Illustribus* 57. Papus: Polybius 2, 31, 1–6.

27. This is the implication of Festus p. 430L; the inscription quoted by Livy (41, 28, 8–10) from the Temple of Mater Matuta in Rome, commemorating Gracchus' victory, does refer to booty, but leads with the total of more than 80,000 enemy killed or captured.

28. Livy 30, 45, 4–5 (though at 45, 39, 7 Livy too refers to his appearance in the triumph). Livy also offers two different versions of the fate of Hamilcar: killed in battle (31, 21, 18); taken alive and paraded in triumph (32, 30, 12; 33, 23, 5).

29. Augustus, *RG* 4, 3.

30. Livy 45, 39, 7.

31. Anicius Gallus: Livy 45, 43, 6; Velleius Paterculus 1, 9, 5–6. Bituitus: Florus, *Epit.* 1, 37 (3, 2, 5). Jugurtha: Plutarch, *Mar.* 12; Livy, *Periochae* 67. Arsinoe etc: Dio Cassius 43, 19, 2–4; Plutarch, *Caes.* 55; Appian, *BC* 2, 101; Florus, *Epit.* 2, 13 (4, 2, 88).

32. Distinguished prisoners: Livy 10, 46, 4; 33, 23, 5; *De Viris Illustribus* 17, 3. Scipio's triumph: Livy 37, 59, 5. *Duces ducti:* Livy 3, 29, 4; 4, 10, 7.

33. Recording the triumph of Manius Acilius Glabrio in 190.

34. Pliny, *Pan.* 17; SHA, *Lucius Verus* 8, 7. See also Persius 6, 43–50.

35. Florus, *Epit.* 1, 30 (2, 14, 5).

36. Lactantius, *Divinae Institutiones* 1, 11.

37. SHA, *Aurelian* 33–4; *Tyranni XXX (Thirty Pretenders)* 30, 24–6.

38. Vergil, *Aen.* 8, 722–8. Gurval (1995) 34–6, 242–4; Toll (1997) 45–50; Östenberg (1999).

39. Velleius Paterculus 2, 121. Dench (2005) 76–80.

40. Lucan 1, 12.

41. Appian, *BC* 2, 101.

42. "Cover-up": Poduska (1970); with more nuance, Toll (1997) 48.

43. E.g., Ovid, *Am.* 1, 2, 30; *Tr.* 4, 2, 46 (Germania). Pompey's triumph: Appian, *Mith.* 117.

44. Literary texts: e.g. Cicero, *Pis.* 60; Livy 4, 10, 7; 6, 4, 2; Seneca, *Ep.* 71, 22; Valerius Maximus 4, 1, 8. Inscriptions: in addition to Augustus' *RG* 4 (a text known to us entirely epigraphically), Degrassi, *Inscr. It.* XIII. 3, no. 17 and 83 (texts derived from the *elogium* of Marius in the Forum of Augustus, including details of the victory over Jugurtha "led in front of his chariot"). Seneca, *Dial.* 10 *(De Brevitate Vitae)*, 13, 8 half jokes on the familiar

expression, referring to the "120 . . . elephants" in front of the chariot of Lucius Caecilius Metellus in 250 BCE. Victims behind chariot: Lucan 3, 77–8.

45. Ryberg (1955) 150–4; Rotili (1972) 106–12; Adamo Muscettola (1992); Rivière (2004) 31–3. Only fragments of other such friezes survive, from (for example) the Temple of Apollo Sosianus in Rome (Fig. 23) and the Arch of Titus (Fig. 30).

46. Admitting adjustments for "decorative purposes" (as do Ryberg [1955] 150 and Rivière [2004] 32–3) can obscure the more general questions of the nature of the documentary realism of sculptures of this type. So too does the usual claim that this frieze is a version of the particular occasion of Trajan's triumph over the Dacians and Germans in 106 CE.

47. Josephus, *BJ* 7, 153–5.

48. Zonaras, *Epitome* 7, 21; Cicero, *Ver.* 2. 5, 77.

49. Rivière (2004) 52–3; Rüpke (1990) 210–1; Bonfante Warren (1974) 580.

50. Pontius: Livy, *Periochae* 11. Pirate chiefs: Cicero, *Ver.* 2. 5, 66–7. Vercingetorix: Dio Cassius 40, 41, 3; 43, 19, 4. Adiatorix and Alexander: Strabo 12, 3, 6; Dio Cassius 51, 2, 2. Even in these cases it is not entirely clear whether they were put to death—as Josephus claims was the case for Simon—during the procession itself, or at some point soon afterwards and not directly associated with the triumph.

51. Appian, *Mith.* 117; Dio Cassius 37, 16, 4; 39, 56, 6; 41, 18, 1; Josephus, *AJ* 14, 79, 92–9, 123–4; *BJ* 1, 158, 171–3, 183–4.

52. Livy, *Periochae* 67; Plutarch, *Mar.* 12. Similar doubts about the fate of Aristonicus (in 126 BCE): Velleius Paterculus 2, 4, 1; Eutropius 4, 20 (who has picked up the idea that although he was killed, he was not displayed in a triumphal procession).

53. Gentius: Livy 45, 43, 9. Zenobia: SHA, *Tyranni XXX (Thirty Pretenders)* 30, 27. There are many other examples of captives surviving the procession, including: King Perseus and his sons in 167 (Plutarch, *Aem.* 37; Livy 45, 42, 4), Arsinoe in 46 (Dio Cassius 43, 19, 4), Bato in 12 CE (Suetonius, *Tib.* 20).

54. *Panegyrici Latini* 6 (7), 10.

55. Eutropius 10, 3, 3.

56. Simon: Josephus, *BJ* 7, 153–5. John Chrysostom, *In Praise of St. Paul* 2, 3. Also: Silius Italicus 17, 629–30; Seneca, *Tr.* 150–6; *Phoen.* 577–8; Horace, *Ep.* 2, 1, 191; Plutarch, *Aem.* 33–4; Cicero, *Ver.* 2. 5, 66.

57. *Panegyrici Latini* 6 (7) 10; see also Cicero, *Cat.* 4, 21.

58. Quote: Florus, *Epit.* 1, 38 (3, 3, 10); also Eutropius 5, 1; Orosius, *Historia Adversus Paganos* 5, 16 (who has him killed on the battlefield).

59. Florus, *Epit.* 1, 37 (3, 2, 5).

60. SHA, *Aurelian* 34, 3, *Tyranni XXX (Thirty Pretenders)* 30, 24–6. Gold chains on Syphax in 201 BCE: Silius Italicus 17, 630.

61. Florus, *Epit.* 1, 37 (3, 2, 5).

62. Dio Cassius 63, 1, 2.

63. Ovid, *Tr.* 4, 2 (quotes 19–24, trans. A. D. Melville; 27–8); the description of the prisoner is closely related to that of the emperor (47–8; dubbed *dux* in l. 44). See Beard (2004) 124.

64. Dio Cassius 43, 19. The form and use of *fercula:* Abaecherli (1935–6).

65. Plutarch, *Aem.* 33, 4.

66. Plutarch, *Aem.* 34, 1.

67. Plutarch, *Aem.* 35, 1–2; Livy 45, 40, 7–8; Valerius Maximus 5, 10, 2. They differ on the question of whether the younger son did (Valerius Maximus) or did not (Livy) appear in the triumphal chariot with his father before his death. Eutropius 4, 8 has both sons in the chariot—and does not seem to know of the deaths.

68. Livy 45, 41, 10–11; Plutarch, *Aem.* 36, 6.

69. Seneca, *Ep.* 71, 22.

70. Seneca, *Dial.* 7 *(De Vita Beata)*, 25, 4. The usual translation, "*a* Socrates" (that is, a typical sage), conceals the anomaly of The Latin expression.

71. Among a vast literature, seminal contributions include: Brunt (1963); (1978); (1990) 433–80; Harris (1979) 9–41; Hopkins (1978) 25–8.

72. Dio Cassius 12, 50, 4 (from Byzantine epitome); Florus, *Epit.* 1, 20 (2, 4). It is tempting to see a connection here with Horace's famous phrase about "captive Greece" making her "savage conqueror captive" (Horace, *Ep.* 2, 1, 156).

73. Dio Cassius 43, 23, 4 (though it is not explicitly stated that these "prisoners" had previously been paraded in the triumph).

74. Plutarch *Aem.* 37; Zonaras, *Epitome* 9, 24; Diodorus Siculus 31, 9 (from Byzantine excerptions).

75. Plutarch, *Caes.* 55; Appian *BC* 2, 46; Christ (1920) 401–3.

76. Valerius Maximus 6, 2, 3.

77. Suetonius, *Jul.* 80 ("swanky": literally "broad-striped" referring to the distinctive senatorial toga).

78. Valerius Maximus, 6, 9, 9 ("prison"/*carcer* evokes the threat of execution); Aulus Gellius 15, 4, 4; Velleius Paterculus 2, 65, 3; Pliny, *Nat.* 7, 135.

79. Ovid, *Am.* 2, 12, 1–2 and 5–6 (trans. P. Green).

5. THE ART OF REPRESENTATION

1. Dio Cassius 51, 21, 8; Propertius 3, 11, 53–4. Nisbet and Hubbard (1970) 410 surprisingly regard Propertius' reference here as merely "dutiful."

2. Haskell and Penny (1981) 184–7; Barkan (1999) 246–7. Appropriately enough, this "Cleopatra" was for a time displayed in the Belvedere courtyard of the Vatican, supported on a second-century CE Roman sarcophagus with triumphal scenes (Köhler [1995] 372–3).

3. Original Latin text: Perosa and Sparrow (1979) 193–5. Pope's translation: Ault and Butt (1954) 66–8. Castiglione also plays on the ambivalence between victim and general: at one point (line 19) the Latin adjective "unhappy"/"unlucky" *(infelix)* can be apply equally to the "unhappy" statue—or to the general "unlucky" in not being able to show the living queen in his procession.

4. Sartain (1885).

5. Appian, *BC* 2, 101. Cf. the tears prompted by the model of the town of Massilia (Marseilles) also in 46 BCE: Cicero, *Phil.* 8, 18; *Off.* 2, 28.

6. Josephus, *BJ* 7, 139–47.

7. The dangers of falling off a *ferculum:* Obsequens 70.

8. Livy 26, 21, 1–10; Plutarch, *Marc.* 21–2; Valerius Maximus 2, 8, 5.

9. Plutarch, *Marc.* 21, 1–2. The pun on "booty" and "beauty" is in the original Greek.

10. Florus, *Epit.* 1, 13 (1, 18, 27).

11. Notably Gruen (1992) 84–130—though, in fact, he comes up with rather few clear and uncontentious examples. McDonnell (2006) restates the innovation of this occasion.

12. Plutarch, *Marc.* 21, 3–4. Other criticisms of Marcellus: Polybius 9, 10; Livy 34, 4, 4. A more favorable view: Cicero, *Ver.* 2. 4, 120–3 (using Marcellus as a foil for the depredations of Verres). Discussions of the complex historiographical tradition (including the contrast with Fabius Maximus, often portrayed as a respectful and pious conqueror): Gros (1979); Ferrary (1988) 573–8; Gruen (1992) 94–102; McDonnell (2006) 78–81.

13. Livy 26, 21, 7–9.

14. Cicero, *Rep.* 1, 21. The complex story of the refoundation of the temple: *LTUR* s.v. Honos et Virtus, aedes.

15. *ILLRP* 218, 295.

16. Plutarch, *Marc.* 30, 4–5; Livy 25, 40, 3. Marcellus' booty in general: Pape (1975) 6–7 and *passim*.

17. E.g., Dionysius of Halicarnassus, *Ant.* 6, 17, 2 (499 or 496 BCE); Livy 9, 40, 15–16 (309 BCE).

18. Seneca, *Dial.* 10 *(De Brevitate Vitae),* 13, 3; Eutropius 2, 14; Pliny, *Nat.* 8, 16; 7, 139.

19. Appian, *Pun.* 66.

20. Livy 34, 52; Plutarch, *Flam.* 14; Cicero, *Ver.* 2. 4, 129.

21. Plutarch, *Aem.* 32–3.

22. Pliny *Nat.* 12, 111–2.

23. Josephus, *BJ* 7, 132–52; Beard (2003b).

24. Josephus, *BJ* 7, 158–62; Millar (2005) 107–12.

25. Summary of the controversies, back to Reland (1716): Yarden (1991); see also Pfanner (1983) 73–4; Gibbon (1776–88) 4, ch. 36, p. 6; Miller (2005) 127–8 and below, pp. 318–9. Kingsley (2006) claims to have run the holy objects to ground on the West Bank. There is disagreement too about which menorah is represented on the arch, and whether it was that from the Temple at all.

26. In addition to a plethora of often highly partisan websites detailing the various theories and developments, Fine (2005) offers a sane overview.

27. Dio Cassius 43, 19–21 (Arsinoe, axle); Plutarch, *Caes.* 55; Appian, *BC* 2, 101 (paintings of Romans); Suetonius, *Jul.* 37, 2 (axle, "I came . . ."); 49, 4 and 51 (songs); Florus, *Epit.* 2, 13 (4, 2, 88–9) (representation and models).

28. Full discussion of the *Triumphs:* Martindale (1979) esp. chap. 5 for the classical sources (and p. 136 for the *pegmata*).

29. E.g. Brilliant (1999) 223–4.

30. In general: Ryberg (1955) 141–62. The small frieze on Trajan's Arch at Beneventum (Figs. 21, 22; including several loaded *fercula*): Rotili (1972) 106–12; Adamo Muscettola (1992). The severely damaged small frieze on the Arch of Titus (Fig. 30; including a plausible model of a river): Pfanner (1983) 82–90. Sculptural decoration of the Temple of Apollo Sosianus (Fig. 23; including small triumphal frieze): Heilmeyer, La Rocca and Martin (1988) 121–48. The small friezes on the Arch of Septimius Severus, often described as "triumphal" (but equally plausibly—if we are to take them as narrowly "documentary"—a representation of the journey home of the victorious army): Brilliant (1967) 137–47. The only surviving representation of any architectural model is a fragment of late imperial sculpture (possibly a forgery) from North Africa, showing a bridge—identified as the Milvian Bridge—carried in procession on a *ferculum* (illustrated by Künzl [1988] 78–9, fig 47).

31. Martindale (1979) 109–22.

32. *ESAR* I, 126–38 ("National Income and Expenses, 200–157," relying heavily on literary records of triumphal booty).

33. Pollitt (1978) 157.

34. Pollitt (1983) 63–74. Evidence for particular works of art on display in individual processions and their subsequent history: Pape (1975) 41–71 (with Yarrow [2006], attempting to track the final destination of Mummius' booty). Significant contributions to the debates on the changes in artistic practice and "appreciation" especially among the Roman elite at this time: Hölscher (1978); Pollitt (1978); MacMullen (1991); Gruen (1992) 84–130. The complexity of the cultural change which underlies claims (or denials) of "Hellenization": *HSCPh* (1995) and Habinek and Schiesaro (1997).

35. E.g. Holliday (1997); (2002) 22–62. The triumph has also been linked to the development of Roman traditions in portraiture and honorific statuary, on the grounds that the first statues of living people erected in Rome appear to have been of generals who had triumphed: Rüpke (2006) 261–5. Hölkeskamp (2001) 111–26 links honorific statues to (what he sees as) the triumphal route.

36. Murphy (2004) 155 and 160; Hardie (2002) 310.

37. Velleius Paterculus 2, 56, 2. Cf. accounts of the triumph of Aemilius Paullus: displaying some 56,250 kilos of silver coin (to translate Plutarch's account, *Aem.* 32, 5), or, according to Velleius (1, 9, 6), exceeding all previous triumphs in the display of money (with 200 million sesterces transferred to the treasury); Pliny (*Nat.* 33, 56) refers to 300 million sesterces.

38. Suetonius, *Aug.* 41, 1.

39. Pliny, *Nat.* 33, 148 (though he goes on to say that the legacy to Rome of the kingdom of Asia by Attalus had even worse effects); 33, 151.

40. "Tax-paying subjects" *(servit nunc haec ac tributa pendit):* Pliny, *Nat.* 12, 111–2.

41. Polybius 6, 15, 8.

42. Josephus, *BJ* 7, 133–4; Beard (2003b) 551–2.

43. Plutarch, *Luc.* 36, 7.

44. Florus, *Epit.* 1, 13 (1, 18, 27). Retrojection of opulence: Valerius Maximus 6, 3, 1b (502 and 486 BCE); Livy 4, 34 (426); Dionysius of Halicarnassus, *Ant.* 6, 17, 2 (499 or 496); though in discussing Romulus' spoils in 753 Dionysius (*Ant.* 2, 34, 3) drives home the moral contrast between the modesty of early triumphs (as he assumed them to be) and the ostentatious pomp of his own day. Florus, *Epit.* 1, 18 (2, 2, 30–2) refers to a triumph in 245 BCE aborted because all the booty had been lost at sea.

45. Livy 31, 49, 3; cf. 40, 38, 9.
46. Cicero, *Att.* 4, 18, 4; *Q. fr.* 3, 4, 6; Dio Cassius 37, 47–8; 39, 65; *Scholia Bobiensia* (Stangl) 149–50.
47. Appian, *Mith.* 115.
48. Östenberg (2003) 60.
49. Livy 45, 35, 6; Plutarch, *Aem.* 29, 3. The procedure for plundering defeated cities: Ziolkowski (1993), rightly challenging the orderly picture offered by Polybius 10, 15, 4–16, 9 (referring to the sack of New Carthage in 209).
50. Shatzman (1972) and Churchill (1999) represent the two main sides of the argument, with full references to other contributions.
51. Livy 37, 57, 12–58, 1; Astin (1978) 69–73; Briscoe (1981) 390–2.
52. Gabelmann (1981).
53. Östenberg (2003) 264–6. Itgenshorst (2005) 82–8; 192–3 is more skeptical of any detailed reconstructions.
54. For variations in the "literary order" of the procession, compare Appian, *Pun.* 66 (trumpeters, wagons of spoils, images of cities, pictures of the war, bullion and coin, golden crowns, sacrificial animals, elephants, prisoners) with Livy 39, 5, 13–17 (golden crowns, bullion, coin, statues, captured weapons, prisoners) or Tacitus, *Ann.* 2, 41 (spoils, captives, images of mountains, rivers, and battles). Plutarch, *Luc.* 37, 2 (perhaps the Circus Flaminius held the booty before the parade too).
55. Livy 9, 40, 16; Rawson (1990), suggesting that often such stories were invented, *ex post facto,* to explain and give a history to spoils on display in the city. Cistophori: Harl (1991); Kleiner and Noe (1977). Triumphs: Livy 37, 46, 3; 37, 59, 4; 38, 58, 4–5; 39, 7, 1.
56. Livy 10, 46, 5.
57. Callixeinos, *FGrH* 627 F 2 (=Athenaeus, *Deipnosophistae* 5, 197C–203B). Rice (1983) is a full discussion of the text which energetically searches out parallels for the objects in the procession and other reasons to believe. The statue is "one of many historically attested automata" (p. 65); ostriches are shown pulling "the chariot of Eros" (hardly much of a proof!) on an imperial gem from Munich and feature in ostrich carts in California and Nevada (p. 90); the wine sack is "of the size, material, and ostentation suited to the Grand Procession" (p. 71). The appendix on "the credibility of Athenaeus and Kallixeinos," pp. 138–50, by and large gives both author and excerptor a clean bill of health. More recent discussions of this text take it similarly as a more or less accurate documentary account: Stewart (1993) 253–4; Thompson (2000)—though Itgenshorst (2005) 214

is more circumspect. My calculations of comparability are based on Thompson (2000) 370, where she reckons the capacity of the wine sack at 116,340 litres (assuming 38.78 litres = 1 measure/*metreta*).

58. Athenaeus, *Deipnosophistae* 197D; though this reference is a long way from proving (as Rice [1983] 171–5 would have it) that Callixeinos' account was based on an official record of the occasion.

59. Cicero, *Ver.* 2. 1, 57.

60. Epigraphical hints at record-keeping: *ILLRP* 319, commemorating the naval triumph of Duilius in 260 BCE. Literary precision: Livy 34, 10, 4 (195BCE); Livy 39, 5, 15 (187 BCE). Documents on Pompey's booty in 61: above, pp. 38–40.

61. In detail, the pattern of Livy's account is complicated. There are similarly precise figures in his text occasionally before 207 BCE (for example, 10, 46, 5 and 14 on the triumphs of 293 BCE); books 11–20 are lost; the series of regular standard notices, with precise figures, starts only in 207 BCE (Livy 28, 9, 16–7)—triumphs in any case not having been frequent in the period covered by Books 21–27. In its most skeletal form, the standard information is: sums of coin or bullion put into the treasury, the amount distributed to the troops; though from 190 BCE numbers of gold crowns are regularly included, as are occasionally numbers of standards captured or statues. Triumphal notices as part of Livy's rhetorical purposes: Phillips (1974).

62. Nature of Servilius' list: Bradford Churchill (1999) 105–6. New Carthage: Livy 26, 47. 5–8. Livy 45, 40, 1 cites the earlier writer Valerius Antias as source for his figures for booty.

63. Diodorus Siculus 31, 8, 10–2 (from the Byzantine excerption of George Syncellus).

64. Plutarch, *Aem.* 32–3 (the only exact match with Diodorus is the 120 sacrificial oxen and 400 garlands or gold crowns). Östenberg (2003) 23–4, 27 sees the difference in terms of their different uses and understanding of their common source, Polybius.

65. Livy 36, 21, 11; 36, 39, 2.

66. Plutarch, *Flam.* 14; Livy 34, 52, 4–7.

67. Briscoe (1981) 128–9.

68. Briscoe (1981) 252, 254, 278–9.

69. Pompey's "eight cubit" statue: Plutarch, *Luc.* 37; above, p. 9.

70. Livy 6, 29, 8–10.

71. Pliny, *Nat.* 34, 54. The exact location is contested: *LTUR* s.v. Fortuna Huiusce Diei, Templum and Fortuna Huiusce Diei, Templum (in Palatio).

72. Haskell and Penny (1981) 108–24 (quote p. 111); McClellan (1994) 120–3.

73. This is not to say that there was no appreciation of Greek art. Discussion: Gruen (1992) 84–130.
74. E.g., Livy 45, 33, 1–2; Rüpke (1990) 199–202.
75. Plutarch, *Luc.* 37, 3; Diodorus Siculus 31, 8, 11–2 (from the excerption of George Syncellus); Livy 34, 52, 5–7.
76. Plutarch, *Aem.* 32, 3–4; Propertius 2, 1, 34.
77. Trophies *(tropaea):* Picard (1957). Images: Holliday (2002) 57–60.
78. E.g., Livy 9, 40, 15–7 (shields from the triumph of Papirius Cursor in 309 said to have decorated the Forum); Livy 10, 46, 7–8 (Papirius Cursor junior decorates the Temple of Quirinus, the Forum, and the temples and public places of the allies with *spolia*—probably here in the limited sense of arms and armor). *Columnae rostratae* ("beaked columns") featured a display of "beaks" (or rams) captured from enemy ships.
79. Livy 38, 43, 10 suggests that the spoils attached to houses might be a more varied selection than just captured weapons.
80. Livy 24, 21, 9.
81. Pliny, *Nat.* 34, 43. Livy's notice of Carvilius' triumph (10, 46, 13–5) does not refer to this.
82. Plutarch, *Mor.* 273 C–D (*Quaestiones Romanae* 37).
83. Livy 23, 14, 4.
84. Plutarch, *CG* 15, 1 and 18, 1; Velleius Paterculus 2, 6, 4.
85. Livy 24, 21, 9–10.
86. Appian, *Pun.* 135.
87. Polybius 9, 10 (quotation, section 13). Though not explicitly about the triumph, this is a crucial passage for the darker side of victory.
88. Smith (1981) 30–2.
89. Pliny, *Nat.* 35, 135; Quintilian, *Inst.* 6, 3, 61 (cf. Velleius Paterculus 2, 56, 2—a slightly different version).
90. Künzl (1988) 117–8; Ling (1991) 9–11; Holliday (2002) 19, 50–5, 87–90.
91. Pliny, *Nat,* 35, 22–3; Livy 41, 28, 8–10 (Gracchus).
92. Ovid, *Tr.* 4, 2 (esp. line 65). Beard (2004) 118–21; Oliensis (2004) 308–17; Hardie (2002) 308–11 (quotation, p. 309). The context is a triumph expected, but not celebrated, in 10 CE.
93. Ovid, *Pont.* 2, 1, 37–8 (few scholars have been convinced either by the reading *victis* ["conquered"] or by Heinsius' emendation of *fictis* ["made up," "imaginary"] for *pictis;* see Galasso [1995] 115). The phrase *pictis . . . viris* echoes the *pictas . . . vestes* ("painted clothes") of the general, another nice example of the slippage between conqueror and conquered. See Beard (2004) 116.
94. Appian *Mith.* 117 (most translations attempt to reduce the peculiarity of

the Greek by turning it into "his silent flight by night" *vel sim.*) with Beard (2003a) 31–2. Hölscher (1987) 29 incautiously leaps to the conclusion that this description is good evidence for increasingly sensational effects sought by art in the late Republic.

95. Appian, *Mith.* 117 with Beard (2003a) 32. Divine image-making in general: R. Gordon (1979).

96. Josephus, *BJ* 7, 136.

97. Ovid, *Ars* 1, 223–8 (trans. P. Green, adapted).

98. Tigris and Euphrates: Lucan 3, 256–9.

99. Suetonius, *Cal.* 47; Persius 6, 46–7

100. Tacitus, *Ag.* 39, 1; Pliny, *Pan.* 16, 3; Dio Cassius 67, 7. 4.

101. Dio Cassius 79, 16, 7; 72, 17–20.

6. PLAYING BY THE RULES

1. Plutarch, *Crass.* 32–3.

2. The letters between Cicero in Cilicia and friends in Rome are clustered in his *Letters to Atticus (Att.),* Books 5 and 6 (with the return journey continuing into Book 7) and *Letters to Friends (Fam.),* Books 2, 3, 8, and 15, largely comprising numbers 66–118 in Shackleton Bailey (1977). On the principles of selection: Beard (2002), 116–43.

3. *Fam.* 8, 5, 1.

4. *Fam.* 2, 10, 2–3. The usual assumption is that Scipio's acclamation in 208 was the first: Livy 27, 19, 4; Combès (1966) 51–9; Auliard (2001) 18–9.

5. *Att.* 5, 20, 3; *Fam.* 2, 10, 3.

6. Concise narratives: Rawson (1975b) 164–82; Mitchell (1991) 204–31. Wistrand (1979) offers a detailed reconstruction; Marshall (1966) is an excellent account of his nonmilitary activity.

7. *Fam.* 3, 6, 3–5. Cicero assumes malevolence on Appius' part, but it is not inconceivable that Appius was as much ignorant of Cicero's arrival as malevolent.

8. *Fam.* 2, 10, 2; 15, 14, 3 (quoted); in *Att.* 5, 18, 1 he also takes the Parthian threat seriously at its outset—and similarly, later, in *Phil.* 11, 35.

9. *Att.* 5, 20, 3; 21, 2; *Fam.* 3, 8, 10; 8, 10, 2. Misinformation from the frontiers (leading to a triumph) in the Empire: Dio Cassius 68, 29, 1–3; Ando (2000) 126, 182.

10. *Att.* 5, 16, 2; *Fam.* 3, 10, 1; 3, 9, 2.

11. *Att.* 5, 20, 4; 6, 5, 3; 6, 8, 5; 7, 2, 6; *Fam.* 8, 6, 4. Cicero's tone changes according to the recipient: his official dispatch to the senate (*Fam.* 15, 1, 5) refers to Bibulus as "very brave" *(fortissimus).* Cake recipe: Cato, *Agr.* 121.

12. Halkin (1953) discusses what (little) we know of the ritual (99–105); for Cicero's supplication, 48–58.
13. *Att.* 7, 1, 8.
14. *Fam.* 15, 10 (to Marcellus); 15, 13 (to Paullus, markedly more fulsome; quoted).
15. *Fam.* 15, 4, discussed in detail by Wistrand (1979) 10–18; Hutchinson (1998) 86–100.
16. *Fam.* 8, 11. Curio: Lacey (1961).
17. *Fam.* 15, 5. Judgments: Tyrrell and Purser (1914) xxxiii; Rawson (1975b) 170; Boissier (1870) 294, showing perhaps a more nineteenth-century sympathy for Cato's rhetoric.
18. *Fam.* 15, 11; 3, 13.
19. *Fam.* 15, 6.
20. *Att.* 6, 3, 3; 6, 6, 4; 6, 8, 5; *Fam.* 2, 12, 3.
21. *Att.* 7, 1, 7; 7, 2, 6–7; 7, 4, 2; the text of the numeral at 7, 2, 7 is disputed.
22. *Att.* 7, 8, 5; with 6, 9, 2; 7, 1, 9.
23. *Att.* 7, 1, 5.
24. *Att.* 7, 4, 2; Cicero did attend the senate (presumably meeting outside the *pomerium*) in January 49, *Att.* 9, 11a, 2).
25. *Att.* 7, 7, 4.
26. *Att.* 7, 3, 2.
27. *Fam.* 16, 11, 3.
28. E.g., *Att.* 7, 10; 8, 3, 6; 9, 2a, 1; 9, 7, 5; 11, 6, 2–3; *Fam.* 2, 16, 2. The circumstances of Cicero's laying down his *imperium* and abandoning his triumphal hopes are (hypothetically) explored by Wistrand (1979) 200–2.
29. Halkin (1953), whose focus is the *supplicatio* rather than the triumph, is a partial exception; and, briefly, Itgenshorst (2005) 67–9.
30. E.g., Ogilvie (1965) 679; Versnel (1970) 172–3.
31. Phillips (1974) 267–8.
32. Suetonius (quoted in Isidore, *Orig.* 18, 2, 3) hedged his bets: the *tri*umph owes its name to the fact that it was awarded by *three* bodies—army, senate, and people.
33. E.g., Livy 2, 20, 13; 2, 31, 3.
34. Dionysius of Halicarnassus, *Ant.* 6, 30, 2–3.
35. Livy 3, 63, 5–11.
36. The "standard procedure" is summarized by, for example, Ehlers, *RE* 2. VIIA, 1, 497–9, Weinstock (1971) 60 and, at greater length, Auliard (2001) 133–67.
37. Dio Cassius 48, 4. Dio also, unusually in a republican context, refers to Pompey "accepting" (rather than asking for) his third triumph (37,

21, 1)—a sign maybe of Dio's imperial perspective. A little earlier Marius refused or postponed a triumph (Livy *Periochae* 68; Plutarch, *Mar.* 24, 1).

38. Bonnefond-Coudry (1989) 143–9 (location of debates); 269–74 (timing).

39. Halkin (1953) 80–3; 109–11; Combès (1966) 118–20 suggests the importance of such an acclamation in gaining a triumph, but the link is only rarely and tenuously suggested by ancient writers—by Cicero's loaded claim that a thanksgiving is regularly preceded by an acclamation (*Phil.* 14, 11) and by Zonaras, *Epitome* 7, 21, derived presumably from Dio.

40. Plautus, *Am.* 188–92 (with Christenson [2000] 174–6); see also 655–7 and *Pers.* 753–4. Plautine triumphal parodies: Fraenkel (1922) 234–40; Halkin (1948). The distinctive style (including series of ablative absolutes): Livy 10, 37, 8 (with Oakley [2005b] 375); 40, 52, 5–6; 41, 28, 8–9 (with Galli [1987–8]); *ILLRP* 122. Livy 38, 48, 15 claims to quote part of the official phraseology of the senatorial vote.

41. See, e.g., Livy 45, 35, 4: "The praetor, Quintus Cassius, was assigned the task of arranging with the tribunes that, following a resolution of the senate, they should propose a motion to the people that the generals should possess *imperium* on the day that they rode into the city in triumph" (167 BCE). It seems that the senate might also authorize additional honors to accompany a triumph: Dio Cassius 43, 14, 3.

42. Apart from Livy 45, 35, 4, the only direct evidence is a similar reference concerning Marcellus' ovation in 211 (Livy 26, 21, 5). The accounts of Pomptinus' triumph in 54 BCE (see esp. Cicero, *Q. fr.* 3, 4, 6) imply a potentially illegitimate vote of *imperium.*

43. This theory, in its essentials, goes back to Laqueur (1909). Recent refinements and restatements: Brennan (2000) 52–3; Linderski (1990) 44–6 (prompted by the question of why those who held the office of consular tribune did not, and so perhaps *could not,* triumph, despite having *imperium*). The basic controversy, *imperium* vs *auspicia,* is reviewed by Versnel (1970) 164–95; it is further and minutely dissected by Vervaet (2007) 41–85.

44. From the many accounts of petitioning a triumph, these are mentioned only by Livy 5, 28, 13 (an obvious anachronism), 45, 1, 6–7, and Cicero, *Pis.* 39. Pliny, *Nat.* 15, 133 refers to this as one of the uses of the laurel tree, but from what date and how regularly is unclear; Appian, *Mith.* 77 refers to it as "the custom" for victors. The idea (Livy 30, 43, 9) that the fetial priests carried their own sacred boughs *(verbenae)* with them might just provide a parallel for the general and his laurels.

45. In addition to the early triumphs imagined to have taken place against the will of the senate: Livy 7, 17, 9 (Caius Marcius Rutilus, 356); 10, 37, 6–12

(Lucius Postumius Megellus, 294), with Oakley (1997) 721. One way round this has been to claim that the senate acquired its triumphal authority only later (perhaps under Sulla): Ogilvie (1965) 513, following Mommsen (1887) 3, 1233–4.

46. Polybius 6, 15, 8 (though he appears to allow the possibility of proceeding without funds). Self-funding: Orosius, *Historia Contra Paganos* 5, 4, 7 (Appius Claudius, 143 BCE); also Livy 33, 23, 8 (Alban Mount, 197 BCE).

47. Cicero, *Cael.* 34; Valerius Maximus 5, 4, 6; Suetonius, *Tib.* 2, 4; Dio Cassius 22, fr. 74 (from a Byzantine excerption); Orosius, *Historia Contra Paganos* 5, 4, 7.

48. Brennan (1996) 319–20.

49. Develin (1978) 437–8.

50. Mommsen (1887) 1, 132; Versnel (1970) 191–3; Brennan (1996) 316. It is partly with these problems in mind that the key role in the triumph of *auspicia* (rather than *imperium*) has been stressed; though, so far as I can see, that only raises further slippery issues.

51. Versnel (1970) 384–8; J. S. Richardson (1975) 59–60.

52. The legal and constitutional notion of *imperium* (as well as of the supposed subdivisions, *imperium domi* and *imperium militiae*) has been the subject of innumerable learned but inconclusive discussions over the last two centuries at least (largely building on or refining the work of Mommsen). Useful introductions to the subject include: Drummond (1989) 188–9; J. S. Richardson (1991).

53. The one major exception is the debate on the triumph of Aemilius Paullus in 167 BCE, which is set by Livy in the popular assembly convened to extend his *imperium* (45, 35, 5–39, 20).

54. Livy 26, 21, 1–6.

55. Livy 31, 20.

56. Recent contributions to the traditional industry include: Petrucci (1996); Auliard (2001). Gruen (1990) 129–33 is a rare case of dissent, though may overstate the case.

57. Mommsen (1887) 1, 126–36; Laqueur (1909) (with n. 43, above).

58. J. S. Richardson (1975); and, with even greater emphasis on flexibility, Brennan (1996), with quotation, p. 317.

59. Changing requirements to bring home the army: J. S. Richardson (1975) 61. The Mommsen "rule" (that even magistrates whose victory occurred in the period directly after their year of office, when their *imperium* had been seamlessly prorogued, could not triumph): Mommsen (1887) 1, 128–9; Versnel (1970) 168–9.

60. Harris (1979) 255 argues for the "partial confidentiality" of senatorial debates—though how long that lasted, or how strictly it was enforced, is unclear.

61. Valerius Maximus 2, 8. *Ius triumphale* is Valerius' term.

62. Orosius, *Historia Contra Paganos* 5, 4, 7. For the "what-if?" style of legal conundrum, see the *Declamationes* of the Elder Seneca and Pseudo-Quintilian.

63. On Valerius' evidence the date would be 62 BCE, the date of Cato's tribunate. Lucius Marcius or Marius (the text is uncertain) is otherwise unknown—though he creeps into reference works on the basis of this passage.

64. Brennan (2000) 83–5 is the sharpest analysis of Valerius Maximus' account of the controversy. Vervaet (2007) 59–64 is a less skeptical discussion.

65. Harris (1979) 123. The classic case of a triumph awarded for the recovery of territory is Livy's account (5, 49, 7) of the triumph of Camillus in 390: "Having won his country back from the enemy, the dictator returned to Rome in triumph."

66. Modern writers have also disagreed over the ovation awarded to Marcellus, but for different reasons: J. S. Richardson (1975) 54–5 sees it as driven by narrowly political concerns, Develin (1978) 432 as a proper application of the rules. Different controversies surround Scipio's triumph: against Valerius Maximus and Livy (26, 21, 1–5), both Polybius (11, 33, 7) and Appian (*Hisp.* 38) claim that he celebrated a triumph.

67. The role of precedent (and innovation) in Livy: Chaplin (2000) 137–67.

68. Livy 28, 38, 4; 34, 10, 5.

69. Concern with the fair apportioning of triumphal glory: Livy 28, 9; 33, 22, 2.

70. Livy 31, 48–49, 3 (with Brennan [2000] 197–200 for a full discussion of the many factors that might have been at work here); 38, 44, 9–50, 3.

71. The need to assert authoritative command perhaps lies behind the list of terms used to refer to military leadership in several records of victory, and parodied by Plautus: in its fullest form (found only once, Livy 40, 52, 5), "under the command, the auspices, the authority and through the success of so-and-so" *(ductu, auspicio, imperio, felicitate)*. Predictably enough, this phrase and its variants (see, for example, Livy 41, 28, 8; *ILLRP* 122; Plautus, *Am.* 192, 196, 657) have been minutely scrutinized for what they might reveal about the precise legal or other qualifications for a triumph (Versnel [1970] 176–81; 356–71). But the point may be far less technical than that: by piling up different ways of expressing the general's responsi-

bility for his victory, it may serve rather to make that responsibility seem uncontestable.

72. Livy 40, 38. Despite Livy's claim of a triumphal innovation here, there are stories of earlier triumphs said to have involved no fighting (Dionysius of Halicarnassus, *Ant.* 8, 69, 1–2; Livy 37, 60, 5–6).

73. Livy 31, 48, 5; 49, 8–11.

74. Livy 33, 22, 9.

75. Livy 35, 8.

76. The same theme is reflected in Cato the Elder's speech, "On false battles," delivered against the triumphal claims of Quintus Minucius Thermus in 190; *ORF* Cato, fr. 58.

77. Greater strife: Livy 39, 5, 12. The prospect of a triumph: Livy 28, 38, 4. Nasica: Livy 36, 39, 8. "Desire for (true) glory": Sallust, *Cat.* 7, 3; Harris (1979) 17–32.

78. Attacks on those who had come to terms: Suetonius, *Jul.* 54, 1; Dio Cassius 36, 18, 1.

79. Livy 2, 47, 10–11. Among vain attempts to account for this: Auliard (2001) 140–1; and see below, p. 300–1.

80. Valerius Maximus 2, 8, 3.

81. *Pis.* 44; reminiscent of Caelius' quip (see above, n. 3).

82. Nisbet (1961) 172–80.

83. Cicero, *Pis.* 37–8; 54.

84. Cicero, *Pis.* 51–2 (Cicero's return); 53–64 (Piso's return). Piso's return as "anti-triumph": Itgenshorst (2005) 82–8.

85. Griffin (2001) is a careful analysis of the Epicurean elements in the speech, attempting to reveal both Piso's own philosophical position and the original audience's philosophical familiarity and understanding.

86. Cicero, *Pis.* 60. This section is so expertly parodic that it has been taken for Cicero's own philosophical critique of triumphal trinkets (Brilliant [1999] 225). The passage continues, dropping the parody, to make Piso "put his own case in the worst light" (Nisbet [1961] ad loc.).

87. Cicero, *Pis.* 56.

88. Cicero, *Pis.* 62, 58.

7. PLAYING GOD

1. Cafiero (1986) 38–9.

2. A particular puzzle is their relationship to eight similar reliefs, originally depicting Marcus, later incorporated into the Arch of Constantine. Dif-

ferent solutions: Ryberg (1967) 1–8, 84–9; Angelicoussis (1984); Cafiero (1986).

3. Schollmeyer (2001) 152–68. Examples include: Arch of Germanicus: Crawford *et al.* (1996) 1, no. 37, 18–21; Arch of Nero: F. S. Kleiner (1985) 78–9.

4. This is another of those *faux,* or nearly *faux,* Latin terms that litter modern writing in ancient history (*Romanitas, lararium* are others). So far as I have been able to discover, in surviving classical Latin it is used twice by Apuleius (*Apol.* 17 of Manius Curius; *Mun.* 37 of Jupiter), once by Minucius Felix (*Octavius* 37 of a Christian). From the late third century CE it is commonly found in inscriptions among the titles of emperors (*triumphator perpetuus/aeternus/semper*—that is "perpetual triumphator"): e.g., *CIL* VI 1141, 1144, 1178; *CIL* VIII, 7011 (= *ILS* 698, 700, 5592, 715). From the fourth century, it is found similarly in coin legends: e.g., *RIC* VIII, 410, Constantius II and Constans (*triumfator gentium barbarum*—that is, "triumphator over barbarian tribes"); *RIC* X, 325–6, Honorius *(triumfator gent[ium] barb[arum]).*

5. Suggestions include the arch spanning the road up the Capitoline hill with the nearby Temple of Jupiter Tonans (the Thunderer) or alternatively Jupiter Custos (the Protector); the Arch of Augustus in the Forum, with the nextdoor Temple of Divus Julius; the Porta Triumphalis with its supposed neighbor Fortune the Home-Bringer; the Temple of Bellona. General review: Ryberg (1967) 19–20; Cafiero (1986) 39. Arch of Augustus: M. R. Alföldi (1999) 93.

6. Diodorus Siculus 31, 8, 10 (from the excerption of George Syncellus); Plutarch, *Marc.* 22, 2; Appian, *Pun.* 66. Musicians at various Roman ceremonies, including the triumph: Fless (1995) 79–86.

7. The relief: Fless (1995) pl. 10. 2. It is dated, stylistically, to the mid-first century BCE. Musicians also appear in a relief now in Spain, which almost certainly depicts the procession of Augustus' triumph of 29 BCE (Trunk [2002] 250–4; pl. 68, 71a; *ThesCRA* I, 48, no. 75) and the manuscript copy of a lost processional relief (Pfanner [1980] 331).

8. Zonaras, *Epitome* 7, 21. Roman and Italic chariots of various types: Emiliozzi (1997).

9. Suetonius, *Nero* 25, 1; Dio Cassius 63, 20, 3 (from a Byzantine abridgment). J. F. Miller (2000) 417–9. A different version is offered by the biographer of the late third-century emperor Aurelian (SHA, *Aurelian* 33, 2): that in his triumph Aurelian used a chariot captured from the king of the Goths.

10. Ginzrot (1817) 2, 41.

11. Suetonius, *Vesp.* 12. Similar problems: SHA, *Severus* 16, 6.

12. Appian, *Mith.* 117; Diodorus Siculus, 31, 8, 12 (from the excerption of George Syncellus); Livy 10, 7, 10. Among the host of other references to gold, gilded, or ivory chariots: Horace, *Epod.* 9, 21–2; Florus, *Epit.* 1, 1 (1, 5, 6); Tibullus 1, 7, 8; Ovid, *Tr.* 4, 2, 63.

13. Propertius 4, 11, 11–2. See also Cicero, *Fam.* 15, 6, 1; Florus, *Epit.* 2, 13 (4, 2, 89); Pliny, *Nat.* 5, 36.

14. Valerius Maximus 1, 1, 10.

15. Ryberg (1967) 17–8; Chilosi and Martellotti (1986) 48.

16. Germanicus: Tacitus, *Ann.* 2, 41. Scipio: Appian, *Pun.* 66. Aemilius Paullus: Livy 45, 40, 7–8. Flory (1998) doubts that girls were part of the triumph until the imperial period, and (not implausibly) considers that Appian and Dio (Zonaras, *Epitome* 7, 21) are retrojecting imperial practice into the Republic.

17. Briefly reported by Murray (2004) 9.

18. Suetonius, *Tib.* 6, 4.

19. E.g., Gnecchi (1912) pl. 60, 7; *RIC* III, Marcus Aurelius, no. 1183.

20. Boscoreale: Kuttner (1995) 145.

21. Livy 10, 7, 10.

22. Frazer (1911) 174–8.

23. Religious representation: Scheid (1986). Other advocates of the general's divine status include: Wissowa (1912) 126–8; Strong (1915) 64–5; with further references in Versnel (1970) 62.

24. Seminal critics include: Reid (1916); Warde Fowler (1916) (from whom the challenge, p. 157); Deubner (1934); most recently Rüpke (2006) 254–9. Full review of the debate: Versnel (1970) 56–84; (2006), specifically in response to Rüpke. Dionysius of Halicarnassus, *Ant.* 3, 61–2; with 4, 74, 1 and similarly Florus, *Epit.* 1, 1 (1, 5, 6).

25. Versnel (1970) 84–93; Bonfante Warren (1970a).

26. Ovid, *Ars.* 1, 214; *Tr.* 4, 2, 48; Livy 45, 39, 2; 45, 40, 6; Silius Italicus 17, 645.

27. Livy, *Periochae* 67; Plutarch, *Mar.* 12, 5. Variants include *cultus triumphantium* (Velleius Paterculus 2, 40, 4); *habitus triumphalis* (Pliny, *Nat.* 34, 33).

28. I am not including here images of late antique consuls dressed in costume which may mirror triumphal costume; below, pp. 277–9.

29. The repertoire is fully rehearsed by Ehlers, *RE* 2. VIIA, 1, 504–8, with references. As usual the evidence is more fragile than the reconstruction

tends to imply: the amulet is, for example, referred to once by Macrobius (1, 6, 9), the iron ring by Pliny only (*Nat.* 33, 11–2). The sanest modern account, though not quite skeptical enough for my taste: Oakley (2005b) 100–4.

30. Ehlers, *RE* 2. VIIA, 1, 505–6; Versnel (1970) 74–7.

31. Festus, p. 228L; Martial 7, 2, 8; Apuleius, *Apol.* 22. Less precise: Oakley (2005b) 101 (of course, we have no idea how precise the terminology was in, say, the third century BCE).

32. Festus, p. 228L.

33. Livy 10, 7, 10; see also Juvenal 10, 38 (the praetor leading the games in the "tunic of Jupiter"), a passage quoted by Servius (*Ecl.* 10, 27) who refers to triumphing generals having "all the insignia of Jupiter"; in the dream of Augustus' father (Suetonius, *Aug.* 94, 6), his son holds the "thunderbolt, scepter, and attributes of Jupiter" (the closest we come to answering Warde Fowler's challenge, n. 24).

34. Tertullian, *De Corona* 13, 1, with Versnel (1970) 73–4; (2006) 302–3. By contrast, Andreas Alföldi, among others, seems to have envisaged a costume store-cum-dressing-up box in the Capitoline temple (A. Alföldi [1935] 28).

35. There is very little evidence for the appearance of the cult statue; but it would be surprising if (at least those versions installed after 83 BCE) were only life-size (Martin [1987] 131–44).

36. Triumphal impersonations at funerals: Polybius 6, 53, 7; Pompey's pyre: Lucan 9, 175–9. None of this is easily compatible with a puzzling passage in the late imperial life of Gordian I (SHA, *Gordians* 4, 4): "He was the first private citizen among the Romans to possess his own *tunica palmata* and *toga picta,* for previously even emperors had taken them from the Capitol or from the palace." It is possible that the author has the ceremonial/inaugural dress of the imperial consuls in mind.

37. As a technical term, Versnel (1970) 58 (and *passim*); (2006) 295–6, 301 (and *passim*); Bonfante Warren (1970a) 59 ("the Romans often refer to the *insignia* of the triumphator as the 'ornatus' of Jupiter Optimus Maximus").

38. Pliny, *Nat.* 33, 111–2 (the full quotation is rarely given by modern theorists; in particular, Pliny's expression of bafflement is almost never included); see also 35, 157 where he explains the coloring of the original statue of Jupiter as necessary because it was made of terracotta. Later writers: Servius (auct.), *Ecl.* 6, 22; Isidore, *Orig.* 18, 2, 6; Tzetzes, *Epistulae* 97.

39. Statue of Jupiter: Versnel (1970) 78–84, with discussion of other theories.

The most extreme argument for the equivalence of the general with commemorative statuary more widely is Rüpke (2006), countered by Versnel (2006) esp. 304–8. Scheid (1986) esp. 221–4 offers a more subtle version.

40. Quotation: Wagenvoort (1947) 167. Austronesian idea of *mana* as a useful term in the analysis Roman religion (and as an equivalent of the Latin word *numen*): H. J. Rose (1948) 12–49; Wagenvoort (1947) 5–11; with the devastating critique of Dumézil (1970) 18–31.

41. Martin (1987) 131–44.

42. The difficulties of identifying a clear Etruscan prehistory for the triumph is discussed below, pp. 306–12.

43. Beard, North, and Price (1998) 1, 84–7; 140–9; 2, 216–28. Deification as a problematic Roman category: Beard and Henderson (1998).

44. Note, however, that the especially splendid head of the outermost horse is restoration of the late sixteenth century (La Rocca [1986] col. pl. 3).

45. SHA, *Aurelian* 33, 3.

46. Dio Cassius 43, 14, 3.

47. Camillus: Livy 5, 23, 5–6; Plutarch, *Cam.* 7, 1; see also Dio Cassius 52, 13, 3 and Diodorus Siculus, 14, 117, 6 (with a variant tradition that Camillus did not triumph at all). Full discussion of Caesar, Camillus, and the divine associations of white horses: Weinstock (1971) 68–75, which is part of a sustained argument for Caesar's personal ambition to become a god during his lifetime. Different emphasis, critiques, and further references: Versnel (1970) 67–8; North (1975) 173.

48. Quotation: Weinstock (1971) 68. Any such argument relies on the convenient assumption that no writer bothered to mention the usual, but only drew attention to the exceptions.

49. Propertius 4, 1, 32; Ovid, *Fast.* 6, 723–4; Tibullus 1, 7, 7–8 (translating *nitidis,* though the variant reading *niveis* would make them more securely white); Pliny, *Pan.* 22, 1. Servius, *Aen.* 4, 543 asserts the general rule that "the triumphing general uses four white horses."

50. Suetonius, *Aug.* 94, 6; though four horses are the usual number, several visual representations multiply the animals, as here (e.g. *RIC* II, Trajan, no. 255; IV Septimius Severus, no. 259); see also SHA, *Gordians* 27, 9.

51. Whether elephants were more a feature of triumphal imagination than triumphal reality is a moot point. But various later emperors are (reliably or not) said to have succeeded where Pompey failed: SHA, *Gordians* 27, 9; *Severus Alexander* 57, 4 (an empty chariot); cf Lactantius *De Mortibus Persecutorum* 16, 6.

52. Arch of Titus: Cassiodorus, *Variae* 10, 30, 1; Pfanner (1983) 3, 99; *LTUR*

s.v. Arcus Titii (Via Sacra). Domitian: Martial 8, 65; above pp. 98–9. Augustus: De Maria (1988) 269; pl. 43.4; *BMCRE* I, Augustus, no. 432 (= Fig. 18); Rich (1998) 119, suggesting that the triumph voted to Augustus in 19 BCE, but not celebrated, included the use of elephants.

53. Above, p. 17.

54. Pfanner (1983) 76–9; Beard and Henderson (1998) 209–10.

55. See, for example, Figs. 23, 26, and 30. It is hard to determine exactly the status of these men, but a case has been made for identifying some as equestrian officials (Gabelmann [1981]).

56. "The whole senate": Valerius Maximus 7, 5, 4. Magistrates: Dio Cassius 51, 21, 9. Messalina: Suetonius, *Cl.* 17, 3; Flory (1998) 492–3. Carpentum: Boyce (1935–6) 5–7. Julia Domna represented in a triumphal context (on the arch at Lepcis Magna): Strocka (1972) 154–7; Kampen (1991) 233–5. Other visual images, "accurately" or not, including women in the general's group: Crawford *et al.* (1996) 1, no. 37, 19–21; Furtwängler (1900) 1, tab. 66 (a cameo, possibly a modern fake).

57. Plutarch, *Flam.* 13, 3–6; Livy 34, 52, 12 (they had been sold into slavery after capture by Hannibal); two other such occasions are noted, both (suspiciously?) within a decade (201: Livy 30, 45, 5; Valerius Maximus 5, 2, 5. 197: Livy 33, 23, 6).

58. Suetonius, *Jul.* 78, 2. Ancient scholars puzzled too. Aulus Gellius (5, 6, 27) quotes the (unlikely) view of Masurius Sabinus, who had probably never witnessed an ovation, that in an ovation the general was followed by the whole senate, not by his soldiers as at a triumph.

59. Dio Cassius 43, 19, 2–4; above, p. 136–7.

60. Dio Cassius 51, 21, 9. Quotation: Reinhold (1988) 158.

61. Livy 28, 9, 11–16; Valerius Maximus 4, 1, 9.

62. Valerius Maximus 3, 2, 24; Pliny, *Nat.* 7, 101–3.

63. Livy 45, 38, 12–14. A fragment of what appears to be a representation of triumphal soldiers: De Maria (1988) 280–2, pl. 61–2 (from Claudius' Arch in Rome for his British victory).

64. Appian, *BC* 2, 93.

65. 201–167 BCE: Brunt (1971) 394. First century BCE: Brunt (1962) 77–9; *ESAR* I, 323–5.

66. Livy 37, 59, 6, for example, arouses suspicion (a donative is recorded, but at a triumph at which no troops were present; Briscoe [1981] 394). Emendations: Livy 33, 37, 11; 34, 46, 3; the ratio of 1:2:3 is attested on numerous occasions, but this is no reason to distrust or emend away variants.

67. Not always: Livy (45, 38, 14) represents Aemilius Paullus' troops as hanging around the city before the triumph (albeit in special circumstances).

68. Livy 45, 35, 5–39, 20; Plutarch, *Aem.* 30–32. At a reported 100 denarii for each of the common soldiers, the donative offered was larger than any recorded before—but then the spoils were unprecedentedly lavish too.

69. Livy 45, 40, 4; Plutarch, *Aem.* 34, 4; Plutarch, *Marc.* 8, 2.

70. Soldiers' chant: Livy 45, 38, 12; Tibullus 2, 5, 118. Derivation: Varro, *LL* 6, 68. Obscure hymn (of the Arval Brethren): Scheid (1990) 616–23; 644–6; (1998) no. 100a.

71. Latest linguist: Biville (1990) 220–1. Other theories: Bonfante Warren (1970b) 112; Versnel (1970) 38–55; (2006) 309–13 ("there is only one way in which Latin *triumpe* can have been derived from Greek *thriambe,* and that is via the Etruscan language," p. 309).

72. Livy 45, 38, 12.

73. A male head, with the legend "TRIUMPUS" on a silver denarius issued around the time of Julius Caesar's triumph in 46 BCE (*RRC* no. 472.2) has been taken to be the personification of the triumph; though there is no further evidence for or against such an identification.

74. Servius (auct.), *Ecl.* 8, 12; Isidore, *Orig.* 17, 7, 2.

75. Pliny, *Nat.* 15, 133–5; Festus (Paulus) p. 104L (the assumption has been that this "information" goes back to the Augustan scholar Verrius Flaccus); Pliny later (15, 138) does himself refer, in general, to the use of the plant in "purifications." The triumph as a rite of purification: (for example) Warde Fowler (1911) 33, Lemosse (1972) 448. The passage through the *porta triumphalis* as purificatory: Warde Fowler (1920) 70–5.

76. Myths of Delphi, in particular stories of the purification of Orestes and of the god Apollo himself (Pausanias 2, 31, 8; Aelian, *VH* 3, 1) may have been influential on them too. Reid (1912) 45–7 is refreshingly skeptical about the original purificatory significance of the triumph ("mere guesswork").

77. Above, pp. 50–1. The connection between the triumph and the myth of Apollo and Daphne: Barkan (1986) 225–6.

78. See, e.g., Livy 4, 20, 2; 53, 11; 5, 49, 7 etc. The potentially dangerous popular politics implied by the term *inconditus:* O'Neill (2003a) 6 with (2003b) 157–62.

79. Suetonius, *Jul.* 51.

80. Suetonius, *Jul.* 49, 4.

81. Dio Cassius 43, 20.

82. Livy 28, 9, 18.

83. Livy 10, 30, 9. Decius Mus senior, when a tribune, was similarly marked out in a triumph (7, 38, 3). He later also sacrificed himself for Roman victory (8, 9) and Livy stresses that in 295 the songs concern-

ing the son evoked the father's memory as well. The tradition of self-sacrifice *(devotio),* which suspiciously clusters in this particular family: Beard, North, and Price (1998) 2, 157–8. Other instances of the songs, in different ways, "re-hierarchizing" the ceremony: Livy 4, 20, 2; 53, 11–3.

84. Versnel (1970) 70; Richlin (1983) 10, 94; O'Neill (2003a) 3–4.

85. Plutarch, *Aem.* 34, 7; *Marc.* 8, 2; Dionysius of Halicarnassus, *Ant.* 2, 34, 2; Livy 4, 53, 11–2.

86. I am closer here to the other view expressed in O'Neill (2003a) 4, namely that the songs had a sociological function. They contributed, he argues, to the reincorporation of the glorious general "whose outstanding fortune threatened to place him above his peers in the senatorial aristocracy" (drawing on Kurke [1991], who discusses the function of Pindaric Odes in the reintegration of the victor into the life of the city). Rüpke (2006) 268 sees a satiric "rite of reversal" in the soldiers' mockery (including their shouts of *triumpe*) and points in a similar direction.

87. Caesar: Dio Cassius 43, 21, 2. Claudius: Dio Cassius 60, 23, 1. The sacrifice is mentioned only by Josephus (*BJ* 7, 155).

88. Triumphal dedication: Ovid *Tr.* 4, 2 56 and *Pont.* 2, 1, 67. Dedication of laurel could also take place outside a triumph proper: Suetonius, *Nero* 13, 2; *Dom.* 6, 1; Pliny, *Pan* 8, 2–3; Dio Cassius 55, 5, 1.

89. The connection with the Temple of Jupiter is reviewed, skeptically, in *CIL* I. 1, 78 (2nd ed.).

90. This is implied by Plutarch's description of Aemilius Paullus' triumph: *Aem.* 32–4.

91. Valerius Maximus 4, 1, 6 (though Livy 38, 56, 12–3 claims that Scipio refused the statue); Sehlmeyer (1999) 112–31; 134–41. Such connections between general and commemoration do not entail adopting the radical position of Rüpke (2006), of the ritual links between the ceremony as a whole and commemorative statuary.

92. *CIL* XIV, 3606 and 3607 = *ILS* 921 and 964.

93. E.g. Livy 35, 10, 5–9; Cicero, *Mur.* 15.

94. Harris (1979) 32; though Rosenstein (1990), esp. 9–53, stresses how military defeat appears not decisively to blight a man's further political career. There are not enough surviving examples to draw any meaningful conclusions from a comparison of the careers of those victors who celebrated a triumph and those who did not.

95. Florus, *Epit.* 1, 34 (2, 18, 17).

96. Camillus: Livy 5, 23, 5; Plutarch, *Cam.* 7, 1–2. Scipio: Livy 38, 52–3, with Astin (1989) 179–80.

97. Plautus, *Am.* 186–261; above pp. 201–2.
98. Janne (1933); Hermann (1948); Galinsky (1966); P. Harvey (1981); O'Neill (2003a) 16–21.
99. Dupont (1976); O'Neill (2003a) 7–16.
100. Beard (2003a) 39–43.

8. THE BOUNDARIES OF THE RITUAL

1. Dio Cassius 67, 9.
2. "Autocratic sadism": Murison (1999) 239–42. Elegant wit or philosophical fantasy: Waters (1964) 75–6; Dunbabin (1986) 193–5.
3. Either two separate triumphs or a single, joint celebration: Griffin (2000) 63.
4. Plautus, *Bac.* 1072–4 (the "triumph" and "soldiers" in question are part of an elaborate comic metaphor).
5. Dionysius of Halicarnassus, *Ant.* 2, 34, 2; 5, 17, 1–2; Livy 3, 29, 4–5.
6. Lavish celebration: Dio Cassius 43, 42, 1; Suetonius, *Jul.* 38, 2 (though it is not certain that these "dinners" *[prandia]* are closely connected with his triumphs). *Triclinia:* Plutarch, *Caes.* 55, 2. Wine: Pliny, *Nat.* 14, 97. Lampreys: Pliny, *Nat.* 9, 171.
7. "Greatest occasions": Purcell (1994) 685. "Capstone": D'Arms (1998) 35 (the capstone of major public holidays and funerals too, he claims).
8. Polybius 30, 14 (from a Byzantine excerption); Livy 45, 32, 11; Purcell (1994) 686.
9. Athenaeus, *Deipnosophistae* 5, 221f; 4, 153c, with Kidd (1988) 282–3 (a passage which could refer to elite dining only).
10. Varro, *RR* 3, 2, 16; 3, 5, 8.
11. Plutarch, *Luc.* 37, 4. The claims that Sulla and Crassus also held mass triumphal banquets depend on interpreting the feasts they offered on dedicating a tenth of their property to the god Hercules (Plutarch, *Mor.* 267E–F (= *Quaestiones Romanae* 18) as simultaneously triumphal celebrations (Plutarch, *Sull.* 35, 1; *Crass.* 12, 2).
12. Tiberius: Dio Cassius 55, 2, 4. Vespasian and Titus: Josephus, *BJ* 7, 156. Domitian: above, n. 1.
13. Livy 39, 46, 2–3.
14. There is a clash here, I suspect, between an ideal of the commensality of the whole people (as fantasized by Martial of a later victory celebration of Domitian: "the knights, and the people, and the senators all eat with you," 8, 49, 7) and the political reality of hierarchy and separation. Hand-

outs for the people (versus feasting for the elite) feature on other occasions in the Empire (e.g., Suetonius, *Cal.* 17, 2).

15. Appian, *Pun.* 66; Dionysius of Halicarnassus, *Ant.* 5, 17, 2; Dio Cassius 55, 8, 2 (a ladies' occasion was hosted by Livia elsewhere).

16. Livy 45, 39, 13.

17. Valerius Maximus 2, 8, 6 (quoted); Plutarch, *Mor.* 283A (= *Quaestiones Romanae* 80).

18. Scheid (1988).

19. *Ludi triumphales:* Stern (1953) 82; McCormick (1986) 37–9. Modern writers (e.g. Klar [2006]) are too eager to use the adjective "triumphal" for any celebration connected with military victory. The closest suggestion of earlier "triumphal" games are the "victory games" of L. Anicius in 167 (Polybius 30, 22 quoted by Athenaeus, *Deipnosophistae* 14, 615a–e)—as the Greek word "epinikioi" could also, but need not, refer to a "triumphal" celebration. Tacitus, *Ann.* 14, 21 implies a connection between triumph and drama, but does not clearly state that the actors performed at Mummius' triumph.

20. Dio Cassius 43, 23, 4.

21. Gruen (1990) 93–4; Flower (1995) esp. 181–3; Klar (2006) 168–70.

22. Flower (1995) 184–6. Triumph: Livy 39, 5, 13–7. Games: Livy 39, 5, 7–10; 22, 1–2. Temple: *LTUR* s.v. Hercules Musarum, aedes.

23. Horace, *Ep.* 2, 1, 187–93. Spoils: Brink (1982) 431–2. Chariots: above, pp. 53, 125.

24. Pliny, *Nat.* 15, 125; though, of course, part of the point of emphasizing this as an "exception" is to preserve the general rule that myrtle was worn at ovations.

25. Aemilius Paullus: Plutarch, *Aem.* 30, 1–3. Flamininus: Livy 34, 52, 2 *(prope triumphantes).* Junior officer, Decius Mus: Livy 7, 36, 8 (with Oakley [1998] 349, who points to further triumphal terminology in Livy's description). See also Cicero, *Ver.* 2. 5, 66; *Phil.* 14, 12–3 (with Sumi [2005] 174–7); Suetonius, *Nero* 2, 1; *Vit.* 10, 2.

26. Josephus, *BJ* 7, 96; 147; Ando (2000) 256–7.

27. Caesar's hybrid (which seems to have been in some way connected with the ceremony of the *feriae latinae,* held at the Alban Mount): Dio Cassius 44, 4, 3. Octavian and Antony: Dio Cassius 48, 31, 3. Sumi (2005) 196 stresses the use of the ovation rather than the "full triumph" in framing these political or dynastic celebrations unrelated to military victory in the strict sense of the word.

28. Dio Cassius 49, 40, 3–4; Plutarch, *Ant.* 50, 4; Velleius Paterculus 2, 82, 3–4; Strabo 11, 14, 15.

29. Suetonius, *Nero* 25, 1–2; Dio Cassius 63, 20.
30. Syme (1939) 270 ("hostile propaganda has so far magnified and distorted these celebrations that accuracy of fact and detail cannot be recovered"); Huzar (1978) 182–3; Pelling (1988) 241, Woodman (1983) 213–5. It is not, however, absolutely clear that Velleius' Dionysiac procession is to be equated with the "triumphal" ceremony.
31. Dio Cassius 63, 8, 3.
32. Answer: Griffin (1984) 230–1. Insult: Edwards (1994) 90.
33. Merging: Bradley (1978) 148–9, with Vitruvius 9, *praef.* 1 (Gagé [1955] 660–2 sees it as a parody of both ceremonies). Theater: Champlin (2003b) 233–4. Nonmilitary achievement: Morford (1985) 2026.
34. J. F. Miller (2000).
35. Tacitus, *Ann.* 3, 47.
36. Dio Cassius 60, 8, 6 (though Pliny *Nat.* 5, 11 has a different story: that these campaigns in Mauretania were a *bona fide* Claudian war).
37. Caligula: Suetonius, *Cal.* 19; Dio Cassius 59, 17. Nero: Tacitus, *Ann.* 14, 13, 2–3; Champlin (2003b) 219–21.
38. Tacitus, *Ann.* 15, 1–18, 24–31; Dio Cassius 62, 19–23; Griffin (1984) 226–7.
39. Tacitus, *Ann.* 15, 29, 7 *(ostentui gentibus);* Dio Cassius 63, 1, 2.
40. Suetonius, *Nero* 13; Dio Cassius 63, 6, 1–2. Champlin (2003b) 221–9.
41. Pliny, *Nat.* 30, 16; Dio Cassius 62, 23, 4. Griffin (1984) 232–3: "Nero does not appear to have held a triumph, though he dressed up in triumphal garb"—*contra* Champlin (2003b) 329, n. 23.
42. The implication of Dio Cassius 48, 16, 1; though it is uncertain from what date. *Contra* Weinstock (1971) 107–8, I see no reason to suppose (on the basis of Polybius 6, 39, 9) that men who had triumphed would have been entitled to wear their laurel wreaths at the games.
43. Aemilius Paullus: *De Viris Illustribus* 56, 5. Pompey: Velleius Paterculus 2, 40, 4; Dio Cassius 37, 21, 4. Marius: Plutarch, *Mar.* 12, 5. Metellus Pius: Valerius Maximus 9, 1, 5; Plutarch, *Sert.* 22, 2; Sallust, *Hist.* 2, 59. I am not convinced by Sumi (2005) 37 that Cato the Younger was granted a similar honor.
44. Only the clipped account of Aemilius Paullus' honor implies no unfavorable moral judgment.
45. Polybius 6, 53, 7.
46. E.g., Rawson (1975a) 155: "the gift of the trappings of a triumphator to foreign kings."
47. Massinissa, 203: Livy 30, 15, 11–2 (also 31, 11, 11–2, under 200 BCE); Appian, *Pun.* 32 (though listing a different set of gifts). Honors to Syphax and others, 210 BCE (with nothing specifically triumphal, though

Deubner (1934) 318 would see purple tunic and toga here as a reflection of early triumphal dress): Livy 27, 4, 8–10. Honors to Eumenes, 172, and Ariarathes, 160 (curule chair and scepter; the scepter may, or may not, specifically evoke the triumph): Livy 42, 14, 10; Polybius 32, 1, 3. Mythical regal examples: Dionysius of Halicarnassus, *Ant.* 3, 61; 5, 35, 1. Other gifts of chairs or thrones: Weinstock (1957) 148. Despite a tendency to treat it as a similar example, Caesar, *Gal.* 1, 43 (gifts to Ariovistus) does not specify what the gifts were.

48. Tacitus, *Ann.* 4, 26 (Dolabella is also contrasted earlier, 4, 23 with those generals who left the enemy alone once they had done enough to earn triumphal *insignia*); Martin and Woodman (1989) 155–60.

49. Maxfield (1981) 105.

50. Whether the Augustan triumphal ornaments could have influenced Livy's account depends on the (disputed) date of their first award, which could have been before or after the composition of this section of Livy's *History.* Suetonius, *Tib.* 9, 2 states that the first award went to Tiberius, but whether that was in 12 BCE (Dio Cassius 54, 31, 4) or earlier is uncertain; see Taylor (1936) 168–70.

51. Statue: Dio Cassius 55, 10, 3. Dress: Suetonius *Cl.* 17, 3, with discussion above, p. 70.

52. Dio Cassius 43, 44, 2; Suetonius, *Jul.* 76, 1 both claim that this title went back to Caesar. Modern scholarship (critically reviewed by Weinstock [1971] 106–11) has suspected a retrojection from an Augustan innovation—which was fully established practice by the end of the Julio-Claudian dynasty.

53. A. Alföldi (1935) 25–43.

54. Dio Cassius 43, 43, 1; 44, 4, 2; Appian, *BC* 2, 106.

55. Dio Cassius 48, 16, 1; 49, 15, 1; 51, 20, 2; 53, 26, 5. Date of Tiberius' triumph: Dio Cassius 55, 8, 1–2. Augustus' absence on Jan. 1, 7 BCE: Halfmann (1986) 159.

56. Royal costume: Dio Cassius 44, 6, 1. Confusion: Mommsen (1887) 1, 416. Two separate decrees: Weinstock (1971) 271.

57. Plutarch, *Ant.* 12, 1; Dio Cassius 44, 11, 2.

58. Weinstock (1971) 270–5. Quotation: Pelling (1988) 145.

59. Suetonius, *Cal.* 52; Dio Cassius 59, 26, 10.

60. Dio Cassius 67, 4, 3; 60, 6, 9.

61. Claudian: *Panegyricus de IV Consulatu Honorii* esp. 1–17, 565–656; *De VI Consulatu Honorii* esp. 560–602, with MacCormack (1981) 52–4; Dewar (1996) 370–97. Corippus: *In Laudem Justini Minoris* 4, with Cameron

(1976) 194–211. Discussions of the *processus,* with further references: Jullian (1883); Meslin (1970) 55–9.

62. Cameron (1976) 12.

63. Corippus, *In Laudem Justini Minoris.* 4, 80, 227, 101. Claudian too presents a triumphal image: *Panegyricus de IV Consulatu Honorii* 14; *De VI Consulatu Honorii.* 579–80; and through analogy with triumphal Bacchus (below, pp. 315–8). Triumphal/consular toga: Delbrueck (1929) esp. 65–6; Stern (1953) 152–68 (though exactly how close any of these version are to the strictly triumphal *toga picta* is unclear).

64. Other poems of Claudian celebrate the inauguration of consuls other than the ruling emperor (e.g. *De Consulatu Stilichonis* 2, 356–69) and these are less emphatically triumphal. However, Stern (1953) 152–68 suggests an increasing divergence between the dress of emperor-consuls and others—the latter remaining more strictly "triumphal."

65. Ovid, *Pont.* 4, 4, 27–42; 9, 1–56. Livy 21, 63, 8 may perhaps have a republican version of such a ceremony in mind. The scanty other evidence for consular inauguration is assembled by Mommsen (1887) 1, 615–7.

66. Martial 10, 10, 1.

67. Documentary depiction: D. E. E. Kleiner (1983) 81–90. Metaphor/literalization: Schäfer (1989) 380–1; Smith (1998) 71 (though exactly what Smith means by "a metaphorical consular *pompa*[?]" [sic] is not clear). Stern (1953) 158–63 argues strongly that the ceremonial of consular inauguration did not involve a chariot, and would see in this a representation of the procession at the consular games. Others, including Schäfer, are warm to this possibility, even though consular games were not at this date a regular obligation of the office and despite the clear reference to the Arch of Titus.

68. Cameron (1976) 196, 201, 202.

69. Marius: Sallust, *Jug.* 114, 3; Velleius Paterculus 2, 12, 1; Plutarch, *Mar.* 12, 2; Dio Cassius 48, 4, 5. Pompey: Velleius Paterculus 2, 30, 2. Lepidus: Degrassi, *Inscr. It.* XIII. 1, 567; Antonius: Dio Cassius 48, 4, 3–6; Censorinus: Degrassi, *Inscr. Ital.* XIII. 1, 568; Maximus: Degrassi, *Inscr. Ital.* XIII. 1, 567, in October roughly at the beginning of his "three-month consulship" (Suetonius, *Jul.* 80, 3). Lucius Munatius Plancus also triumphed in 43 just a few days before his consulship (Degrassi, *Inscr. It.* XIII. 1, 567). Sumi (2005) 248 and Hölscher (1967) 85 see some of the importance of the connection; Mommsen (1887) 1, 127 n. 1 predictably tries to link it to the *imperium* of the general/consul.

70. Juvenal 10, 36–46.

71. It is often taken for granted that Juvenal is referring to the *Ludi Apollinares* (e.g. Versnel [1970] 130); but other games were conducted by a praetor (Dio Cassius 54, 2, 3). Unconvincingly, "consul" has been taken as an interpolation (Courtney [1980] 458) or a desperate attempt to avoid too much alliteration with the letter "p" (Ferguson [1979] 258).

72. Versnel (2006) 294 sums up trenchantly: "The idea that the *pompa circensis* and the triumph belong in some way together is one of the universals in the discussion of the triumph."

73. Mommsen (1859), quotation p. 81. He also pointed to the fact that Livy claims that the "*ludi Romani* alternatively called *magni*" (Livy 1, 35, 9) were founded to celebrate a military victory and that the starting point of the *pompa circensis* was the same as the endpoint of the triumphal procession, namely, the Temple of Jupiter Optimus Maximus. Modern accounts: Künzl (1988) 105; *New Pauly* VII s.v. Ludi Romani.

74. Versnel (1970) 103–15 (critique of Mommsen); 255–303 (alternative version). Versnel's stress on the primitive New Year festival allows him economically to incorporate the *processus consularis* on January 1 as a simultaneously new and old aspect of triumphal style celebration (pp. 302–3).

75. One literary account: Dionysius of Halicarnassus, *Ant.* 7, 72, 1–13. Conflicting views: Piganiol (1923) 15–31 (general reliability of Dionysius), 84–91 (plebeian agricultural origin); Thuillier (1975) esp. 577–81 (inadvertent reliability of Dionysius); Bernstein (1998) 254–68 (Greek character of Dionysius' account, in the context of a largely skeptical discussion overall).

76. Livy 1, 35, 9 (on the foundation of the games under King Tarquin): "sollemnes deinde annui mansere ludi Romani magnique varie appellati." With no comma, it means "From then on the solemn games, known alternatively as the *ludi Romani* or *magni,* were celebrated annually." With a comma after *solemnes,* it would mean "the games known alternatively as the *ludi Romani* or *magni* became a solemn ritual, and later they became annual." Only the second is compatible with Mommsen's theory.

77. Juvenal 11, 194–5 (note the pun on *praetor* and *praeda*).

78. Tacitus, *Ann.* 1, 15; Dio Cassius 56, 46, 5. Other evidence commonly cited does not bear the weight that has been laid on it. Livy 5, 41, 2 need not mean that the "stately robes" were the *same* for those triumphing and those conducting the games (nor, *contra* Versnel [1970] 130, does he refer to "triumphal *ornatus*"). Dionysius of Halicarnassus, *Ant.* 6, 95, 4 does not say "that the *aediles plebis* during the games wore triumphal garb" (Versnel [1970] 130); he says that they were honored with a purple robe

and "various insignia which the kings had had" (which could refer to different types of ceremonial dress). Martial 8, 33, 1 refers only to a leaf from a praetor's *corona,* with the implication that it is gold; any allusion to games must be understood from that alone. Pliny, *Nat.* 34, 20 refers only to praetors riding around the Circus in a chariot, not to triumphal attire. Mayor (1881) 76–7 is a particularly splendid *farrago* of inaccuracy on this subject.

79. Drawings: *Codex Coburgensis* fol. 75, 3; *Codex Pighianus* fol. 99 v. 100r; *Codex Vat. lat.* 3439 (Ursinianus) fol. 58a v. 58b r. Engraving: Dupérac in O. Panvinio, *De Ludis Circensibus* (Padua, 1642) 7 (original engraving 1566). Discussion: Rodenwaldt (1940) 24–5 (Figs. 10 and 11); Wrede (1981) 111–2; Ronke (1987) 219–20, 236–7, 716.

80. General discussions: Stern (1953) 158–63; Ronke (1987) 221–55; *ThesCRA* I, 46–50. These include some brave but ultimately unconvincing attempts to distinguish triumphal from circus processions by, for example, the form of the scepter carried (topped by a bust in the case of the circus procession, by an eagle in the case of a triumph?) or the types of chariot (two-horse for the circus, four horse for the triumph?). In addition to the monument of Philopappos, disputed images include: a sarcophagus fragment in Berlin, Pergamum Museum, inv. 967 (Ronke [1987] 735, n. 200), and even the famous *opus sectile* image of Junius Bassus (now in the Museo delle Terme, Rome, MNR 375831), which has been seen both as a circus image and less plausibly as a *processus consularis* (Becatti [1969] 196–202).

81. Dionysius of Halicarnassus, *Ant.* 7, 72, 10–2; Dionysius surprisingly does not refer to—and maybe does not know of—the satyr dances reported by Appian (*Pun.* 66) at the the triumph of Scipio in 201. These would fit his model even more closely.

82. Flower (1996) 107; Bömer, *RE* XXI, 2, 1976–7. Flaig (2003a) 34–8; (2003b) 301–3 urges a semiotic connection between the three processions.

83. Versnel (1970) 115–29 dissects the similarities between the two rituals optimistically assembled by Brelich (1938); though, as Flower (1996) 101 implies, perhaps throwing the baby out with the bathwater.

84. Flower (1996) 109, 113. Dionysius of Halicarnassus, *Ant.* 8, 59, 3, which she cites in support, in fact refers to the funeral of the traitor Coriolanus, who never celebrated a triumph at all (though it does refer in general terms to "what was needed to do proper honor to excellent men"); and the observation that the troops marched at the funeral of Sulla "as they had done in earlier triumphs" is not made by Appian (*BC* 1, 105) but by

Flower alone (p. 101). The closest we have to any such practice is the clothing used at Julius Caesar's funeral: below, n. 87.

85. Suetonius, *Aug.* 100, 2 (proposal on triumphal gate and statue of Victory); Tacitus, *Ann.* 1, 8 (proposal on triumphal gate and placards); Dio Cassius 56, 34. Dio's account of the funeral ceremony of Pertinax (74, 4–5) includes some similar triumphal elements. Modern discussion: Flower (1996) 244–5.

86. Richard (1978) 1122–5 (overstating the case); Arce (1988) 35–7 (warning against taking the practical parallels too far). The (tomb) monument of Philopappos appropriates these ideas in a private context.

87. Suetonius, *Jul.* 84, 4.

88. Seneca, *Dial.* 6 *(Ad Marciam)*, 3, 1; the triumphal theme is also developed—albeit in a different direction, predicting a triumph to avenge Drusus' death—in the poem of consolation to his mother Livia, once attributed to Ovid (Ps. Ovid, *Consolatio ad Liviam* esp. 271–80).

89. Plutarch, *Phil.* 21, 2–3.

9. THE TRIUMPH OF HISTORY

1. Pliny, *Nat.* 15, 136–7.
2. Suetonius, *Gal.* 1.
3. Dio Cassius 48, 49, 2–52.
4. Bruhl (1929); Bonfante Warren (1970a) 64–6.
5. Bonfante Warren (1970a) 49 ("the gradual transformation . . . from a purification ritual . . . into a purely honorific ceremony"). Similarly McCormick (1986) 12; Nicolet (1980) 353; Künzl (1988) 7; Holliday (2002) 22–3; and many more.
6. Alban Mount: Brennan (1996), though Livy (45, 38, 4) claims—in an admittedly tendentious context—that "many" had triumphed on the Alban Mount. Chronology of ovations: Rohde, *RE* XVIII, 2, 1900–3. Aulus Plautius: Tacitus, *Ann.* 13, 32; Suetonius, *Cl.* 24, 3. Rise and fall of *insignia*: A. E. Gordon (1952) 305–30; Maxfield (1981) 105–8; *CIL* XI, 5212 = *ILS* 1058 (last known award, 138 CE). "Undeserved" awards: Dio Cassius 58, 4, 8; Tacitus, *Ann.* 12, 3; 13, 53.
7. Brennan (1996) 329 (Caius Cicereius was a former scribe).
8. A view implied by A. Alföldi (1934) 93.
9. J. S. Richardson (1975) esp. 56–7.
10. Hobsbawm and Ranger (1983), especially Cannadine (1983) on royal ritual.

11. The stronger version of this point would be to argue that "cultural conservatism" is always a state of mind, not a description of practice. Paradoxically, a society which did not change any of its ritual practice would be the most innovatory of all.

12. Propertius 4, 10, 45–8; Livy 1, 10, 6, with Ogilvie (1965) 70–1; Festus (Paulus) p. 81L (bringing [ferre] peace); Plutarch, *Marc.* 8, 4 (adding an even more unlikely possibility).

13. The three celebrations: Propertius 4, 10; Valerius Maximus 3, 2, 3–5; Plutarch, *Rom.* 16, 5–8; *Marc.* 8, 1–5; Festus pp. 203–4L. Debates on the nature of the ceremony (especially on eligibility and the different protocols for different ranks of dedicator): Dumézil (1970) 166–8; Versnel (1970) 308–9; Rich (1996) 88–9, 123–6.

14. Florus, *Epit.* 1, 33 (2, 17, 11). Dismissed: Astin (1967) 46; Rich (1996) 89. Versnel (1970) 309 imagines that, like others, Scipio won the *spolia,* but was not allowed to dedicate them (following Valerius Maximus 3, 2, 6a). Oakley (1985) 398 hazards many now lost dedications, at least in the early period.

15. Picard (1957) 130–3; Bonfante Warren (1970a) 50–7; Versnel (1970) 306–13.

16. Flower (2000).

17. Livy 4, 20, 5–7. The Crassus "controversy": Dio Cassius 51, 24, 4; Rich (1996); Flower (2000) 49–55; less skeptically, Vervaet (forthcoming). The importance of the *spolia* in Augustan culture more generally: Harrison (1989); Rich (1999); R. M. Schneider (1990). The fact that temple had been in ruins at one stage in the first century BCE, before restoration by Augustus (Livy 4, 20, 7; Nepos, *Att.* 20, 3) makes the survival of any fifth-century corselet even more unlikely.

18. Overview: Hickson (1991). Forum of Augustus: above, pp. 43–4. Coins: e.g., *BMCRE* I, Augustus, 36, 384–6, 390–402. Arches: Rich (1998) 97–115. *Imperator* (and acclamations): above, p. 275, and Augustus, *RG* 4, 1. Laying of laurels: Dio Cassius 54, 25, 1–4; 55, 5, 1. Triumphal poetry: Galinsky (1969) with pp. 48–52. 111–4, 142 above. A range of triumphal ceremonies is stressed in Augustus, *RG* 4.

19. Tibullus 1, 7, esp. 1–22; 2, 5, 113–20. Messalinus' *insignia:* Velleius Paterculus 2, 112, 2; Ovid, *Pont.* 2, 2, 75–90.

20. Syme (1939) 404 (lapidarily; "Nor any more triumphs"); Eck (1984) 138–9; Hickson (1991) 138.

21. "Since they did not possess independent *auspicia,* none of these generals received triumphs," Hickson (1991) 128; Brunt (1990) 447; with slightly different emphasis, J. S. Richardson (1991) esp. 8.

22. Velleius Paterculus 2, 115, 2–3; Augustus, *RG* 4, 2.

23. Dio explicitly points to the subordinate status of the triumphing general: 48, 42, 4 (Cnaeus Domitius Calvus); 49, 21, 2–3 (Publius Ventidius Bassus).

24. Or so Syme (1979) 310–1 over-confidently asserts: "An axiom stands. No triumph can be celebrated without an antecedent acclamation, no acclamation taken without the possession of a pronconsul's *imperium.*" Lucius Passienus Rufus was clearly acclaimed *imperator* and went on to receive triumphal *insignia:* Schumacher (1985) 215–8. Rich (1990) 202 points to examples of campaigns which one might have expected would have led to triumphs.

25. Tacitus, *Ann.* 2, 41. Brunt (1974) reviews some of the (unfathomable) difficulties of the legal status of the imperial princes. J. S. Richardson (1991) 8 tries to get round such difficulties by postulating "delegation" of auspices by the emperor himself. The problematic case of Drusus: Rich (1999) 552.

26. Acclamations: Schumacher (1985) arguing strongly that Dio is "anachronistic," *contra* Combès (1966) 155–86. Recent discussion of auspices in this period: Giovannini (1983) 43–4, 77–9; Rich (1996) 101–5 (quote p. 104). The account of Ventidius' triumph (49, 21) is a classic case of Dio's muddle.

27. Refusals: Dio Cassius 53, 26, 5; 54, 10, 3; 54, 31, 4; 54, 33, 5; 55, 6, 6; Florus, *Epit.* 2, 33 (4, 12, 53). Blazoning: Augustus, *RG* 4, 1.

28. Dio Cassius 54, 12, 1–2.

29. Dio Cassius 54, 24, 8.

30. Suetonius, *Aug.* 38, 1.

31. Pliny, *Nat.* 5, 36; Velleius Paterculus 2, 51, 3.

32. *CIL* 1, 1, 78 (2nd ed.), also noting the theory that the Egyptian and Actian victories were similar enough to count as one. Whether we should give any significance to the omission of "palmam dedit" in the second entry is unclear.

33. Of course, practical considerations may help to explain the quality (the original location may have been inconveniently placed for a neat inscription)—but can hardly be a sufficient explanation on their own. This is only one of several mysteries about this text: the date of carving is another.

34. Rüpke (2006), with the detailed point by point critique of Versnel (2006). Though Versnel fires some mortal blows at Rüpke's thesis, this

learned debate as a whole, framed in these precise chronological terms, seems a sadly fruitless one.

35. Durante (1951) 138–43; Wallisch (1954–5) arguing also for an origin as late as the third century BCE.

36. Bonfante Warren (1970a) esp. 57–64 (seeing the "triumphal route" established in the pre-Etruscan phase, but culminating at the Temple of Jupiter Feretrius); Versnel (1970) esp. 255–303 (Etruscan link); 306–13 *(spolia opima);* (2006) 295–304.

37. Bonfante Warren (1970a) 64–5; Holliday (2002) 65–74.

38. Etruscan triumph: *ThesCRA* I, 22 and 28 (Cerveteri: no. 56; Perugia: no. 57). Praeneste: Torelli (1989) 28–30; Chateigner (1989) esp. 127–30, 137–8; Colonna (1992) 39–43. Rome: Carandini and Cappelli (2000) 322–8.

39. Florus, *Epit.* 1, 1 (1, 5, 6).

40. Holliday (2002) 73 nonetheless asserts that he is wearing a *toga picta.* The other painted scenes in the tomb do not give a clear guide to the interpretation of Vel Saties: they depict scenes of warfare from the Homeric to the more recent Etruscan past, but only provide a general background of military activity to the figure, who is in any case isolated from them on a separate panel.

41. Del Chiaro (1990). The condition of the object is poor and, as it is in a Swiss private collection, re-examination is not easy. Sino (1994) discusses a similar frieze from Murlo (Poggio Civitate), briefly reflecting (esp. 112–3) on the difficulties of such identifications.

42. Jannot (1984) 42–4; Cherici (1993), sympathetic to the triumphal interpretation (because of the ordering of the prisoners and spoils), but noting several very different interpretations.

43. Andrén (1974) reviews several similar objects, suggesting that the Praenestine examples depict a simple warrior scene. The interpretation of most such processional scenes is controversial. Winged horses sometimes seem to indicate a mythological scene, sometimes not.

44. No less fragile are the constructions based on the puzzling iconography of the famous *cista Praenestina.* This has been seen as a representation of some form of triumph (e.g., Bonfante Warren [1964]); but a variety of other interpretations, mythical and theatrical, have been proposed (e.g. Adam [1989], with review of earlier literature). I am likewise unconvinced by other attempts to see triumphs in early Roman tomb painting (Holliday [2002] 33–43).

45. Ryberg (1955) 16–7; Holliday (1990) 86–90. In fact Vel Saties too may be

of Roman date. The tomb was built in the fifth century BCE, but—as Bonfante Warren (1970a) 65 briefly discusses—the paintings have been variously dated between the fourth and first centuries BCE.

46. This would be taken as self-evident in the case of poetic or obviously mythic aetiologies of rituals, such as we find in Ovid's *Fasti (Calendar Poem)* and elsewhere. Convenient summary: Graf (2002) 115–21.

47. Africa: Servius (auct.), *Aen.* 4, 37 (in the context of Virgil's description of Africa as "rich in triumphs"). Tripartite honor: Isidore, *Orig.* 18, 2, 3.

48. Varro, *LL* 6, 33; Cicero, *Leg.* 2, 54.

49. An idea echoed in Plutarch, *Rom.* 16; Dionysius of Halicarnassus, *Ant.* 2, 34.

50. Dionysius of Halicarnassus, *Ant.* 5, 47; Festus (Paulus) p. 213L.

51. Plutarch, *Marc.* 22, 4.

52. Servius, *Aen* 4, 543.

53. Pliny *Nat.* 7, 191.

54. Euripides, *Ba.* 13–19.

55. Nock (1928) 21–30; Bowersock (1994) 157.

56. Curtius 3, 12, 18.

57. In addition to that illustrated, Matz (1968) 271–3, pl. 156–9 (prisoners and spoils); 263–7, pl. 144, 152–6 (procession and Dionysiac "general").

58. Pliny, *Nat.* 8, 4.

59. Another case of an originary story being reinscribed in the ritual as performed is hinted at by Appian (*Pun.* 66). He refers to lyre players and pipers "acting out" an Etruscan procession, as if they were putting on a show of imitating Etruscan origins.

60. Celebration: Procopius, *Vand.* 2 (*Bella* 4), 9, with McCormick (1986) 65–6, 125–9. Mosaic: *Aed.* 1, 10, 16–18, with MacCormack (1981) 74–5.

61. Graves (1954) foreword; Cameron (1976) 119.

62. "Post-Roman" victory celebrations in Constantinople and elsewhere: McCormick (1986) esp. 36–78 (for developments from the fourth to eighth centuries).

63. John Lydus, *De Magistratibus* 2, 2 (triumphal vocabulary, but focused on Justinian); Jordanes, *Getica* 171–2 (*MGH* AA 5.1, 102–3); John Malalas 18, 81; Marcellinus Comes, year 534.

64. Barini (1952) 161–200; some celebrations may have fallen out of the record.

65. SHA *Aurelian* 33–4; *Tyranni XXX (Thirty Pretenders)* 30, 4–11, 24–6.

66. Merten (1968) 101–40; Paschoud (1996) 160–9. A particular target has been the stags pulling the chariot, often thought to be the author's confu-

sion of a Greek source referring to elephants (Greek *elaphos* = stag; *elephas* = elephant); though stags are defended by A. Alföldi (1964) 6–8 and Alföldi-Rosenbaum (1994).

67. SHA, *Severus Alexander* 56.
68. Dio 76, 1; Herodian 3, 10, 1–2; SHA, *Severus* 16, 6–7.
69. MacCormack (1981) 17–61.
70. Ammianus Marcellinus 16, 10, 10 and 1.
71. Ammianus Marcellinus 16, 10, 2.
72. MacCormack (1981) 51.
73. Dionysius of Halicarnassus, *Ant.* 2, 34, 2; 5, 17, 1–2; Livy 3, 29, 4–5. Ando (2000) 257.
74. *Panegyrici Latini* 11, 4; Eutropius 9, 27, 2; Chrongraphus anni 354 = *MGH* AA 9, 148; Cassiodorus, *Chronica* = *MGH* AA 11, 150; with Nixon (1981).
75. *Panegyrici Latini* 4, 30, 4–32, 3 (quotation 31, 1), Lactantius, *De Mortibus Persecutorum* 44, 10; Zosimus 2, 17, 1; Eusebius, *Historia Ecclesiastica* 9, 9, 9; *Vita Constantini* 1, 39. Omission of sacrifice: Straub (1955), with criticism of McCormick (1986) 101; Nixon and Rodgers (1994) 323–4; Fraschetti (1999).
76. Claudian, *Panegyricus de VI Consulatu Honorii* 369–70, 404–6, 393.
77. *Currus:* McCormick (1986) 87. *Ioci: Panegyrici Latini* 12, 18, 3. Early Roman precedents: Procopius, *Vand.* 2 (*Bella* 4), 9, 2; Priscian, *De laude Anastasii* 174–7.
78. Thesiger (1987) 54–6; Maitland (2006) 44–5.

Bibliography

A number of fundamental works on the Roman triumph stand behind most of what I say in this book. The annotated chronology of republican Roman ceremonies in A. Degrassi, *Inscriptiones Italiae* XIII.1 (Rome, 1947), and on the CD accompanying T. Itgenshorst, *Tota illa pompa: der Triumph in der römischen Republik* (Göttingen, 2005), can be taken as the first port of call for the basic information on any individual ceremony. I have not normally referenced these in the endnotes. Throughout my research I have had at my side W. Ehlers' entry, "Triumphus," in Pauly-Wissowa, *Real-Encyclopädie (RE)* 2. VIIA, 1, 493–511; H. S. Versnel, *Triumphus: an inquiry into the origin, development and meaning of the Roman triumph* (Leiden, 1970); E. Künzl, *Der römische Triumph: Siegesfeiern im antiken Rom* (Munich, 1988); and in the later stages Itgenshorst's *Tota illa pompa* and I. Östenberg, *Staging the world: Rome and the other in the triumphal procession* (diss. Lund, 2003; rev. ed. Oxford, forthcoming). These are usually referenced only in the case of particular disagreement, to highlight a discussion that might otherwise be hard to locate, or—especially in the case of Versnel—where his treatment of the topic has become the starting point of modern debate.

Abaecherli, A. L. 1935–6. *"Fercula, carpenta,* and *tensae* in the Roman procession." *Bollettino dell'Associazione Internazionale degli Studi Mediterranei* 6, 1–20.

Aberson, M. 1994. *Temples votifs et butin de guerre dans la Rome républicaine.* Rome.

Adam, R. 1989. "Faux triomphe et préjugés tenaces: la ciste Berlin misc. 3238." *MEFRA* 101, 597–641.

Adamo Muscettola, S. 1992. "Per una riedizione dell'arco di Traiano a Benevento: appunti sul fregio trionfale." *Prospettiva* 67, 2–16.

Agnoli, N. 2002. *Museo Archeologico Nazionale di Palestrina: le sculture.* Rome.

Alföldi, A. 1934. "Die Ausgestaltung des monarchischen Zeremoniells." *MDAI(R)* 49, 1–118.

———— 1935. "Insignien und Tracht der römischen Kaiser." *MDAI(R)* 50, 1–171.

———— 1964. "Zwei Bemerkungen zur Historia Augusta." *Historia Augusta Colloquium 1963*. Bonn. 1–8.

Alföldi, M. R. 1999. *Bild und Bildersprache der römischen Kaiser*. Mainz.

Alföldi-Rosenbaum, E. 1994. "Heliogabalus' and Aurelian's stag chariots and the Caesar contorniates." *Historiae Augustae Colloquium Genevense*. Macerata. 5–10.

Ammerman, A. 2006. "Adding time to Rome's *imago*," in L. Haselberger and J. Humphreys, eds. *Imaging ancient Rome: documentation—visualization—imagination. JRA* supplement 61, Portsmouth, RI. 297–308.

Anastasiadis, V. I., and G. A. Souris. 1992. "Theophanes of Mytilene: a new inscription relating to his early career." *Chiron* 22, 377–83.

Anderson, W. S. 1963. "Pompey, his friends and the literature of the first century BC." *University of California Publications in Classical Philology* 19, 1, 1–81.

Ando, C. 2000. *Imperial ideology and provincial loyalty in the Roman Empire*. Berkeley.

Andreae, B. 1979. "Zum Triumphfries des Trajansbogens von Benevent." *MDAI(R)* 86, 325–9.

Andrén, A. 1974. "Osservazioni sulle terrecotte architettoniche etrusco-italiche." *ORom* 8, 1–16.

Angelicoussis, E. 1984. "The panel reliefs of Marcus Aurelius." *MDAI(R)* 91, 141–205.

Arce, J. 1988. *Funus imperatorum: los funerales de los emperadores romanos*. Madrid.

Astin, A. E. 1967. *Scipo Aemilianus*. Oxford.

———— 1978. *Cato the censor*. Oxford.

———— 1989. "Roman government and politics, 200–134 BC," in A. E. Astin et al., eds. *Cambridge Ancient History* VIII. 2nd ed. Cambridge. 163–96.

Athanassaki, L. 1992. "The triumph of love and elegy in Ovid's *Amores* 1, 2." *MD* 28, 125–41.

Auliard, C. 2001. *Victoires et triomphes à Rome: droit et réalités sous la République*. Besançon.

Ault, N., and J. Butt, eds. 1954. *The poems of Alexander Pope, vol. 6: Minor poems*. Twickenham.

Badian, E. 1955. "The date of Pompey's first triumph." *Hermes* 83, 107–18.

———— 1961. "Servilius and Pompey's first triumph." *Hermes* 89, 254–6.

Barchiesi, A. 2000. "Rituals in ink: Horace on the Greek lyric tradition," in M. Depew and D. Obbink, eds. *Matrices of genre: authors, canons, and society.* Cambridge. 167–82.

———— 2002. "Martial arts: Mars Ultor in the Forum Augustum," in G. Herbert-Brown. *Ovid's Fasti: historical readings at its bimillennium.* Oxford. 1–22.

Barchiesi, A., J. Rüpke, and S. Stephens, eds. 2004. *Rituals in ink: a conference on religion and literary production in ancient Rome held at Stanford University in February 2002.* Stuttgart, 2004.

Barini, C. 1952. *Triumphalia. Imprese ed onori militari durante l'Impero Romano.* Turin.

Barkan, L. 1986. *The gods made flesh: metamorphosis and the pursuit of paganism.* New Haven and London.

———— *Unearthing the past: archaeology and aesthetics in the making of Renaissance culture.* New Haven and London.

Barnes, T. D. 1971. *Tertullian: a historical and literary study.* Oxford.

Baumstark, R., and F. Büttner, eds. 2003. *Grosser Auftritt: Piloty und die Historienmalerei.* Exhibition catalogue. Munich.

Bayet, J. 1940. "16 août 48: la date de la mort de Pompée d'après Lucain," in *Mélanges de philologie, de littérature et d'histoire anciennes offerts à A. Ernout.* Paris. 5–10.

Beacham, R. C. 1999. *Spectacle entertainments of early imperial Rome.* New Haven and London.

Beard, M. 1987. "A complex of times: no more sheep on Romulus' birthday." *PCPhS* n.s. 33, 1–15.

———— 2002. "Ciceronian correspondences: making a book out of letters," in T. P. Wiseman, ed. *Classics in progress: essays on ancient Greece and Rome.* Oxford. 103–44.

———— 2003a. "The triumph of the absurd: Roman street theatre," in C. Edwards and G. Woolf, eds. *Rome the cosmopolis.* Cambridge. 21–43.

———— 2003b. "The triumph of Flavius Josephus," in A. J. Boyle and W. J. Dominik, eds. *Flavian Rome: culture, image, text.* Leiden and Boston. 543–58.

———— 2003c. "Picturing the Roman triumph: putting the *Fasti Capitolini* in context." *Apollo* 158, no. 497, 23–8.

———— 2004. "Writing ritual: the triumph of Ovid," in Barchiesi, Rüpke, and Stephens. 2004. 115–26.

Beard, M., and J. Henderson. 1998. "The emperor's new body: apotheosis from Rome," in M. Wyke, ed. *Parchments of gender: deciphering the bodies of antiquity.* Oxford. 191–219.

Beard, M., J. North, and S. Price. 1998. *Religions of Rome,* 2 vols. Cambridge.

Becatti, G., ed. 1969. *Scavi di Ostia 6: Edificio con opus sectile fuori Porta Marina.* Rome.

Bell, C. 1992. *Ritual theory, ritual practice.* New York and Oxford.

Bellemore, J. 2000. "Pompey's triumph over the Arabs," in C. Deroux, ed. *Studies in Latin literature and Roman history,* Vol. 10. Brussels. 91–123.

Beloch, K. J. 1926. *Römische Geschichte bis zum Beginn der Punischen Kriege.* Berlin.

Bennett, J. 1997. *Trajan: optimus princeps.* London.

Bernardo, A. S. 1962. *Petrarch, Scipio and the "Africa": the birth of humanism's dream.* Baltimore.

Bernstein, F. 1998. *Ludi publici: Untersuchungen zur Entstehung und Entwicklung der öffentlichen Spiele im republikanischen Rom.* Stuttgart.

Biondo, F. 1459. *De Roma triumphante libri decem.* Brescia. 1503 ed. cited.

Birley, A. R. 1997. *Hadrian: the restless emperor.* London.

Biville, F. 1990. *Les emprunts du latin au grec: approche phonétique* 1. Leuven.

Boissier, G. 1870. *Cicéron et ses amis: étude sur la société romaine du temps de César.* 2nd ed. Paris.

Bonfante Warren, L. 1964. "A Latin triumph on a Praenestine cista." *AJA* 68, 35–42.

———— 1970a. "Roman triumphs and Etruscan kings: the changing face of the triumph." *JRS* 60, 49–66.

———— 1970b. "Roman triumphs and Etruscan kings: the Latin word *triumphus,*" in R. C. Lugton and M. G. Saltzer, eds. *Studies in Honor of J. Alexander Kerns.* The Hague and Paris. 108–20.

———— 1974. Review of Versnel. 1970. *Gnomon* 46, 574–83.

Bonneau, D. 1961. "Nouvelles données sur la crue du Nil et la date de la mort de Pompée." *REL* 39, 105–11.

Bonnefond-Coudry, M. 1989. *Le sénat de la République romaine de la guerre d'Hannibal à Auguste: pratiques délibératives et prise de décision.* Rome.

Bowersock, G. 1994. "Dionysus as an epic hero," in N. Hopkinson, ed. *Studies in the Dionysiaca of Nonnus.* Cambridge Philological Society Supplement 17. 156–66.

Boyce, A. Abaecherli. 1942. "The origin of *ornamenta triumphalia.*" *CPh* 37, 130–41.

Braccesi, L. 1981. *Epigrafia e storiografia: interpretazioni augustee.* Naples.

Bradley, K. R. 1978. *Suetonius' Life of Nero: an historical commentary.* Brussels.

Braund, S. Morton. 1996. "Ending epic: Statius, Theseus and a merciful release." *PCPhS* n.s. 42, 1–23.

Brelich, A. 1938. "Trionfo e morte." *SMSR* 14, 189–93.

Brennan, T. C. 1996. "Triumphus in Monte Albano," in R. W. Wallace and E. M. Harris, eds. *Transitions to empire: essays in Greco-Roman history, 360–146 BC.* Oklahoma. 315–37.

———— 2000. *The praetorship in the Roman Republic.* Oxford.

Brilliant, R. 1967. *The Arch of Septimius Severus in the Roman Forum.* Rome.

———— 1999. "'Let the trumpets roar!' The Roman triumph," in B. Bergmann and C. Kondoleon, eds. *The art of ancient spectacle.* CASVA Studies in the History of Art, Symposium Papers 34. Washington/New Haven and London. 221–9.

Brink, C. O. 1982. *Horace on poetry: Epistles Book II: The letters to Augustus and Florus.* Cambridge.

Briscoe, J. 1981. *A commentary on Livy Books XXXIV–XXXVII.* Oxford.

Bruhl, A. 1929. "Les influences hellénistiques dans le triomphe romain." *MEFRA* 46, 77–95.

Brunt, P. A. 1962. "The army and the land in the Roman revolution." *JRS* 52, 69–86. Repr. in *The fall of the Roman Republic, and related essays.* 1988. Oxford. 240–80.

———— 1963. Review of H. D. Meyer, *Die Aussenpolitik des Augustus und die Augusteische Dichtung. JRS* 53, 170–6. Repr. in Brunt. 1990. 96–109.

———— 1971. *Italian manpower, 225 BC–AD 14.* Oxford.

———— 1974. "C. Fabricius Tuscus and an Augustan dilectus." *ZPE* 13, 161–85.

———— 1978. "Laus imperii," in P. D. A. Garnsey and C. R. Whittaker, eds. *Imperialism in the ancient world.* Cambridge. 159–91. Repr. in Brunt. 1990. 288–323.

———— 1990. *Roman imperial themes.* Oxford.

Buchan, M. 1995. "Ovidius Imperamator: beginnings and endings of love poems and empire in the *Amores.*" *Arethusa* 28, 53–85.

Buchheit, V. 1972. *Der Anspruch des Dichters in Vergils Georgika.* Darmstadt.

Cafiero, M. L. 1986. "I rilievi della chiesa di S. Martina: documentazione storica etc," in La Rocca. 1986. 38–45.

Cameron, A. 1976. *In laudem Iustini Augustu minori libri IV, Flavius Cresconius Corippus.* London.

Campbell, J. B. 1984. *The emperor and the Roman army 31 BC–AD 235.* Oxford.

Cannadine, D. 1983. "The context, performance and meaning of ritual: the British monarchy and the 'invention of tradition,' c. 1820–1977," in Hobsbawm and Ranger. 1983. 101–64.

Capoferro Cencetti, A. M. 1979. "Variazioni nel tempo dell'identità funzionale di un monumento: il teatro di Pompeo." *RdA* 3, 72–85.

Carandini, A., and R. Cappelli, eds. 2000. *Roma: Romolo, Remo e la fondazione della città.* Exhibition catalogue. Milan.

Champlin, E. 2003a. "Agamemnon at Rome: Roman dynasts and Greek heroes," in D. Braund and C. Gill, eds. *Myth, history and culture in republican Rome: studies in honour of T. P. Wiseman.* Exeter. 295–319.

———— 2003b. *Nero.* Cambridge.

Chaplin, J. D. 2000. *Livy's exemplary history.* Oxford.

Chastel, A. 1983. *The sack of Rome, 1527.* Princeton.

Chateigner, C. 1989. "Cortèges en armes en Étrurie: une étude iconographique de plaques de revêtement architectoniques étrusques du VIe siècle." *RBPh* 67, 122–38.

Cherici, A. 1993. "Per una lettura del sarcofago dello Sperandio." *XAnt.* 2, 13–22.

Chilosi, M. G., and G. Martellotti. 1986. "Dati sulle techniche esecutive etc," in La Rocca. 1986. 46–52.

Chilver, G. E. F., and G. B. Townend. 1985. *A historical commentary on Tacitus' Histories 4 and 5.* Oxford.

Chioffi, L. 1996. *Gli elogia augustei del Foro Romano: aspetti epigrafici e topografici.* Rome.

Christ, W. von, et al. 1920. *Geschichte der Griechischen Litteratur.* Part II. 6th ed. Munich.

Christenson, D. 2000. *Plautus Amphitruo.* Cambridge.

Churchill, J. B. 1999. "*Ex qua quod vellent facerent:* Roman magistrates' authority over *praeda* and *manubiae.*" *TAPhA* 129, 85–116.

Coarelli, F. 1968. "La Porta Trionfale e la Via dei Trionfi." *DdA* 2, 55–103.

———— 1971–72. "Il complesso pompeiano del Campo Marzio e la sua decorazione scultorea." *RPAA* 44, 99–122.

———— 1985. *Il Foro Romano II: periodo repubblicano e augusteo.* Rome.

———— 1992. *Il Foro Boario: dalle origini alla fine della repubblica.* 2nd ed. Rome.

———— 1997. *Il Campo Marzio: dalle origini alla fine della repubblica.* Rome.

Colilli, P. 1990. "Scipio's triumphal ascent in the *Africa*," in Eisenbichler and Iannucci. 1990. 147–59.

Colonna, G. 1992. "Praeneste arcaica e il mondo etrusco-italico," in *La Necropoli di Praeneste: periodo orientalizzante e medio repubblicano.* Atti del 2− Convegno di Studi Archeologici. Palestrina 21/22 Aprile 1990, Palestrina. 13–51.

Combès, R. 1966. *Imperator: recherches sur l'emploi et la signification du titre d'imperator dans la Rome republicaine.* Paris.

Connor, W. R. 1987. "Tribes, festivals and processions: civic ceremonial and political manipulation in archaic Greece." *JHS* 107, 40–50.

Cornell, T. J. 1986. "The value of the literary tradition concerning archaic Rome," in K. A. Raaflaub, ed. *Social struggles in archaic Rome: new perspectives on the conflict of the orders.* Berkeley. 52–76.

Courtney, E. J. 1980. *A commentary on the satires of Juvenal.* London.

Crake, J. E. A. 1940. "The annals of the pontifex maximus." *CPh* 35, 375–86.

Crawford, M. H., et al. 1996. *Roman statutes.* London.

D'Arms, J. H. 1998. "Between public and private: the *epulum publicum* and Caesar's *Horti trans Tiberim*," in M. Cima and E. La Rocca, eds. *Horti romani.* Rome. BCAR Supp. 6, 33–43.

Daut, R. 1984. *"Belli facies et triumphus." MDAI(R)* 91, 115–23.

Degrassi, A. 1943. "Le sistemazioni dei Fasti Capitolini." *Capitolium* 18, 327–35. Repr. in Degrassi, *Scritti vari.* 1962. Rome. 229–38.

Delbrueck, R. 1929. *Die Consulardiptychen und verwandte Denkmäler.* Berlin.

Del Chiaro, M. 1990. "An Etruscan funerary 'naiskos.'" *NAC* 19, 51–8.

De Maria, S. 1988. *Gli archi onorari di Roma e dell'Italia romana.* Rome.

Dench, E. 2005. *Romulus' asylum: Roman identities from the age of Alexander to the age of Hadrian.* Oxford.

Deubner, L. 1934. "Die Tracht des römischen Triumphators." *Hermes* 69, 316–23.

Deutsch, M. E. 1924. "Pompey's three triumphs." *CPh* 19, 277–9.

Develin, R. 1978. "Tradition and development of triumphal regulations in Rome." *Klio* 60, 429–38.

Dewar, M. 1996. *Claudian, Panegyricus de sexto consulatu Honorii Augusti.* Oxford.

Dillon, S., and K. E. Welch, eds. 2006. *Representations of war in ancient Rome.* Cambridge.

Dreizehnter, A. 1975. "Pompeius als Städtegründer." *Chiron* 5, 213–45.

Drummond, A. 1989. "Rome in the fifth century 1: the social and economic framework; 2: the citizen community," in F. W. Walbank et al., eds. *The Cambridge Ancient History* VII 2. 2nd ed. Cambridge. 113–204.

Dumézil, G. 1970. *Archaic Roman religion.* Chicago.

Dunbabin, K. M. D. 1986. "Sic erimus cuncti . . . : The skeleton in Graeco-Roman art." *JDAI* 101, 185–255.

Duncan-Jones, R. 1990. *Structure and scale in the Roman economy.* Cambridge.

———— 1994. *Money and government in the Roman empire.* Cambridge.

Dupont, F. 1976. "Signification théâtrale du double dans l'Amphitryon de Plaute." *REL* 54, 129–41.

Durante, M. 1951. "*Triumpe* e *triumphus:* un capitolo del più antico culto dionisiaco latino." *Maia* 4, 138–44.

Ebert-Schifferer, S. 1988. "Ripandas Kapitolinischer Freskenzyklus und die Selbstdarstellung der Konservatoren um 1500." *Römisches Jahrbuch für Kunstgeschichte,* 23/24, 75–218.

Eck, W. 1984. "Senatorial self-representation: developments in the Augustan period," in F. Millar and E. Segal, eds. *Caesar Augustus: seven aspects*. Oxford, 1984. 129–67.

———— 1999. "Kaiserliche Imperatorenakklamation und ornamenta triumphalia." *ZPE* 124, 223–7.

———— 2003. *The age of Augustus*. Oxford.

Edwards, C. 1994. "Beware of imitations: theatre and the subversion of imperial identity," in J. Elsner and J. Masters, eds. *Reflections of Nero*. London. 83–97.

Egan, R. B. 1977. "Lexical evidence on two Pauline passages." *NT* 19, 34–62.

Eisenbichler, K., and A. A. Iannucci, eds. 1990. *Petrarch's Triumphs: allegory and spectacle*. Toronto.

Emiliozzi, A. 1997. *Carri da guerra e principi Etruschi*. Exhibition catalogue. Rome.

Evangelides, D. E. 1958. "Anaskaphe tou theatrou Mytilenes." *PAAH,* 230–32.

Faccenna, D. 1956. "Il Pompeo di Palazzo Spada." *ArchClass.* 8, 173–201.

Favro, D. 1994. "The street triumphant: the urban impact of Roman triumphal parades," in Z. Çelik et al., eds. *Streets: critical perspectives on public space*. Berkeley. 151–64.

———— 1996. *The urban image of Augustan Rome*. Cambridge.

Ferguson, J. 1979. *Juvenal. The Satires*. Basingstoke.

Ferrary, J.-L. 1988. *Philhellénisme et impérialisme: aspects idéologiques de la conquête romaine du monde hellénistique, de la seconde guerre de Macédoine à la guerre contre Mithridate*. Rome.

Fine, S. 2005. "The Temple Menorah—where is it?" *Biblical Archaeology Review* 31.4, 18–25, 62–3.

Flaig, E. 2003a. *Ritualisierte Politik: Zeichen, Gesten und Herrschaft im Alten Rom*. Göttingen.

———— 2003b. "Warum die Triumphe die römische Republik ruiniert haben," in K.-J. Hölkeskamp et al., eds. *Sinn(in) in der Antike*. Mainz. 299–313.

Fless, F. 1995. *Opferdiener und Kultmusiker auf stadtrömischen historischen Reliefs*. Mainz.

Flory, M. B. 1998. "The integration of women into the Roman triumph." *Historia* 47, 489–94.

Flower, H. I. 1995. "*Fabulae praetextae* in context: when were plays on contemporary subjects performed in Republican Rome?" *CQ* n.s. 45, 170–90.

———— 1996. *Ancestor masks and aristocratic power in Roman culture*. Oxford.

———— 2000. "The tradition of the *Spolia Opima*: M. Claudius Marcellus and Augustus." *ClAnt.* 19, 34–64.

Forsythe, G. 2005. *A critical history of early Rome: from prehistory to the First Punic War.* Berkeley.

Fraccaro, P. 1957. "The history of Rome in the regal period." *JRS* 47, 59–65.

Fraenkel, E. 1922. *Plautinisches im Plautus.* Berlin. Translated as *Plautine elements in Plautus.* 2007. Oxford.

Fraschetti, A. 1999. "Veniunt modo reges Romam," in W. V. Harris, ed. *The Transformations of urbs Roma in late antiquity. JRA* Supplement 33. Portsmouth, RI. 235–48.

Frazer, J. G. 1911. *The magic art and the evolution of kings.* Part 1, Vol. 2 of *The golden bough: a study in magic and religion.* 3rd ed. London.

Frier, B. W. 1979. *Libri annales pontificum maximorum: the origins of the annalistic tradition.* Rome.

Fuchs, M. 1982. "Eine Musengruppe aus dem Pompeius-Theater." *MDAI(R)* 89, 69–80.

Furtwängler, A. 1900. *Die antiken Gemmen.* Berlin.

Gabba, E. 1956. *Appiano e la storia delle guerre civili.* Florence.

Gabelmann, H. 1981. "Römische ritterliche Offiziere im Triumphzug." *JDAI* 96, 436–65.

Gagé, J. 1955. *Apollon romain: essai sur le culte d'Apollon et le développement du "ritus Graecus" à Rome des origines à Auguste.* Paris.

Gagliardo, M. C., and J. E. Packer. 2006. "A new look at Pompey's theater: history, documentation and recent excavation." *AJA* 110, 93–121.

Galasso, L. 1995. *P. Ovidii Nasonis, epistularum ex Ponto Liber II.* Trieste.

Galinsky, K. 1966. "Scipionic themes in Plautus' *Amphitruo.*" *TAPhA* 97, 203–35.

—— 1969. "The triumph theme in the Augustan elegy." *WS* n.s. 3, 75–107.

—— 1996. *Augustan culture.* Princeton.

Galli, F. 1987–8. "L'iscrizione trionfale di T. Sempronio Gracco (Liv. XLI. 28)." *AION(filol)* 9–10, 135–8.

Geertz, C. 1973. *The interpretation of culture: selected essays.* New York.

—— 1983. "Centers, kings and charisma: reflections on the symbolics of power," in *Local knowledge: further essays in interpretative anthropology.* New York. 121–46.

Gibbon, E. 1776–88. *The history of the decline and fall of the Roman empire.* Cited from J. B. Bury, ed. 7 vols. 1896–1900. London.

—— 1796. *Miscellaneous works of Edward Gibbon.* John Lord Sheffield, ed. London.

Ginzrot, J. C. 1817. *Die Wagen und Fahrwerke der Griechen und Römer und anderer alten Völker.* Munich.

Giovannini, A. 1983. *Consulare imperium.* Basel.

Girardet, K. M. 1991. "Der Triumph des Pompeius im Jahre 61 v. Chr.—*ex Asia?*" *ZPE* 89, 201–15.

Gleason, K. 1990. "The garden portico of Pompey the Great." *Expedition* 32. 2, 4–13.

———— 1994. "*Porticus Pompeiana:* a new perspective on the first public park of ancient Rome." *Journal of Garden History* 14, 13–27.

Gnecchi, F. 1912. *I medaglioni romani* 2. Milan.

Goldhill, S. 1987. "The Great Dionysia and civic ideology." *JHS* 107, 58–76.

Gordon, A. E. 1952. *Quintus Veranius consul AD 49: a study based upon his recently identified sepulchral inscription. University of California Publications in Classical Archaeology* 2. 1934–52. 231–341.

Gordon, R. L. 1979. "The real and the imaginary: production and religion in the Greco-Roman world." *Art History* 2, 5–34. Repr. in *Image and Value in the Graeco-Roman World: studies in Mithraism and Roman art.* I. 1996. Aldershot.

Graf, F. 2002. "Myth in Ovid," in P. Hardie, ed. *The Cambridge companion to Ovid.* Cambridge. 108–21.

Graves, R. 1954. *Count Belisarius.* Harmondsworth.

Greenhalgh, P. 1980. *Pompey: the Roman Alexander.* London.

———— 1981. *Pompey: the republican prince.* London.

Griffin, M. 1984. *Nero: the end of a dynasty.* London.

———— 2000. "The Flavians," in A. K. Bowman, P. Garnsey, and D. Rathbone, eds. *Cambridge ancient history* XI. 2nd ed. Cambridge. 1–83.

———— 2001. "Piso, Cicero and their audience," in C. Auvray-Assayas and D. Delattre, eds. *Les polémiques philosophiques à Rome à la fin de la République: Cicéron et Philodème de Gadara.* Paris. 85–99.

Gros, P. 1979. "Les statues de Syracuse et les 'dieux' de Tarente." *REL* 57, 85–114.

Gruen, E.. 1990. *Studies in Greek culture and Roman policy.* Leiden.

———— 1992. *Culture and national identity in republican Rome.* Ithaca.

Guilhembet, J.-P. 1992. "Sur un jeu de mots de Sextus-Pompée: *domus* et propagande politique lors d'un épisode des guerres civiles." *MEFRA* 104, 787–816.

Gurval, R. A. 1995. *Actium and Augustus: the politics and emotions of civil war.* Ann Arbor.

Habinek, T. 2002. "Ovid and empire," in P. R. Hardie, ed. *The Cambridge companion to Ovid.* Cambridge. 46–61.

Habinek, T., and A. Schiesaro, eds. 1997. *The Roman cultural revolution.* Cambridge.

Halfmann, H. 1986. *Itinera principum: Geschichte und Typologie der Kaiserreisen im römischen Reich.* Wiesbaden.

Halkin, L.-E. 1948. "La parodie d'une demande de triomphe dans l'*Amphitryon* de Plaute." *AC* 17, 297–304.

——— 1953. *La supplication d'action de graces chez les Romains.* Paris.

Hanson, J. A. 1959. *Roman theater temples.* Princeton.

Hardie, P. 1993. "After Rome: Renaissance epic," in A. J. Boyle, ed. *Roman epic.* Cambridge. 294–313.

——— 2002. *Ovid's poetics of illusion.* Cambridge.

——— forthcoming. "Poet, patrons, rulers: the Ennian traditions."

Harl, K. W. 1991. "Livy and the date of the introduction of the cistophoric tetradrachma." *ClAnt* 10, 268–97.

Harris, W. V. 1979. *War and imperialism in republican Rome: 327–70 BC.* Oxford.

Harrison, S. 1989. "Augustus, the poets and the *Spolia Opima*." *CQ* n.s. 39, 408–14.

Harvey, F. D. 1983. "Cognati Caesaris: Ovid *Amores* 1.2.51/2." *WS* n.s. 17, 89–90.

Harvey, P. 1981. "Historical allusions in Plautus and the date of the *Amphitruo*." *Athenaeum* 59, 480–9.

Haselberger, L. 2002. *Mapping Augustan Rome. JRA* Supplement, 50. Portsmouth, RI.

Haskell, F., and N. Penny. 1981. *Taste and the antique: the lure of classical sculpture 1500–1900.* New Haven and London.

Heilmeyer, W.-D., E. La Rocca, and H. G. Martin. 1988. *Kaiser Augustus und die verlorene Republik.* Mainz.

Helbig, W. 1966. *Führer durch die öffentlichen Sammlungen klassischer Altertümer in Rom.* Rev. ed. Tübingen.

Henderson, J. 2002. "A doo-dah-doo-dah-dey at the races: Ovid *Amores* 3.2 and the personal politics of the Circus Maximus." *ClAnt* 21, 41–66.

Herrmann, L. 1948. "L'actualité dans l'*Amphitryon* de Plaute." *AC* 17, 317–22.

Hickson, F. V. 1991. "Augustus *Triumphator*: manipulation of the triumphal theme in the political program of Augustus." *Latomus* 50, 124–38.

Hobsbawm, E. J., and T. O. Ranger, eds. 1983. *The invention of tradition.* Cambridge.

Hölkeskamp, K.-J. 1987. *Die Entstehung der Nobilität: Studien zur sozialen und politischen Geschichte der Römischen Republik im 4 Jhdt V. Chr.* Stuttgart.

——— 2001. "Capitol, Comitium und Forum. Öffentliche Räume, sakrale Topographie und Erinnerungslandschaften der römischen Republik," in S. Faller, ed. *Studien zu antiken Identitäten.* Würzburg. 97–132.

——— 2006. "History and collective memory in the Middle Republic," in N.

Rosenstein and R. Morstein-Marx, eds. *A companion to the Roman republic*. Oxford. 478–95.

Holliday, P. J. 1990. "Processional imagery in Late Etruscan funerary art." *AJA* 94, 73–93.

——— 1997. "Roman triumphal painting: its function, development and reception." *Art Bulletin* 79, 130–47.

——— 2002. *The origins of Roman historical commemoration in the visual arts*. Cambridge.

Hölscher, T. 1967. *Victoria Romana*. Mainz.

——— 1978. "Die Anfänge römischer Repräsentationskunst" *MDAI(R)* 85, 315–57.

——— 1987. *Römische Bildsprache als semantische System*. Heidelberg. Translated as *The Language of Images in Roman Art*. Cambridge, 2004.

——— 2004. "Provokation und Transgression als politischer Habitus in der späten römischen Republik." *MDAI(R)* 111, 83–104.

——— 2006. "The transformation of victory into power: from event to structure," in Dillon and Welch. 2006. 27–48.

Hopkins, K. 1978. *Conquerors and slaves*. Cambridge.

——— 1980. "Taxes and trade in the Roman Empire. 200 B.C.–A.D. 400. *JRS* 70, 101–25.

——— 1983. *Death and renewal*. Cambridge.

HSCPh. 1995. *Greece in Rome. Harvard Studies in Classical Philology*, 97. Cambridge.

Humphrey, C., and J. Laidlaw. 1994. *The archetypal actions of ritual: a theory of ritual illustrated by the Jain rite of worship*. Oxford.

Hutchinson, G. O. 1998. *Cicero's correspondence: a literary study*. Oxford.

Huzar, E. G. 1978. *Mark Antony: a biography*. Minneapolis.

Itgenshorst, T. 2004. "Augustus und der republikanische Triumph." *Hermes* 132, 436–57.

——— 2005. *Tota illa pompa: der Triumph in der römischen Republik*. Göttingen.

Jacquot, J., ed. 1956–75. *Les fêtes de la Renaissance*. Paris.

Janne, H. "L'*Amphitryon* de Plaute et M. Fulvius Nobilior." *RBPh* 34, 515–31.

Jannot, J. R. 1984. *Les reliefs archaïques de Chiusi*. Rome.

Jost, M. 1994. "The distribution of sanctuaries in civic space in Arkadia," in S. E. Alcock and R. Osborne, eds. *Placing the gods: sanctuaries and sacred space in ancient Greece*. Oxford. 217–30.

Jullian, C. 1883. "Processus consularis." *RPh*. 7. 145–63.

Kampen, N. B. 1991. "Between public and private: women as historical subjects in Roman art," in S. B. Pomeroy, ed., *Women's history and ancient history.* Chapel Hill and London. 218–48.

Kelly, C. 2006. *The Roman empire: a very short introduction.* Oxford.

Kidd, I. G. 1988. *Posidonius II. The Commentary: i Testimonia and Fragments 1– 149.* Cambridge.

Kierdorf, W. 1986. "Apotheose und postumer Triumph Trajans." *Tyche* 1, 147–56.

Kimpel, H., and J. Werckmeister, eds. 2001. *Triumphzüge: Paraden durch Raum und Zeit.* Marburg.

Kingsley, S. 2006. *God's gold: the quest for the lost temple treasure of Jerusalem.* London.

Klar, L. S. 2006. "The origins of the Roman *scaenae frons* and the architecture of triumphal games in the second century BC," in Dillon and Welch. 2006. 162–83.

Klein, J. 1889. "Die kleineren inschriftlichen Denkmäler des Bonner Provinzialmuseum." *Jahrbücher des Vereins von Alterthumsfreunden in Rheinlande. BJ* 87, 60–86.

Kleiner, D. E. E. 1983. *The monument of Philopappos in Athens.* Rome.

Kleiner, F. S. 1985. *The arch of Nero in Rome: a study of the Roman honorary arch before and under Nero.* Rome.

———— 1989. "The study of Roman triumphal and honorary arches 50 years after Kähler." *JRA* 2, 195–206.

Kleiner, F. S., and S. P. Noe. 1977. *The early cistophoric coinage.* New York.

Köhler, J. 1995. "Zur Triumphalsymbolik auf dem Feldherrnsarkophag Belvedere." *MDAI(R)* 102, 371–9.

Köves-Zulauf, T. 1972. *Reden und Schweigen: römische Religion bei Plinius Maior.* Munich.

Künzl, E. 1988. *Der römische Triumph: Siegesfeiern im antiken Rom.* Munich.

Kurke, L. 1991. *The traffic in praise: Pindar and the poetics of social economy.* Ithaca.

Kuttner, A. L. 1995. *Dynasty and empire in the age of Augustus: the case of the Boscoreale cups.* Berkeley.

———— 1999. "Culture and history at Pompey's Museum." *TAPhA* 129, 343–73.

Lacey, W. K. 1961. "The tribunate of Curio." *Historia* 10, 318–29.

Lankheit, K. 1984. *Karl von Piloty, Thusnelda im Triumphzug des Germanicus.* Bayerische Staatsgemäldesammlungen Künstler und Werke 8. Munich.

Laqueur, R. 1909. "Über das Wesen des römischen Triumphs." *Hermes* 44, 215– 36.

La Rocca, E. 1986. *Rilievi storici capitolini: il restauro dei pannelli di Adriano e di Marco Aurelio nel Palazzo dei Conservatori.* Exhibition catalogue. Rome.

———— 1995. "Il programma figurativo del foro di Augusto," in E. La Rocca et al., eds. *I luoghi del consenso imperiale: il foro di Augusto; il foro di Traiano*. Rome. 74–87.

Lebek, W. D. 1987. "Die drei Ehrenbogen für Germanicus." *ZPE* 67, 129–48.

———— 1991. "Ehrenbögen und Prinzentod." *ZPE* 86, 47–78.

Lemosse, M. 1972. "Les éléments techniques de l'ancien triumphe romain et le problème de son origine." *ANRW* I, 2. Berlin and New York. 442–53.

Le Roy Ladurie, E. 1979. *Carnival in Romans: a people's uprising at Romans 1579–80*. Harmondsworth.

Levick, B. 1976. *Tiberius the politician*. London.

Linderski, J. 1990. "The auspices and struggle of the orders," in W. Eder, ed. *Staat und Staatlichkeit in der frühen römischen Republik*. Stuttgart. 34–48. Repr. in *Roman questions: selected papers*. Stuttgart, 1995. 560–74.

Ling, R. 1991. *Roman painting*. Cambridge.

Luce, T. J. 1965. "The dating of Livy's first decade." *TAPhA* 96, 209–40.

Lyngby, H. 1954. *Beiträge zur Topographie des Forum-Boarium-Gebietes in Rom*. Lund.

MacCormack, S. G. 1981. *Art and ceremony in late antiquity*. Berkeley.

MacMullen, R. 1991. "Hellenizing the Romans (2nd century B.C.)." *Historia* 40, 419–38.

Madonna, M. L. 1980. "L'ingresso di Carlo V a Roma," in M. Fagiolo, ed. *La città effimera e l'universo artificiale del giardino: la Firenze dei Medici e l'Italia del '500*. Rome. 63–8.

Maitland, A. 2006. *Wilfred Thesiger: the life of the great explorer*. London.

Makin, E. 1921. "The triumphal route, with particular reference to the Flavian triumph." *JRS* 11, 25–36.

Malamud, M. Forthcoming. *New Romes for a new world: ancient Rome and imperial America*.

Marquardt, J. 1884. *Römische Staatsverwaltung* II. 2nd ed. Leipzig.

Marshall, A. J. 1966. "Governors on the move." *Phoenix* 20, 231–46.

Martin, H. G. 1987. *Römische Tempelkultbilder: eine archäologische Untersuchung zur späten Republik*. Rome.

Martin, R. H., and A. J. Woodman. 1989, eds. *Tacitus, Annals Book IV*. Cambridge.

Martindale, A. 1979. *The triumphs of Caesar by Andrea Mantegna in the collection of Her Majesty the Queen at Hampton Court*. London.

Mattingly, H. 1936–7. "The tale of a triumph." *GandR* 6, 94–102.

———— 1963. "Notes on late republican coinage." *NC,* 7th series, 3, 51–4.

Matz, F. 1968. *Die dionysischen Sarcophage II*. Berlin.

Maxfield, V. A. 1981. *The military decorations of the Roman army.* London.

Mayor, J. E. B. 1881. *Thirteen satires of Juvenal,* 2. 3rd ed. London.

McClellan, A. 1994. *Inventing the Louvre: art, politics, and the origins of the modern museum in eighteenth-century Paris.* Cambridge.

McCormick, M. 1986. *Eternal Victory: triumphal rulership in late antiquity, Byzantium, and the early medieval West.* Cambridge.

McCuaig, W. 1991. "The Fasti Capitolini and the study of Roman chronology in the sixteenth century." *Athenaeum* 79, 141–59.

McDonnell, M. 2006. "Roman aesthetics and the spoils of Syracuse," in Dillon and Welch. 68–90.

McGowan, M. M. 1973. *L'entrée de Henri II à Rouen 1550.* Facsimile and Introduction. Amsterdam.

——— 2000. *The vision of Rome in late Renaissance France.* New Haven and London.

——— 2002. "The Renaissance triumph," in J. R. Mulryne and E. Goldring, eds. *Court festivals of the European Renaissance: art, politics and performance.* Aldershot. 26–47.

McKeown, J. C. 1987–. *Ovid, Amores: text, prolegomena and commentary.* Liverpool and Leeds.

Merten, E. W. 1968. *Zwei Herrscherfeste in der Historia Augusta: Untersuchungen zu den pompae der Kaiser Gallienus und Aurelianus.* Bonn.

Meslin, M. C. 1970. *La fête des kalendes de janvier dans l'empire romain. Étude d'un rituel de nouvel an.* Brussels.

Millar, F. 2005. "Last year in Jerusalem: monuments of the Jewish War in Rome," in J. Edmondson, S. Mason, and J. Rives, eds., *Flavius Josephus and Flavian Rome.* Oxford. 101–28.

Miller, A. 2001. *Roman triumphs and early modern English culture.* Basingstoke and New York.

Miller, J. F. 1995. "Reading Cupid's triumph." *CJ* 90, 287–94.

——— 2000. "Triumphus in Palatio." *AJPh* 121, 409–22.

Mitchell, T. N. 1991. *Cicero: the senior statesman.* New Haven and London.

Mommsen, T. 1859. "Die *ludi magni* und *Romani.*" *RhM* 14, 79–87. Repr. in *Römische Forschungen* 2. 1879. Berlin. 42–57.

——— 1887. *Römisches Staatsrecht.* 3rd ed. Leipzig.

Moretti, L. 1925. "Urbisaglia—frammento di una redazione locale di Fasti Triumphales Populi Romani." *NSA,* 114–27.

Morford, M. P. O. 1985. "Nero's patronage and participation in literature and the arts." *ANRW* II, 32, 3. Berlin and New York. 2003–31.

Morgan, M. G. 1973. "Villa Publica and Magna Mater." *Klio* 55, 215–45.

Morpurgo, L. 1908. "La porta trionfale e la via dei trionfi." *BCAR* 36, 109–50.

Muir, E. 1981. *Civic ritual in Renaissance Venice.* Princeton.

Mulryne, J. R., H. Watanabe-O'Kelly, and M. Shewring, eds. 2004. *Europa triumphans: court and civic festivals in early modern Europe.* Aldershot.

Murison, C. L. 1999. *Rebellion and reconstruction: Galba to Domitian: an historical commentary on Cassius Dio's Roman History book 64–67 (AD 68–96).* Atlanta.

Murphy, T. M. 2004. *Pliny the Elder's Natural History: the empire in the encyclopaedia.* Oxford.

Murray, W. M. 2004. "Birthplace of empire: the legacy of Actium." *Amphora* 3, 2, 8–16.

Murray, W. M., and P. M. Petsas. 1989. *Octavian's campsite memorial for the Actian War.* Philadelphia. *TAPhS* 79, 4.

Musso, L. 1987. "Rilievo con pompa trionfale di Traiano al museo di Palestrina." *Bollettino d'Arte* 72, n. 46, 1–46.

Nedergaard, E. 1994–5. "La collocazione originaria dei *Fasti Capitolini* e gli archi di Augusto nel Foro Romano." *BCAR* 96, 33–70.

Nibby. 1821. *Le mura di Roma.* Rome.

Nicolet, C. 1980. *The world of the citizen in republican Rome.* Berkeley.

———— 1991. *Space, geography, and politics in the early Roman empire.* Ann Arbor.

Nisbet, R. G. M. N., ed. 1961. *M. Tulli Ciceronis, in L. Calpurnium Pisonem Oratio.* Oxford.

Nisbet, R. G. M. N., and M. Hubbard, eds. 1970. *A Commentary on Horace, Odes Book I.* Oxford.

Nisbet, R. G. M. N., and N. Rudd, eds. 2004. *A commentary on Horace, Odes, Book III.* Oxford.

Nixon, C. E. V. 1981. "The panegyric of 307 and Maximian's visits to Rome." *Phoenix* 35, 70–6.

Nixon, C. E. V., and B. S. Rodgers. 1994. *In praise of later Roman emperors: the Panegyrici Latini: introduction, translation and historical commentary.* Berkeley.

Nock, A. D. 1928. "Notes on ruler cult I–IV." *JHS* 48, 21–43. reprinted in Z. Stewart, ed. *Essays on religion and the ancient world.* 1972. Oxford. 134–44.

North, J. A. 1975. "Praesens Divus." *JRS* 65, 170–77.

———— 1976. "Conservatism and change in Roman religion." *PBSR* 44, 1–12.

Oakley, S. P. 1985. "Single combat in the Roman republic." *CQ* n.s. 35, 392–410.

——— 1997. *A commentary on Livy Books VI–X,* Vol. 1: Introduction and Book VI. Oxford.

——— 1998. *A commentary on Livy Books VI–X,* Vol. 2: Books VII and VIII. Oxford.

——— 2005a. *A commentary on Livy Books VI–X,* Vol. 3, Book IX. Oxford.

——— 2005b. *A commentary on Livy Books VI–X,* Vol. 4: Book X. Oxford.

Ogilvie, R. M. 1965. *A Commentary on Livy Books 1–5.* Oxford.

Oliensis, E. 2004. "The power of image-makers: representation and revenge in Ovid *Metamorphoses* 6 and *Tristia* 4." *ClAnt* 23, 285–321.

O'Neill, P. 2003a. "Triumph songs, reversal and Plautus' *Amphitruo.*" *Ramus* 32, 1–38.

——— 2003b. "Going round in circles: popular speech in ancient Rome." *ClAnt* 22, 135–65.

Orlin, E. 1996. *Temples, religion, and politics in the Roman Republic. Mnemosyne* Supplement, 164. Leiden.

Östenberg, I. 1999. "Demonstrating the conquest of the world: the procession of peoples and rivers on the shield of Aeneas and the triple triumph of Octavian in 29 B.C. (*Aen.* 8, 722–728)." *ORom* 24, 155–62.

——— 2003. *Staging the world: Rome and the other in the triumphal procession.* Diss. Lund; rev. ed. Oxford, forthcoming.

Pais, E. 1920. *Fasti Triumphales Populi Romani.* Rome.

Palmer, R. E. A. 1990. *Studies of the northern Campus Martius in ancient Rome.* Philadelphia. *TAPhS* 80, 2.

Panvinio, O. 1558. *Fastorum libri V a Romulo rege usque ad Imp. Caesarem Carolum V Austrium Augustum.* Venice.

Pape, M. 1975. *Griechische Kunstwerke aus Kriegsbeute und ihre öffentliche Aufstellung in Rom.* Hamburg.

Paschoud, F. 1996. *Histoire Auguste, vies d'Aurélien, Tacite.* Paris.

Payne, R. 1962. *The Roman triumph.* London.

Pecht, F. 1873. *Kunst und Kunstindustrie auf der Wiener Weltausstellung.* Stuttgart.

Pelling, C. 1988. *Plutarch, Life of Antony.* Cambridge.

Perosa, A., and J. Sparrow. 1979. *Renaissance Latin verse: an anthology.* London.

Peter, H. 1865. *Die Quellen Plutarchs in den Biographieen der Römer.* Halle. Repr. Amsterdam. 1965.

Petrucci, A. 1996. *Il trionfo nella storia costituzionale romana dagli inizi della Repubblica ad Augusto.* Milan.

Pfanner, M. 1980. "Codex Coburgensis Nr 88: die Entdeckung der Porta Triumphalis." *MDAI(R)* 87, 327–34.

——— 1983. *Der Titusbogen*. Mainz.

Phillips, J. E. 1974. "Form and language in Livy's triumph notices." *CPh* 69, 265–73.

Picard, G.-C. 1957. *Les trophées romains: contribution à l'histoire de la religion et de l'art triomphal de Rome*. Paris.

Piganiol, A. 1923. *Recherches sur les jeux romains*. Strasbourg and Paris.

Pinelli, A. 1985. "Feste e trionfi: continuità e metamorfosi di un tema," in S. Settis, ed. *Memoria dell'antico nell'arte italiana* 2. Turin. 279–350.

Poduska, D. M. 1970. "*Ope barbarica* or *bellum civile?*" *CB* 46, 33–4 and 46.

Polignac, F. de. 1995. *Cults, territory and the origins of the Greek city-state*. Cambridge.

Pollitt, J. J. 1978. "The impact of Greek art on Rome." *TAPhA* 108, 155–74.

——— 1983. *The art of Rome c753 BC–AD 337: sources and documents*. Cambridge.

Price, S. R. F. 1984. *Rituals and power: the Roman imperial cult in Asia Minor*. Cambridge.

Purcell, N. 1994. "The city of Rome and the *plebs urbana* in the late Republic" in J. A. Crook, A. Lintott, and E. D. Rawson, eds. *The Cambridge ancient history* IX. 2nd ed. Cambridge. 644–88.

Putnam, M. C. J. 1973. "Horace C. 3. 30: the lyricist as hero." *Ramus* 2, 1–19.

Rawson, E. 1971. "Prodigy lists and the use of the *Annales Maximi*." *CQ* n.s. 21, 158–69. Repr. in Rawson. 1991. 1–15.

——— 1975a. "Caesar's heritage: Hellenistic kings and their Roman equals." *JRS* 65, 148–59. Repr. in Rawson. 1991. 169–88.

——— 1975b. *Cicero: a portrait*. London.

——— 1990. "The antiquarian tradition: spoils and representations of foreign armour," in *Staat und Staatlichkeit in der frühen römischen Republik*. Stuttgart. 157–73. Repr. in Rawson. 1991. 582–98.

——— 1991. *Roman culture and society: collected papers*. Oxford.

Reid, J. S. 1912. "Human sacrifices at Rome and other notes on Roman religion." *JRS* 2, 34–52.

——— 1916. "Roman ideas of deity." *JRS* 6, 170–84.

Reinhold, M. 1988. *From republic to principate: an historical commentary on Cassius Dio's Roman History books 49–52 (36–29 BC)*. Atlanta.

Reland, A. 1716. *De spoliis templi Hierosolymitani in arcu Titiano, Romae conspicuis liber*. Utrecht.

Rice, E. E. 1983. *The grand procession of Ptolemy Philadelphus*. Oxford.

Rich, J. 1990. *Cassius Dio: the Augustan settlement (Roman History 53–55, 9)*. Warminster.

———— 1996. "Augustus and the *spolia opima.*" *Chiron* 26, 85–127.

———— 1998. "Augustus's Parthian honours, the temple of Mars Ultor and the arch in the Forum Romanum." *PBSR* 66, 71–128.

———— 1999. "Drusus and the *spolia opima.*" *CQ* n.s. 49, 544–55.

Rich, J., and G. Shipley, eds. 1993. *War and society in the Roman world.* London.

Richard, J.-C. 1966. "Les funérailles de Trajan et le triomphe sur les Parthes." *REL* 44, 351–62.

———— 1978. "Recherches sur certains aspects du culte impérial: les funérailles des empereurs Romains aux deux premiers siècles de notre ère." *ANRW* II, 16, 2, 1121–34.

———— 1994. "À propos du premier triomphe de Publicola." *MEFRA* 106, 403–22.

Richardson, J. S. 1975. "The triumph, the praetors and the senate in the early second century BC." *JRS* 65, 50–63.

———— 1983. "The triumph of Metellus Scipio and the dramatic date of Varro RR 3." *CQ* n.s. 33, 456–63.

———— 1991. "*Imperium Romanum:* empire and the language of power." *JRS* 81, 1–9.

Richardson, L., Jr. 1987. "A note on the architecture of the *Theatrum Pompei* in Rome." *AJA* 91, 123–6.

Richlin, A. 1983. *The garden of Priapus: sexuality and aggression in Roman humor.* New Haven and London.

Ridley, R. T. 1983. "*Falsi triumphi, plures consulatus.*" *Latomus* 42, 372–82.

Rivière, Y. 2004. *Le cachot et les fers: détention et coercition à Rome.* Paris.

Rodenwaldt, G. 1940. "Römische Reliefs, Vorstufen zur Spätantike." *JDAI* 55, 12–43.

Rodríguez Almeida, E. 1982. *Forma urbis marmorea: aggiornamento generale 1980.* Rome.

Ronke, J. 1987. *Magistratische Repräsentation im römischen Relief.* BAR International series. Oxford.

Rose, C. B. 2005. "The Parthians in Augustan Rome." *AJA* 109, 21–75.

Rose, H. J. 1948. *Ancient Roman religion.* London.

———— 1958. "The dream of Pompey." *AClass* 1, 80–84.

Rosenstein, N. 1990. *Imperatores victi: military defeat and aristocratic competition in the middle and late Republic.* Berkeley.

Rotili, M. 1972. *L'arco di Traiano a Benevento.* Rome.

Rüpke, J. 1990. *Domi Militiae: die religiöse Konstruktion des Krieges in Rom.* Stuttgart.

———— 2006. "Triumphator and ancestor rituals: between symbolic anthropology and magic." *Numen* 53, 251–89.

Ryberg, I. S. 1955. *Rites of the state religion in Roman art, MAAR* 22.

———— 1967. *Panel reliefs of Marcus Aurelius.* Archaeological Institute of America. New York.

Sartain, J. 1885. *On the antique painting in encaustic of Cleopatra, discovered in 1818.* Philadelphia. Available at http:// penelope.uchicago.edu/oddnotes/cleoinencaustic/cleopatraencaustic.html.

Sauron, G. 1987. "Le complexe pompéien du Champ de Mars: nouveauté urbanistique à finalité idéologique," in *L'urbs: espace urbain et historique. Ier siècle av. J.-C.—IIIe siècle ap. J.-C.* Rome. 457–73.

———— 1994. *Quis Deum? L'expression plastique des idéologies politiques et religieuses à Rome à la fin de la République et au début du Principat.* Rome.

Schäfer, T. 1989. *Imperii Insignia: Sella Curulis und Fasces. Zur Repräsentation römischer Magistrate.* Mainz.

Scheid, J. 1986. "Le flamine de Jupiter, les Vestales et le général triomphant: variations romaines sur le thème de la figuration des dieux," in C. Malamud and J.-P. Vernant, eds. *Corps des dieux (Le temps de la réflexion 7).* Paris.

———— 1988. "La spartizione sacrificiale a Roma," in C. Grottanelli and N. F. Parise, eds. *Sacrificio e società nel mondo antico.* Bari. 267–92.

———— 1990. *Romulus et ses frères: le college des frères arvales, modèle du culte public dans la Rome des empereurs.* Paris.

———— 1998. *Commentarii fratrum arvalium qui supersunt.* Rome.

Scheidel, W. 1996. "Finances, figures and fiction." *CQ* n.s. 46, 222–38.

Schmidt, T. E. 1995. "Mark 15, 16–32: the crucifixion narrative and the Roman triumphal procession." *NTS* 41, 1–18.

Schneider, L. 1973. "Donatello's bronze David." *Art Bulletin* 55, 213–6.

Schneider, R. M. 1990. "Augustus und der frühe römische Triumph." *JDAI,* 105, 167–205.

Schöffel, C. 2002. *Martial, Buch 8: Einleitung, Text, Übersetzung, Kommentar.* Stuttgart.

Schollmeyer, P. 2001. *Antike Gespanndenkmäler.* Antiquitates 13. Hamburg.

Schumacher, L. 1985. "Die imperatorischen Akklamationen der Triumvirn und die *auspicia* des Augustus." *Historia* 34, 191–222.

Seager, R. 2002. *Pompey the great: a political biography.* Rev. ed. Oxford.

———— 2005. *Tiberius.* Rev. ed. Oxford.

Sehlmeyer, M. 1999. *Stadtrömische Ehrenstatuen der republikanischen Zeit:*

Historizität und Kontext von Symbolen nobilitären Standesbewusstseins. Stuttgart.

Shackleton Bailey, D. R., ed. 1977. *Cicero: epistulae ad familiares,* Vol. 1. Cambridge.

Shatzman, I. 1972. "The Roman general's authority over booty." *Historia* 21, 177–205.

Simpson, C. J. 1993. "The original site of the *Fasti Capitolini.*" *Historia* 42, 61–81.

Sino, R. H. 1994. "Godlike men: a discussion of the Murlo procession frieze," in R. D. de Puma and J. P. Small, *Murlo and the Etruscans: art and society in ancient Etruria.* Madison. 100–17.

Sjöqvist, E. 1946. "Studi intorno alla Piazza del Collegio Romano." *Oarch* 4, 47–155.

Skutsch, O. 1985. *The Annals of Quintus Ennius.* Oxford.

Smith, R. R. R. 1981. "Greeks, foreigners and Roman Republican portraits." *JRS* 71, 24–38.

——— 1998. "Cultural choice and political identity in honorific portrait statues in the Greek east in the second century AD." *JRS* 88, 56–93.

Spannagel, M. 1999. *Exemplaria principis: Untersuchungen zu Entstehung und Ausstattung des Augustusforums.* Heidelberg.

Sperling, C. M. 1992. "Donatello's bronze 'David' and the demands of Medici politics." *Burlington Magazine,* 218–24.

Stenhouse, W. 2005. *Reading inscriptions and writing ancient history: historical scholarship in the late Renaissance.* London.

Stern, H. 1953. *Le calendrier de 354: étude sur son texte et ses illustrations.* Paris.

Stewart, A. 1993. *Faces of power: Alexander's image and Hellenistic politics.* Berkeley.

Straub, J. 1955. "Konstantins Verzicht auf den Gang zum Kapitol." *Historia* 4, 297–313.

Strocka, V. M. 1972. "Beobachtungen an den Attikareliefs des severischen Quadrifrons von Lepcis Magna." *AntAfr.* 6, 147–72.

Strong, E. (Mrs. A. S.). 1915. *Apotheosis and after life.* London.

Stuart Jones, H. 1926. *A catalogue of the ancient sculptures preserved in the municipal collections of Rome: Palazzo dei Conservatori.* Oxford.

Suerbaum, W. 1972. "Ennius bei Petrarca. Betrachtungen zu literarischen Ennius-Bildern," in O. Skutsch, ed. *Ennius.* Entret. Fondation Hardt 17, Geneva. 293–352.

Sumi, G. S. 2002. "Spectacles and Sulla's public image." *Historia* 51, 414–32.

——— 2005. *Ceremony and power: performing politics in Rome between republic and empire.* Ann Arbor.

Swan, P. M. 2004. *The Augustan succession: an historical commentary on Cassius Dio's Roman History, Books 55–56 (9 BC–AD 14)*. Oxford and New York.

Syme, R. 1939. *The Roman revolution*. Oxford.

——— 1979. "Some imperatorial salutations." *Phoenix* 33, 308–29. Repr. in A. R. Birley, ed. *Roman Papers* 4. 1894. Oxford. 1198–1219.

Taisne, A. M. 1973. "Le thème du triomphe dans la poésie et l'art sous les Flaviens." *Latomus* 32, 485–504.

Taylor, L. R. 1936. "M. Titius and the Syrian command." *JRS* 26, 161–73.

——— 1946. "The date of the Capitoline *Fasti*." *CPh.* 41, 1–11.

——— 1950. "Degrassi's edition of the consular and triumphal Fasti." *CPh* 45, 84–95.

——— 1951. "New indications of Augustan editing in the Capitoline *Fasti*." *CPh.* 46, 73–80.

Thesiger, W. 1987. *The life of my choice*. London.

Thompson, D. J. 2000. "Philadephus' procession: dynastic power in a Mediterranean context," in L. Mooren, ed. *Politics, administration and society in the Hellenistic and Roman world*. Leuven. 365–88.

Thuillier, J.-P. 1975. "Denys d'Halicarnasse et les jeux Romains. *Antiquités Romaines*," VII, 72–3. *MEFRA* 87, 563–81.

Timpe, D. 1968. *Der Triumph des Germanicus*. Bonn.

Toll, K. 1997. "Making Roman-ness and the *Aeneid*." *ClAnt.* 16, 34–56.

Torelli, M. 1989. "Topografia sacra di una città latina—Praeneste," in *Urbanistica ed Architettura dell'Antica Praeneste*. Atti del Convegno di Studi Archeologici, Palestrina 17/17 Aprile 1988, Palestrina. 15–30.

Trunk, M. 2002. *Die "Casa de Pilatos" in Sevilla. Madrider Beiträge* 28. Mainz.

Tufi, S. R. 2002. "Foro di Augusto in Roma: qualche riflessione." *Ostraka* 11, 177–93.

Tyrrell, R. Y., and L. C. Purser, eds. 1914. *The correspondence of Cicero*, Vol. III. 2nd ed. Dublin.

Ungaro, L., and M. Milella, eds. 1995. *The places of imperial consensus: the Forum of Augustus and the Forum of Trajan*. Exhibition catalogue. Rome.

Valentini, R., and G. Zucchetti. 1940. *Codice topografico della città di Roma* I. Rome.

Versnel, H. S. 1970. *Triumphus: an inquiry into the origin, development and meaning of the Roman triumph*. Leiden.

——— 2006. "Red herring? Comments on a new theory concerning the origin of the triumph." *Numen* 53, 290–326.

Vervaet, F. J. 2007. "The principle of the *summum imperium auspiciumque* under the Roman Republic." *SDHI* 73, 1–148.

——— forthcoming. "Varro, Augustus and the Spolia opima."

Vogel-Weidemann, U. 1985. "The dedicatory inscription of Pompeius Magnus in Diodorus 40.4. Some remarks on an unpublished manuscript by Hans Schaefer." *AClass* 28, 57–75.

Wagenvoort, H. 1947. *Roman dynamism*. Oxford.

Walde, C. 2001. *Die Traumdarstellungen in der griechisch-römischen Dichtung*. Munich.

Wallace-Hadrill, A. 1990. "Roman arches and Greek honours: the language of power at Rome." *PCPhS* n.s. 36, 143–81.

Wallisch, E. 1954–55. "Name und Herkunft des römischen Triumphes." *Philologus* 98, 245–58.

Warde Fowler, W. 1911. *The religious experience of the Roman people, from the earliest times to the age of Augustus*. London.

——— 1916. "Iuppiter and the triumphator." *CR* 30, 153–7.

——— 1920. *Roman essays and interpretations*. Oxford.

Watanabe-O'Kelly, H. 2002. "Early modern European festivals—politics and performance, event and record," in J. R. Mulryne and E. Goldring, eds. *Court festivals of the European Renaissance: art, politics and performance*. Aldershot. 15–25.

Waters, K. H. 1964. "The character of Domitian." *Phoenix* 18, 49–77.

Weinstock, S. 1957. "The image and chair of Germanicus." *JRS* 47. 144–54.

——— 1971. *Divus Julius*. Oxford.

Whitehorne, J. E. G. 1994. *Cleopatras*. London.

Whitmarsh, T. 2001. *Greek literature and the Roman empire: the politics of imitation*. Oxford.

Wilkins, E. H. 1962. *The triumphs of Petrarch*. Chicago.

Wiseman, T. P. 1987. "*Conspicui postes tectaque digna deo:* the public image of aristocratic and imperial houses in the late republic and early empire," in *L'urbs: espace urbain et histoire. Ier siècle av. J.-C.–IIIe siècle ap. J.-C.* Actes du Colloque International Organisé par le Centre National de la Recherche Scientifique et L'Ecole Francaise de Rome. Rome. 393–413.

——— 1995. *Remus: a Roman myth*. Cambridge.

——— forthcoming. "Three notes on the triumphal route," in A. Leone et al., eds. *Res Bene Gestae. Ricerche di storia urbana su Roma antica in onore di Eva Margareta Steinby*. Rome.

Wissowa, G. 1912. *Religion und Kultus der Römer*. 2nd ed. Munich.

Wistrand, M. 1979. *Cicero imperator: studies in Cicero's correspondence 51–47 BC*. Göteburg.

Woodman, T. = A. J. 1974. "*Exegi monumentum:* Horace, *Odes* 3. 30," in T.

Woodman and D. West, *Quality and pleasure in Latin poetry.* Cambridge. 115–28.

Woodman, A. J. 1983. *Velleius Paterculus: the Caesarian and Augustan narrative.* Cambridge.

Wrede, H. 1981. "Scribae." *Boreas* 4, 106–16.

Wyke, M. 2002. *The Roman mistress: ancient and modern representations.* Oxford.

Yarden, L. 1991. *The spoils of Jerusalem on the Arch of Titus.* Stockholm.

Yarrow, L. 2006. "Lucius Mummius and the spoils of Corinth." *SCI* 25, 57–70.

Zanker, P. 1968. *Forum Augustum.* Tübingen.

Ziolkowski, A. 1993. "*Urbs direpta,* or how the Romans sacked cities," in Rich and Shipley. 69–91.

Acknowledgments

A book long in the making incurs many debts. I am extremely grateful that John North, my fellow explorer of Roman religion over the last thirty years, was able to read—and improve—the whole in typescript. Others commented, critically and generously, on large or small chunks: Clifford Ando, Corey Brennan, Christopher Kelly, and Joyce Reynolds. Across the years I have been advised, helped, reassured, and informed on triumphal matters large and small by Peter Carson, Robin Cormack, Lindsay Duguid, Miriam Griffin, John Henderson, Richard Hewlings, the late Keith Hopkins, Tom Laqueur, Paul Millett, Helen Morales, Stephen Oakley, Ida Östenberg, Clare Pettitt, Michael Reeve, Frederik Vervaet, Terry Volk, Andrew Wallace-Hadrill—and many audiences on whom I have inflicted my triumphal concerns. Emma Buckley was a tower of strength as a research assistant in the final stages. Other students and friends who helped out then include Nick Dodd, Suzy Jones, Kristina Meinking, Marden Nichols, and Libby Wilson. It has once again been a pleasure to work with Harvard University Press. My thanks go especially to Susan Wallace Boehmer, David Foss, Gwen Frankfeldt, Margaretta Fulton, Mary Kate Maco, Alex Morgan, Sharmila Sen, William Sisler, and Ian Stevenson—as well as to the astute referees for the Press, whose comments were enormously helpful on the very last lap and on more than one point saved me from myself.

This project was made possible thanks to the award of a Senior Research Fellowship by the Leverhulme Trust (a brave and generous charitable institution to which I have several times been indebted). As ever, I have been supported in more ways than I can count by the Faculty of Classics in Cambridge and by Newnham College; I cannot think of better places to spend a working life. The later chapters were drafted while enjoying the splendid hospitality and research facilities of the Getty Research Institute in Los Angeles. My own research on the triumph began with an essay, "The Triumph of the Absurd," in C. Edwards and G. Woolf, eds., *Rome the Cosmopolis* (Cambridge: Cambridge University Press, 2003); some of that material is reworked here.

Illustration Credits

FRONTISPIECE (caption on p. iv): G. B. Tiepolo, *The Triumph of Marius*, 1729. 5558.8 x 326.7 cm. The Metropolitan Museum of Art, Rogers Fund, 1965 (65.183.1) Image © The Metropolitan Museum of Art.

FIGURE 1: Boris Drucker, *So far so good. Let's hope we win.* © The New Yorker Collection 1988 Boris Drucker from cartoonbank.com. All Rights Reserved.

FIGURE 2: Bronze vessel (krater), late second–early first century BCE, inscribed as a gift of Mithradates VI Eupator (reigned 120–63 BCE). Handles and foot restored. 70 cm. Rome: Musei Capitolini, Inv. MC 1068.

FIGURE 3: *Aureus*, minted at Rome c80, 71 or 61 BCE. *RRC* 402. 1b. © Copyright the Trustees of the British Museum.

FIGURE 4: Reverse types of *denarii*, minted at Rome, 56 BCE. *RRC* 426, 3 and 4b. © Copyright the Trustees of the British Museum.

FIGURE 5: Three-dimensional reconstruction of the Theatre of Pompey (based on the 1851 study by Luigi Canina), created by Martin Blazeby, King's College, University of London. Courtesy of Richard Beacham.

FIGURE 6: Colossal male statue ("Palazzo Spada Pompey"). First century BCE–first century CE; head modern. 345 cm. Salone del trono, Palazzo Spada, Rome. Alinari / Art Resource, NY.

FIGURE 7: C'est la deduction du sumpteux order plaisantz spectacles et magnifiques theatres dresses . . . par les citoiens de Rouen . . . a la sacrée maieste du tres christian roy de France, Henry seco[n]d . . . (Rouen, 1551), F, 2r. Courtesy Houghton Library, Harvard University.

FIGURE 8: Passage relief from Arch of Titus, Rome ("Triumph of Titus"), early 80s CE. 202 x 392 cm. Scala / Art Resource, NY.

FIGURE 9: Passage relief from Arch of Titus, Rome ("Spoils relief"), early 80s CE. 202 x 392 cm. Werner Forman / Art Resource, NY.

FIGURE 10: Arch of Trajan at Beneventum (Benevento), 114–118 CE. Scala / Art Resource, NY.

FIGURE 11: Silver cup from Boscoreale ("Tiberius cup"), c. 7 BCE or later. Height, 10 cm. Musée du Louvre, Paris, Inv. BJ 2367. Réunion des Musées Nationaux / Art Resource, NY.

FIGURE 12: "The Triumph of Love," engraving from a design by M. van Heemskerck, 1565. 19.2 x 26.4 cm. Rijksmuseum, Amsterdam, RP-P-1891-A-16463.

FIGURE 13: From O. Panvinio, *Amplissimi ornatissimiq triumphi* (Rome, 1618; copy of earlier edition, Antwerp, c. 1560); engravings after M. van Heemskerck. Courtesy Houghton Library, Harvard University.

FIGURE 14: Sala della Lupa, Palazzo dei Conservatori, Musei Capitolini, Rome. Werner Forman / Art Resource, NY.

FIGURE 15: C. Huelsen, reconstruction of the Regia (showing the placement of the *Fasti Capitolini*), CIL I, 1, 2nd ed., pl. 16 (from Degrassi, *Inscr. It,* XIII, 1, pl. IV). Courtesy of the Istituto Poligrafico e Zecca dello Stato, Rome.

FIGURE 16: A. Degrassi and G. Gatti, reconstruction of the Augustan Arch commemorating the battle of Actium, late first century BCE (showing the placement of the *Fasti Capitolini*), RPAA 21, 1945–46, 93, Fig. 11 (from Degrassi, *Inscr. It.* XIII, 1, pl. IX). Courtesy of the Istituto Poligrafico e Zecca dello Stato, Rome.

FIGURE 17: Relief showing the triumph of Trajan. Early second century CE. 169 x 117 cm. Museo Prenestino Barberiano, Palestrina. Inv. 6520. Alinari / Art Resource, NY.

FIGURE 18: Reverse of *aureus*, minted in Spain 17–16 BCE. *BMCRE* I, Augustus no. 432. © Copyright the Trustees of the British Museum.

FIGURE 19: Reverse of *denarius*, minted at Rome, 101 BCE. *RRC* 326, 1. © Copyright the Trustees of the British Museum.

FIGURE 20: K. T. von Piloty, *Thusnelda in the Triumphal Procession of Germanicus*. 1873. Oil on canvas. 490 x 710 cm. Neue Pinakothek, Munich, Inv. WAF 771. Foto Marburg / Art Resource, NY.

FIGURE 21: M. Pfanner, *Der Titusbogen* (Mainz: Verlang Philipp von Zabern, 1983), supplementary ill. 3. Drawing courtesy of M. Pfanner.

FIGURE 22: Detail from small frieze of the Arch of Trajan at Beneventum. Alinari / Art Resource, NY.

FIGURE 23: Detail from fragmentary frieze of the Temple of Apollo Sosianus, Rome. 34–25 BCE. Height, 86 cm. Musei Capitolini, Rome, Inv. 2776.

FIGURE 24: Campana plaque, showing prisoners in a triumph. Early second century CE. 32.5 x 39 cm. British Museum, London, GR 1805.7-3.342, Terracotta D625 (Townley collection). HIP / Art Resource, NY.

FIGURE 25: "Sleeping Ariadne." Roman version of Greek original, third–second century BCE. Length, 195 cm. Pio Clementino, Vatican Museums. Inv. 548. Scala / Art Resource, NY.

FIGURE 26: Fragmentary relief, showing "prisoners" and trophy, late second century CE. 114 x 103 cm. Museo Nazionale Romano (Terme di Diocleziano) Inv. 8640. Rome. Alinari / Art Resource, NY.

FIGURE 27: A. Mantegna, *Triumphs of Caesar* IX, *Caesar on his triumphal chariot*, 1484–92. 270.4 x 280.7 cm. The Royal Collection © 2007, Her Majesty Queen Elizabeth II, Hampton Court Palace, London, RCIN 403966.

FIGURE 28: A. Mantegna, *Triumphs of Caesar* II, *The bearers of standards and siege equipment*, 1484–92. 266 x 278 cm. The Royal Collection © 2007, Her Majesty Queen Elizabeth II, Hampton Court Palace, London, RCIN 403959.

FIGURE 29: A. Mantegna, *Triumphs of Caesar* I, *The picture-bearers*, 1484–92. 266 x 278 cm. The Royal Collection © 2007, Her Majesty Queen Elizabeth II, Hampton Court Palace, London, RCIN 403958.

FIGURE 30: Detail from fragmentary frieze of the Arch of Titus, Rome, early 80s CE. Schwanke, Neg. D–DAI–Rom 1979. 2324.

FIGURE 31: *The triumph of Marcus Aurelius,* 176–80 CE. 350 x 238 cm. Musei Capitolini, Rome, Inv. MC 808. Erich Lessing / Art Resource, NY.

FIGURE 32: Relief panel from vault of the Arch of Titus, early 80s CE. Alinari / Art Resource, NY.

FIGURE 33: Painting from room n, House of the Vettii (VI, 15, 1), Pompeii, 62–79 CE. Scala / Art Resource, NY.

FIGURE 34: "Of the Monument of Philopappus . . . The elevation of the front, restored so far as the authorities we found will justify." J. Stuart and N. Revett, *The Antiquities of Athens* (London, 1794), chap. V, pl. III.

FIGURE 35: E. Dupérac (d. 1604), engraving of sarcophagus in the Maffei collection. Original engraving 1566, in O. Panvinio, *De Ludis Circensibus* (Padua, 1642), p. 7. Courtesy Houghton Library, Harvard University.

FIGURE 36: *Fasti Triumphales Capitolini,* Parast. IV, Frag. XLI, from Degrassi, *Inscr. It.* XIII, 1, p. 86. Courtesy of the Istituto Poligrafico e Zecca dello Stato, Rome.

FIGURE 37: *Fasti Triumphales Barberiniani,* Frags. CIII, CIV, from Degrassi, *Inscr. It.* XIII, 1, p. 344. Courtesy of the Istituto Poligrafico e Zecca dello Stato, Rome.

FIGURE 38: Painting of Vel Saties, from the François Tomb, Vulci, between fourth and first centuries BCE. Neg. D–DAI–Rom 1963. 0790.

FIGURE 39: Sarcophagus from Sperandio necropolis, Perugia, late sixth century BCE. Limestone. Length: 191 cm. Museo archeologico, Perugia. Neg. D–DAI–Rom 1931. 2184.

FIGURE 40: Architectural terracotta, from Praeneste (Palestrina), sixth or fifth century BCE. 44 cm. Museo di Villa Giulia, Rome. Alinari / Art Resource, NY.

FIGURE 41: Etruscan funerary urn, with triumphal scene, second century BCE. 40 x 84 cm. Museo archeologico, Florence. Neg. D–DAI–Rom 07766.

FIGURE 42: Sarcophagus, mid-second century CE. Length: 183 cm. Villa Medici, Rome. Kopperman, Neg. D–DAI–Rom 1963. 1238.

PLAN: Designed and created by Isabelle Lewis.

Index